Egypt:
"Image of Heaven"

Frontier Publishing

To Hendrine

Willem H. Zitman

Egypt:
"Image of Heaven"

*The Planisphere and
the Lost Cradle*

Frontier Publishing

Translation: Peter Rijpkema
Cover: Henk Heijblok
Editor: Gay Roberts
Publisher: Philip Coppens & Herman Hegge

Originally published as Het Sterrenbeeld van Horus (Baarn: Tirion, 2000). The work has been slightly adapted.

© Willem Zitman 2006; Picture Credits see p. 311.
ISBN 1-931882-54-1

www.zitman.org

Cover: see figure 28 inside for further explanation.

Frontier Publishing
Postbus 10681
1001 ER Amsterdam
the Netherlands
fp@fsf.nl
http://www.frontierpublishing.nl

printed in China

Contents

Foreword

One summer night in 1986, I awoke with a start. In a dream, or possibly in a state of wakefulness such that I had never experienced before, I was told in penetrating words that the history of the world and the development of Mankind as we know it did not correspond with reality.

I wondered what this message meant. It held me in its grip. Was I supposed to perform a certain role in this, and if so, would I be able to fulfil it? Since my youth in the university town of Leiden, I had often visited the various museums on which this town prides itself, such as the National Museum of Antiquities with its Egyptian collection, which had stimulated a lively curiosity in the development of the Earth and Mankind. It had already aroused in me a permanent interest in these subjects, an interest which intensified after the message I had received.

The fascinating revelations of the ancient Egyptian way of life, the structure of their culture and their religion, the campaigns of Alexander the Great and, many centuries later, of Napoleon appealed to my imagination. What form of wisdom and what riches did they expect to find there?

The ancient Egyptians bequeathed to us an unparalleled heritage of colossal and monumental buildings. For centuries, these fascinating monuments, pyramids and temples have held us all in their spell. Is it true that the pyramids were only monumental tombs or did they fulfil some other function? Many questions have been raised that, until now, could not always be answered satisfactorily. The theories are almost inexhaustible, frequently incomplete and definitely not consistent.

How do we acquire this knowledge called Egyptology? Our present level of knowledge of the Egyptian civilisation is based upon texts and source material, supplemented with archaeological as well as other forms of scientific analyses that serve to gain insight into its origin and development. In spite of this cautionary approach, many aspects still remain unclear, caused, amongst others, by numerous destructions, the ravages of time and an omission on the part of the ancient Egyptians to make a concise record of their own history. Yet we must ask ourselves whether the method described above is adequate to discover the potential power behind the unique culture and religion of Egypt. If we are unable to fathom the meaning of the Egyptian texts to a satisfactory degree, the results will be reflective of this, since the relationship cannot be established and the context will remain concealed.

However, their primary heritage consists of *their buildings with astronomical inscriptions and the remaining foundations*. Their cosmological heritage and order have been hidden from view, probably tucked away on purpose.

This order is concealed in the choice of their locations and the orientation of certain building plans. The Egyptians determined the locations of the pyramids on the Pyramid Field in accordance with cosmological order, which bestowed a cosmic reflection upon this building plan. As soon as we relate this order to their religion and their texts, we will definitely gain more understanding.

This relationship, in which the Egyptians expressed their cosmological development, seems crucial to me. In essence, Egyptian civilisation did not express itself solely in its predominantly shrouded and vague texts but all the more astutely in the application of their real talents, namely in their geometric order based on a cosmological order, the principle of which they literally founded their State on, and which may be discerned in their architecture.

That skill should be interpreted and understood from an iconographical point of view. This cosmological structure intrinsically reveals their religious disposition. From a historical point of view, it affords proof of their universal wisdom and demonstrates their intention to hand their knowledge down to Mankind for all eternity.

In the last thirty years, my studies of architecture as well as a long-lasting intensive interest in astronomy and Egyptology provided me with the necessary basic knowledge for my researches. During this spiritual voyage, I encountered books of great interest, and even highly promising titles such as **Kingship and the Gods, A Study of Ancient Near Eastern Religion as the Integration of Society and Nature** (1948), **Ancient Egyptian Religion** (1948) by Professor H.Frankfort, and **Ancient Egypt, Anatomy of a Civilization** (1989) by Field Director B.J.Kemp. These authors tried, each in their own manner, to lay the foundation for a scientific look at Egyptology. Unfortunately, their efforts did not bear satisfactory fruit.

In his comprehensive work, **Einführung in die Ägyptologie** (1967), Professor E.Hornung deals as extensively as possible with all branches of the field, thereby supplying an overview of the state of affairs in Egyptology, its methods and the tasks that it has set itself. Amongst other aspects, Hornung describes the origin, the development during the 19th and the 20th centuries, as well as the chronological and spatial limits, value, and meaning of the science of Egyptology. Yet it lacks an axiom on which this science ought to be founded.

According to insiders, these books provide a cultural and scientific concept of great importance, in particular to archaeology. This is also due to Frankfort's comparison between Egypt and Mesopotamia in his previously mentioned **Kingship and the Gods**. The design, constructions and realisation of the entire Pyramid Field prove that some five to six thousand years ago, the Egyptians already possessed a highly advanced level of knowledge of project development, construction methods, architecture, geometry, land-surveying, stereographic skills and organisational capabilities. They built an enormous constellation on earth as Pyramid Field with the temple locations of Memphis, Heliopolis and Letopolis. It reflects their cosmological model and order and allowed them to express a permanent structure, which I will label their *"Existential Structure"*.

Every science requires an axiom. In my opinion, a concise and clear axiom that acknowledges their religion as its basis and does justice to their cosmological insight can be briefly phrased in the expression: "**as above, so below**", which enhances the analogy that they consciously sought between the macrocosm and the microcosm. Actually, the wording of this basic principle existed long before 332 BCE, although it is not recognised and accepted as such. It can be found in the Hermetic texts and is couched in the following words by Hermes Trismegistus, addressed to Asclepius: *"Or are you ignorant, Asclepius, that Egypt is the image of heaven? Moreover, it is the dwelling-place of heaven and all the forces that are in heaven. If it is proper for us to speak the truth, our land is the temple of the world."*

This text is from the *Nag Hammadi Library*, which was found near Hiw in December 1945, the town of the *Perfect Word*. According to the high priest Manetho, the contents of the Hermetic writings can be traced back at least to the vizier Imhotep and Pharaoh Djoser.

I have researched into the truth of this axiom, which is thousands of years old, and the present book contains the fruits of my investigation. This divine axiom can resurrect the Hermetic Words of the God Thoth and instigate a new Renaissance. Hence, the meaning of the Ancient Egyptian writings and the source material are placed in their correct context, which also applies to the interpretation of the iconographical depictions. Astronomy as they knew it and used it within their religion can be brought back to life once again.

The first such theory was put forward by Bauval and Gilbert (**The Orion Mystery**, 1994). Although it seemed spectacular, it had not been thoroughly deliberated. They attempted to demonstrate that the three stars of Orion's Belt correlated with the positioning of the three pyramids of Giza. Furthermore, they claimed to have established a correlation of two other stars, Saiph and Bellatrix, with the pyramids at Abu Rawash and Zawyet el Aryan respectively, as well as between the Hyades and the two pyramids near Dahshur. However, their theory was too limited in view and was therefore not accepted. The constellation Orion consists of more stars than accounted for by their theory. Accordingly, their Orion-correlation hypothesis is actually incomplete and contains incorrect interpretations, such as the stereographic projection of the constellation onto the Earth. This is dramatic because *the ancient Egyptians actually did use twelve pyramids, one pyramid city and three temple locations to build an enormous constellation on earth*. The website www.zitman.org or *Egypt: image of Heaven* demonstrates this and serves to clarify the subject matter. This whole concept is a highly sensitive matter due to the extensive implications in various scientific domains, which might easily obstruct scientific progress, to say the least.

During my research, I did not limit myself to existing texts and source material, but I also used ancient traditional knowledge regarding the origin and meaning of names of stars and constellations. The question which I attempt to answer in Part 1 of this book is: when and why was the Pyramid Field built? In this book, part of that question has been answered. Apart from its remarkable planological location, the Pyramid Field contains the crucial core of the technocratic, religious, ideological, cultural, and economic dynamics of ancient Egypt.

After the publication of the Dutch edition in 2000, I continued my research, which, between autumn of 2003 and spring of 2004 (cf. paragraph 4.29), resulted in new facts and justifications that serve to clarify the original question: when and why was the Pyramid Field built? This clarification will place the birth of our human history and its theory of evolution - and the profound influence which the cosmological myth exerted on it - further back in time and thereby shed an entirely different light on prehistory and history.

Since about 1950, Egyptologists have focused exclusively on the theory that the will of the Gods played no particular role in Egyptian life. Modern scholars in this field maintain that Egypt kept silent about signs in the heavens (see ***Ägypten Eine Sinngeschichte***, Part IV,2, J.Assmann) such as eclipses of the Sun and the Moon and earthquakes - the very signs that divinatory cultures studied meticulously and recorded. In fact, evidence points in the opposite direction, as is clearly shown both in the work, ***Lives of Eminent Philosophers***, Book I, 2 by the Greek biographer Diogenes Laertius (early 3rd century CE), who confirmed that the Egyptians recorded 373 eclipses of the sun and 832 eclipses of the moon, and in the Ipu-wer papyrus, which gives a description of destruction and horror towards the end of the Old Kingdom. Cosmology played an important role in the development of the ancient cultures of Mesopotamia and Egypt and even made itself felt up to the Renaissance.

A remarkable detail is that up to now, ancient Egyptian geographic/planological abilities have hardly attracted any attention. Nevertheless, according to ancient source material from Herodotus and Aristotle, the origin and practice of geometry or land-surveying was a typical ancient Egyptian skill. Its knowledge and mastery resulted in environmental planning, which constituted the first basic principle in urban and rural planning and architecture and may be based on a standard measurement, a module.

In ancient Egyptian architecture, we clearly discern a near obsession with structure, pattern systems and zoning. If we happen to encounter these features during a journey through ancient Egypt, we are amazed at the awe-inspiring skilfulness, all the more so when we take into account the means and methods that were available at the time. In my opinion, this tendency towards structure already dominated the infrastructure they applied to the zones of their territory during prehistoric and protohistoric times.

In my estimation, the preparations made by the Egyptians for the building of this project go back very far in time. The specification of the sites of the first prehistoric capitals in both Upper and Lower Egypt are the fundamental roots of that development. This also applies to the choice of location of the first pyramid complex of Pharaoh Djoser as the cornerstone of the State of Egypt, which is a highlight in the formation period.

During my long years of study, I discovered the methical approach behind the development of their territory. That is how I discovered the proof - hardly discernible at first sight - of their planological and iconographical skills, which was based on astronomical knowledge. The Egyptians apparently developed the complex technique of astronomical iconography, which enabled them to project a celestial star pattern (constellation) onto the surface of the Earth. This ability provided them with a framework for the development of their culture. The ancient Egyptians were the first geographical planners to develop this system to establish an "image of heaven" on Earth.

When the Egyptians built the Pyramid Field as the "Image of Heaven" on Earth, they revealed the essence of what later would be known as a Hermetic tradition, which is at least 5,000 to 6,000 years old, and contains the order and all the qualities inherent in Universal Spirituality. Here, Asclepius' words were realised in stone. This Hermetic tradition offers an important contribution to a better understanding of our western cultural and religious inheritance. After an initial rebirth in the Renaissance, the Hermetic tradition is now experiencing its second revival.

Up to the year 1999, my research for this book resulted in a chain of "innovations". These consisted mainly of the discovery of the true identity of Osiris and the correlation of his constellation with the river Nile, the "Osiris meridian" as the zero meridian of the Ancient World, the concept of the two "heavens", the meaning of the name Giza, the constellation Orion and the iconography of the Pyramid Field as the god Horus, the pharaoh being his personification in his regal, ritual posture denoting "I shall maintain". Presumably, it is prehistoric and once ranked as the emblem of their ancestors, the Followers of Horus.

My work also incorporated the birth of (dynastic) kingship at the time of a solar eclipse, the transition from star-cult to sun-cult and the ensuing chronological implications, the development of the calendar and the observation-tracks of the star Sirius including the view of their infrastructure. The latter innovation enabled me to make a fruitful analysis of a Mesopotamian planisphere found in the British Museum. This analysis allowed me trace the origin of the Followers of Horus, and in Part 2, I postulate that this planisphere is an atlas of the prehistoric world. The written confirmation of Plato's dialogue about a sunken Fatherland, discovered in an Egyptian temple, marks the climax of this investigation.

This book is meant for university graduates as well as for all those with an interest in a new and above all, a broader outlook on the development of Mankind. Detailed proof is included in the extensive appendix and chronology, and can also be found on my website www.zitman.org, where an animation demonstrates the correlation of the sites of the pyramids and the temple-cities with the celestial constellations. The sub-pages of the website contain numerous Pyramid Texts and other accounts that serve as reliable substantiation of the propositions I have set forth in this book.

Acknowledgements

My study would not be complete without expressing my gratitude towards my family, friends and relatives who, each in their own characteristic way, have supported and helped me in the course of many years to make this book into a reality. I am the only one who bears responsibility for whatever idea is brought forward in this study.

My special thanks go to Philip Coppens, who, in the beginning of my research, was always prepared to exchange mutual thoughts about the purpose of this book and to judge its contents critically. Wolf Edlinger was willing to translate Old German texts. A different form of help was offered by Maurice Foulon, by advising and assisting with any computer work. During the long period of research, Rob van Gent supplied up-to-date information, either in the form of lunar tables or other useful astronomical material. Diny de Groot attended to the translation of various French texts. Koen Koenders, in his own refined manner, produced the necessary slides that were required at lectures, thereby casting his light over ancient Egypt. I am also very grateful to him for his co-operation in the production of the illustrations. The same applies to Henk Heijblok, for creating my website and producing the complicated illustrations in my book. For some time, Dick van Koten acted as a sounding board and gave useful hints concerning my writing-style. Remco de Maayer provided me with the necessary information about the latest scientific research on the Planisphere. In his continuous drive for perfection, Gé van Oosterhout kept on urging me to increase the profundity of my investigations and to achieve greater distinction in my formulations. His research into the chronology of ancient Egypt, based on the heliacal risings of Sirius, made an important contribution to the progressive stages of my research on this special phenomenon and to its particular significance for the origin of civilisation. The comments and criticisms that Herman Traas and Ad Paulen made were highly constructive. Their meticulous and discerning suggestions were an impetus to bring the inventiveness of the ancient engineers more to the forefront. In that same area, Rob Schuurkes proved to be a moving spirit whose intellect, along with his imagination, kept on kindling my enthusiasm for the research in that field.

A contribution of a different kind came from Hans van Tekelenburg, who on various occasions offered useful information. Harry Verwiel corrected the manuscript twice in a very creditable manner. My cooperation with Yolande Michon, the Dutch publisher's general editor, was not only pleasant; like also with the English editress Gay Roberts, their concern and commitment aimed predominantly at achieving a high-quality result. At the *Bibliotheca Philosophica Hermetica* in Amsterdam, the founder, Joost Ritman, arranged a meeting with Jacob Slavenburg and his wife Annine van der Meer. The meeting was so fruitful that afterwards, Jacob wrote his book **De Herme-tische Schakel (The Hermetic Link)**.

I would also like to express here my appreciation for the translator Peter Rijpkema. Each time another instalment with alternatives arrived, I was astonished at his boundless capacity for work. He was clearly taken by the subject. I am truly grateful to him. I have, of course, taken the liberty of adopting a different choice of words at a few points in the text, so that if there are errors in the English rendering, I trust the reader will attribute them to me personally.

Lastly, the original Dutch text was published in 2000 by Tirion Publishers. Since then, I have reconsidered certain passages in my work, which sometimes reached different or further conclusions.

Above all, I wish to thank my loving wife Hendrine for her support, interest and unremitting stimulations.

Eindhoven,
the Netherlands,
January 2005

Part I

Egypt: *"Image of Heaven"*

(*NHC Library*; Asclepius 21-29 (VI,8) line 70)

"Without some broader view, the culture-history of Egypt and the continuity between its prehistory and history will ever elude us."
Michael A.Hoffman, *Egypt before the Pharaohs*, p. 241

Fig. 1. Upper part of the statue of Pharaoh Khafre with the Horus falcon on his shoulder as a protection of kingship; origin: the Temple of the Death at Giza, Fourth Dynasty. Egyptian Museum in Cairo.

Introduction

Is there a civilisation missing from the history of Mankind? Was there an extinct race and a culture that once stood at the cradle of the ancient familiar civilisations of Egypt and Sumeria, as some have speculated? The Turin papyrus, a chronological list of the kings that ruled over ancient Egypt, mentions a tribe called the Shemsu Hor, the Followers of Horus. Were they the ancestors of the Egyptians?

More than a hundred years of research on this presumed, extinct civilisation have, up to the present day, hardly provided us with notable results. But now the tables have turned. Renewed research on a Sumerian Planisphere - a depiction of a celestial hemisphere - has revealed substantial cartographic indications that finally made it possible to pinpoint their former dwelling-place, a location in what is now the Sahara desert. It can therefore be no coincidence that recently, the oldest pottery on earth was found in that dwelling-place. The spectacular discovery of this oldest map of the prehistoric world provides us with an amazing new view on our origins and our history. It appears that the ancestors of our civilisation possessed an advanced level of astronomical knowledge, which enabled them to draw up a plan to build *"Heaven on Earth"*.

Climatological circumstances forced the ancestors of the Egyptians to abandon their dwelling-place and establish a new home in the land of Egypt, which they reached around 5300 BCE. Approximately two millennia later, they created an eye-catching representation of a constellation of the heavens on the surface of the earth by designing and building the Pyramid Field.

The function of the oldest pyramids was not restricted to that of royal tombs. The fact is that the design of the Pyramid Field corresponds with the depiction on the palette of Pharaoh Narmer, on display in the Egyptian Museum in Cairo. The outline and design of the Pyramid Field is a rendering of the god Horus in a ritual pose. This ritual pose on the palette of Pharaoh Narmer and the design of the Pyramid Field both represent the posture which, in concise terms, is nowadays called "smiting the enemy", a pose that continued to exist for almost four thousand years. It symbolises the power which the Ancient Egyptian Empire wielded over the world.

Furthermore, the Followers of Horus developed a geographical/planological framework that was inspired by the cosmos, on which they based their religious notions. Many millennia before they moved to Egypt and Sumeria, these ancestors of our civilisation, who descended from the Followers of Horus, experienced a catastrophe on Earth. More than two thousand years ago, they described this event on the walls of the "Temple of Horus" at Edfu. These chronicles - The Sacred Books of Edfu - show that the account by Plato of a war and the decline of a very early culture is a rendering of their history. New and fascinating insights into this matter have their repercussions in this book, which strives to provide an answer to many intriguing questions that are still very much alive....

Chapter 1

Lost Species
Turning Points and a New Beginning

It was the day on which "Osiris is raised from the dead. The sky reels and the earth quakes [...]."[1] These are the opening words of one of the Pyramid Texts. The first time the Egyptians gave publicity to their Pyramid Texts occurred when they inscribed them on the walls of the pyramid of Pharaoh Unas, the last ruler of the Fifth Dynasty. Hence, these texts date back authentically to the Pyramid Age.

What did the ancient Egyptians intend the opening words from this Pyramid Text to convey? Were they meant to point to a catastrophe, which was subsequently followed by some creative act that would restore the earth to its former state of equilibrium? Might those who wrote them have witnessed this event? And why did the Egyptians celebrate New Year twice annually on separate days? Does that additional celebration allude to a much earlier cultural period of which we have no knowledge? Maybe a New Year's Day from bygone times, from the "Golden Age of Osiris"? After all, the Egyptians are well-known for their deeply-rooted traditions.

Their first annual New Year was celebrated in conjunction with the first "brilliant" visible rising of the star Sirius after it had remained out of sight for nearly seventy days (a heliacal rising). From times beyond recall, this New Year's Day was celebrated as the Day of Creation and as the beginning of the Egyptian calendar year and the annual cycle of the Egyptian year. It was a festive day, dedicated to Thoth, the god who was believed to have made an orderly division of time, to mention just one of his deeds.

Four months afterwards, immediately after the Osiris festival, they celebrated their second New Year's Day. According to mythical tradition, on that New Year's Day, the god Horus had agreed to succeed Osiris, his father.[2] To them, this festivity recalled (or maybe "recalled by re-enactment") the mythical "First Era of Osiris" i.e. Zep Tepi, and the beginning of the rule of Horus. Yet where do we place that period? The Greek historian Herodotus has provided us with an answer.

1.1 Lost Species, Neanderthal and Cro-Magnon man

The chronology of the Egyptians, as it has been handed down to us, dates back to approximately 28,000 BCE. The Sumerian King-List even distinguishes between kings who ruled before the Great Flood and those who ruled afterwards. This King-List mentions an all-encompassing catastrophe, which is supposed to have occurred around 32,000 BCE. This coincides with the extinction of Neanderthal man (named after the site where he was found in the *Neander-thal* in the *Feldhofer* cave near Düsseldorf, Germany in 1856). In **De**

Neandertaler, Dutch author Holleman writes: "Around 30,000 BCE, Modern Man was a very lonesome figure on the global setting."[3] The arrival of Homo Sapiens brought with it the power of imagination, which is discernible in the naturalistic style of cave paintings.

The Sumerian King-List goes even further back in time. The true start of the chronology it tabulates begins around 272,000 BCE. Recent research, conducted on 38 males to examine in particular "a non-recombining component of the Y-chromosome", shows "that Modern Man's genes-kit appears to be a relatively young phenomenon. Its rate of mutation points to an age of approximately 270,000 years."[4] Does the age of Modern Man (Homo Sapiens) happen to coincide with the first entry on the Sumerian King-List? (see Chronology)

Some time after 30,000 BCE, Neanderthal man disappeared from the world scene. Around that same time, Cro-Magnon man made his appearance. It is not known how or where this species came about. L.Lartet named him after the place where he was found in 1868, inside the Cro-Magnon cave at Les Eyzies in France. Cro-Magnon man strongly resembled modern man, yet differed from Neanderthal man. Cro-Magnon man was slender, yet compared to us his build was more muscular and he was considerably taller. Presumably because he was out hunting all day, not sitting in his office like we do.

The disappearance of Neanderthal man coincided with the time of the Great Flood as dated in the Sumerian King-List. Here, the list shows a dividing line which separates the kings who reigned before the Flood from those who reigned after. Accordingly, the era of Homo Sapiens begins at approximately 30,000 BCE.

In the tenth millennium BCE, Cro-Magnon man disappeared rather suddenly from the global scene. He was replaced by Modern Man. On the geological time scale, this marks the end of the Wisconsin or Würm Glacial-Age and draws a dividing line that denotes the transition from the Pleistocene to the Holocene. The geological present started and a blank page lay open in the history of planet Earth. In **Le Tschad depuis 25000 ans**, the French scholar Schneider summarises this as follows: "....the border between the Pleistocene and the Holocene appears to lie closer to 9000 BCE than to 10,000 BCE. Various authors pinpoint this dividing line quite accurately, namely in 8770 BCE (with a margin of 150 years)." Between 9800 and 8800 BCE, the climate improved (known as the warming-up period). Schneider informs us that the Nile caused severe flooding, and that vegetation re-appeared in the Central Mountains of North Africa, especially in the Hoggar Mountains. He dates this transition from the Pleistocene to the Holocene around 9800 BCE.[5] This transition did not happen gradually; it coincided with a natural catastrophe. The transitional period after the catastrophe lasted for about one millennium.

Both the Sumerian King-List and the Chronology of the Egyptians specify the turning-point between the Pleistocene and the Holocene periods. The Second Dynasty of Kish, a town-state in Sumeria, began in approximately 8400 BCE (similar to the Maya chronology, which began approximately 8500 BCE). Egyptian chronology started around 8400 BCE with the rule of the "Race of the Demigods and Other Kings" (chronology of Manetho revised by the Father of Church History, Eusebius; cf. appendix Chronology, especially Egyptian and

Sumerian Chronology I). Again, we notice an almost exact correspondence between the chronology of the ancient cultures and the results of the research mentioned by Schneider and the article by Hammer, Clusen and Tauber, in which they place the transition from the Pleistocene to the Holocene around 8700 BCE.[6]

1.2 Climatological Turning-points

Does the chronology of the Egyptian and Sumerian King-List contain additional turning-points in the course of the history of the Earth and mankind? Do Egypt and Sumeria share a singularity that runs right through the chronology of both cultures? Research shows a synchronicity between the two chronologies that enables us to track down certain catastrophic events. In prehistoric times, climatological circumstances of this type had a considerable impact on mankind. Notable mass migrations are known to have resulted from changes in the climate.

From approximately 7200 until 2500 BCE, climatological conditions in the North African region between the 17th and the 31st parallel were highly congenial. The Sahara desert as we know it now was non-existent; quite the contrary, the tropical and sub-tropical wet climate with favourable temperatures that prevailed in large parts of this region made it into a paradise for man and fauna. In those millennia, this part of the North African continent was crosscut by major rivers, some of which rose on the plateau of the Tassili mountains. In addition, a considerable number of lakes existed in that part of the continent, some of which were as vast as inland seas.

The Paleo-Lake Chad with a surface-area of approximately 330,000 square kilometres ranked as one of those immense expanses of water. It extended from the town of Bogor (10° N) to the town of Borkou (18° N), near the Tibesti mountains.[7] At present, Lake Chad measures no more than approximately 25,000 square kilometres.

Before the beginning of the fifth millennium, Lake Triton, an inlet of the Mediterranean Sea, lay on the southern side of the foothills of the Atlas Mountains, near Gafsa (Tunisia). The town of Gafsa is named after Capsa, where an important cultural group, which may have originated in Europe, developed between approximately 8400 and 5300 BCE. Remainders of this remarkable cultural group were also found near Sebile, a town in the immediate vicinity of Kom Ombo in Upper Egypt.[8]

All that is left of Lake Triton are a few meagre salt marshes in Algeria and Tunisia. From 5700 BCE onward, the sea-level rose considerably. Around 5500 BCE, the land bridge between Tunisia and Italy disappeared. Remarkably, this drastic occurrence appears to coincide with the beginning of the Byzantine World Era in 5508 BCE. The Eurasian and African continents became permanently separated. Between 4000 and 3000 BCE, a connection between the Mediterranean and the Black Sea gradually came about via the Bosphorus. The inland sea of Marmora was transformed into the Sea of Marmora, and via the Dardanelles, a connection was established with the Aegean Sea and subsequently with the Mediterranean.

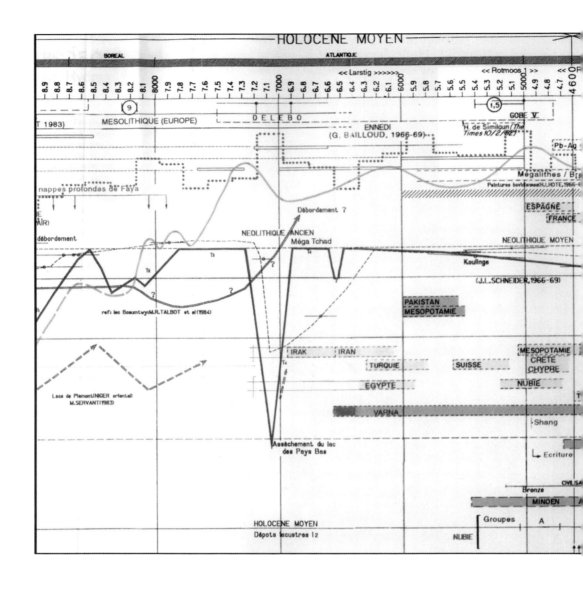

Fig.2. Graphical survey showing climatological changes. Extreme drought between 5300 and 4900 BCE, deduced from the drying-up of paleo-Lake Chad; climatological circumstances in North Africa (Sahara) were comparable to those of the present. The transition from the Middle Holocene to the

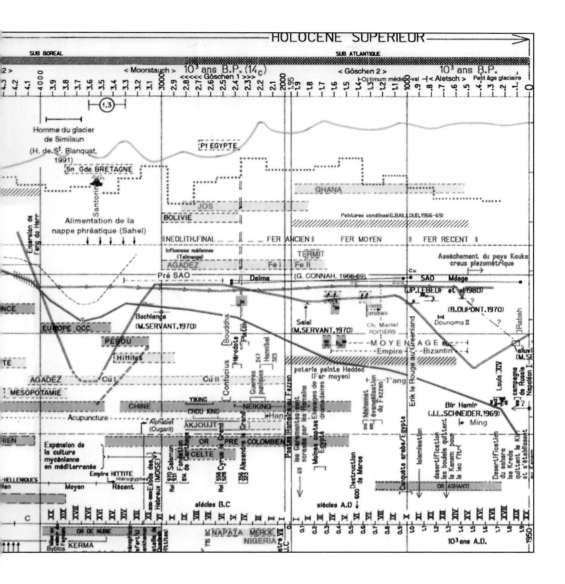

Upper Holocene - between 2600 and 2500 BCE (Biblical Deluge) - shows a permanent climatological change in the northern part of Africa leading to present-day conditions.

Le Tschad depuis 25000 ans contains a graphic overview that shows how a radical, unique, and quite sudden change in the climate took place at some point between 7200 and 2500 BCE - the only one to have occurred within a period of around 4,700 years. More precisely, this drastic change, comparable to the present extreme dehydration of the Sahara, occurred between 5300 BCE and 4900 BCE (cf. fig. 2).[9] It was this catastrophic change (similar to Hekla5/Thjorsa, seen in the Greenland ice-core borings, Hammer et al.) that drove the inhabitants of the Sahara to the banks of the major rivers of Africa and Asia, a migration that developed into the river cultures of Sumeria and Egypt. This climatological catastrophe led to the "Big Bang" of civilisation.

In Sumeria, the town-states of Ur, Erech, Ubaid and Eridu were founded on the rivers Euphrates and Tigris. This is recorded in the Sumerian King-List as the beginning of the reign of the First Dynasty of Erech (Uruk), dated approximately 5200 BCE.

Presumably due to catastrophic flooding of the Nile between 10,000 and 6,000 BCE, no evidence has (yet) been found in Egypt of extensive forms of habitation prior to 5300 BCE.[10] From approximately 5300 BCE onward, the first settlements were established near Lake Fayum and Merimde on a tributary of the Nile. In that same period, Memphis and El Badari were founded.

1.3 Chronological Entanglements

Eusebius, the Father of Church History (circa 264 - 349 CE), rewrote or revised the chronological work **Aegyptiaca**, which the Egyptian high priest Manetho (circa 280 BCE) had compiled. The task of recording the history of Egypt is believed to have been assigned to Manetho by Pharaoh Ptolemy I Soter, the first pharaoh of the Ptolemaic Dynasty (332 - 31 BCE).

Manetho's original work was lost in the course of the centuries. However, excerpts have been preserved that were recorded in the works of the Jewish historian Flavius Josephus (1st century CE). Manetho also drew up a list of dynasties and included the number of years of each pharaoh's rulership; this was preserved in the **World Chronicle** by Julius Africanus (3rd century CE), the founder of Christian chronography, thereby enabling the data to be handed down to Eusebius. We owe this classification of Egyptian history into thirty dynasties to these specific circumstances.

Apart from the list in Manetho's lost work, other fragments of Pharaonic King-Lists also exist, such as the Turin Canon. Unfortunately, most of this manuscript fell apart into minute fragments while being transported to Italy in the 19th century. Specifically, the beginning of this papyrus, which describes the prehistory of the Egyptians, suffered the most damage. A team of Egyptologists managed to accomplish a reconstruction that, unfortunately, in spite of their strenuous efforts, does not supply any decisive clues to Egyptian chronology.

Fortunately, Eusebius had access to Manetho's work when he rewrote the chronology of the Egyptians. According to Eusebius, the part that extends up to the beginning of their First Dynasty runs as follows:[11]

Gods until Bitis	13,900 years
The Empire of Spirits/Demigods	5,813 "
Subtotal	19,713 years
Race of Demigods	1,255 years
Other Kings	1,817 "
30 Kings, reigning from Memphis	1,790 "
Total	24,575 years

Eusebius gave a separate account of ten Thinite Kings who reigned for a period of 350 years, which equals the overall period of rulership of the First and the Second Dynasties. In short, Eusebius classified the various prehistoric eras of the Egyptians as follows: the Era of the Gods began around 28,121 BCE (cf. Appendix I and Chronology) and ended around 14,215 BCE. Then came "The First Era of the Primaeval Age", which continued until approximately 8402 BCE.

At this point, which marked an astronomically significant juncture in time due to the transition of the spring equinox from Leo to Cancer (known as precession), "The Second Era of the Primaeval Age" began in the "Sacred Domains", with its various periods of rulership under the "Race of Demigods and other Kings", which subsequently leads us to the climatological turning-point around 5330 BCE. This was followed by the period known as the "Hinterland", which lasted for 1,790 years, during which time the country was ruled from Memphis by thirty successive kings.

From approximately 3520 BCE onward, their chronology shows a subdivision into thirty Dynasties. The classification into the three aforementioned periods, i.e. the "First Era", the "Second Era", and the "Hinterland", is described in the chronicles of the Temple of Horus at Edfu.[12]

However, according to Egyptian chronology as it is traditionally endorsed, the rule of the First Dynasty is at present assumed to have begun around 3000 BCE. Previously, Egyptologists had based their assumptions on much earlier dating. When chronological research got under way in the 19th century, they had settled on the year 5800 BCE. Towards the middle of the 20th century, this date had been reset to 3400 BCE. However, it seems more than likely that the chronology, which is currently acknowledged, will be changed anew.

What is this all about? Quite recently, renewed research was carried out on the age of pyramids and their annexes. In 1984, Egyptologists R. and D. Klemm applied the Carbon-14 Dating method, also called C-14, to examine a total of 64 organic samples taken from the pyramids. "After calibration, the average age according to these data amounted to 374 years more than had been assumed in existing chronologies."[13]

In 1986, "The Pyramids Carbon-dating Project", supervised by the American Egyptologist M. Lehner, set out in a new attempt to determine the age of 15 samples, which had been taken from the mortar of the Great Pyramid at Giza. Lehner reported that the ensuing results placed the age of the pyramid of Khufu some 400 to 450 years earlier than chronological findings had previously established.[14] According to this provisional result, the beginning of the reign of the Fourth Dynasty would have to be reset to approximately 3000 BCE instead of 2550 BCE.

Such results are apt to rekindle the flame amongst Egyptologists in their discussions on Egyptian chronology. So in 1995, it was decided to extract a further 300 samples from monuments of the First Dynasty up to and including the Sixth Dynasty. The results, which have not yet been published, are expected to throw new light on the Egyptian chronology.

1.4 Two Chronological Turning-points

A: The Installation of Kingship in Egypt coincided with a Solar Eclipse

Will these imminent results force us to make further chronological revisions? Actually, various ancient Egyptian sources indicate that the beginning of Egyptian chronology goes further back by some 500 years, which would bring us to approximately 3500 BCE, instead of approximately 3000 BCE.

1) An ancient Egypt source informs us that the Egyptian year originally commenced around the winter solstice. According to the "adjustable calendar", the beginning of the First Dynasty should consequently be set at around 3518 BCE.[15] Between 3518 and 3514 BCE, their New Year's Day - known to the Egyptians as I Achet 1 - fell on January 16th or 17th (Julian calendar), the day of the winter solstice. (details can be found in Appendix I and Chronology.)

2) On that day, as the Sun rose on Giza's eastern horizon, the star Deneb (alpha Cygni) was no longer visible. Yet a line drawn from the North Pole to the star Deneb would form part of a great circle that crosses the horizon on the spot where the Sun was seen to rise. To the Egyptians, this was the day on which the Sun was symbolically born.

3) Of all the Egyptian legends, that of Nut, the goddess of the sky, and the birth of Ra rank amongst the most prominent. As many images show, the goddess of the sky was depicted naked, stretching herself along the firmament. She represents the Milky Way, and her legs, arms, and head are discernible in figures 3 and 3a. The star Deneb (alpha Cygni) is seen to mark the birth canal.

Here, we want to draw attention to an apparently remarkable correspondence: the time-span between the day on which the Sun reaches its vernal (spring) equinox and the day of the winter solstice, when the Sun emerges from out of the birth canal and is symbolically "born" again, amounts to 273 days. [16] This happens to coincide with the average duration of a human pregnancy, following a conception period of seven days. The ancient Egyptian Law of Hermes Trismegistus – the laws of the Prenatal Epoch, known as the "The Trutine of Hermes" - also states that a human pregnancy lasts 273 days.

Nut's head is located somewhere near the star Alhena and the star constellation Gemini, whilst the Ecliptic is seen to run through her mouth. In distant antiquity, the Ecliptic was known as the "Great Central Circle".[17] The arms are located in the vicinity of the star Sirius.

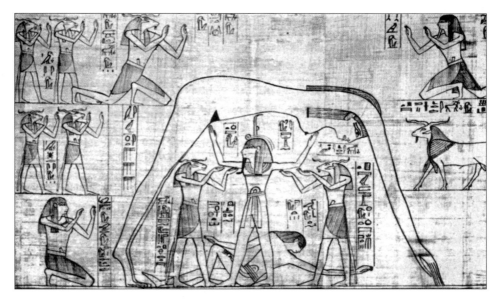

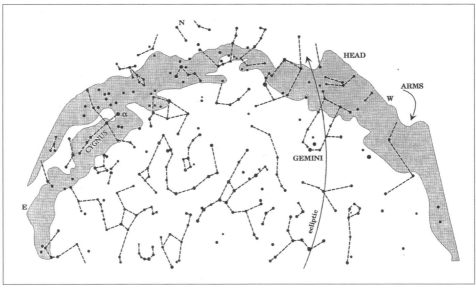

Fig. 3 Shu, god of the air, raises Nut, goddess of the sky, above the earth. Her posture bears a notable resemblance to the image of the Milky Way in fig. 3a.

*Fig. 3a. A contemporary representation of the Milky Way, as it is observed in the northern hemisphere. On the left, the bisection near Cygnus is seen to coincide with the spot where the legs begin. The star Deneb indicates the mouth of the birth canal. On the right, the constellation Gemini marks the head, face-down, which is followed by the arms (adapted from Skymap 4, from **A Field Guide to the Stars and Planets** by D.H. Menzel and J.M. Pasachoff, Boston 1983, p.48, adopted from **Astronomy before the Telescope**, p.30)*

4) The star Deneb fulfilled an additional role by reminding the Egyptians of their mythical "First Era" of Osiris, around 15,000 BCE, when Deneb was in the position of the *pole star*. It was the period in which their origin - their birth as a tribe – occurred.

A fourth notable particularity is the alignment of the south-eastern corners of the three pyramids of Giza, which forms what is known as "the great diagonal of Giza" (cf. fig. 4). This diagonal points north-eastward, at an approximate angle of 45-46° to true north. During the winter solstices around 3000 BCE, the star Deneb rose exactly in the north-east, i.e. at the same angle of approximately 45-46° to true north.[18] Hence, the great diagonal of Giza, which aligns with the obelisk of Heliopolis, standing on the mound of the temple in that town, pointed at that time towards the rising of the star Deneb. In addition, the causeway that leads from the pyramid of Pharaoh Djedefre at Abu Rawash veers off and continues in parallel to the great diagonal of Giza. Hence, beyond that bend, the causeway of Abu Rawash also bore exactly north-eastward and consequently also pointed towards the rising of the star Deneb during the winter solstices around 3000 BCE (cf. fig.4).

These findings suggest a correlation between the "birth" of the state of Egypt and the day of the winter solstice, because at the winter solstice at that time, the star Deneb, the pole star during the "First Era", rose just before sunrise in the exact north-east. Furthermore, around 3518 BCE, the first Egyptian calendar day, I Achet 1 on the "adjustable" calendar, occurred on the day of the winter solstice (appendix II). This narrows the beginning of the First Dynasty down to the period between 3518 and 3514 BCE.

Certain facts that have been handed down to us do not only lend greater credibility to the assumption that the birth and the installation of Kingship in Egypt took place on the day on which the Sun was in the winter solstice, they also point to the fact that this event also coincided with a Solar eclipse that was observed in Egypt. Are there known texts that describe this phenomenon? If that is the case, then we should consider them a godsend, because they would allow Egyptian chronology to be established definitively. Texts in the temples at Edfu and those at Esna do indeed mention this occurrence. What is more: that specific winter solstice also marks the founding of the temple at Karnak by Thutmosis III.

During the reign of Thutmosis III, this winter solstice from times beyond recall was apparently still observed as a commemorative day on which festivities were held – and considered a cause for rejoicing. Even during the Graeco-Roman period, this commemorative festivity was still celebrated in the temples at Edfu and Esna. The same rites were performed in Edfu on I Achet 1 (New Year's Day) as in Esna on III Peret 1 (winter solstice during the Old Kingdom). The French Egyptologist Sauneron actually expressed his astonishment at this similarity (***Esna V***, Le Caire, 1962, p.185) because in Esna, the day marked the Festival of the Potter's Wheel to celebrate the Unification with the Sundisc and the Birth and Installation of Kingship ("l'instauration de la royauté").

In my hypothesis, I argue that III Peret 1 appears to have been the day on which the commemorative festival of the installation of Kingship was held. The

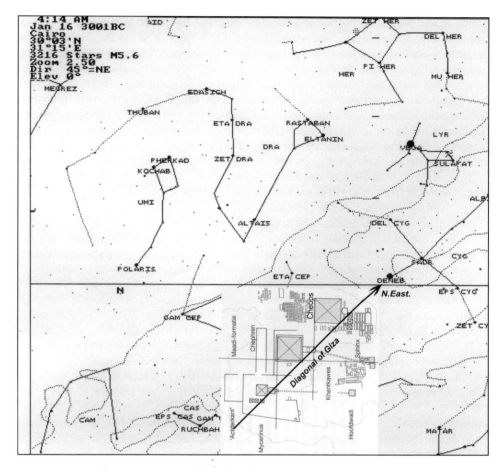

Fig. 4. Around 3000 BCE, whilst the three pyramids of Giza were being built, the end of the winter solstice night was marked by the rising of the star Deneb in the exact north-east. The diagonal of Giza as well as the first part of the causeway to the pyramid of Abu Rawash were directed at the rising of Deneb.

extreme significance that was evidently attached to this day is confirmed by the founding of the temple at Karnak by Pharaoh Thutmosis III, which occurred on the previous day: II Peret 30. Additionally, this specific day is mentioned twice in ***The Book of the Dead***, namely in the Chapters 125 and 140: "[...] who maketh all mankind to live on the day when the Eye (Utchat) of Ra is full in Annu (Heliopolis) at the end of the second month of the season Pert" and "The Book which is to be recited on the last day of the second month of the season Pert when the Utchat is full in the second month of the season Pert."

As suggested above, I Achet 1, along with III Peret 1, played an important role in the Egyptian calendar. We recognise this graphically in the Mammisis of Denderah (***Studien zur Ägyptischen Astronomie***, Leitz, p.19, illustration by Daumas, pl. LXI bis), where these days are pictured side by side. That founding day in Karnak, II Peret 30, and the birthday of Kingship on III Peret

1 gain even more importance as the installation of Kingship in the Old Kingdom apparently occurred on that day. (Apocatastasis = restitutio in pristinum statum [Latin] = return to the original or previous condition in memory of the founding-day of the Old Kingdom; ibid, Leitz, p.87).

The Egyptians developed a unique, "adjustable" calendar, which was based on the principle that every four years, all calendar-days moved forward by one day in relation to the fixed civil calendar. In the following Sirius-calendars (either in the year 4242 BCE, 2782 BCE, or 1322 BCE; sources pertaining to this calendar cited by the Roman writer Censorinus and the Roman Emperor Diocletianus), the fixed civil calendar began on New Year's Day on the calendar-day I Achet 1 (July 19th) and ended on Epagomene day 5 (July 18th).

It took 1,460 years (one day per 4 yrs. = 365 days x 4 yrs. = 1,460 yrs.) for the calendar to return to its starting-point, whereupon the next Sirius year started. This was their method of calculation, strange though it may seem to us. It forms a link to the famous words spoken by Pythagoras, that "all things are numbers", and there is no question where this line of thinking came from.

After 724 years (=181 days x 1 leap-day in every 4 years, [181 x 4 = 724]), I Achet 1 on the "adjustable" calendar (New Year's Day, July 19th on the Julian calendar) fell on III Peret 1 (winter solstice, January 16th or 17th on the Julian calendar; II Peret 30 or III Peret 1 on the fixed civil calendar).

I postulate that this particular exchange was intended. Hypothetically, the Egyptian calendar began in 4242 BCE, so that 724 years later, only the years 3518, 3517, 3516, and 3515 BCE qualify. Only in those years, on January 16th or 17th, could a solar eclipse have been visible in Heliopolis in Egypt. The subsequent years that might theoretically be considered to relate to the birth of kingship would be 2058 up to and including 2055 BCE (1,460 years after 3518 and 3515 BCE respectively). However, this possibility must be categorically excluded because Pharaonic Egypt lasted for an overall period of around 3,000 to 3,500 years, ending when Cleopatra committed suicide in 31 BCE.

The chances of a solar eclipse occurring on that winter solstice day in one of those years (3518, 3517, 3516, and 3515 BCE) and being observable in Egypt are extremely small. Still, its potential implications would be very significant. Even more notably, the solar eclipse which I hypothetically assume to have occurred is described as follows: "You have wounded the sacred Eye of Heliopolis on the Day of the Festivity of the Face ("am Tage des Festes der Gesichter") (Urkunde VI, Sethe, 138: 19-22).

The phrase "Festivity of the Face" alludes to the Eyes, in particular to those of the Sun and the Moon. In addition, the 19th century German Egyptologist J. Krall wrote (cf. **Studien zur Geschichte des alten Ägypten I**, Krall, p.868, which renders an unusual image): "In that case, the Festivity to commemorate the suspension of the Heavens by the ancient God Ptah, who was venerated as the Creator of the World [Hephaestus, Memphis], would present us with a remnant from the time when, on the winter solstice, the young Sun, according to the testimonies of Macrobius (ibid, Krall 837-838) [cf. also Plutarchus, *De Iside et Osiride*, Griffith, 1970, 221 and 530], set out on its annual course and simultaneously pointed to the start of the year and the creation of the world (a mere hypothesis)".

Krall's hypothesis and mine prove to be correct; the specific date on which the solar eclipse was visible in Heliopolis and on which the Installation of Kingship in Egypt occurred is 17th January 3517 BCE (J.D. 436,855). This is clearly illustrated by the Vignette of Chapter 140 in the *Book of the Dead*. The solar eclipse occurred on the winter solstice (0° Capricorn) and is indicative of the aforementioned texts, their astronomical knowledge, and of the ancient Egyptians' way of thinking. It marks a new beginning.

Referring to the results of "The Pyramids Carbon-dating Project" (cf. § 1.3 Chronological Entanglements), recent excavations at Abydos, which were carried out under the supervision of the Egyptologist Dreyer, revealed amazing objects of excellent workmanship from the Naqada I period (before approximately 3600 BCE). These objects bear the oldest hieroglyphs known to us, which puts the date of the transition from Egyptian prehistory to history back by some 500 years to around 3500 BCE.

This outcome definitively changes the present chronology of Egypt, as well as that of Sumeria/Babylonia. The present chronology of Egypt has to be back-dated by approximately 500 years. The occurrence of this eclipse offers important information to geophysicists. Professor Stephenson, a specialist on eclipses, unaware of the above results, is therefore wont to point out that "in no other science [with the exception of geophysics and astronomy], do observations, made two to three thousand years ago, still retain their value for research that we undertake at present."

Armed with this new information, the inconstancy of the rotation of the Earth can be calculated anew. This very important discovery will produce interesting implications. Not only have convincing documents been found concerning the observation of a very ancient solar eclipse that may be called unique in its class, but two dates have now been established. The beginning of the Egyptian calendar on 19th July 4242 BCE (J.D. 172,232) marks the first date of the History of the World. Secondly, the installation date of the Birth of Kingship of the First Dynasty fell on 17th January 3517 BCE. As a result, the Egyptian Chronology has now been established conclusively.

B: From Star-cult to Sun-cult

The addition of the suffix *Re* to the name of a pharaoh was introduced during the reign of the Fourth Dynasty, with Pharaoh Djedef-*Re*. This addition points to the origin of the sun-cult and a simultaneous astronomical event. The uniqueness of this phenomenon, which occurred between approximately 2930 and 2900 BCE, lay in the Sun's appearance at exactly 0° of the zodiacal sign Cancer, i.e. at the summer solstice, immediately before dawn of the day on which the heliacal rising of the star Sirius was seen in Heliopolis (cf. appendix III).[19] This had *never* occurred before in ancient Egypt's history. It proves that from Djedefre's reign onward (circa 2900 BCE), the star-cult was gradually replaced by the sun-cult. It marked a highly significant turning-point, which caused their religion to become involved in various entanglements.

The star-cult that prevailed at that time merged with the sun-cult that would subsequently gain great importance. Previously, the Sun had appeared in the zodiacal sign Gemini on the days of Sirius' heliacal rising. The transition of the Sun's location to Cancer, specifically in the degree that pertained to the summer solstice (0° Cancer), was an exceptional astronomical event to the Egyptians and bore such tremendous significance that it even caused them to change their religion. At that eventful moment, the sun-cult was introduced and then gradually brought into force, becoming permanently installed around 2825 BCE towards the beginning of the Fifth Dynasty (which has now been set at 2465 BCE). The sun-cult of the god Re (Sun) definitively ousted the star-cult of the god Atum (Sirius, cf. § 3.5).

This led to the conception of the falcon-headed Re-Horakhti being born around 2900 BCE (cf. fig. 5). Henceforth, the Egyptians called the last month of their calendar "Mesore", a word meaning "birth of the sungod Re".[20] This phrase is self-explanatory, and enables an even more precise dating. It tells us that the first year of the sun-cult dates back to approximately 2922 BCE, when Atum, the star Sirius, the great Creator, truly merged with Re.

The installation of this combined Atum-Re cult in Heliopolis marked a transition point. The merging of the star Sirius with the Sun is recited in the Pyramid Texts (Utterance 600), § 1652 in particular: "O Atum-Khoprer, you became high on the height, you rose up as the *bnbn*-stone in the Mansion of the 'Phoenix' in On [Heliopolis]." In other words, on the day of the heliacal rising of Sirius (Atum) in Heliopolis, the Sun (Re) which was positioned in the summer solstice (0° Cancer, the constellation representing Kheper and the scarab beetle), rose in the east and at a certain moment seemed to rest on top of the Benben column (phallus with conical top) in the temple of the "Phoenix" in Heliopolis. Symbolically, the star Sirius copulated with the Sun, which resulted in the creation of the sun-cult. The fact is that the star Sirius correlated with the temple of Heliopolis (cf. chapter 4 and the correlation theory).

It follows from our current observations that the above climatological turning-point, as well as the indication that the Egyptian year began at the winter solstice, and the transition from star-cult to sun-cult, rank as permanent points of chronological calibration.

The results of the carbon dating will undoubtedly have an effect on the chronology of Egypt and of other ancient cultures with which it is chronologically linked.

1.5 A New Geographic Framework and a New Setting

The climatological turning-point in 5300 BCE resulted in the birth of the river cultures of Sumeria and Egypt. The ancestors of the Egyptians, the Followers of Horus, founded their first settlements in the region of Memphis, whereupon thirty kings reigned for a period of 1,790 years before the first Dynasty of Egypt came to power around 3518 BCE. The Followers of Horus were to recognise Osiris symbolically in the geography (geomorphologic structure) of Egypt, their new country. There, they would experience the religious ideas of their god Osiris anew. Thousands of years later, they were to build pyramids and thereby create what is now known as the Pyramid Field in a manner that would set the ritual pose of their god, Horus, in stone for eternity." They were to choose the locations in accordance with the landscape of their new country.

The town-states of Sumeria came about in that same period. Their inhabitants mingled with the population of the Kish region and subsequently founded Ur, Erech, Ubaid and Eridu in the Garden of Eden of Mesopotamia, our proverbial paradise.

These facts show the development of civilisation in a new perspective. To start with, they break through that rigid boundary which is set at 3000 BCE. From 5300 BCE onward, civilisation on the Euphrates, Tigris and the Nile went through stages of development that were triggered off by an extreme change in the climate. In this context, we refer to the "out-of-Africa theory", which will be shown to gain surprising support and acquire a powerful new impetus from current research, described in Chapter 5, on what is known as the Sumerian planisphere.

During the sixth millennium, the ancestors of the Egyptians had already experienced tumultuous times. Now, this natural catastrophe drove them from their habitat. Again they were forced to create a new framework and a new setting in unknown territory, in the land we now know as Egypt. They continued

Fig. 5. Statue of the God Re-Horakhti with the head of a falcon. Royal Museum for Art and History in Brussels.

to observe their traditions whilst they adapted themselves to the distinctive features of their new environment. They set up a new calendar, which was based on the heliacal rising of the star Sirius and marked the start of the first season (I Achet 1), coinciding with the flooding of the river Nile.

The first day of the Egyptian civil calendar was 19th July 4242 BCE, a New Moon-day (J.D. 172,232). They celebrated their annual New Year on this date, prior to yet another traditional New Year's Day, dating back to their distant past. This second New Year's Day, which occurred at the beginning of the second season, was celebrated immediately after the Osiris festival (I Peret 1), when they commemorated the rising of the land from the primaeval waters. To them, this annual event was a symbolic reminder of the first period of their civilisation and of the natural catastrophe that drove their ancestors from the "islands at the edge of the world". From that second New Year's Day onward, the waters of the Nile gradually subsided. Like the year before, the land slowly re-emerged. The sowing season set in, announcing the creation of new life. The Nile and the Osiris festival were inextricably linked up with one another. Thus, Egypt was not only a gift of the Nile, as Herodotus stated: the Nile was literally and figuratively the personification of Osiris, something that appeared to be unknown and, up to now, even incomprehensible, because since time immemorial, it has remained buried under the dust of the centuries.

Chapter 2

Osiris and the Cosmic Geography

Histories, the work by the famous Greek historian Herodotus (circa 485-425 BCE) provides us with vital information on ancient Egypt. Egyptian priests presented him with an image that is now nearly 2,500 years old. This enabled Herodotus to offer us a glimpse into the daily life and the ideas of ancient Egypt. However, his information seems to suffer from a lack of sufficient confidence in its trustworthiness, if the following quotation carries any weight: *"So far, the historical capita of Herodotus' second book (II, 99-182) have, quite legitimately in our view, been considered to consist of two clearly distinguishable parts, namely II, 99-146 and II, 147-182. The first part hardly contains any useful historical material and merely amounts to a sequence of accounts which, in spite of their general historical authenticity, were frequently spun out by popular fantasy and became mutilated to such an extent that it has now become difficult to distinguish history from legend."* [1]
The opinion of the Egyptologist De Meulenaere has caused the loss of important information. What is more, no mention is made of Book II, 1-99. This information by Herodotus is trusted even less by Egyptologists. In general, his manuscripts are regarded as " the source of numerous errors and hackneyed phrases, which quite commonly still receive credit." [2] This attitude leads unwittingly to the gradual dismissal of fundamental information on astronomical-cum-religious knowledge of the Egyptians and their chronology.

2.1 Herodotus and the Golden Era of Osiris

The Egyptians used chronological transition-points to mark the beginning of their eras. Herodotus tells us about these points in their chronology:
" I was told that Heracles [Hercules and the zodiacal sign Sagittarius] was one of the Twelve Gods, but I could not hear anything anywhere in Egypt about the other Heracles, the one familiar to the Greeks. Now, I could supply a great deal of evidence to support the idea that the Greeks got the name of Heracles from Egypt, rather than the other way round, and that the Greeks then applied the name Heracles to the son of Amphitryon. I have a great deal of evidence pointing in this direction. Here is just one item: both parents of the Greek Heracles, Amphitryon and Alcmene, trace their lineage back to Egypt. Moreover, the Egyptians claim not to know the names of Poseidon and the Dioscuri, and these gods are not to be found in their pantheon. But if the Egyptians had borrowed the name of any deity from the Greeks, Poseidon and the Dioscuri would not have been overlooked, but would have stuck in their minds more than any other Greek deity - if I am right in my view that even in those days the Egyp-

tians were making sea voyages and so were some of the Greeks. From this it follows that the Egyptians would be more aware of the names of these gods than they would of Heracles. No, in fact Heracles is a very ancient Egyptian god; as they themselves say, it was *17,000* years before the reign of King Amasis [Pharaoh Amasis ruled from 570 - 526 BCE] when the Twelve Gods descended from the Eight Gods, and they regard Heracles as one of the Twelve."[3] (cf. chapter 4.2).

Herodotus also referred to said beginning of the reign of Pharaoh Amasis in the following fragment:

" They demonstrated, then, that all the people portrayed by these statues were mortal human beings, bearing no relation to gods. They claimed, however, that before these men gods had been the kings of Egypt - that they had lived alongside human beings and that at any given time one of them had been the supreme ruler. The last of these divine kings of Egypt, they said, had been Horus the son of Osiris, whom the Greeks call Apollo. He had deposed Typhon and become the last divine king of Egypt. In Greek, Osiris is Dionysus." [4]

Further on, Herodotus continues:

" In Greece, the youngest gods are considered to be Heracles, Dionysus, and Pan, but in Egypt Pan is regarded as one of the Eight Primal Gods (as they are called), and therefore as the oldest of the three, because Heracles is thought to belong to the second group (called the Twelve) and Dionysus to the third group, who were descendants of the Twelve. I have stated earlier how many years there are, according to the Egyptians, from Heracles to the time of King Amasis [fragment 1]; Pan is supposed to be even earlier, and although the interval between Dionysus and Amasis is the smallest of the three, they calculate it at *15,000* years. The Egyptians claim to have precise knowledge of all this, because they have always kept count of and continuously chronicled the passing years."[5]

Hence, Herodotus is seen to revert twice to the beginning of the reign of Pharaoh Amasis in 570 BCE as a chronological pointer within his historiography. Since Herodotus lived nearly a hundred years after the reign of Amasis, they were not contemporaries. Nevertheless, he mentions this specific pharaoh on two occasions, thereby bringing this significant juncture in the history of Egypt to the reader's notice.

In point of fact, he actually draws attention to a moment of extreme importance in the history of the entire world, as 570 BCE or thereabouts marked the dawn of a new era in which Greek culture went through a rapid development, in which villages were cleared in accordance with the urban planning, which itself foresaw the creation of the future town of Rome, the cradle of what developed later into the Roman Empire. It also marked the point in time when the supremacy of the state of Egypt began irrevocably to crumble. The old world announced its end. The classical era of Greeks and Romans was now ushered in.

We notice how Herodotus pointed out chronological periods that were apparently of great astronomical importance to the ancient Egyptians and old world. We will go on to show that the start of these periods happened to coincide with astronomical phenomena to which the Egyptians attached such significance, and that these provided them with the foundation on which they based their religion. In other words, Herodotus' account leads us to the fundamental driving forces behind Egyptian religious belief (cf. especially chapter 4.2, 4.3 and 4.4).

Evidently, Herodotus calculated that the beginning of the Golden Era of Osiris was in 15,570 BCE. In addition, the Egyptians based their chronological calculations on the start of the reign of Pharaoh Amasis and in doing so, revealed a few chronological transition points in their own history.

In order to count their years, the Egyptians used, amongst other things, the Sirius-Moon calendar. This calendar had fixed periods of 25 years. Detailed investigations show that the beginning of the reign of Pharaoh Amasis coincided with the start of a new 25-year period on this Sirius-Moon calendar, namely at sunrise on 5th January 569 BCE (Julian Calendar, Julian Day = JD 1,513,600). It was a New-Moon day, and at the end of the afternoon, exactly at sunset, the New Moon occurred. This was the day and the moment in time that the Egyptian priests had referred to in their conversation with Herodotus.

The Egyptians apparently used these fixed periods to synchronise their calendar: 25 Egyptian years of 365 days amount to a total of 9,125 days, which coincides exactly with 309 Moon-periods. Since the duration of the lunar orbit is freakish and varies, a high standard of astronomical observation and knowledge is required to determine the precise number of solar years in which an exact number of lunar orbits can be calculated. Exact calculations of this kind concerning the lunar orbit prove unquestionably that the ancient Egyptians had attained a highly advanced level of astronomical knowledge.

2.2 The Golden Era of Osiris and the Zodiac of Denderah

We have already quoted Herodotus, Book II-144, where he stated that the Greek Dionysos and the Egyptian Osiris are one and the same deity. Obviously, Herodotus' account implies that the Era of Osiris began in the year 15,570 BCE. Egyptian religious texts often refer to this period as the paradisaical "Era of Osiris", also known as the "First Era" or Zep Tepi,[6] the First Golden Century. "The rule of Osiris on Earth was seen as Egypt's happiest and most noble epoch and was believed to have existed in the distant abyss of time [...]"[7] We may therefore conclude, theoretically at least, that the history of the Egyptians dates back to 15,570 BCE. Furthermore, they claimed that a world era had begun around 17,570 BCE.

Denderah prides itself on an important temple, which was dedicated to Hathor. It once contained a stone plaque, known as the round Zodiac, *showing the image of Osiris*. This plaque had been placed in the roof-chapel of the sanctuary, where the semen of Osiris sprouted annually. At present, the original plaque is on display in the Louvre museum in Paris. That Osiris (cf. fig. 6) is depicted on this plaque is by all means a stroke of luck. It allows for a definitive identification of Osiris with a constellation, which, incredible though it may seem, has still not been correctly established up to this very day. Obviously, previous research on the identity of Osiris either overlooked his presence on the plaque, or the object itself was persistently disregarded. Osiris' effigy is shown diametrically opposite to Sahu-Orion. Hence, Osiris, having been

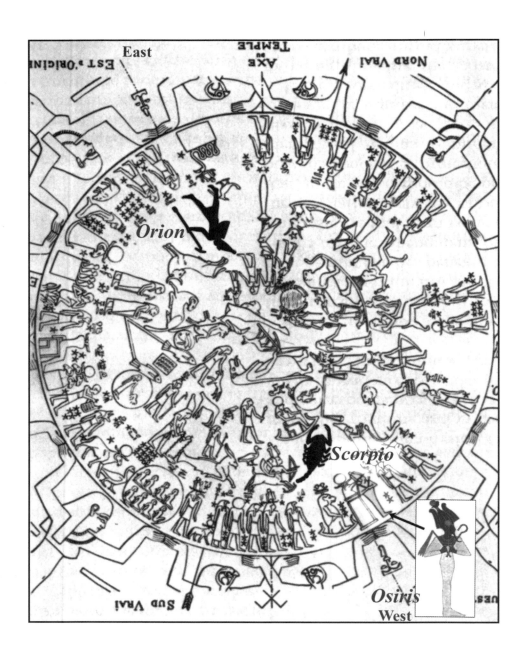

Fig. 6. Plaque of Denderah, a round Zodiac with celestial constellations. The temple complex was built around 100 BCE. On the outer edge, Osiris (below, to the right) is pictured diametrically opposite Orion (top part, to the left). This temple replaced a much older sanctuary; according to information which was handed down and to inscriptions in and around the temple. Pharaoh Khufu and Pepi I are said to have founded a building in which rituals were held that can be traced back to the pre-dynastic Followers of Horus (WdO, column 2982). The Horus falcon on the papyrus stalk is pictured between Orion and Sothis (Sirius).

pictured on the opposite side to Orion, definitely *cannot* be identical with the latter (cf. fig. 6).

In the 1960s, the astronomer Neugebauer and Egyptologist Parker carried out combined research, subsequently publishing their findings in **Egyptian Astronomical Texts**. In this book, Osiris is repeatedly identified with Orion. As a consequence, we nowadays even find the names of Osiris, Orion and Sahu bracketed together. In their book, Neugebauer and Parker argue their case as follows: "In the Pyramid Texts, Sahu [Orion] is identified with Osiris which fits well with its depiction as a human figure on the coffins and ceilings."[8] However, the illustration on the plaque clearly renders Neugebauer and Parker's conclusion doubtful, to say the least. The plaque shows Osiris and Sahu-Orion depicted separately, spaced apart as two separate, divine personifications.

Nevertheless, Neugebauer and Parker's statements have been adopted by a considerable number of scientists, resulting in a large-scale acceptance that the constellation Orion - the Hunter with his upraised arm - corresponds in all respects with Osiris.[9] This view dovetailed squarely with the correlation-theory which Bauval and Gilbert developed in their book **The Orion Mystery**. They adopted this disputable concept and based their theory relating to Osiris-Orion on the verbatim link between these two characters.

However, this link is incorrect. To our knowledge, the only scientist who took a different approach in his search for the origin of Osiris, and who did not share Neugebauer and Parker's conclusion, was the Egyptologist Piankoff. He postulated correctly that Orion-Sahu is the *visible* manifestation of the soul of Osiris. Pyramid Text §819C tells us: "Osiris has come as Orion." Piankoff's metaphor is correct when he spoke of "a visible manifestation".[10]

In order to reach a correct evaluation of these opinions, it should be borne in mind that the visible appearance of the constellation Orion-Sahu on the eastern horizon, just before sunrise, coincides with the setting of the Osiris constellation on the western horizon. That is why Orion-Sahu was and truly remains the "visible manifestation" of Osiris after the latter has set on the western horizon. To the ancient Egyptians, the true image of Osiris, after he had disappeared under the horizon and became invisible to the eye, dwelt in the Netherworld, which corresponds perfectly with the image held by the Egyptians of Osiris: he was the pre-eminent deity of the Netherworld.

The fact that the images of Osiris and that of Orion-Sahu are placed separately on the plaque of Denderah puts an end to all further discussions. Obviously, Osiris is definitely not identical with Orion. The image on the Zodiac of Denderah shows this only too plainly. Both constellations, Scorpio and Taurus, will forever take opposite positions. The Egyptians understood this perfectly: the soul of Osiris rested in Orion. That is why Orion was the "visible manifestation" of Osiris.

As the image on the plaque shows, Osiris (sbssn= Sebshesen) is one of the 36 figures who are the spirits of the decans, and the ruler of the zodiacal sign of Scorpio. One of the astro-religious meanings attributed to this sign is Death, yet so is Resurrection. To the Egyptians, Osiris fulfilled the function of the Judge of the Dead, as well as being the god of Resurrection.

Furthermore, the plaque shows Orion-Sahu apart, between the constellation of Taurus and Gemini, representing germinative power, growth, and development (in fact: life itself), qualities that correspond entirely with the

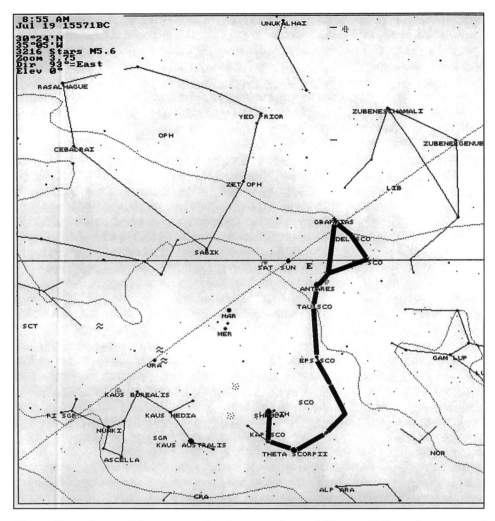

Fig. 7. Star chart of the eastern horizon on the 30° N. parallel on the assumed New Year's day: July 19th in 15,571 BCE. According to Herodotus the Greek, it marked the beginning of Zep Tepi, the Golden Era of Osiris. The constellation Scorpio rises above the horizon whilst the Spring Equinox lies within the sign of Scorpio.

significance and the respective role which the Egyptians attributed to the constellation Orion-Sahu. Life, Death and Resurrection therefore became (jointly) united in the pyramid field, the residence and necropolis of Osiris/Orion-Sahu.

From this perspective, the contents of the quoted fragments from Herodotus' Book II-145 take on a completely different meaning and acquire an increased value. After all, the information he obtained from the Egyptian priests implied that the *Era of Osiris* commenced in the year 15,570 BCE. A star chart set for July 19th of the year 15,570 BCE affirms that Osiris does indeed represent an important part of the constellation Scorpio. On that particular day, immediately before sunrise, the sign Scorpio rose on the eastern horizon (cf. fig. 7).

2.3 The parts of Osiris

Plutarch, the Greek biographer and essayist (46-120 CE), was the author of the famous *Isis and Osiris*. We are forced to rely on his work, since no Egyptian sources are known to exist that render an entirely coherent account on this subject. He wrote that Seth tore the body of Osiris into fourteen parts.[11] Egyptian sources mention either fourteen or sixteen parts.[12]

The constellation Scorpio consists of sixteen stars, including Antares, which is the most prominent. The occasional mention of no more than fourteen stars could be explained by the fact that in those days the naked eye might well have been unable to discern more than that number. What we are suggesting is that there is a correspondence between the body of Osiris and the zodiacal sign, in which every part of Osiris' body is represented by a star of the constellation Scorpio. Osiris is thus shaped by the following *sixteen* stars:

nu Scorpii (Lesath); lambda Scorpii (Shaula); kappa Scorpii; iota Scorpii; theta Scorpii (Sargas); eta Scorpii; zeta Scorpii; epsilon Scorpii; tau Scorpii; alpha Scorpii (Antares); sigma Scorpii (Al Niyat); upsilon Scorpii; beta Scorpii (Graffias); delta Scorpii (Isidis); pi Scorpii; rho Scorpii.

According to Papke's research, the star beta Scorpii (8° Scorpio) is positioned at "the entrance of the Realm of the Dead ",[13] which, amongst other issues, confirms that Scorpio is considered to be the Netherworld, and simultaneously ascertains the identity of Osiris as its ruler.

At that same crucial spot, the path of the Ecliptic (Sinus line) exits the northern hemisphere and enters the southern one. The Ecliptic thereby crosses the Celestial Equator (by projecting the globe of the Earth to the Celestial Sphere, the Earth Equator = the Celestial Equator).

2.4 The Nile and Osiris are one

Geographically, the unique course of the Nile exerted a major influence on religious developments within the Egyptian civilisation. Figures 8 and 9 illustrate convincingly the similarity between the constellation of Osiris in the heavens and the course of the Nile, including its Delta. These figures will serve to place this resemblance in a correct context.

The Egyptians called the Nile 'Jotru'. The term *Hapi* also refers to the river Nile, but stresses its intangible spirit and its inner power. "Hapi was held to be included among the forms of the god [Osiris]."[14] In other words, the river Nile renders the outline (shape) of the god Osiris and calls to mind "[...] that Egypt is [the] image of heaven."[15]

The course of the Nile from the town of Denderah and the wadi Qena down to and including the entire Delta stylistically resembles a *mirrored* image of the constellation Scorpio, i.e. Osiris. This might mean that the Egyptians observed the constellations in the night skies by using a mirror. Figure 9 shows how the location of the towns of Abydos and Thinis (star theta Scorpii is Sargas) were chosen to correspond symbolically with the rear end of Scorpio, which explains

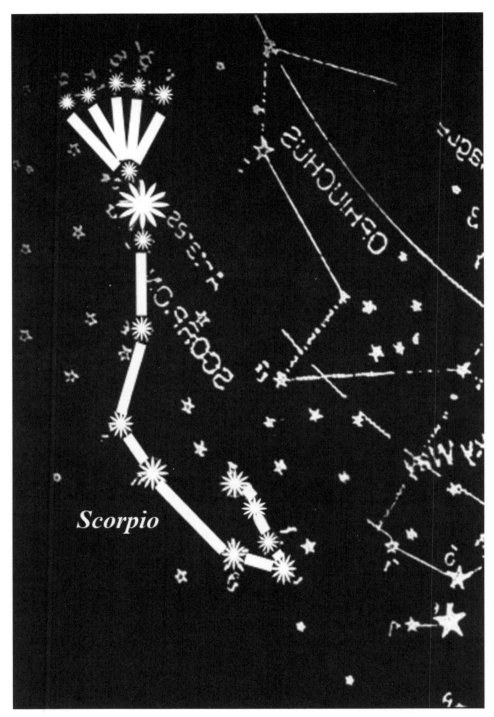

*Fig. 8. Mirrored map of the heavens (from **COSMIC; the Universe of Stars**) of the constellation Scorpio and its correlation with the river basin of the Nile from Thebes up to and including the Delta, and the correspondence between the course of the river and the settlements of ancient Egypt, cf. fig.9).*

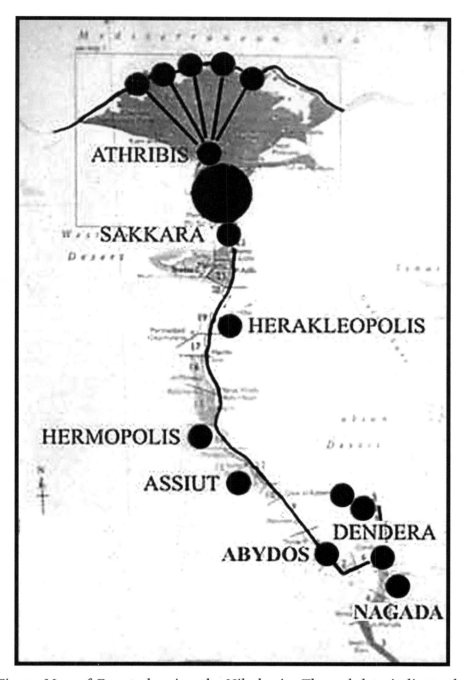

Fig. 9. Map of Egypt showing the Nile basin. The red dots indicate the settlements and correlate with the stars of the constellation Scorpio (see fig. 8). The large dot correlates with the Golden Triangle Letopolis-Heliopolis-Memphis and the Pyramid field on this site. The dots at the endings of the five arms (Delta) are stars, yet obviously do not correlate with previous settlements. Whether the dots above Denderah bear any relevant correspondence remains unknown until further excavations.

the strong link the Egyptians experienced between these towns and the god Osiris.

Abydos ranks amongst the oldest towns of Egypt. It was the unparalleled centre of homage to Osiris. Pilgrimages were undertaken by boat, both upstream to Abydos and downstream from the town Busiris. This journey was known as the "voyage of the dead"; participation in the Osiris festival in Busiris was considered a special privilege. Numerous ancient Egyptian texts mention the remarkable scenic correspondence between the Nile and the sign Scorpio. In *The Book of Two Ways* (circa 2050 BCE) we read verbatim: "I have passed over the paths of Rostau, whether on water or on land, and these are the paths of Osiris, they are [also] in the limit of the sky..."[16]

Similar descriptions are found in the Pyramid Texts §589, 788 and 1360 respectively. "Horus comes and recognises his father in you, you being young in your name of Fresh Water"; "You have your water, you have your flood, the fluid which issued from the god, the exudation which issued from Osiris"; "Your water is yours, your flood is yours, your efflux which issued from the putrefaction of Osiris is yours." In all these texts, it is the river Nile that is being referred to.

The same is found in the cosmogony of the Myth of Horus and Seth. After the battle between Horus and Seth, Seth killed Osiris, cut his body into fourteen parts, which he then scattered into the Nile. Isis searched for the parts and found them, yet the phallus remained untraceable as the fish had devoured it. Numerous texts make it apparent how Osiris could literally be recognised in the shape that is drawn by the course of the river Nile. In Pyramid Texts §1044, this is rendered verbatim: "If I go down into the water, Osiris will lift me up." Here, Osiris appears as a personification of the Nile.[17]

In his *Praeparatio Evangelica,* the Patriarch Eusebius claimed that the classics stated that the legends about Osiris and Isis, as well as all other mythologies, were related to the stars and their configurations, to their rising and their setting.[18] The Egyptians also believed in the existence of a "heavenly" Nile; even now, this is still presumed to allude to water or to rain. However, the Egyptians were definitely not referring either to water or to rain; to them, the Nile was and is also visible in the star-spangled sky. The Egyptologist Daressy starts his article *L'Egypte Céleste* as follows: "It is a known fact that the Egyptian priests were eager to find, either in the sky or in the domain of the Genii, similarities with our Earth; the one world is merely a replica of the other, the Nile is a *'celestial road, which descended on earth'*.[19] A song of praise, known as *"The Great Hymn to the Aten"* from the Amarna period, expresses this with even greater clarity in the following sentences: "You made Hapi (the Nile god) in *dat* (the Netherworld), You bring him [as flood waters] when you will, to nourish the people; [...] You made a heavenly Hapy descend for them."[20] These texts tell us that during the Creation, the celestial Nile descended on Earth in Egypt. The classicists (Eratosthenes, Germanicus and Hyginus) presumed that the constellation Eridanus possessed that function for the Egyptians. However, in view of the remarkable similarity between the constellation Scorpio and the course of the Nile and its delta, it is quite evident that the Egyptians never alluded to the constellation Eridanus, or even to the Milky Way. In the following paragraph, the correlation between stars of the constellation Scorpio and certain settlements along the Nile, which were known to be places dedicated to the Osiris cult, will be demonstrated.

2.5 Strongholds of the Osiris-cult

The geographical similarity between the Nile basin and the mirrored constellation Scorpio as shown on any star map is striking and convincing. The locations of a number of important settlements along the Nile, which were known to the Egyptians as strongholds of the Osiris cult, underline this similarity with additional authority. A projection of the mirrored image of the constellation Scorpio onto the Nile basin reveals that the five branches of the Delta correlate with the five branches of the constellation. The Delta was presumed to harbour the "House of Selket"[21] (Scorpio).

Likewise, the following correlations show up:
- the town of Athribis with the star sigma Scorpio;
- the golden triangle between the towns Letopolis, Heliopolis and Memphis with the stars alpha (Antares) and tau Scorpio;
- the region of Herakleopolis with the star epsilon Scorpio, the region Hermopolis with the star zeta Scorpio;
- the region Asyut-Syut with the star eta Scorpio, as well as the extremely important region Thinis-Abydos-Hiw with the star theta Scorpio.
The tail of Scorpio runs towards Denderah and Coptos (cf. fig. 9), so that after the course of the Nile was known, these surroundings, from Thinis up to and including Edfu, were chosen to become the Proto-Kingdom of Upper Egypt. The focal area was situated between Abydos and Hiw and included the prehistoric settlement El Amra (Amratian, circa 4200 BCE), where the Badarian-Amratian culture, originating in Nubia, attained prosperity.

Osiris was linked with the God Sepa the centipede (in actual fact, this animal, the scolopendra cingulata, possesses 42 legs, a number of considerable importance; cf. sections 4.2, 4.3 and 4.4), that had a sanctuary situated not far from the Heliopolitan harbour on the Nile, near the Nile meter (measuring the height of the river Nile) on the Island Roda.[22] In chapter 4, we will go into the significant role this location played in plotting out the exact position of the various pyramids.

In Athribis, "der grosse Schwarze"[23], the Great Black One, was worshipped, while in Heliopolis relics of Osiris, such as the flail and hook, were kept during the Late Period.[24] In early 2000 AD, a symbolic tomb of Osiris was found on the territory of Giza, which contained a granite sarcophagus. In Herakleopolis, an Osiris tomb was found in which thigh bones, a skull and both lower legbones had been placed as relics.[25] In Hermopolis, the "feather on the shoulder of Osiris"[26] was found. In Asyut, another Osirian tomb was located.[27] At Abydos, where the megalithic Osireion was built, another thighbone was found.[28]

2.6 Constellations on Earth?

The ancient Egyptians evidently applied themselves to the study of the heavens, the stellar constellations, and the course of the planets. They were the very first to have arranged the visible profusion of stars into constellations, to which they subsequently adapted the geographical infrastructure of their country. It will become evident in the course of this book that they actually depicted various constellations on Earth, either by means of specific locations for their settlements, or by pyramids. From the Egyptian point of view, a parallel existed between Heaven and Earth. This is made very clear in the following text: *"Or are you ignorant, Asclepius, that Egypt is [the] image of heaven?"* [29]

How the Egyptians discovered the striking similarity between the course of the Nile and the constellation Scorpio (Osiris) can only have been determined by surveying the territory from a fixed measuring point, for instance a meridian or an axis running through the entire country. In that case, they would have measured the course of the river Nile at regular intervals in reference to this meridian, enabling them subsequently to determine its course. Possibly they drew up a geographic image, which was then compared with the celestial sphere, allowing them to perceive that specific correspondence. By these means, the Egyptians assembled their first constellation, an ability which they had mastered in a far-distant past.

2.7 The "Osiris-meridian"

Egyptologists are willing to recognise the north-to-south course of the Nile as an opportunity for ancient Egyptians to make their river fulfil the function of a meridian,[30] which would then have served them as a means to divide their world into an eastern and a western half. This could, to a certain extent, be compared to the function of the Zero Meridian of Greenwich. Research in that direction brought an even more sensational fact to light, namely the existence of a "meridian" at 31°13' E.[31] Surprisingly, this longitudinal meridian was *not* merely the specific meridian we had been looking for that would divide Egypt into an eastern and a western half, it also proved to define the "Middle of the World", a concept we will come across further on.

Various texts show that the Egyptians believed their country to be the centre of the world. In their own words: Egypt was the heart of the *historical* world, the "Centre" of the world in which the gods (the stars) had their temples. This is apparent in the following texts: "The most sacred land of our ancestors lies in the centre of the world."[32] Furthermore: "The ancient Egyptians considered their country to be the centre of the world",[33] and: "Our temples are your image, your shadow is every god."[34] We postulate that they believed this to be literally true and that they filled this notion with a geographic meaning, which is endorsed by the fact that this meridian marks the location of the Djoser complex, the first and therefore the oldest pyramid of Egypt.

This hitherto unsuspected longitudinal meridian, which began and ended in towns called Abusir and was in fact marked and characterised by settlements that at present bear this Arabic name, will be subsequently referred to as the *"Osiris meridian"*. We extract this term from the meaning of the word Abusir, as set forth by the Egyptologist Lehner: "The Arabic word [Abusir] is derived from the Greek Busiris, which in turn stems from the ancient Egyptian Per Wsir, [of which the meaning is] "house of Osiris". [Hence,] Abusir portrays the myth of Osiris who was murdered, cut into pieces and buried in various pla-

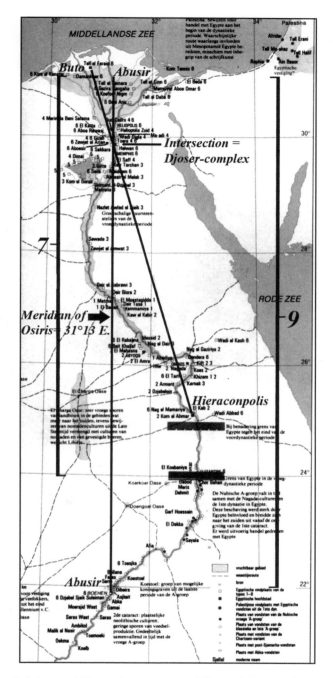

Fig 10. The Osiris meridian: the zero meridian of the ancient world. On the right, the Nine Bows - i.e. precisely nine degrees of latitude - are indicated. Later on, for instance during the New Kingdom, these were reduced to Seven Bows - precisely seven degrees of latitude - (as indicated on the left). Furthermore, the observation track between the prehistoric capitals Hierakonpolis and Buto is shown. It crosses the Osiris meridian at Saqqara in the Djoser complex.

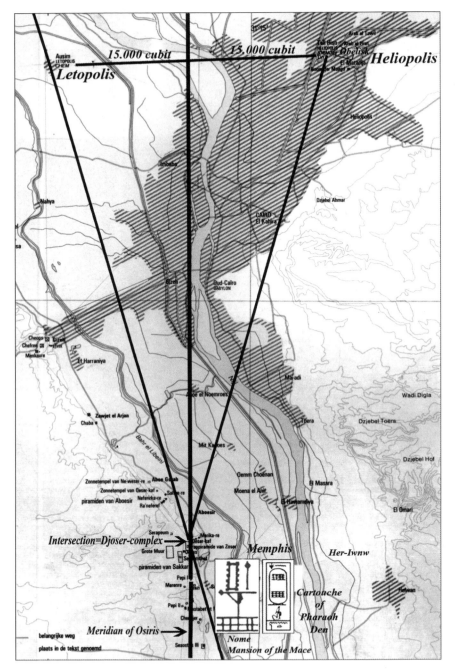

Fig. 11. *The Osiris meridian runs exactly midway between the temple-cities Heliopolis and Letopolis. The observation track extends from Hierakonpolis via the Djoser complex through the temple city Letopolis to Buto. Note the isosceles triangle between Memphis/Helwan (Her-IWNW), Heliopolis and Letopolis. The grid expresses structure and order, achieved with the aid of land-surveying methods that were introduced by Pharaoh Den; cf. his cartouche.*

ces."[35] The "Osiris-meridian" runs from *Abusir* in the extreme north (30°55' N. and 31°14' E.) via the second *Abusir* (29°53' N. and 31°13' E.) and ends near *Abusir* (21°50' N. and 31°13' E.) in the deep south.

In detail, the "Osiris meridian" began at *Abusir* (Busiris, 30°55' N.). On its way towards the deep south it ran across Abusir (29°53' N.), continued in between the Djoser complex and Memphis, via the pyramids of Dahshur (29°48' N.) and the pyramids of Mazghuna (29°46' N.), the pyramids of El Lisht (29°34' N.), the prehistoric settlement of Girza (29°27' N.), then crossed the Nile at El Attawla/ Asyut (27°14' / 27°11' N.). The "Osiris meridian" ended in *Abusir* (21°50' N.) near the fortress-town of Buhen, close to the second cataract in the Nile (cf. fig. 10).

These various places through which the "Osiris meridian" runs, are all located on 31°13' E., and both the beginning and the end of the meridian are notably defined by places bearing the name *Abusir*. The Egyptians accordingly used three "fixed" points, Abusir (Busiris) in the North, the intersection with the Nile near Asyut and Abusir in the south as a reference to chart the course of the Nile and their territory (cf. fig. 10). Hence, this "Osiris meridian" extended across precisely nine zones, between the latitude of Abusir in the north to Abusir near Buhen. Furthermore, the meridian ran in between and at equal distance from Heliopolis and Letopolis (cf. fig. 10 and 11).

It cannot be ruled out that around 5300 BCE, marshes and lagoons dominated the region immediately north of the town of Busiris, which was founded at a later date. At this point, terra firma ended and so did the "Osiris meridian". North of Busiris, the uninhabitable Delta is presumed to have extended down to the Mediterranean Sea. Recent excavations have revealed that the prehistoric capital Buto (circa 3600 BCE) was once located near the coast, yet separated from the sea by marshland. In the course of millennia, large amounts of sludge were carried along by the Nile causing the Delta to spread out towards the north.

The second Abusir is located directly northeast of the Djoser complex. This area, bordering on the Lake of Abusir, not only harbours the pyramids and their annexes of the Fifth Dynasty, it is also the site of the mastabas (tombs) of the First and Second Dynasties. In addition, it is presumed to be the place where archaic Memphis was once located. These facts reveal that the primaeval capital Memphis was once the pulsating heart of their world, a world that came into existence around 5300 BCE. It was a world embued with life, which retained the memory of a catastrophe that had occurred in days of yore. The recollection of that disintegration of the world was kept alive in Busiris by an annual ritual ceremony called "Raising up the Djed pillars". This ceremony, in which the pillars served as columns that were meant to uphold the celestial vault, symbolised the support of the firmament. It was their way of averting the evil forces that had caused a catastrophe of such an extent, and prayers were uttered to invoke stability and permanence.

The "Osiris meridian" is also found on the plaque of Denderah, which was attached to the ceiling of the roof-chapel. This plaque shows the image of a Horus falcon on the stalk of a papyrus. Two children are seen holding each other by the hand; they represent the zodiacal sign Gemini. The Horus falcon marks the axis of the temple (centre line of the pylon) of Denderah, which points to 16° east of north. The north-south axis that runs through the plaque is marked by 0° of the sign Cancer and by 0° of the sign Capricorn (cf. fig. 6). Consequently, the axis of the temple was aligned to and correlated with 14° or 15° of the sign Gemini, i.e. the position of the star Alhena. The sign Aries marked the east.

From approximately 5300 BCE until 5150 BCE, the vernal equinox was in conjunction with the star Alhena. Therefore the characteristic image of the Horus falcon on the stalk of a papyrus on the plaque of Denderah marks the moment when the State of Egypt was founded in Memphis around 5300 BCE. Referring to this Horus falcon, especially to the stalk of the papyrus, the German Egyptologist Kees justifiably remarks: "also considered a star-constellation, and worshipped in Memphis due to its link with a Sokar sanctuary."[36] The Horus falcon, perched on the stalk of a papyrus, correlated with the aforementioned "Osiris meridian", which the Egyptians looked upon as the axis of their country.

Millennia later, the Djoser complex was built in the surroundings of Memphis/Abusir, namely on the intersection of the "Osiris meridian" with the observation track, which we will deal with in Chapter 3. This Djoser complex became the cornerstone of the pyramid field and of the State of Egypt, thereby imbuing the myth of Osiris with new life.

2.8 Nine Bows, or Nine degrees of latitude?

The enormous time-span covered by Egyptian civilisation makes it difficult for us to interpret some of its concepts. New discoveries, such as the "Osiris meridian", which covered nine degrees of latitude, throw a different light on certain notions.

The expression "Nine Bows" is used in the Pyramid Texts, e.g. §1655: "O you Great Ennead which dwells in On: [namely] Atum, Shu. Tefenet, Geb, Nut, Osiris, Isis, Seth, and Nephtys; O you children of Atum, extend his [good] wishes to his child in your name of the nine Bows." The Pyramid Texts date back to circa 2700 BCE, yet the "Nine Bows" are linked with a much older tradition that originated before the First Dynasty.

An even more striking example is provided by the base-plate of a statue of Pharaoh Djoser, which can be admired in the Egyptian Museum of Cairo. The remains of a sculpture of Pharaoh Djoser (circa 3150 BCE) displays the "Nine Bows" pictured under the feet of this pharaoh. The rendering implies that Pharaoh Djoser ruled over the "Nine Bows". But which "Nine Bows" did he rule over?

The term "Nine Bows" can be traced back to ancient times and is, theoretically at least, considered to denote the Egyptian dominion over the tribes they had conquered.[37] In the course of time, the true meaning of this notion faded away and the bow symbolised subjection and foreign enemies.[38] Presumably, in even earlier times, the "Nine Bows" possessed a different meaning, implying rulership over a territory with the size of "Nine Bows", over nine degrees of latitude, namely those between Abusir in the north and Abusir in the south (cf.

fig. 10). Representations are also known from later periods in which the Nine Bows were replaced by nine bars next to a bow.

Research by Egyptologist Säve-Söderbergh has shown that at a certain time (about the time of the New Kingdom), mention was made of "Seven Bows".[39] The history of ancient Egypt is known to have included prolonged periods in which the southern border was located near Philae, close to the first cataract on the Nile. During the New Kingdom for example, the territory of Egypt covered seven degrees of latitude, namely those between Philae and Abusir.

The deeper meaning of the term "Nine Bows" (also known as "People of the Nine Bows") points to the "presumed world dominion" of the Egyptians. During the Old Kingdom, a phrase was born in which the goddess Nechbet of Upper Egypt is said to "bind the bows together", in other words: she subjugated them to the rulership of the pharaoh.[40] Accordingly, the king of Egypt is pictured throughout the entire history in a *Ritual Pose*, in which he uses one fist to hold one or more enemies by the hair, while his other arm is raised, this fist brandishing a battle-axe or some other kind of weapon. This posture became the symbol for invincibility and even appeared in practically the same shape in the time of Roman rulership over Egypt.

This image was maintained for no less than approximately four millennia. This symbolic rendering, expressed in that bodily posture, represents the ritual pose known as "smiting the enemies".

Chapter 3

Sirius, a Geographical Guide

The following warning is said to have capped the entrance to Plato's Academy: *"Let no-one unversed in geometry enter my gates."* Neo-Platonists, orthodox followers of Platonism, based their notion of the world on perfect mathematics. Plato (circa 428-347 BCE) believed that geometry was superior to physics. Proclus (circa 410-485 CE), the last and greatest Greek advocate of Neo-Platonism, proclaimed that "we must follow the teachings of Timaeus." Plato did indeed integrate the principles of geometry into his **Timaeus**, recommending geometry as a preparatory study to philosophy. In his **Letters** III-319, there is a discussion in which geometry is clearly quoted: "Then what should I be instructed in first? In the skills of land-surveying?" In **Timaeus** 53-54, Plato explains: "Every triangle emerges from two triangles of a kind that has one right angle and two acute angles." Here, Plato is referring to the right-angled triangle, the basis on which he builds up his geometry.

The techniques of practising geometry or land-surveying had its roots in Egypt. This is mentioned by Aristotle in his **Metaphysics A1**, as well as by Herodotus in his Book II-109. Nowadays, we define the term *geometry* as "the science of the properties and relations of lines, angles, surfaces and solids".

Originally, geometry meant land-surveying, a skill in which the Egyptians were well-versed. Their surveyors were called "Harpedonapts" (stretchers of the cord). They were equipped with instruments such as a cord, a measuring-tape of a "fixed" length, and a drum with a rolled-up cord and a kind of view-finder mounted on top to take bearings from one gnomon to another (cf fig. 12). These devices allowed a fixed distance to be marked off in the field. The length of their measuring tapes will have had a specific length, for instance 50 meh (26.18 metres). In addition, they used a "Merkhet" to plot angles.

The Egyptologist Goyon believed that the Egyptians had undoubtedly mastered the art of geometry from the third millennium BCE onward,[1] if not already from the fourth millennium BCE. Evidence of this skill in measuring and plotting is found in texts and in the actual construction of the pyramids. In addition, these facts make it clear that they were acquainted with the division of the circle into 360 degrees and that they were also able to carry out angular calculations, further evidence of which we will mention later. This kind of knowledge of plotting and of measuring out specific lengths can be found on the border stelae of Achet-Aten, the present El Amarna. Pharaoh Amenhotep IV gave orders to inscribe on these border stelae how he intended to mark out Achet-Aten, his new residence. It exemplifies the skill and the precision with which they executed their plans, as we will make clear in the course of this book.

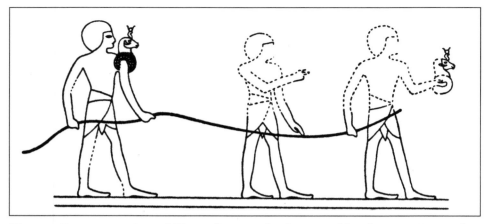

Fig. 12: Representation of Harpedonapts in the act of land-surveying; taken from the grave at Thebes of Amenhotpe-si-se of the XVIIIth Dynasty.

In the **Timaeus**, Plato postulates that "all triangles" derive from the combination of two other triangles that are both right-angled. This notion of Plato is described in the book **Kepler's Geometrical Cosmology**.[2] Kepler sided with Plato and both shared the belief in the Creator being a practitioner of geometry. In the Pythagorean teachings, the right-angled triangle is considered the triangle of God. Remarkably, in contrast to the Greeks, the Egyptians used the isosceles triangle. They called this isosceles triangle "the Triangle of the Deity".[3] The isosceles triangle became the hieroglyph for Sopdet, the star Sirius (see hieroglyph M44 and Z8 in: Survey **Egyptian Grammar**, Sir Alan Gardiner). This golden triangle is a gnomonic figure, highly appropriate for carrying out measurements.

3.1 The Djoser complex, Cornerstone of the State of Egypt

The former capital Memphis, close to the Djoser complex, has not yet been excavated. The site around Memphis also extends further eastward in the direction of the town of Helwan. Excavations have only recently begun, and no results have yet been published. In the meantime, we must base our assumptions on the notion that Egypt was generally still in a pristine condition around 3150 BCE, and that no building activities worth mentioning had yet taken place, with the exception of a few semi-oval clay enclosures, similar to those built within the temple complex of the prehistoric capital Hierakonpolis. Furthermore, burial chambers had been hewn and various mastaba graves had been built in Naqada and in the surroundings of Abydos for the pharaohs of the First Dynasty.

Towards the end of the Second Dynasty, Pharaoh Khasekhemwy built a fortress in the immediate surroundings of Hierakonpolis. In Abydos, remains still exist of the tomb of this last pharaoh of the Second Dynasty, which was constructed in fired flagstone. As far as we know, hardly any other building activities had been undertaken in Egypt at that time, least of all on a monumental scale and in natural stone.

This changed drastically at the start of the Third Dynasty. Plans had been drawn up to shape the Egyptian state. A location had to be determined for the mighty, large-scale Djoser complex, the cornerstone of the future Pyramid Field.

Of course, the obvious and intriguing question is: why was the Djoser complex built precisely on this location? The critical components in the construction of a building invariably consist of first plotting the location and then establishing the main measuring points. These points then serve to mark out the entire building project. Nowadays, a theodolite is used to specify the overall building frame, consisting of pickets that are driven into the ground and to which a lath (a length of wood) is attached. The main measuring points are then indicated in red lead on the lath that serves as tracers.

How could the Egyptians have ever plotted the enormous temple complex of Pharaoh Djoser on that large, pristine plain? Were they able to take measurements in those days? What did they use to do so? Where did they take their bearings from? Or did they start at random? Was their attention drawn perhaps to some natural object which made them decide to choose this particular location? These are questions that have never received an intelligent answer.

The Djoser temple complex is a colossal building complex, consisting of a step pyramid and annexes. The base of the step pyramid measures 121 metres by 109 metres, with a present height of 62 metres. The rectangular enclosure is 545 metres long and 278 metres broad. The enclosing wall, with a total length of 1,646 metres, is 10.5 metres high and harbours 1,680 niches. The core was constructed in masonry, which was covered on both sides with approximately 35,000 square meters of Tura limestone blocks.

The sheer plotting and marking out of this gigantic monumental complex undoubtedly made exceptional demands on the technical abilities of the people in charge of a building project of this size, not to mention the preparation and the time it took to complete the project. Until then, natural stone had only been used in simple projects, to build on a very small scale. Therefore, very little knowledge existed regarding the possibilities of this material, the various types of natural stone and how to apply it on a truly large scale.

Which quarry would be suitable? How could the small blocks of natural stone be hewn and sawn out of the quarry? How could these blocks be tooled and where did they get the idea of polishing them? In short, how was natural stone finished off? How did they transport these blocks from the Tura limestone quarry to the future building complex over a distance of about ten kilometres, partly across the Nile? On site, these natural stone blocks were joined together by means of white gypsum mortar from the Fayum oasis. How did they find the correct composition of the joining mortar? Their fluted, conical pillars remained an integral part of the natural stone walls out of which they had been sculptured, and they were adorned with capitals that had the shape of leaves. How did they ever achieve these delicate technical masterpieces?

Quite understandably, later generations regarded this entire complex with exceptional respect. Even thousands of years afterwards, Egyptians still expressed their admiration for this building in the texts they wrote on walls.

This was where their culture had once begun; this was the location where their civilisation became manifest. Here, the first steps were taken towards an independent unfoldment of the state of Egypt. This building complex represented the "cornerstone", the "first stone" in the execution of the Pyramid Field.

3.2 El Badari and the Development of the Calendar

The disclosure of their knowledge of geometry provides crucial answers to the question of whether they had thoroughly mastered this science and actually put it into practice. The ancient Egyptians had measured their territory using the "Osiris meridian" and had established its size. The length amounted to precisely nine degrees of latitude, from (Abusir) Busiris (30°55' N.) to Abusir near Buhen (21°55' N.), in other words: approximately 1,000 kilometres. The next step was to start from El Badari/Hammamieh.

Around 5300 BCE, an agglomeration of prehistoric settlements sprouted on the 27th parallel, immediately south of Asyut, on the eastern bank of the Nile. The northernmost settlement was Matmar (27°06' N., 31°20' E.). In the south, the settlements are called Mustagidda (27°05' N./31°23' E.), Deir Tasa (27°03' N./31°25' E.), El Badari (27°00' N./31°25' E.), Hammamaija (26°56' N./31°29' E.) and Kaw el Kebi (26°54' N./31°30' E.)

Positioned like a spider in its web, in longitude as well as in latitude, El Badari was located in the exact centre of all these settlements, precisely on the 27th parallel. This latitude almost marks the ideal circumference of the earth (36,000 kilometres). Does this enable us to see this location as a predetermined choice for a settlement?

In any case, an apparent choice was made to settle permanently in one fixed location. Maybe it was decided to give up hunting and to start growing crops. Accordingly, more attention was paid to the climate and to the annual flooding of the Nile. The rise of the water level in the river went hand in hand with flooding, and simultaneously, people observed the heliacal rising of the star Sirius, an event that seemed to have had a special meaning to the inhabitants of these settlements. There are clear indications that this special phenomenon initiated the development of the calendar in the agglomeration of settlements around El Badari. The preceding habitation of the oases at Fayum and Merimde do not show such indications.

Investigations of a kind never carried out before revealed that around 4500 BCE, the phenomenon known as the heliacal rising of the star Sirius, the "first brilliant visibility", could be observed in the settlements around El Badari on July 13th (Julian calendar). After 4242 BCE, this phenomenon was observed one day earlier, on July 12th. On the Egyptian calendar, July 13th coincides with the very last calendar day, the 360th day, IV SMW 30 (cf. appendix IV). It would seem that those agglomerate settlements had been founded deliberately on this parallel, in specific connection with the annual astronomical phenomenon mentioned above.

According to prevailing scientific opinion, calendars, even those of a rudimentary kind, did not exist in the fifth millennium BCE. As to the introduction of the calendar, the Egyptologist Parker mentions in **Calendars** that the civil year (360+5 days) was not established until approximately 2937 BCE.[4] However, it is a fact that on the very last day of the Egyptian calendar, IV SMW 30, the heliacal rising of the star Sirius was observable in the prehistoric settlement of El Badari. We argue that this stellar phenomenon, which was observed in the fifth millennium BCE in El Badari, set off a development that led to the compilation of the Egyptian calendar. Indisputably, "the year ended on the 360th day".[5] With the addition of the five days dedicated to the gods, this adds up to a civil year of 365 days, with the New Year celebration beginning on the last day of the year and continuing over the five epagomene days.[6]

Assuming this hypothesis to be true, then on what day would this special phenomenon of the "first brilliant visibility" of the star Sirius have been observed in Egypt on the presumed New Year's Day (I Achet 1), if we assume that a year was already known to consist of 365 days? The computer star chart pointed precisely to the 30th parallel, in other words: to Giza. With the location of El Badari as the starting point in the cycle of observations and Giza as its final point, it needs to be noted that these two sites are separated by precisely 180 geographical minutes of arc. Over a period of six days, the observation site moved northward by approximately 30 geographical minutes of arc per day. This observation implies that people in those days apparently knew about parallels of latitude and their exact position. But surely, this cannot be true?

The moment had come to consult the **Atlas of Ancient Egypt**. The settlements that qualified as sites from where the heliacal rising of the star Sirius could possibly have been observed were Sheik Atiya, Zawyet el Amwat, El Kom el Ahwar, Maiyana, Tarchan and finally Giza. On this list of places, Zawyet el Amwat and its surroundings, located on the 28th parallel, leaps to the forefront. It is the only place where a pyramid was erected on the eastern bank of the Nile, in the immediate surroundings of Men at Khufu (El Minja), where the "Horizon of Horus" was located.[7] Actually, Maiyana, Tarchan and Giza are also very important due to the archaeological findings from the Naqada II period (circa 3500-3200 BCE). The interim conclusion seemed therefore that in those prehistoric times, a chain of settlements had been built along the Nile that served as observation sites for the heliacal rising of the star Sirius. This hypothetical assumption led to yet another remarkable discovery.

If people had actually planned and organised their infrastructure in prehistoric times, then surely there must be more evidence to prove that fact? Might the heliacal risings of Sirius have been a reason to found settlements? Would that perhaps explain why certain settlements had lost their significance in the course of time? Immediately, a case in point sprung to mind, namely the two prehistoric twin towns of Buto in Lower Egypt and Hierakonpolis in Upper Egypt. They bore the exceptional name of "Thronstätte",[8] "throne state", a name they were entitled to retain for all eternity. Yet it is completely unknown why these places received that name and, even more peculiar, why they were allowed to use it for eternity. This implied the possible existence of a relatively organised society, maybe even of a state, before the First Dynasty commenced its rulership. Could these governmental powers have been exercised by the kings who had their seat in Memphis?

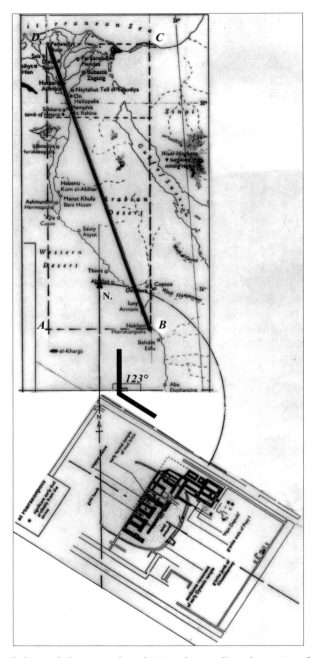

Fig. 13. Groundplan of the temple of Hierakonpolis; the axis of the temple is directed at the heliacal rising of the star Sirius. Observation track from B (Hierakonpolis) to D (Buto). Between 3950 and 3650 BCE, the azimuth of Sirius decreased from 123° to 120°. The axis of the temple runs at an angle of 123° to true north. The dotted rectangle shows the first geographical zoning of Egypt in the design of the Serekh (see 3.11). The dotted borderline between the land of Horus (Lower Egypt) and the land of Seth (Upper Egypt) corresponds with the symbolical zoning within the Serekh.

3.3 Buto and Hierakonpolis: on the right track

In Upper Egypt, we find the predynastic twin towns of Nechen and Necheb, better known to us as Hierakonpolis (Kom el Ahmar) and El Kab. Hierakonpolis was the "cradle of the oldest historical kingdom of the 'Unification of the Two Lands' (Union of Upper and Lower Egypt), and it was linked with a widely dispersed myth: the Creation of the World."[9] The temple of Hierakonpolis seems to have been oriented towards the heliacal rising of the star Sirius. The plan of the temple is rectangular, and its axis was plotted at an angle of 123°, measured clockwise from true north (cf. fig. 13). In the period between approximately 3950 and 3650 BCE, the star Sirius maintained an azimuth which gradually decreased from 123° down to 120° (azimuth is the angle, measured clockwise from true north, towards the point where the celestial body rises). In the course of the centuries, the azimuth kept on decreasing. Accordingly, the specific position of the temple points to the era during which it was founded.

In Lower Egypt, we find the predynastic twin towns of Pe and Dep, better known as Buto. The town of Buto derives its name from Bouto (transcription pr-w3dj.t), which stands for "house of Uto". Uto is the snake goddess, the cobra that later on represented the Delta. Furthermore, Uto is incorporated in the uraeus that adorns the forehead of the pharaohs from the Middle Kingdom (circa 2067 BCE) onward. Buto was the capital of Lower Egypt; its name is connected with the papyrus plant. Uto stood for the power of germination, freshness and fertility.[10] The name of this town could very well have symbolised the freshness and the novelty of the year.

Recent excavations in Buto show layers of habitation that date back to approximately the same period (Naqada IIb, circa 3600-3500 BCE). At that time, Buto was located near the coast of the Mediterranean Sea, from which it was separated by marshes. This location served as an administrative seat for overseas connections.[11] Here, typical ornamental nails known as "Grubenkopfnaegel" were found. These were used in alcove architecture so that this can be presumed to have been the site of a noteworthy, important building, maybe for the use of certain authorities. Alternatively, it may have served as a meeting place for a small group of Sumerian merchants.[12] This shows that links existed with the Uruk culture (especially the Djemdet-Nasr period) of Sumeria. Egyptologists tend to relate this to mercantile connections that ran via Anatolia, the northern part of Syria, although the possibility of a sailing route around the Arabian peninsula is not excluded.[13]

The principal deity of Hierakonpolis was the falcon with two feathers on its head (Necheni, "the Nechenite"). It was assimilated as Horus at a very early date.[14] Excavations in Hierakonpolis towards the end of the previous century revealed the aforementioned temple complex. A large number of votive offerings were found in this temple. The entire structure was surrounded by a clay wall and contained (off-centre, slightly in the western quadrant) a semi-oval earthen mound, which is thought to have been the base of a sanctuary, built of reeds or wood. This, however, is uncertain. East of the centre, close to the remains of a stretch of pavement, a rectangular plinth was found. This is where the Egyptologist Quibell found the famous Narmer Palette.

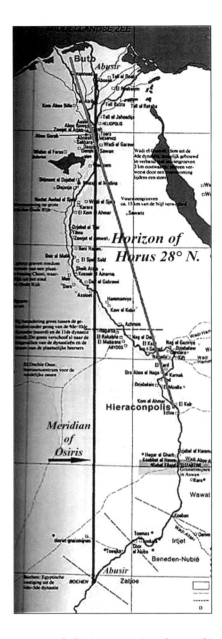

*Fig. 14. The observation track between Hierakonpolis and Buto, after 3650
BCE, with a length of 365/366 geographical minutes of arc. The Horizon of
Horus is the 28th parallel. Note: The Djoser complex is located on the intersection of the Osiris meridian and the observation track. This location divides
the total length of the "Osiris meridian" into two parts, the smaller of which is
in the proportion of 2 : 9 of the total length, while the location of the Djoser
complex also simultaneously divides the "Osiris meridian" into two parts, the
smaller of which is in the proportion of 1: 9 of the total length. The length of
the Osiris meridian between Busiris (Abusir, 30°55' N.) and the fortification of
Buhen (21°55' N.) amounts to precisely 9 degrees (approximately 1000 km).*

The temple complex of Hierakonpolis contains the oldest temple mound known to us. Its diameter measures 49.26 metres and may possibly represent the "primeval mound". It is positioned off-centre within the temple complex and this corresponds closely with the position of the hill within the enclosure of the complex that Pharaoh Khasekhemwy built in Abydos towards the end of the Second Dynasty. The arrangement of the ground plan of these complexes deviates from the ground plan of the Djoser complex. The Djoser complex is also located off-centre within the enclosure, albeit within the southern half. Consequently, the temple complexes mentioned above cannot have served as prototypes for the design of the Djoser complex.

Opposite to Hierakonpolis lies the former site of El Kab, the town that prides itself on a very ancient history. Here, the main goddess was the Vulture, named Nechbet. She was considered to be the supreme goddess of Upper Egypt, and "she was raised to become the tutelary deity of the Egyptian kings (together with the cobra goddess Uadjit [from Buto] of Lower Egypt)".[15]

The following quotation shows how these prehistoric towns played a special role, and how their existence served to honour the ancestors of the Egyptians: "Sethe had ascertained correctly that the Shemsu Hor (Followers of Horus) were kings of Hierakonpolis and Buto",[16] but when this was checked, he failed to mention the decisive proof of his claim. Griffith then pointed out verbally to the author that this proof can be found in a papyrus with hieroglyphs from the Roman period, which undoubtedly contains an amount of commonly known traditional knowledge of the scholars from the time of Cheops (***Two Hieroglyphic Papyri***, Egypt Exploration Fund, London, 1889, Pl.9, fragm.10); here, we find two introductions (1) "Souls of Pe, Followers of Horus as Kings of Lower Egypt" and (2) "Souls of Nechen, Followers of Horus as Kings of Upper Egypt".[17] The Egyptians also pointed out the important role that Hierakonpolis and Buto played in the development of their country: "Egyptian historiography mentions as the principle of its founding: the prehistoric Upper Egyptian Kingdom of Hierakonpolis and the Lower Egyptian Kingdom of Buto, which was conquered by Menes, the Horus King of Hierakonpolis."[18]

Yet there is no mention that these settlements were observation posts. So why were they so important to the development of Egypt? Did this maybe allude to the "Unification of the Two Lands"? After all, Buto and Hierakonpolis were the capitals of Lower Egypt and Upper Egypt respectively. Buto was located in the extreme north on the coast, a natural border. Could Hierakonpolis have been located on the "imaginary" southern border during the preliminary stage of developments towards a single, united Egyptian Kingdom? This presumption put us on the right track to the significance and the function of both towns, since they appear to have fulfilled an extremely important role in the observation of the heliacal rising of the star Sirius. Since the conglomeration of settlements around El Badari and the location of the plateau of Giza pointed conspicuously to their respective parallels of latitude, it seemed desirable to compare the co-ordinates of Buto with those of Hierakonpolis. The geographical co-ordinates of Buto (Pe and Dep) and Hierakonpolis and El Kab (Nechen and Necheb) are:

Buto	31°12' N.	and 30°45'E.
Hierakonpolis	25°05' N.	and 32°47'E.
El Kab	25°07' N.	and 32°48'E.

The difference between the latitude of Buto and Hierakonpolis/El Kab amounts to 06°06' or 06° 05', which equals 366 or 365 minutes of arc. This remarkable result clearly refers to the length of the solar year (tropical solar year = 365.24219879 days). If we connect the two towns, the outcome is astounding: the geodetic connection is that at the intersection of the Osiris-meridian with the observation track between Hierakonpolis and Buto (cf. fig. 11 and 14), the Egyptians built their first pyramid, the Djoser-complex. Hence, that location had already been fixed by astro-geometry before the complex was built (see also www.zitman.org subject, ***Egypt: Image of Heaven***, chapter 3d). In addition, the location of the Djoser complex (the point of intersection mentioned above) divides the distance between Hierakonpolis and Buto into two parts, the smaller one of which is in the proportion of 2 : 9 to the total length, while the location of the Djoser complex simultaneously divides the "Osiris meridian" into two parts, the smaller one of which is in the proportion of 1: 9 to the total length.

Yet for what reason? Egyptologist Lehner posed the same question when he remarked: "Why are the pyramids of Djoser and Sekhemkhet and these mysterious empty rectangles located so far off in the desert?" He assumes that the natural condition of the area played a role in the ancient Egyptians' choice of the location. A detailed map of the area around Saqqara shows a natural bend at that point that may once have been part of the course of the Nile. It is also claimed that a natural wadi would have guaranteed favourable conditions for a solid foundation of the building complex.

Yet another reason is sought in the small lakes that formed after the flooding of the Nile.[19] The Egyptians might well have taken this into account when they planned the partitioning of their country in order to set up the infrastructure. Nevertheless, other fundamental reasons, maybe of a religious nature, could also have played a decisive role. Those decisive reasons are linked with observations of the heliacal rising of Sirius, which were of extreme importance to the ancient Egyptians.

The observation of this spectacular phenomenon acted as their guide in designing and constructing the infrastructure of their entire state, especially in the foundation of Hierakonpolis and Buto, the towns that were considered to be "throne states". Yet, with few exceptions, no mention is made of these observation points. However, the following text by Diodorus Siculus (1st century BCE) mentions Heliopolis: "Diodorus Siculus and Strabo both mention Heliopolis as the place where the priests paid great attention to the observation of the stars."[20] Accordingly, Heliopolis is repeatedly referred to in the relevant literature as a presumed point where the heliacal rising of the star Sirius was observed.

Heliopolis possessed a vast and highly important temple complex, the centre of the established religion and astronomy. The high priest of this temple would appear in a ceremonial garment that was adorned with "five-pointed stars", which obviously alluded to their stellar religion.

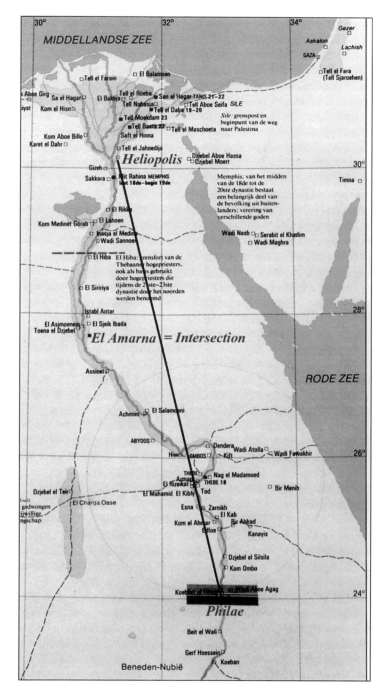

Fig. 15. The observation track between Philae/Elephantine and Heliopolis after 2782 BCE, with a length of 365 minutes of arc. The observation track between Hierakonpolis and Buto intersects that between Philae/Elephantine and Heliopolis on the parallel of El Amarna. During the New Kingdom, this parallel was chosen by Pharaoh Amenhotep IV as the location for his future residence Achet-Aten.

The Sun, even though it is a star, was never pictured as one by the Egyptians; it was rendered as a round disc with a dot in its centre. The five-pointed star refers to activities involving astronomical matters that were carried out for religious purposes. This shows that in former times, the stars were of more importance than the Sun. This is expressed forcefully by the German Egyptologist Kees: "Ancient Heliopolis was, to a great extent, adapted to star constellations, more so than the subsequent, one-sided emphasis on the Sun could ever have brought about."[21] In other words, observations were indeed carried out in Heliopolis. But if there was a link between Hierakonpolis and Buto that concerned observations of the heliacal rising of the star Sirius, then what kind of connection existed with Heliopolis?

The geographical location of Heliopolis is 30°08' N. and 31°18' E., i.e. the prehistoric capital Buto lay 1°04' north of Heliopolis. During an Egyptology congress held in Basel in 1982, the Egyptologist Brack pointed out that "the axis of the Ptolemaic Satis temple in the town of Elephantine and of the cult-alcove directly underneath seem to be directed at the spot on the horizon where the star Sirius formerly rose during the winter solstice."[22] The *Atlas of Ancient Egypt* mentions the co-ordinates: Elephantine at 24°05' N. and 32°53' E. That area contains an agglomeration of settlements along the Nile at the location of the first cataract.

There are two more islands in the Nile next to the island of Elephantine: Sehel and Biga. Slightly to the south of them, we find the town of Philae (24°01' N. and 32°53' E), which was called the "Island of Time" in Antiquity.[23] On an average, Elephantine and Philae are located at 24°03' N. A comparison between the geographical co-ordinates of Hierakonpolis and those of Philae shows that Philae lies 1°04' south of Hierakonpolis.

This result caused a shock of recognition. A connection existed between Hierakonpolis and Buto on the one hand, and between Heliopolis and Elephantine/Philae on the other: the geographical difference between Heliopolis and Elephantine/Philae once again amounts to 365 minutes of arc. The possibility arose that these four places could very well be brought into relationship with the observation of the heliacal rising of the star Sirius.

Consulting the map of ancient Egypt and drawing the two geodetic connecting lines (cf. fig. 15), it appeared that these geodetic lines intersected. Even more remarkably, this intersection is located at 27°37' N. That very point on this parallel marked the location of the residence El Amarna (Achet-Aten) of Pharaoh Amenhotep IV, better known as Akhenaten. By founding this residence on this site, Akhenaten apparently intended to establish the very centre of Egypt. Nevertheless, it has remained a mystery why Akhenaten decided to build his residence right here, on pristine ground. The Egyptologists Baines and Malek stated: "King Akhenaten built his city on pristine grounds which were untainted by the former presence of people and their gods. Yet the exact reasons for choosing precisely this large bend on the eastern bank of the Nile, north of the Dzjebel Abusir Feda Massif are still unknown. Not so long ago, it was suggested that the landscape resembled a large hieroglyph for 'horizon' (cf. hieroglyph N 27, *Egyptian Grammar*), implying that this might well have been be the reason why the city was founded on this site."[24] The name Achet-Aten is assumed to mean "The horizon of the sun disc". The meaning of the name of the residence points to "observation". Hence, the following novel translation of this hieroglyph [25] could be accepted as an addition to the existing one: "horizon where the celestial body rises" or, alternatively: "house or place of observation of natural phenomena, especially of a celestial body on the horizon", in other words: an "observatory". Or could the hieroglyph have been intended to indicate that El Amarna lay in the centre (the navel) of Egypt?

It became increasingly probable that these geodetic connecting lines fulfilled the function of virtual observation tracks. The two observation tracks intersect on the parallel of El Amarna, which explains very clearly why Akhenaten chose this location to found his residence of Achet-Aten (El Amarna 27°38' N. and 30°53' E.). El Amarna was also to serve as a religious centre and was, amongst others, also founded as a place where the heliacal rising of the star Sirius was to be observed.

All this makes it increasingly clear that the Egyptians used astro-geodetic methods to structure and organise their country. However, the residence of El Amarna was founded around 1364 BCE, nearly two millennia after the Djoser complex was built.

El Amarna is situated on the east bank of the Nile and therefore does not coincide literally with the point of intersection. Yet it does lie on exactly the same parallel as the intersection of the two virtual observation tracks (cf. fig. 15). From this, we were led to assume that the settlements along the Nile had been built on places that divided the virtual observation track into equal segments. In that case, the location of those settlements would have been determined by the Egyptians according to observations of the heliacal rising star Sirius. Further research showed that adaptations were made over time. The manner in which these adaptations were carried out reveals that alterations due to precession were noticed by the Egyptians, which caused them to found new settlements. However, after the downfall of the Old Kingdom, this high rate of precision was not maintained. These conclusions apply to both tracks and have been proved by experiment to be correct (cf. appendix V).

The exact location of the Djoser complex, the cornerstone of the concept, coincides with the intersection of the "Osiris meridian" and the observation track between Hierakonpolis and Buto. Obviously, this location had also been determined by means of observations on the day on which the heliacal rising of the star Sirius reached visibility. The length of the observation track between Hierakonpolis - via the Djoser complex and Letopolis - and Buto totals 707 kilometres (1,350,000 royal cubits), a distance that was then divided into nine equilinear segments of 150,000 royal cubits each. The observation of the "first brilliant visibility" of the star Sirius was carried out around 3150 BCE at Saqqara, on the site of the Djoser complex, on the epagomene day of Seth. This was the 363rd day of the Egyptian Year, the day on which a large-scale catastrophe from a distant past was commemorated. And let us not forget: Saqqara lies opposite Memphis, the birthplace of the god Seth.[26]

An outline of the observation tracks illustrates the development over the course of time (see appendix V). First, a prototype was developed, which ran from El Badari to Giza and remained in use until approximately 3650 BCE. From 3650 BCE onward, after the founding of Hierakonpolis and Buto as "throne states", the more elaborate observation track was used.

During the Fourth Dynasty the track was adapted. First, Buto was replaced as an observation post by Xois (31°05' N.), which in turn would be replaced by Sais (30°58' N.). Hierakonpolis was subjected to a similar fate, when Edfu (24°59' N.) took over its function as the southern observation point. In a later stage, when Sais became the northernmost observation site, the site south of Edfu was moved to 24°52' N.

Nevertheless, the total length of the observation track was bound to remain 365/366 minutes of arc. The shift of the observation posts was a consequence of precession, which the Egyptians monitored closely. They could easily have determined a shift - caused by precession - in the observation of the "first brilliant visibility" of the star Sirius from a certain observation post by, for instance, the positioning of a gnomon (a forerunner of the obelisk). The declination (arc distance of a star to the celestial equator) of Sirius obviously changes in the course of millennia as a result of the Earth's precession. This may also be the reason why temples were disassembled. When observations became inaccurate, the building would lose its role as an observation post. The observation track between Philae/Elephantine and Heliopolis was put into use at the beginning of the new Sirius period in 2782 BCE.

3.4 Observations, and New Year's Day

The discovery of a track that could serve to perceive the spectacular "first brilliant visibility" of the star Sirius from a certain location would gradually result in observation posts along the Nile that would grow into settlements. At the same time, this solves a problem that for many decades had been the cause of heated debate. The problem was how the Egyptians across the country could know simultaneously that New Year's Day had arrived. After all, New Year occurred on I Achet 1. Sunrise occurs each and every day, yet a spectacular rising of a large star that has remained invisible for about seventy days was quite a different matter. This star made its first appearance in the south and it took several days before it became visible in the north of Egypt. Yet the remarkable thing was that New Year's Day was celebrated on the same day throughout the entire country.

There is only one explanation: if for example, the heliacal rising of the star Sirius was perceived in Hierakonpolis, then it was a known fact that the heliacal rising would be observed in Buto ten days later. Consequently, New Year's Day occurred on the same day throughout the entire country. Over the millennia, the interval between the first observation in the south and the last observation in the north wandered from nine to eight, to seven and six finally to no more than five days in the Late Period. From the Sirius period in 2782 BCE onward, this interval had decreased to merely eight days (cf. appendix V).

In the introduction, we referred to New Year's Day as a very special day. The same applied to the five days that preceded this festivity, which were known as the epagomene days, when various types of rituals were performed. The New Year ritual focused on the king and his renewed acceptance of rulership. In *Nieuwjaar in het oude Egypte* (New Year in Ancient Egypt), Egyptology professor Borghouts of NINO at Leiden University, explains: "There were periods in which a coronation was chosen to coincide with New Year's

Day." Borghouts chose this subject for his inaugural speech, in which he mentioned the following: "For the last few years, our main source has been a papyrus from the Late Period - contemporary with the Ptolemaic temples - which is kept in the Brooklyn Museum. [This papyrus] also tells us that the rituals began on the last day of the [calendar] year and that they continue over the five epagomene days. The first part is entitled 'the ritual of the Great Seat'. It is devoted entirely to purification, the laying on of the amulet and the anointment of the king. Similar to what is claimed in the **Leidse schrikkeldagentekst** (Leiden-text on intercalary days), [this ritual] aims to bar evil impacts and powers."

Borghouts continues: "Many allusions are made to the defeat of cosmic enemies. The Creator God Atum of Heliopolis is cited in particular. Tacitly, at times explicitly, the king is put on an equal par with him. In line with the utterances on the temple walls in Denderah and Edfu, Apophis and his henchmen are referred to as the potential disturbers of cosmic harmony." Numerous images depict the killing of Apophis by Re. This ritual slaughter was the main theme at the New Year ceremony, "often expressed in a stereotypical manner as 'Re triumphs over Apophis'. In other words: on the location, the creator god has now maintained the upper hand over his main opponent, the snake that represented dangerous chaos. Actually, this implies that the creation of the world occurred anew."[27] This clear description points out that the 360th calendar day of the year was a very memorable day, as this was the time when the rituals began. In prehistoric times, this last calendar day marked the observation of the "first brilliant visibility" of the star Sirius in El Badari and Hierakonpolis; two thousand years later, the same occurred in Philae/Elephantine. After these rituals, which lasted until the morning of New Year's Day, the dominion of the god Horus was once again re-established and kingship safeguarded.

3.5 Sirius is Atum, the God of Creation

Atum was created out of "a void". Atum is the Lord of Heliopolis and Re-Atum was worshipped in the local temple as the Creator of the World. The location of the temple of Heliopolis correlates with the star Sirius (see Chapter 4). During the summer solstice, Atum, the star Sirius, the great Creator, merged with Re, the star known as the Sun (Atum-Re-Kheprer). Around 2900 BCE, this event led to the foundation of the Sun cult in Heliopolis. In about 2825 BCE, at the start of the Fifth Dynasty, it became permanently established. To the Egyptians, the foundation of this combined Atum-Re cult may have signified the merging of specific positive powers, causing a renewed creation in which only order would prosper. Sirius acted as their guide. The great Sphinx of Giza is the "living image of Atum".[28]

3.6 The Pyramid, an iconographic Image of Creation

The open isosceles triangle was the symbol par excellence of Atum the Creator, signifying how Atum (the One) begot Two (Shu and Tefnut) (cf. fig. 16).

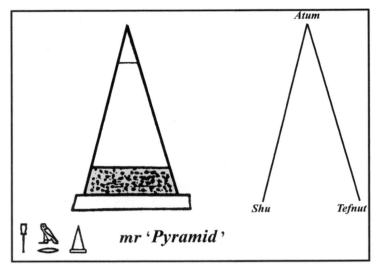

Fig. 16 The open isosceles triangle as the symbol of creation. The top, Atum, creates two elements: the sides, Shu and Tefnut.

"Atum is he who (once) came into being, who masturbated in Heliopolis (On). [He created an] orgasm [...], and so were born the twins Shu and Tefenet." [29]

The original shape of the pyramid is reminiscent of a mountain in the act of creation, a volcano, the "mountain of creation". Hence, the shape of the pyramid represents Creation. Accordingly, due to its shape, each side of the pyramid pays tribute iconographically to Atum, the Creator-God. "O all you gods who shall cause this pyramid and this construction of the King to be fair and endure: You shall be effective, you shall be strong, you shall have your souls, you shall have power [...] you shall have your oblations made to you, you shall take possession of the [...] crown [...]" [30] (cf. fig. 16).

3.7 Towards the Foundation of a State

What mental image have we thus acquired of the path that Egypt followed to flourish into a highly developed civilisation? Questions currently prevailing on this subject were voiced by the Egyptologist Dr. Seidlmayer of the Egyptological department at Berlin University in his contribution to the book **Egypten, Land der Pharaohnen** (Egypt, Land of the Pharaohs). One of the issues he raised concerns the role of the towns in the Delta. "According to later versions of pharaonic traditions that were handed down, towns in the Delta such as Buto and Sais played a major role, next to the extensive royal settlements of Upper Egypt. What prehistoric facts is this based on? How was the Nile Delta organised politically and sociologically during the fourth millennium BCE? Did town states exist or was there one large kingdom?" [31] Seidlmayer asked fundamental questions to gain a correct understanding of the origin of the Egyptian state in the early dynastic period. Nevertheless, we believe that the course of Egypt's history and the development of its civilisation date back to a very distant past. Controversial though it may seem, Egypt owes its existence to a natural catastrophe.

A climatological catastrophe forced the people to move away to the large rivers, of which the Nile was one. From approximately 4900 until 2500 BCE, the climate in Egypt had once again become subtropical, i.e. Mediterranean. At that time, there was no question of the formation of large-scale deserts. Rainfall and annual flooding of the river offered favourable, even vital conditions, for the development of a civilisation.

Chronological information shows that at a very early stage, Memphis and the surrounding region fulfilled the function of a governmental centre. Prior to the pharaonic kingdom, thirty kings are presumed to have wielded the sceptre for an overall period of 1,790 years.[32] Excavations are being carried out at present, which will assess the validity of this data.

The typical Nile basin and its correspondence with Osiris, similar with the celestial constellation Scorpio, furthered their religion and their veneration of the dead. Osiris stood for resurrection, and from time immemorial, death and resurrection belonged to Scorpio.

Since approximately 5000 BCE, the 22nd parallel formed an ecological borderline.[33] Those who once followed the Nile basin discovered a natural narrowing, located close to the 22nd parallel. This natural and strategic point became the southern geographical border of their territory. In addition, this line denoted the transition from the northern, wet and humid area to the southern, dry region. The Delta and its marshes and lagoons formed the northern border. "Egypt" thus covered precisely nine zones within the parallels. In her fascinating book **Secrets du Continent Noir révélés par l'Archéologie**, Cornevin points out that "it seems to become increasingly clear that this 22nd parallel ought to be recognised as a climatologic and ecological border that simultaneously formed an ethnical border between people with a white skin and people with a dark one".[34]

In the course of the fourth millennium, the infrastructure of Egypt took shape. Halfway through the fourth millennium, the towns of Thinis and Abydos were founded on the banks of the Nile, correlating with the star theta Scorpii at the hind part of Scorpio. Hierakonpolis became the first central town in Upper Egypt. Buto followed, as the central town of Lower Egypt at the edge of the Delta. Around 3150 BCE, the Djoser complex was built immediately to the west of Memphis as the cornerstone of the future Pyramid Field. Sirius served to guide them in their accomplishment.

By approximately 3600 BCE, the structure and the political and social shape of Egypt had progressed to such an extent that the town state of Thinis developed into a kingdom in the making. The idea originated, or the need was born, to unite "The Two Lands". This "Unification of The Two Lands" was preceded by a campaign of conquest and/or war.

3.8   The "Unification of The Two Lands" and the Plaque of Denderah

The "Unification of The Two Lands" was accomplished in 3516 BCE (see Chronology). This historic moment in Egypt's development was immortalised on the plaque of Denderah by the insertion of the Horus-Lotus line, which is indicated on the outline (cf. fig. 6). It runs past Osiris, through the constellation of Scorpio and continues via the hindlegs of the constellation of the Bull [Taurus] and through the left foot of Orion. The main stars Betelgeuse and Rigel are the two most brilliant stars of Orion. In Arabic, Rigel means foot and Rigel is thus the footstar of Orion. Rigel's significance to the Egyptians lay in the fact that its heliacal rising took place on virtually the same position as that of Sirius.[35] In about 2000 BCE, Rigel rose exactly one hundred minutes before the heliacal rising of Sirius, which caused the Egyptians to consider Rigel as Sirius' guiding star.

After 3516 BCE, during the period in which "Unification of The Two Lands" was realised, the precession of the equinox came into conjunction with this star Rigel. Accordingly, the Horus-Lotus line on the plaque marks that special moment in history, namely the foundation of the State of Egypt. That was the setting against which the Egyptian state came into being after a preceding development that had lasted nearly two millennia. The ritual Horus-pose of the pharaoh that typifies the founding of this state was to be immortalised during the reign of the third and the fourth Dynasty (cf. www.zitman.org, *Egypt image of Heaven*, chapter 8a – 8y.)

3.9 The Development of the First Geographical Frame

Memphis, the first capital of Egypt, was founded in the area called Mechattawi, i.e. "that which unites the Two Lands". South of Memphis, we find Dahshur and the Red Pyramid and the Bent Pyramid. This Pyramids marked the border between Upper and Lower Egypt (see chapter 4). In Antiquity, this town was called Inheb-heg or "White Walls", which according to Herodotus referred to a dam that had been built to protect the town against the waters of the Nile. In a later period, the town was named Anch-tawi, "the life of Two Lands".

The Memphis/Giza region belonged to a single province, called a "nome" by the Egyptians. This was depicted by means of the sign in the lower part of the hieroglyph pictured in figure 11. Seen from bottom to top, the complete hieroglyph consisted of a grid or matrix - the "nome" - which served as a base for the standard or seat, consisting amongst others of a right-angled triangle. Above the standard we see the hieroglyph for "fortification and enclosure" depicted beside the papyrus stalk of Lower Egypt. The hieroglyph O36 (see *Egyptian Grammar*) for "fortification [residence, mansion] and brick enclosure" is linked with Nome 1 of Dahshur/Memphis from Lower Egypt.

The three locations which appear to enclose the general area around the pyramid field of Giza (Rostau) are Memphis, Letopolis, and Heliopolis. The map of this region (fig. 11) shows how these three locations, due to their geographical position, form an isosceles triangle. The emblem of the nome consists of a horizontal platform supporting the standard, with a fortification (man-

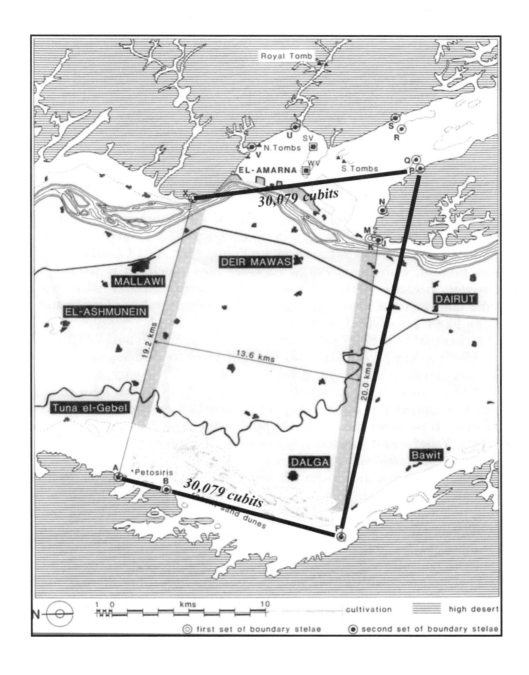

Fig. 17. Survey of the region around El Amarna, including the fourteen boundary stones. The map shows the entire territory to the west and the east of the Nile. The distance between the boundary stones X and P and between A and F both amount to 30,079 royal cubits (approximately 15,750 metres).

sion) and a mace above.[36] As such, the first nome of Lower Egypt is called the "Mansion of the Mace" (see section 4.22).

The hieroglyph for "nome" consists of a grid. The Egyptians used this special sign to denote organised structure. In hieroglyphic script, word and image always build a unity (a word is expressed by means of one or more images). In other words, the visual arts were simultaneously script and sign and these served to convey written information. The grid expresses structure and conquers chaos.[37] This hieroglyph appeared explicitly for the first time in the cartouche of Pharaoh Semti, alias Den, of the First Dynasty (cf. hieroglyph N 24, *Egyptian Grammar*), who was also known as Hesepti. Around 3400 BCE, this pharaoh applied this grid-shaped pattern to the structure and partition of his territory. His cartouche (cf. fig. 11) ranks as the fifth on the kinglist of Abydos. Even after his death, Pharaoh Den was held in reverence because of his outstanding service to his country. Certain passages in the Book of the Dead (30b, 64 and 130) are attributed to him, while other parts are believed to stem from Pharaoh Djedefre and Menkaure from the Fourth Dynasty. The Book of the Dead as such was compiled two millennia later and dates back to the New Kingdom.

It is worth mentioning that the word for desert was commonly written as hieroglyph AA8, *Egyptian Grammar*. Various variations of this hieroglyph form the name *Semti*. The cartouche of Semti shows distinctly that he was the one who ordered that the entire country, Upper as well as Lower Egypt, should be geometrically surveyed, since his cartouche contains two hieroglyphs denoting this grid (cf. fig. 11). Over time, surveying and partitioning the land gained such importance that Pharaoh Semti is even regarded as the "Founder of Egypt", as the chronological lists that were drafted prior to the "Turin Canon" (King-List) show.[38] He was the first to bear the title "King of Upper and Lower Egypt".[39] It is an established fact that Pharaoh Semti determined definitively the framework that structured the land of Egypt. The way Pharaoh Semti demarcated the territory can only have been carried out by land surveyors. The geometric knowledge of the surveyors (or Harpedonapts) evidently existed long before work was started on the Pyramid Field. This opinion was also shared by the French Egyptologist Goyon.[40]

3.10 The Boundary Stones of El Amarna

El Amarna appeals to our imagination because it was founded on "pristine" soil by the renowned Pharaoh Amenhotep IV (1367-1351/49 BCE) and his wife Nefertiti. For a short while, Achet-Aten became the capital of the Egyptian Kingdom and the centre of the new religion. This was where the well-known Amarna letters were dispatched to the vassals and kings of the neighbouring countries. Fifteen years later, after the king died, the town was deserted. Some time afterwards, Horemheb, a former general under Pharaoh Amenhotep IV, subjected the place to systematic destruction. The foundation of this town on "pristine" soil took place around 1364 BCE, on IV Peret 13, in the fifth year of Amenhotep's rule. On that day, the exact position of the first boundary stone was determined (point X; cf. fig. 17), followed by points K and M. One year later, the positions of P, A and F and remaining boundary stones were fixed. In the end, it appears that the boundary stones X and P determined the eastern border of the residence, while the stones A and F defined the western border.

The manner in which measurements were plotted during the New Kingdom can be inferred from texts on the boundary stelae of the residence of Achet-Aten (El Amarna). Pharaoh Amenhotep IV performed this act in his chariot, which was made of electrum (an amalgam of gold and silver). The residence was marked out by fourteen boundary stones; their exact positions were determined by Amenhotep IV himself. Unfortunately, so far it has proved impossible to establish from which boundary stone he started to plot and measure out. We will therefore begin with a close examination of the text in an attempt to determine that location.

According to this text, Pharaoh Amenhotep IV marked off this town by determining the position of a certain number of "fixed" boundary stones. In all, fourteen of these stones were found.[41] He probably started by determining the corners of his residence, such as boundary stone X (phase I), followed at a later stage by boundary stone P (phase II), and boundary stones A and F, which were also marked out in phase II (cf. fig. 17). The fact that Amenhotep IV determined these spots beforehand can be deduced from the text on the boundary stones themselves: "My father Aten brought me to Achet-Aten. No nobleman brought me here, no-one brought me here, while Aten said: 'This is a suitable place where His Majesty can build Achet-Aten.' The territory did not belong to a god; it did not belong to a goddess. No-one has the right of ownership."[42] Excavations have confirmed that precise determination went into the location of the boundary stones. According to the texts on boundary stones K, M, and X, these are the three oldest stones. Boundary stone X is located on the eastern bank of the Nile and it is the northernmost one on that side of the river. This stone may well be the basic demarcation, the first measuring point that served to mark off the remaining boundary stones as subsequent measuring points for the building activities of the town.

One year after his first visit, Amenhotep IV returned to the site and beheld the activities that were to shape his future Achet-Aten. On that occasion, eleven further spots where boundary stones should be placed were determined, and the text on one of these stones reads: "the north-eastern boundary stone of Achet-Aten, where I stopped, is the northern boundary stone. I never travel downstream. Set up the northern boundary stone in the western mountains exactly opposite to it. Achet-Aten extends from the southern boundary stone to the northern boundary stone over a length of 6 iter, ½ and ¼ chet and 4 meh." In a similar manner, Amenhotep IV carried out the plotting activities in the opposite, eastern mountains. Again, the linear distance amounted to 6 iter, ½ and ¼ chet and 4 meh.[43]

These texts make it clear that Amenhotep IV determined the four points on the compass where the respective boundary stones were to be placed, and that four different boundary stones, those running from south to north (probably from P to X) and those from the south-western to the north-western boundary stone in the western mountains (probably from F to A) encompassed the settlement of Achet-Aten. According to this text, the two boundary stones of both pairs are separated from one another by the same distance of 6 iter, ½ and ¼ chet and 4 meh.

Unfortunately, the length of the iter (plural: iter) is unknown, although is it usually presumed to equal 10,500 metres.[44] However, the Egyptologist Borchardt believed that the "iter" used in Achet-Aten amounted to 5,000 royal cubits.[45] The applied real length of the iter can be deduced by comparing it with a length that the Egyptologist Kemp determined on site. In his book **Ancient Egypt**, he mentions a measured distance between the boundary stones A and X of about 19,200 metres (approximately 36,670 royal cubits). [46] Yet a distance of that length occurs only once. Therefore, we must look for a combination of two boundary stones that are in both cases separated by the same distance. Assuming that Borchardt did in fact determine the correct length of the iter, then the total length mentioned in the text is as follows:

1 meh = 1 royal cubit = 52.4 centimetres
1 chet = 100 royal cubits = 52.4 metres (1 chet = 100 meh)
or 1 royal cubit = 52.36 centimetres (Goyon), on average: 52.38 centimetres[47]

Assuming that 1 iter   = 5,000 royal cubits = 2618 metres,
then   6 iter   =   15,708.00 metres
                        50 meh=   26.18 metres
                        25 meh=   13.09 metres
                        4 meh =   2.09 metres
Total   15,749.36 metres = 30,079 royal cubits

1 royal cubit = 15,749.36 metres : 30,079 royal cubits = 0.5236m

Having obtained this result, we then search for two sets of two boundary stones, each at a distance of about 15,750 metres. We find this distance, accurate to a royal cubit, between two pairs of stones, namely P - X and A - F. The boundary stones are easy to find on a plan with the help of a pair of compasses. No other pair of boundary stones can be found that are separated by the above distance. Hence, Borchardt is right on this issue: 1 iter equals 5,000 royal cubits.

Apart from sacrificial texts, the boundary stones also contain instructions concerning the delimitation of the site. The crucial text is to be found on the boundary stones that were the first to be laid out: K, M and X. The essence is basically sacrificial in character. "His Majesty offered a sacrifice to his father Aten, consisting of bread, horned and hornless bulls, other animals, birds, wine, fruit, incense, herbs and flowers." The text pertaining to the delimitation of the urban agglomeration reads as follows: "My father Aten brought me to Achet-Aten. I will build Achet-Aten for him neither to the south, nor to the north, nor to the west, nor to the east of this site."[48] This is merely a small excerpt of the text, which, incidentally, was seriously damaged so that our knowledge of it is incomplete. The text shows once again that boundary stone X occupies the northernmost position. Consequently, boundary stones K and M, together with X, belong to the measuring points that were laid out first.

The fact that the position of boundary stone X is mentioned explicitly and separately leads us to assume that the position of this stone was used as a starting point to determine the positions of the other boundary stones, including those of the three later boundary stones P, A and F. The text goes on to tell us that this happened in the following year. First, the location of boundary stone P was determined. Subsequently, again starting from position X, the location of boundary stone A was marked out, followed by that of F. The text on the eleven boundary stones, to which group P, A and F belong, is known as the second text. This second text was probably inscribed exactly one year later. It provides us with detailed information about the manner in which this task was carried out and how the exact distances between the four boundary stones mentioned above as well as their locations were determined.

In short, the second text, which deviates in some points from the first, reads as follows: "Year 6, 4th month of the 2nd season, the 13th day [IV Peret 13]. On this day, His Majesty was in Achet-Aten in a brightly-coloured pavilion, which had been made for His Majesty in Achet-Aten and bore the name 'Aten is content'. The pharaoh mounted a chariot made of electrum and drawn by a team of horses. Pharaoh rode in a southerly direction and stopped his chariot near the south-eastern mountains of Achet-Aten. Subsequently he stopped at the southern boundary stone P. He then gave orders to position the south-western boundary stone F in the western mountains, exactly opposite boundary stone P. Thereupon, the pharaoh rode in his chariot to the spot where he wished the north-eastern boundary stone X to be placed. He called this the northern boundary stone of Achet-Aten, whereupon he gave instructions to set up boundary stone A precisely opposite boundary stone X in the western mountains, in a north-western direction. Accordingly, Achet-Aten extended from the southern boundary stone up to the northern one. The distance between the two boundary stones X and P in the eastern mountains measures 6 iter, ½ and ¼ chet and 4 meh. This measurement equals the length between the boundary stones A and F in the south-western mountains, also 6 iter, ½ and ¼ chet and 4 meh".[49] Only in the latter two sets are the two boundary stones equidistant (cf. fig. 17).

3.11 Measuring leads to Knowledge

The previous example of the foundation of El Amarna is the only large-scale land surveying feat known to have been carried out in ancient Egypt. Of some buildings, however, the construction plans have been preserved. Now and then, data also becomes available relating to a ceremony held during the marking up and measuring out of the foundation of a temple. Descriptions are known that reveal a glimpse of their method of land surveying. The Egyptians are also known to have made designs and to have drawn up construction plans. In Saqqara, a single remarkable diagram was once found. It was written in red ink on one side of a lump of limestone, apparently intact, and may date back to the era of Pharaoh Djoser. This building plan may possibly have been used to construct an arch or a roof in stone masonry. If this is true, then a calculation method was used to determine and plot such arches.[50]

"The only records of the means used by the Egyptians for surveying are found in the tomb-scenes and in certain statuettes."[51] Territories were surveyed with the help of a cord. This is illustrated by a scene on the tomb of Amenhotpe-si-se in Thebes. Similar scenes from other graves tell us that the cord was sometimes divided up into regular stretches by means of knots. On the picture showing the surveyors, the one at the rear has a viewfinder attached to his left shoulder. The instrument consists of a ram's skull that has a viewfinder mounted on top. The surveyor at the front carries the instrument with the viewfinder in his left hand (cf. fig. 12). In this way, gnomons could be aligned and placed to demarcate or measure a certain territory. The fixed standard they used to measure the surface area of a piece of land was known as the "stat", equal to the Greek "aroura", equivalent to 2,735 square metres or 100 square cubits.

However, the linear measuring standard, amounting to 21 rods of cord,[52] was even more appropriate for land surveying, equalling 2,100 royal cubits or almost 1,100 metres. Various texts reveal that the land on which crops were grown was partitioned into strips with a width of 10 royal cubits (5.24m) or multiples of this unit. The length of those strips might, for example, amount to 100 royal cubits or 2,100 royal cubits, equalling approximately 1,100 metres.

The text mentioned above states: "I made a wide road for my offerings of 21 rods of cord."[53] 21 rods of cord not only approximates 1,100 metres but almost amounts to 1/100th of the distance between two parallels of latitude (1 degree= 111.331 kilometres). In our opinion, this standard unit was the modular unit that the Egyptians used in order to map their territory geographically.

Surveying the territory also had an economic component, as it related to the levying of taxes. This economic relevance, which was linked to the produce of the land, depended on the flooding of the Nile, which in turn took care of fertility. Obviously, one needed to know when the annual flooding would occur, which could only be predicted with the help of a calendar. The beginning of the flooding of the Nile would occur approximately in synchronisation with the heliacal rising of the star Sirius. The flood season, called Achet, started on New Year's Day and lasted for four months. Hence, observation of the "first brilliant visible rising" of this star was extremely important.

The map of Egypt in figure 13 shows the observation track between Hierakonpolis and Buto. If we imagine this track to be the diagonal B-D of a rectangle, then a geographical frame is formed that reminds us of the Serekh (coat of arms, in which the country is shown to be divided into Lower and Upper Egypt). Horizontally, the rectangle is defined by the southern and the northern borders, while the vertical sides of the rectangle mark the western and the eastern borders of Egypt. The respective co-ordinates of the four corners A, B, C and D are:

A:	25°06' N. and 30°45' E.
B: Hierakonpolis/El Kab	25°06' N. and 32°47' E.
C:	31°12' N. and 32°47' E.
D: Buto	31°12' N. and 30°45' E.

The above territory measures approximately 678 kilometres (1,296,000 royal cubits) in length and around 200 kilometres (384,000 royal cubits) in width. This rectangle was developed to serve as a preliminary geographical framework (cf. fig. 13). The diagonal B-D had a length of approximately 707 kilome-

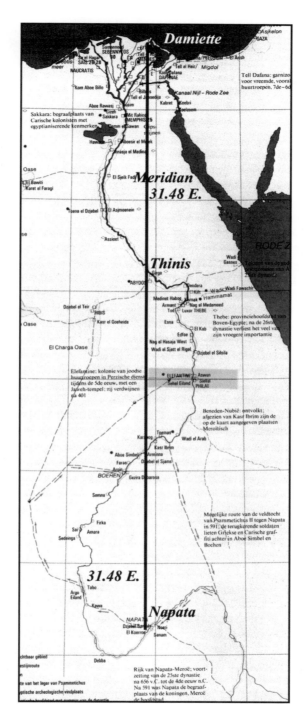

Fig. 18. General map of Egypt and Nubia between approximately 31° N. and 18° N., including the meridian at 31°48' E., running from the coastal town Damiette, via the early dynastic sanctuary Tell Ibrahim Awad and that of Thinis and ending up at the holy table mountain near Napata.

tres (1,350,500 royal cubits). The total length of the territory from B to C consisted of nearly 618 strips of land, each with a length of 1,100 metres. The width of the territory was divided into approximately 38,400 strips of land, each measuring 5.24 metres. Assuming a team to be capable of measuring an area of 1,100 x 1,100 metres a day, the overall surveying of this land could have been carried out by 90 teams in less than four years.

3.12 Expanding the Geographical Frame

The observation track between Hierakonpolis and Buto, based on the heliacal rising of the star Sirius, served to shape the infrastructure of Egypt. This shape functioned as an initial geographical frame that was apparently also instrumental in mapping other localities, both within the country and far beyond its borders.

The Delta derives its shape from the two branches of the Nile, at the extremities of which the towns of Rosetta and Damiette were founded (cf. fig. 18). In the geography of Egypt, the estuary of what is known as the Damiette branch was a region of strategic significance. Damiette is located at 31°25' N. and 31°48' E.; Rosetta, situated on the estuary of the Rosetta branch, is located at 31°25' N. and 30°25' E. Both towns are on the same latitude. The co-ordinates from the *Atlas of Ancient Egypt* have been rounded off to the nearest minute of arc, which means that a margin of no more than two minutes of arc should be taken into account while comparing the co-ordinates. In Antiquity, the settlements extended across a vast territory, which also applies to Hierakonpolis, Memphis and Thinis.

According to the kinglist of Manetho, kingship during the First and Second Dynasties had its seat in Thinis, north-east of the more familiar town of Abydos. Thinis is located between the present El Birba and Girga on the western bank of the Nile. Damiette and Thinis are on the same meridian. This meridian also happens to run across four hill tops that are all situated between Damiette and Thinis in the Eastern Desert, namely those of Gebel Abu Tireifiya (height?), Gineinet el Atash (318 metres), Khasma el Raqaba (483 metres) and Tilat Hassan (476 metres). Via these hill tops, the meridian seems to rush on southward, crossing Thinis on its way and finally ends in Napata, near the towns of El Kurru and Dzjebel Barkal (31°46' N./31°48' E.). These Nubian towns owe their fame to the secret of the sacred table mountain of Dzjebel Barkal and to the relationship between the god Amun of Napata and Amun-Re of Thebes. This is where Pharaoh Thutmosis III (approximately 1485 - 1430 BCE) ended his campaign and established the Amun-Re cult at the foot of the table mountain. 750 years later, a major part of Egypt was to be ruled by the Nubian pharaohs.

Further on in the south, we find the pyramids of Meru (Bagrawia, 16°59' N./ 33°45' E.). During the New Kingdom, but especially during the Kingdom of Kush and Napata and Meru, the meridian (31°48' E.) from Damiette to Napata formed the "heart" of the Egyptian/Nubian kingdoms on the Nile (cf. fig. 18).

Evidently, the plan for the partition of ancient Egypt's infrastructure had already been drawn up by the Egyptians some five thousand years ago. Obvi-

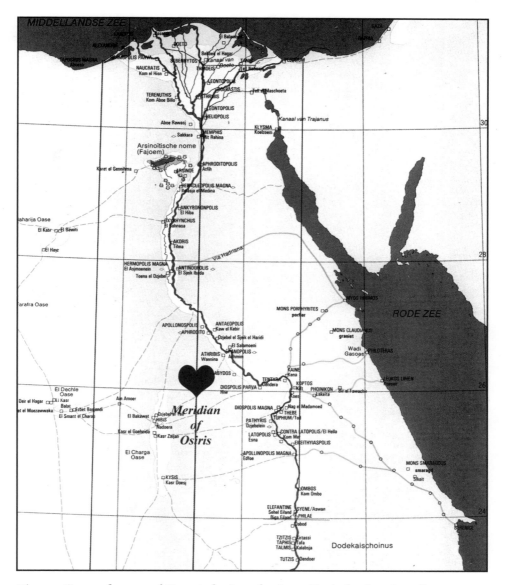

Fig. 19 General map of Egypt during the Late Period, showing the extreme western (29°31' E.) and eastern meridian (32°56' E.). Running through the centre is the Osiris meridian at 31°13' E.

ously, this cannot be achieved without the help of meridians, yet according to modern insights, it was precisely this vital knowledge that was lacking in those days. Nonetheless, various instances illustrate convincingly how knowledge of parallels of longitude as well as their locations did exist at that time. Apparently, these people were quite capable of using longitude to determine locations. The locations of the prehistoric twin towns of Hierakonpolis and Buto are a clear case in point. Of course, there is no doubt that the technical methods that the ancient Egyptians used differed from ours.

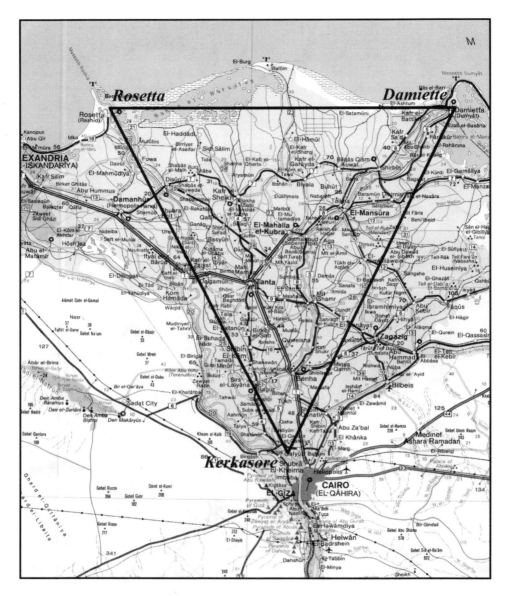

Fig. 20. Triangular layout of the Nile Delta formed by Rosetta and Damiette at the base and the Cercasorus (observation tower?) at the apex. The top of the triangle and its axis are in alignment with the pyramid field of Giza.

In the Western world, the necessary knowledge to determine meridians was not accumulated until late in the eighteenth century. A reward had to be offered before a methodology to determine the degree of longitude of a ship's position had been developed. Previously, the correct longitude could not be determined. But with the help of some basic instruments, the northern and southern parallel could be calculated, with reference to the equator, by specifying the angle in relation to the sun or the stars.

Maps drawn up before the eighteenth century that show degrees of longitude and latitude with any accuracy are therefore unique. Yet they do exist, witness Professor Hapgood who stated that the Dulcert Portolano map from 1339 was one of such maps that had been drawn up with the help of a grid consisting of lines that showed longitude and latitude. Hapgood explains: "We have already noted that A.E. Nordenskiöld [an authority in this field from the 19th century] in his essay on the portolan charts stated that they were too accurate to have originated in the Middle Ages. He found evidence that they probably existed in classical times, alongside the inferior maps of Eratosthenes, Pomponius Mela and Ptolemy. He even hinted that he thought they were of Carthaginian origin. It is our purpose now to examine a number of these charts, to see how accurate they really are, and how far they may be related to a possible world-wide system of sophisticated maps deriving from pre-Greek times." Hapgood then continues: "The Dulcert Portolano of 1339 is an early version of the 'normal portolano' - the highly accurate map that suddenly appeared in Europe in the early 14th Century, seemingly from nowhere. This kind of map did not evolve further but was simply copied and recopied during the rest of the Middle Ages and during the Renaissance."[54] Maps of this kind suggest that knowledge once existed that made it possible to calculate meridians and parallels with accuracy.

But can this knowledge really be thousands of years old? And what was the extent of their precision? These examples, calculated down to minutes of arc, confirm this observation (cf. fig. 19):

Abusir, the former Taposiris, is located at   29°31' E.
Kom Ombo is located at   32°56' E.

In ancient Egypt, Abusir lay at the extreme west and Kom Ombo at the extreme east. The two towns could be said to mark respectively the western and eastern borders of Egypt. The meridian in between and equidistant from these two is located at 31°13' E and is identical with the "Osiris meridian", on which the Djoser complex was located. This Abusir is the fourth town of the same name, which is related to Osiris.

Professor Stecchini, who obtained his doctorate at Harvard University with a thesis on classical metrology, claimed that the Delta had also been partitioned geometrically. He based his theory on the location of Alexandria and that of Thebes. However, these locations have nothing to do with each other. All the same, the Delta was definitely partitioned geometrically, yet in a different manner. Rosetta and Damiette are both situated on the estuaries of the branches of the Nile and on precisely the same parallel.

Rosetta is located at   31°25' N. and 30°25' E.
Damiette is located at   31°25' N. and 31°48' E.

The points in between and at equal distance from these two towns have a longitude of 31°06/07' E. This is the precise geographical position of the pyramid field of Giza with the Great Pyramid of Khufu (Cheops). We can thus connect Rosetta and Damiette with the apex of the Delta (where the observation

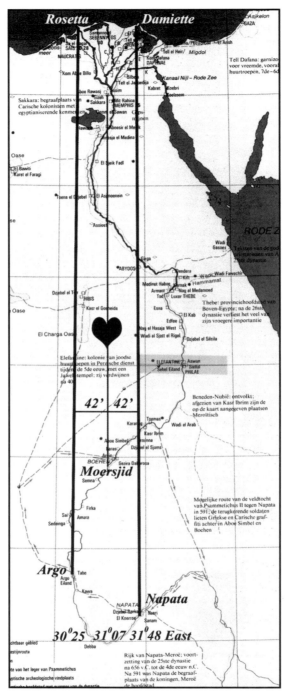

*Fig. 21. The territory of Egypt was divided into two strips of equal size. The geographical frame between Rosetta/Damiette and Murshid, close to the 22° latitude (2nd cataract), served as the basis for hieroglyph N24 (view from above) and AA8 (side view of the ideogram N24; for hieroglyphs, see **Egyptian Grammar**)*

tower of Cercasorus is believed to have stood - we will refer to this later on), thereby forming a triangle. In other words, the Great Pyramid, the geodetic beacon, is situated on the correct location.

The reason for the singularity of the pyramid of Khufu lies in its location on both the apex and the axis of the Delta, which is formed by the mouth of the two branches of the Nile that discharge into the Mediterranean Sea, and by the two towns that were founded on their respective banks: Rosetta and Damiette. The Egyptologist Goyon did not overlook that fact: "When this axis is extended to the Mediterranean Sea, then this straight line runs exactly across the apex of the Delta, which is situated close to the estuary of the Rosetta and the Damiette branches [of the Nile] respectively."[55]

 A general map shows that the territory of Egypt was basically divided into two equal strips of land. Each strip had a width of 42 minutes of arc (cf. fig. 21). The westernmost meridian runs from the town of Rosetta, via Karun to the island of Tabo in the Nile. The central meridian runs from the apex of the Delta via the pyramids of Giza and Asyut to Murshid-West. The eastern meridian runs from the town of Damiette via Fakus (including the important temple Tell Ibrahim Awad, possibly the oldest one in Lower Egypt, built around 3400 BCE), across Thinis and on to Napata. Thus, the meridians continue into the kingdom of Kush and end at the pyramids of Nubia. The short, easternmost meridian runs from Kulzum, the gateway of the Sinai, over a relatively short distance to the temple city of Esna.

3.13 Forgotten sources?

The Egyptians appear to have made ingenious use of the Nile basin. In the northern part, they recognized Osiris by surveying the course of the Nile. This course obviously had to be charted before the correspondence between the celestial constellation of Scorpio (Osiris) and the Nile could be perceived.

Stecchini reports the existence of Egyptian sources from the early dynastic period, which are presumed to have passed into oblivion. According to him, these sources show that from the Equator down to the Mediterranean Sea, the Egyptians had determined points of vital importance along the course of the Nile in degrees of longitude and latitude. However, he quotes no sources or texts, nor does he provide further information on these subjects.

Did Stecchini happen to find his information in the work of Nicolas Fréret, entitled **Mémoires, Académie des Inscriptions XXIV** (1756)? The said Fréret (1688-1749) was the first permanent secretary of the Académie des Inscriptions and he is known as one of the most illustrious scholars France ever brought forth. Fréret wrote "an essay on antique geodesy, in which he stated that not only was the length of the circumference of the Earth known in ancient times, the Egyptians even knew the size of their country down to a royal cubit."[56] In 1816, after having closely examined the entire documentation on the subject, Letronne (1787-1848) came to the conclusion, that "Fréret's declaration ought to be verified, or one should at least refrain from claiming it to be exaggerated."[57]

All this shows convincingly that in a far distant past, a geographical frame was created in which cultural efforts could develop. The ancestors of the Egyptians must have had highly developed astronomical knowledge at their disposal. Without this astronomical and geodetic knowledge, as well as a knowledge of architecture, construction and materials, the pyramids could never have been realised. What is more, civilisation might never have reached that level. The next chapter will reveal the true meaning of these immense buildings, which was a well-kept secret. Are they really nothing more than the regal tombs of the deceased pharaohs?

Chapter 4

Egypt: "Image of Heaven"

In his foreword to **Astronomy before the telescope**, the astronomer P. Moore writes: "To the Egyptians, the sky was formed by the arched body of the goddess Nut, and the sky was solid - a belief which was continued for a surprisingly long time." He also states that "The Egyptians had no real concept of the nature of the universe, but their precision was amazing by any standards, and there is no doubt that the Pyramids were astronomically aligned, even if their exact role is still a matter for debate."[1] The second chapter of this book bears the title **Astronomy in Egypt**, in which the astronomer R. Wells, author of various books on astronomy, astrology and technology, begins: "Historians often underestimate, while others frequently exaggerate the capabilities of the ancient Egyptians."[2] With these words, Wells typifies the continuous battle that has been going on for centuries concerning the standard of the ancient Egyptians' capabilities.

Obviously, these capabilities find their roots in everyday life, yet it means that their development must have been spread out over a very long period of time. This period is much longer than Wells presumes when he writes: "More than six millennia ago in the Nile Valley and Delta, man's primal gleanings from the night sky crystallised into a variety of myths that formed the basis of Egyptian religion." In the end, presumably these observations led to a comprehensive astronomy because "the priesthood mastered the ability to predict the time and place of their gods' appearances [in the heavens]."[3] Later on in this book, a prehistoric rock-painting will be shown to demonstrate that this knowledge existed at least nine millennia ago. Many ancient Egyptian texts mention gods and the heavens. The Pyramid Texts from the Old Kingdom and Coffin Texts from the Middle and End of the Old Kingdom provide appropriate examples. Furthermore, texts also exist that mention a link between heaven and earth.

What is more, some texts even mention *two* heavens. These "two heavens" were subject to an order of precedence, which is described in the Louvre Papyrus: "one sky for this Earth, one for the Duat [netherworld]." What is meant by "one sky for this Earth and one for the Netherworld"? What do these confusing words refer to? Do they conceal some profound, hidden significance that could explain why the Pyramid Field was built? Once again, Herodotus supplies the answer. In his book **Histories**, he spoke about one of these heavens and not only does he mention the exact era, he even specified the precise celestial sector that pertained to the "First Era", Zep Tepi, the Era of Osiris...

In other ancient texts, Egyptologists are confronted with additional hard-to-solve problems concerning the relationship of the heavens with various locations in ancient Egypt. An intriguing ancient text mentions a special bond between heaven and earth: "Or are you ignorant, Asclepius [possibly Imhotep, son of Pharaoh Djoser and his chief master-builder], that *Egypt is the image of heaven?* Moreover, it is the dwelling-place of heaven and all the forces that are in heaven. If it is proper for us to speak the truth, our land is the temple of the world."[4] Does this text infer that Egypt is literally an image of heaven? For many, this conclusion is too far-fetched. Only a handful of scholars are inclined to give it the benefit of the doubt. Nevertheless, the text provides sufficient grounds for a thorough and conscientious examination of the Pyramid Field.

4.1 Egypt, a Gift of Osiris

What could be the deeper meaning of the phrase *"our land is the temple of the world"*? In chapter 2, we pointed to the similarity between the course of the river Nile from Denderah to the Delta, and the constellation Scorpio, identified with Osiris. From this, the celestial sector of Osiris (Scorpio) was represented literally on the surface of Egypt. The constellation Scorpio, the constellation of the Netherworld, governed the "First Era".

To the Egyptians, Osiris represented the primaeval powers. He was the god of the first cultural period of the Egyptians, Zep Tepi (circa 15,500 BCE), and he lived on as the deity who incarnated during their second cultural period (circa 5300 BCE). Initially, he symbolised the fertility of the Earth and its vegetation. Every year, Osiris' festivities were held as a tribute to Nature that would recover and flourish again. It also reminded the Egyptians of the prime days of the "First Era".

The words used by Herodotus, *"Egypt, a gift of the Nile"*[5] imply that after his rebirth, Osiris granted the land of Egypt to Mankind. As such, the Egyptians saw their country as the habitat of the heavens and of all the powers that were represented therein. It gave them the feeling that they belonged to a "Cosmic" Empire. There is ample evidence of this attitude on the famous palette of Pharaoh Narmer, on which he is displayed in a ritual pose known as "smiting the enemy". This pose symbolises power and rulership over the world.

4.2 The Heavens of the Underworld (Netherworld)

The First Era, the Era of the Gods, during which the heavens of Osiris were visible on the eastern horizon on New Year's Day, belongs to the period between approximately 17,500 and 14,000 BCE. At that time, the star Deneb was the Pole Star. This star marked the birth-channel of Nut, the goddess of the heavens. The start of that period was mentioned by Herodotus.[6] It ended with the rulership of the God Bitis around 14,200 BCE.

The celestial map on the assumed New Year's Day around 16,000 BCE, from a viewpoint in Egypt facing towards the eastern horizon, shows the constellations identified in figure 22. The constellation Herakles or Hercules is located near the eastern horizon, at the beginning of the zodiacal sign of Sagittarius. Sagittarius contains the star mu Sagitarii, "known by the Copts, priests from Koptos, as Polis", at approximately 8° Sagittarius.[7] In 17,500 BCE, the vernal equinox was in conjunction with this same star, Polis (see list in Appendix VI).

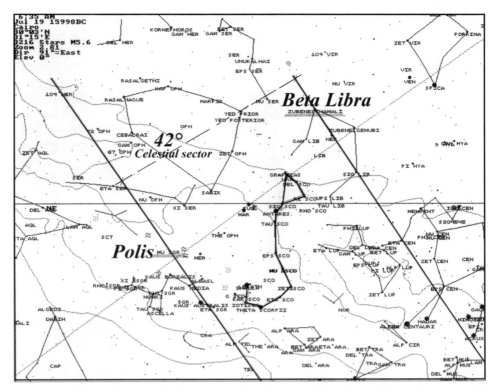

Fig. 22: Celestial map of the eastern horizon on New Year's Day in approximately 16,000 BCE. The figure shows the celestial sector of the First Era, that of Osiris, as described by Herodotus, at the rising of the constellation Scorpio (in the centre) = Osiris, as the heavens of the netherworld.

Polis is situated on the celestial meridian and this meridian (primus verticalis) indicates the nadir of the celestial sphere. This is emphasised by the word Polis, meaning pole – an obvious name. Hence, the position of this star on the celestial meridian provides us with a fixed measuring point. This star points to the beginning of Osiris' netherworld.

Herodotus provides us with additional information to establish the limitation of this specific celestial sector of the netherworld, when he mentions Typho(o)n and Hooros,[8] currently known as Typhon and Horus. Typhon is synonymous with the constellation Serpentis (located at approximately 28° Libra), since Typhon is known as a monster with the head of a dragon and the feet of a snake; it begot a great number of dragon-vermin by a snake-like monster.[9] Horus, or Haroeris, is synonymous with the northern scale of Libra, beta Libra (approximately 25° Libra).

The extreme limits of the celestial sector, "the heavens of the netherworld", based on Herodotus' detailed information, can thus be determined. The sector is contained between 8° Sagittarius and 25° Libra, which means that it extends across 42 degrees and comprises part of Sagittarius and part of Libra. In be-

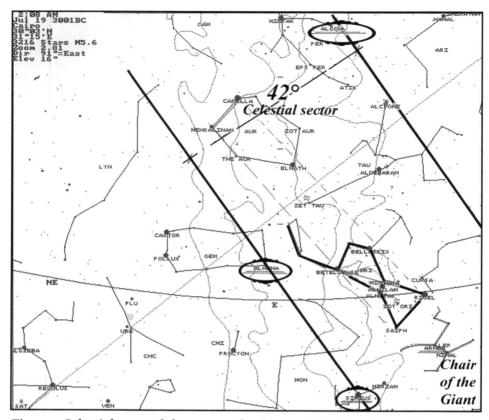

Fig. 23: Celestial map of the eastern horizon on New Year's Day in approximately 3000 BCE. The figure shows the celestial sector of the Second Era, that of Horus, at the rising of the constellation Orion (in the centre) i.e. Horus the Younger, as the heavens of the 'Upper-world' (the Earth).

tween, in a central position, we find Scorpio, the constellation of Osiris. The size of the celestial sector therefore corresponds to the 42 assessors (Judges of the Dead) mentioned in ***The Book of the Dead*** (Proverb 125), the 42 books by Hermes, and the 42 provinces (Nomes) of Egypt. The duration of this era amounts to 3,000 years (appendix VI: 42° x 71.4285 yrs/degree = 3,000 years).

4.3 The Heavens of the 'Upper-world' (Earth)

Before the start of the Second Era, the Followers of Horus experienced a transitional period that began approximately 8400 BCE and ended around 5300 BCE (cf. part 2 of this book). The Second Era of the Followers of Horus is situated between approximately 5300 and 2200 BCE. During this period, about 3000 BCE, the star Thuban (alfa Draconis) became the Pole Star. In this Second Era, another celestial sector gained importance. This sector, containing the constellation Orion, also extended over 42 degrees (see fig. 23). Due to the shifting of the vernal equinox, the overall view of the stars as they were observed from Earth had, in the course of approximately 13,000 years, rotated exactly 180 degrees, resulting in an entirely different image of the celestial sky. At all times, the celestial sector of the Second Era lies diametrically opposite to that of the First Era.

During this Second Era, from 5300 until 2200 BCE, the vernal equinox moved from 15° Gemini (the position of the star Alhena) to 2° Taurus (the position of the star Algol). This means that around 5300 BCE, the vernal equinox was in conjunction with the star Alhena (cf. list in appendix VI), while from 2200 BCE, the vernal equinox came into conjunction with the star Algol. Accordingly, the limits of this celestial sector lie between 15° Gemini and 2° Taurus. The central position is now occupied by the constellation Orion, on top of the seat of Horus, represented by the star Arneb in the constellation Lepus. The name of this main star Arneb is derived from the Greek word *Arnebeschènis*, i.e. "Horus, the First and Foremost of Letopolis",[10] also known as the "chair of the Giant" and "the throne of Jauzah".[11] The Copts called Orion the star [constellation] of Horus.[12]

Once again, the celestial sector in question measures 42 degrees and consists of a part of the sign Gemini and almost the entire sign of Taurus. The duration of the era amounts to approximately 3000 years. This celestial sector is the heavens of the 'Upper- world' (the Earth) (see fig. 23), the Era of Ra, which commenced around 2900 BCE (cf. chapter 1.4).

4.4 The Link between the Upper-World and the Netherworld

Thus, the ancient Egyptians were familiar with two celestial sectors of equal expanse, each consisting of 42 assessors: one that referred to their archaic first cultural period, the First Era of Osiris; the other to their subsequent second cultural period, the Second Era, which pertained to Horus the Younger. This is what the concept of "the two heavens" signifies.

The archaic celestial sector was represented in fact on the ground in the soil of their land, by the course of the river Nile. The celestial sector from the second cultural period was given factual shape by the pyramids that were built close to the isosceles triangle formed by the towns of Memphis, Letopolis and Heliopolis (cf. fig. 11). On this site, they built a necropolis as an *"Image of Heaven"* to pay tribute to Osiris. They expressed their extraordinary enthusiasm by drafting a large scale, ingenious building plan of the pyramids. The function of this immense necropolis was closely related to Osiris as the god of the dead and the netherworld. Their decision to build the pyramids near the Nile enabled them to achieve a relationship between the Upper-world of Horus and the Netherworld of Osiris.

4.5   Giza stands for Orion

The names of geographical locations usually possess a historical background that sometimes reveals interesting information. This is also the case with the name Giza, the village in the immediate proximity of Cairo, where we find the pyramids of Khufu, Khafre and Menkaure (Cheops, Chefren and Mycerinos). During the 19th century, the name of that village was Jeezeh. The following orthographic variations are known to have existed at that time: Gyzeh, Ghizeh, Gizeh, Jeezeh, Gheezeh, Jizeh, Djiza, Dsjise, Dschiseh, Geezeh, El-Geezeh, Dzireth, etc. According to Dr. J.A.S.Grant, *Jeezeh* or *Geezeh* was the correct English spelling.[13] The present name of Giza in Arabic is Ahramat Al Jizah.[14] Some hundred years have gone by since people took the trouble to pronounce Arabic names correctly in English. Nowadays, the only name by which we know it is *Giza*.

Phonetically, *Jizah* and *Jeezeh* more than likely derive from the ancient Arabic Al Jauzah, which simply means *Orion*. "In early Arabic, Orion was Al Jauzah, a word also used for stars in Gemini [Twins]".[15] Assuming that the phonetic interpretation is correct, then this would prove that more than a thousand years ago, the Arabs still knew the true meaning of this location, namely Orion. Consequently, there is hardly any sense in debating whether the pyramids of Giza correlate with the Belt of Orion or not. The fact is that Giza means Orion.

4.6   Jauzah and the Great Central Circle

The Egyptians attached great importance to the central image of the heavens that pertained to the First Era of Osiris (Scorpio). This central image consisted of 42 assessors. It was considered to be the centre of the heavens of the First Era. The same principle also applied to the central image of the heavens from the second cultural period, that of Horus (Orion). This latter image of the heavens also consisted of 42 assessors and was subsequently defined by astronomers as the "Centre of the Heavens". This is certified by the following passage: "In early [Arabic] desert astronomy their two bright stars [Castor and Pollux] formed one of the forepaws of the great ancient Lion; although they also were Al Burj al Jauza, the Constellation of the Twins. On the other hand, the English Orientalist Thomas Hyde (1636-1703), - [called] Jauzah, the Centre, - as designating these stars' position *in medio coeli*, or in a region long viewed as the centre of the heavens; either because they were a zenith constellation, or from the brilliancy of this portion of the sky".[16] This entire celestial area was known as the "great central circle",[17] since the orbit of the ecliptic is visible directly above it.

The opinion of other Arab astronomers in Antiquity focused with even greater acuity on the profound inherent meaning of this constellation. They specifically called the stars in Orion's Belt "the golden walnuts", which they knew to have originally borne the name *Jauzah*. Other sources testify to the exceptional religious significance that this "great central circle" had for Mankind. This must have been one of the motives that led to the development of an astronomical quantifying grid that was based on that specific celestial sector.

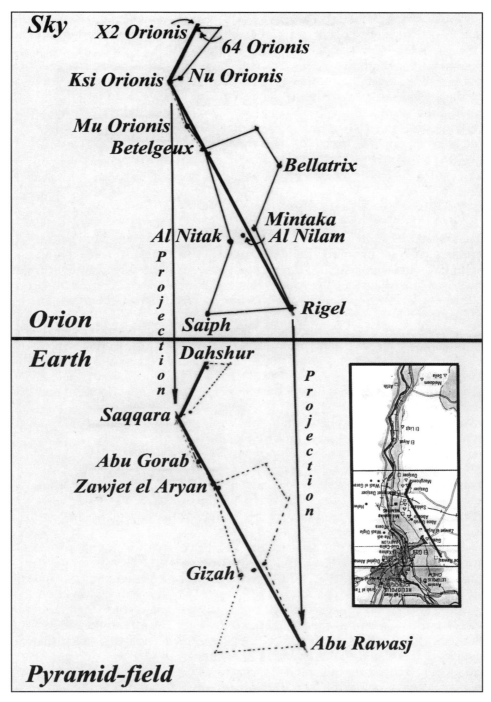

Fig. 24. Upper part: Image of the southern sky with the constellation Orion at night fall (approximately 23h30) during the celebration of the Osiris festival around 3000 BCE. Lower part: The Egyptians drew the constellation Orion downward, as shown by the arrows, and subsequently projected the Main Outline onto the surface of the Earth.

This grid was the basis on which the plan of the Pyramid Field was drawn up, and it was specified in detail in accordance with the positions of certain stars in this celestial sector. The plan took the shape of the landscape and geological factors were taken into account. Subsequently, the Egyptians based the design of the Pyramid Field on the southern celestial heavens as they had been visible in the late evening hours (circa 23h00) during the Osiris festival. On those nights, the constellation Orion could be seen in all its radiant beauty. Orion (Horus) was projected on the Earth, as shown in figure 24. They immortalised the celestial sector of Jauzah by the pyramids that they built. Egypt was indeed an *"Image of Heaven"*.

4.7 The Plan of the Pyramid Field

The Pyramid Field consisted of colossal monuments, such as the royal necropolis with its pyramid complexes, satellite pyramids, queen's pyramids, sphinxes, boat-pits, temples, ceremonial causeways, mastabas, harbours near the various temples of the dead, canals and sacred lakes (cf. e.g. **The Complete Pyramids** by Lehner and **Guide to the Pyramids of Egypt** by Siliotti).

It was built in the royal necropolis, close to the triangle formed by the towns of Memphis, Letopolis and Heliopolis. The Djoser complex is the cornerstone of the Pyramid Field and a forerunner of the classical pyramid era. That era began approximately 3153 BCE, with the start of the Third Dynasty, and ended during the Sixth Dynasty, due to the end of the catastrophic floods in approximately 2521 BCE.

(See section Chronology, especially the passage of the mysterious chronological coincidence in Manetho's **History of Egypt:**

Third Dynasty:	214 "yrs" x 2/3 = approximately 143 Solar years
Fourth Dynasty:	277 "yrs" x 2/3 = approximately 185 Solar years
Fifth Dynasty:	248 "yrs" x 2/3 = approximately 165 Solar years
Sixth Dynasty:	203 "yrs" x 2/3 = approximately 135 Solar years.)

According to the Turin papyrus, the Third Dynasty ruled for approximately 102 years.[18] (In his **History of Egypt** chronology, the Egyptian high priest Manetho recorded that the Third Dynasty ruled for a period of approximately 143 Solar years). The duration of the Fourth Dynasty is unknown, since relevant information concerning the individual periods of the kings has been lost. However, we linked the beginning of the Fifth Dynasty to the birth of the Sun cult, which was introduced around 2825 BCE. Hence, the period that remains for the total duration of the Fourth Dynasty is approximately 185 years. (Manetho recorded that the Fourth Dynasty lasted for a period of 185 approximately Solar years.) In his book **Die Ägyptischen Pyramiden**, Stadelmann had already come to the conclusion that the duration of the Fourth Dynasty ought to be linked to the construction time of the pyramids and he claims to have good reasons to estimate the duration of the Fourth Dynasty at approximately 155 years,[19] thus considerably extending the rule of this Dynasty. Evidently, our calculated estimate surpasses his.

As to the Fifth Dynasty, the data supplied by the Kinglist in the Turin papyrus, combined with the Kinglists of Abydos and Saqqara, result in a period of approximately 180 years[20] (Manetho recorded that the Fifth Dynasty lasted approximately 165 Solar years.) The Turin papyrus lists the period from the First to the Fifth Dynasties as one sub total figure; after Pharaoh Unas, the last king on the list, a red line is drawn under the column of years of rulership (appendix VII). Unfortunately, the total number is lost, yet this line becomes so intriguing after our discovery of the following quotation: "According to Syncellus (p.193, Bonn)., the start of the rulership of the first *Egyptian king* [whose name was Mestraim] began in the year 2776 of the world [start of the world according to Syncellus in 5508 BCE]."[21] In other words, the first king of *Egyptian descent* began his reign around 2732 BCE. This point in time does not coincide with our calculation of the approximate year in which the Fifth Dynasty ended (2825 BCE – 165 years = 2660 BCE, a difference of approximately 72 years). The Sixth Dynasty ruled for approximately 181 years[22] (Manetho recorded that the Sixth Dynasty lasted for a period of approximately 135 Solar years.) The line in the Turin papyrus after Unas is significant. It could mean that the pharaohs of the Third (pharaoh Djoser's name was also indicated in red) to the Fifth Dynasties were not of Egyptian descent. According to the aforementioned source, those of the Sixth Dynasty definitely *were* of Egyptian origin.

This information provides a solid foundation to make a cautious re-assessment of the chronology of the pharaohs from the Third to the Sixth Dynasty, the actual builders of the Pyramid Field:[23]

Dynasty 0   before 3517 BCE

Dynasty I to Dynasty III   3517-3153 BCE
(Thinites, approximately 350 years)   (Manetho mentioned 370 years)

In fact, the *solar eclipse* on the winter solstice (17th January, 3517 BCE) was the beginning of Kingship of Egypt, Dynasty I.

Dynasty III to Dynasty IV   ca.   3153-3010 BCE

 Nebka, Djoser, Sekhemet, Chaba, and Huni

Dynasty IV to Dynasty V   ca.   3010-2825 BCE

 Snofru, Khufu, Djedefre, Khafre, Baka, Menkaure, Sjepseskaf, Khentkawes?

Dynasty V to Dynasty VI   ca.   2825-2660 BCE

Userkaf, Sahure, Neferirkare, Sjepseskare, Raneferef, Niuserre, Menkauhor, Djedkare Izezi, Unas

Dynasty VI to the fall of   ca.   2660-2527 BCE
the Old Kingdom

Teti, Userkare, Pepi I, Merenre I, Pepi II, Merenre II, Nitokerty.

Interruption by Flood 6 years   until 2521 BCE

4.8 The catastrophic decline of the Old Kingdom

The reason why the Old Kingdom collapsed, and the manner in which it happened, is a mystery. Its fall is attributed to decentralisation of the political and economic system, which started during the Fifth Dynasty, with the crumbling of totalitarian pharaonic power.

However, during the reign of the Fifth and the Sixth Dynasties, considerable climatological changes occurred that affected the harvests. The level of the Nile dropped drastically. Contemporary depictions show that in certain years the population was stricken by famine. These climatological changes were the forerunner of a transformation that would gradually create the desert circumstances with which we are now familiar.

Somewhere in the past, from about 4900 BCE to 2600 BCE, this belt had a Mediterranean climate that, at its height, prevailed down to the 20th parallel and may have been caused by an increase in temperature of the Atlantic Ocean. This coincides with the renderings of tropical animals on rock paintings in the Central Mountain Ridge of North Africa. The mountain range had many rivers. The meaning of the name of the Tassili mountains (rise of rivers) reminds us of that fact. This part of North Africa was covered with enormous lakes, which were more like inland seas, such as Lake Triton and Lake Chad, which extended up to the Tibesti mountains.

Between 8000 and 3000 BCE, the Mediterranean climate caused vast oak and cedar woods, as well as all other forms of vegetation, to flourish in this climatological belt. Towards 3000 BCE, this climate gradually retreated northward, and flora began to appear that was resistant to more arid conditions, such as the aleppo, the olive tree, and the cypress.[24] "From about 2700 BC, Quézel reports, there is evidence that the *pinus halepensis* gradually disappeared and that the *acacia*, the *salvadora* and the *balanites* penetrated the area. This savannah phase did not put an immediate end to the earlier forms of vegetation, yet it managed to establish itself firmly and endured until well into the early stages of Christianity."[25]

Quézel carried out drillings in the Hoggar and the Tibesti. Similar types of flora were also encountered in the south of Palestine and the Sinai. Tussocks of pine were also found in the Egyptian Delta, this during a limited investigation that was carried out by Professor Saad of the Botanical Department of the University of Alexandria.[26]

The results showed that the Delta and the neighbouring areas were definitely forested by pine trees, cedars, juniper bushes and oak trees.[27] Furthermore, it became apparent that climatological circumstances, similar to the present conditions, did not begin until around 2600 BCE and that these kept on deteriorating, in spite of a short-lived revival around 1500 BCE. At present, Egypt consists of approximately 97 percent desert area, which was definitely not the case during a major part of the pharaonic era.

These drastic climatological changes coincided with a catastrophic flood (Tsunami) around 2527 BCE, which caused the collapse of the Old Kingdom (precession in conjunction with the constellation Pleiades, see Chronology). Evidence for this radical climatological deterioration has been reported in a series of important investigations by Butzer, Trigger, B.Bell, Lauffray and Vercoutter.[28] Schneider concluded that "the fundamental incision in the climatological circumstances corresponds with 2600 BCE as the optimal time limit of the Middle Holocene", and continues: "An unfavourable alteration in the climate suddenly put an end to the Old Kingdom of Egypt. Up to 1500 BCE, all African lakes showed a rapid decrease in surface area."[29] In addition, he tells us that another unfavourable change occurred in the climate around 1150 BCE (see diagram in fig. 2).[30]

The date of the catastrophic end of the Old Kingdom is also fully corroborated by the results of research by Dansgaard et al. in the climatological record of the Greenland ice sheet. They discovered that what may have been an abrupt climatological change occurred between 2600 and 2500 BCE. During that century, the geological period known as the Middle Holocene changed to the Upper Holocene.[31,32]

The collapse of the Old Kingdom towards the end of the Sixth Dynasty had such far-reaching consequences that it caused a chronological gap of six years, which was marked by a total absence of pharaonic rule.[33] The continuing downfall of this culture (between approximately 2400 – 2150 BCE) manifested itself primarily after the Eighth Dynasty. It took centuries before a renewed revival occurred, this at the very beginning of the Middle Kingdom, around 2067 BCE.

It is not only the demise of a culture that provides evidence of a catastrophe; the simultaneous appearance of other cultures, in numerous areas, following this catastrophe substantiates this conclusion. The following overview of contemporary births of civilisations depicts an intriguing situation:

Rise of the Akkadian civilisation	ca.	2400 BCE
Rise of the Nagar/Ebla/Mari civilisation	ca.	2300 BCE
Rise of the Early-Minoan civilisation	ca.	2400 BCE
Rise of the Indus Valley civilisation	ca.	2400 BCE
Rise of Troy II	ca.	2300 BCE
Rise of Bahrain	ca.	2400 BCE

These events do not match current views on Egyptian chronology, in which no margin has been left for a catastrophic event of such proportions. Such facts might completely change the now accepted Egyptian chronology. Furthermore, contemporary publications on Egypt show that the present interpretation is based on a climate with a desert-like vegetation, combined with an annual flooding of the Nile, which provided the necessary conditions for survival in the valley. However, this notion is now superseded by the results of recent paleo-climatological investigations.

4.9 The Concept of Eternal Egypt

There has never been an inventory of the entire Pyramid Field as one system, although Goyon's research did tend in that direction. Obviously, such an approach would assume that the Egyptians had a complete design at their disposal before they chose the site on which to build a pyramid complex (a pyramid complex consists of a valley temple, a ceremonial causeway, a commemoration temple and a pyramid). This would mean that they had drawn up a detailed plan beforehand. In turn, this would imply that more than 5,000 years ago, the Egyptians were able to work out an entire concept on an extremely large scale. And this could lead to the conclusion that prior to the design, all necessary land-surveying and research on soil conditions in that territory had been carried out, thus resulting in detailed knowledge of the entire terrain on which the Pyramid Field would be erected. If this is the case, the level of Egyptian culture would have to be re-assessed and reckoned to be more advanced than previously presumed. The resulting implications are indeed far-reaching.

Let us consider this possibility in further detail. In outline, a design of such magnitude would have to be based on an analysis of the subsoil, to account for the buildings' foundations. Knowledge of road and waterway construction in order to handle the transport of building materials would also be required, as well as methods of calculation to construct the actual buildings. In addition, a rough estimate would be needed of the amount of building materials necessary to accomplish the entire project, including the choice of the quarries for the appropriate material and the roads and/or waterways for transportation. Moreover, it would require a supply of thousands of cubic metres of construction timber, such as roundwood for the necessary lifting-tackle, tens of millions of hardwood wedges for quarrying and sledges, roundwood for scrolling and towing, and plenty of rope. In order to build the ramps for the transport of material to and from the pyramids, tens of thousands of cubic metres of earth, rubble or alternative material would be needed, as well as wood, which had to be removed and redistributed after the work had been finished.

Tens of thousands of workmen, with a diversity of knowledge of the various crafts were necessary to achieve such a complex plan. These men needed the necessary tools to perform the measuring, digging, hacking and splitting. Undoubtedly, this variety of labourers would have consisted, amongst others, of specialised stonecutters to complete the projects, and to create the reliefs, sculptures and statues. Knowledge of pigmentation and the manufacture of paint were also required. Supervision of the work, as well as the organisation and the methodical way of tackling the various components must have been immense. These people lived on site or in the immediate surroundings of the project and obviously had to be supplied with food and drink – requiring further logistic problems for the project management.

During the Third and the Fourth Dynasties, twelve pyramids with annexes were erected at Abu Rawash (1), Giza (3), Zawyet el Aryan (2), Saqqara (2), Dahshur (2), Meidum (1) and Seila (1). They consumed more than ten million cubic metres of stone. The pyramids and annexes that were built during the

Fifth (Abu Gorab), Sixth and Twelfth Dynasties contain "a mere" four million cubic metres of stone.[34] The gigantic proportions and the awe-inspiring character of the Pyramid Field dwarf our presumed superiority over older cultures. Evidently, the magnificence of the entire complex is almost beyond our comprehension. So maybe there is more to it than we thought.

During the predynastic and early dynastic period, before the introduction of the sun-cult at the beginning of the Fifth Dynasty, the astro-religion of the Egyptians played a fascinating and highly significant role in the design of the Pyramid Field. This required the influx of astronomical knowledge. Egypt's astronomical religion implies that the twelve pyramids of the Third and Fourth Dynasties, as well as the Abu Gorab pyramid of the Fifth Dynasty, had a different function. The fact is that the pyramids of the Third and Fourth Dynasties fulfilled various functions, from the creation of a link between heaven and earth to the demarcation of the necropolis.

The pyramids and the sun temples of the Fifth Dynasty between Abu Gorab and Abusir were built on one central site. The overall function of this pyramid site, known as Abu Gorab (the necropolis of Abusir), included that of a link between heaven and earth. The building quality of these pyramids and sun temples actually differed from that of the Third and the Fourth Dynasties, as did the quality of the pyramids of the Sixth Dynasty, though they contributed to the fulfilment of the iconographic function of the Pyramid Field. On the other hand, the construction of the pyramids of the Twelfth Dynasty led to an expansion of the Pyramid Field as a whole. It extended its total length and enhanced their astronomical religion. The design was finally completed by the pharaohs of the Twelfth Dynasty.

Unfortunately, these pyramids were not built to last forever either. The core generally consisted of brickwork buttresses that ran from the centre to the four corners, as well as additional buttresses that supported the four sides. This created inner vacuums, which were filled with debris or blocks of stone or clay. Obviously, this type of construction was unable to withstand the ravages of time.

A brief review of the Pyramid Field gives the impression of haphazard building activities between Abu Rawash and Meidum, without the slightest trace of any underlying master plan. The area in which the pyramids were built covers an space of approximately 88 x 30 kilometres, or a total of 2,640 square kilometres. The formidable task of supplying the building site with timber, tools and all kinds of other material, as well as craftsmen, must lead to the assumption that this plan was based on a specific system or a specific train of thought.

After all, if these pyramids had merely been intended to function as tombs, they would surely have been built in the direct vicinity of an available quarry? After the completion of one pyramid, the problems involved in moving to the next building site many kilometres away would have been extremely complicated, expensive and unreasonable from a logistics point of view. If the sole function was to act merely as a tomb, this would have led, in the absence of an underlying plan, to the construction of an agglomeration of pyramids on one single site in the immediate surroundings of a natural stone quarry. The chaotically assembled pyramids on the fields of Napata, Nuri and Meru in former Nubia illustrate this fact more than clearly. Yet the Egyptians spared neither trouble nor expense to give shape to their thoughts and ideals. Hence, the design of the Pyramid Field must have been inspired by a deliberate motive, an intention that reaches further than merely the glorification of their deceased pharaoh. In short, is there any demonstrable evidence to corroborate conceptions of a more profound nature and if so, can it be revealed?

4.10 Territory and Landscape

In chapter 2 of this book, we revealed the relationship between Osiris and the Nile, which makes it clear that Osiris is, as it were, to be found on the land surface of Egypt. Later, the concept of the "two heavens" was also explained. It is clear that the course of the Nile plays a crucial role and it is equally clear that the shape of its riverbed was determined by, amongst other factors, the surrounding rock formations.

North of Memphis, before the river reaches the branches of the Delta, the Nile bends gently north-west and continues more or less parallel to the slowly receding rock formation that fences it off from the lowlands. This natural, slight bend in the rock formation was accentuated by the erection of a number of pyramids that were arranged to form a similar bend. One of the pyramids that are part of this bend is the Djoser complex, the cornerstone of the Pyramid Field. Its location was determined by the prominent intersection of the "Osiris meridian" with the observation track of the star Sirius. The complex was built on that intersection, practically on the slight bend of the rock formation.

The rock formation then extends in a north-westerly direction towards Alexandria. Some of the pyramids were built on the edge of this rock formation, yet the building sites of other pyramids do not follow this edge entirely. The pyramid of Abu Rawash was built about two kilometres from the eastern edge, on a relatively small hill. Seen from the bend of the rock formation near the Djoser complex (which is situated at a height of about 20 metres), this formation rises very gradually in the direction of Zawyet El Aryan where the southern pyramid was built on a mountain ridge, then goes on towards Giza where it turns into the Mokattam plateau (its height varying between 40 and 60 metres) and finally reaches a height of between 60 and 80 metres at Abu Rawash. Accordingly, the pyramids of Abu Rawash, Giza and the southern pyramids of Zawyet el Aryan were all located on natural vantage points.[35]

From the strategic point of the pyramid of Abu Rawash, one enjoyed a majestic view of the pyramids of Giza; the eyes could also wander along the southeastern horizon towards Zawyet el Aryan. In those days, visibility under clear weather conditions may even have allowed the Djoser complex to come into view. If so, it would provide a line of sight of about 22 kilometres. This line ran at an angle of approximately 52° with the exact east (see fig. 27; also note the relationship with the constellations during the Osiris festival, and the text pertaining to fig. 40, §4.28). This angle corresponds with the angle of the slope of most pyramids.

The following pyramids are "aligned" on this line of sight: from the pyramid

Fig. 25 Panoramic view from the pyramid of Abu Rawash towards the Pyramid Field of Giza, looking in a south-easterly direction.

of Abu Rawash, this imaginary line runs via the pyramid of Menkaure at Giza and via the pyramids of Zawyet el Aryan to the Djoser complex, allowing an observer to look diagonally towards the south-east (cf. fig. 25). It was precisely in that south-easterly direction that the heliacal rising of the star Rigel and Sirius was observed.

The town of Memphis was also built on a rocky elevation, a kind of "island" within the Nile basin. To the Egyptians, the term "island" raised an issue that played an important role in the myth of the "creation of the world". According to Professor Lehner of the University of Chicago, the site of classical Memphis was located exactly within the slight bend where the mastabas of the First and Second Dynasties (at that place of the Strong Arm, Nekhet) are to be found.[36],[37] The most prominent area where ruins are found around Memphis is the rocky elevation, the "island", immediately to the east of the Djoser complex. This complex, located on the Osiris meridian (31°13' E.), cuts the distance between Letopolis and Heliopolis into two equal halves. The co-ordinates for Letopolis are 30°08' N. and 31°08' E., for Heliopolis they are 30°08' N. and 31°18' E. By theoretically connecting these three towns with each other, an isosceles triangle is formed (cf. fig. 11).

The observation track of Sirius runs through Letopolis to Buto and thus follows one of the sides of the isosceles triangle. The location of the temple of Heliopolis with its benben stone was aligned on the 45 degrees diagonal that runs from the pyramids of Giza (see chapter 1).

Once again, the account given so far illustrates how the physiognomy of the territory was used and combined with human activities in order to shape the idea that "Egypt is the dwelling place of heaven and all the forces that are in heaven … our land is the temple of the world".

4.11 The Golden Section and the Obelisk of Aswan

There are certain indications that the proportions of the Golden Section were known to the Egyptians. These proportions are said to have been integrated into the Great Pyramid of Khufu. The height of each side and half the base of that side area are in the proportion of 1.61899, or Phi. In *Ancient Egyptian Construction and Architecture,* architects Somers Clark and Engelbach report that the Egyptians were able to calculate the cubic volume of a truncated pyramid. They called this one of the most surprising solutions.[38] The proportion of the Golden Section is the division of a line segment into a mean and extreme ratio; the exact proportion is 1.618033. This "sacred proportion" is mentioned in the Rhind papyrus, which dates back to approximately 1700 BCE. Although the indications it contains allude to their technical knowledge, they are no more than hints.

A decisive piece of evidence of the ancient Egyptians' familiarity with the Golden Section is the figure portrayed on the upper side of the "unfinished obelisk", still visible in the granite quarry in Aswan. This obelisk measures 41.75 metres in length and is thought to weigh around 1,168 tons.[39] While work was being carried out on the obelisk, a crack or other imperfection (due to its stratal structure) appears to have been discovered in the granite, so that a decision was made to discontinue further work.

On the upper side of this colossal obelisk, a pattern of grooves and notches was applied. The indented pattern represents the Golden Section in two different ways (see fig. 26). This is factual proof of their knowledge of the Golden Section. Its use resulted in a specific proportional division the application of which achieved the harmony and beauty that is so appealing in Egyptian architecture and sculptures. Once again, a component of their imposing monuments becomes apparent. Their technical ingenuity and artistic abilities in the field of architecture are essentially unsurpassed.

4.12 The Discovery of Structure in the Plan

The early phases of modern building projects are marked by the use of matrices, linear patterns or frames. The Egyptians of the Old Kingdom were already acquainted with these methods. At present, these matrices are generally drawn up without any specific proportional division. The designer uses these means to introduce a certain system into the overall plan. This is also applied in designs for infrastructure and town planning. Whenever systems of this kind are introduced, they will always remain apparent.

Some contemporary architects are known to strive for a modular system. One notorious example is the architect Le Corbusier, who, after a long period of joint research into aesthetics with the psychologist Fechter, came to the conclusion that his modular system was to be founded on two basic principles. Le Corbusier constructed two separate series, one which was based on raising figures to the mathematical powers of the Golden Section, while in the other model, these figures were doubled. One of his colleagues discovered simultaneous influences of both Gothic and of Renaissance origin in these series

Fig. 26, showing the top of what is known as the "unfinished Obelisk" in the quarry at Aswan. The dots indicate where a line was chiselled into the surface. The photo also shows a deep incision, which is seen to continue on the side of the obelisk. The figure contains the proportion Phi; the dimensions are fictitious. The deep incision divides the length of the dotted line in accordance with the Golden Section.

and confirmed inherent qualities which induce harmony. This led to a renewed interest in the ideal right-angled triangle, in which the proportion of the sides is in accordance with the Golden Section. It is not known to what extent the Egyptians used this type of triangle. Yet it poses a challenge to try to discover the system behind their building plan which covered the entire Pyramid Field, all the while taking the characteristics of the land into account.

We cautiously conclude that the Egyptians appear to have had the knowledge to integrate utilitarian projects - including the pyramids and their annexes - into the territory and the landscape in a natural way, whereby they even took advantage of natural elevations and other inherent conditions. The natural elevations within the rock formations were used specifically to give the pyramids a majestic appearance. From a practical point of view, the rock formation obviously provided a solid foundation to build on. Starting at the Djoser complex, the theoretical line of vision runs via the southern pyramid of Zawyet el Aryan of pharaoh Chaba on to the pyramid of pharaoh Menkaure and ends at Abu Rawash. The total length of this line, extending across the rock formation on which these pyramids were built, is divided up geodetically by these pyramids according to the aforementioned mean and extreme ratio Phi.

The building sites of the pyramids in question, which can be found on the map and are mutually aligned, divide that imaginary line into segments that

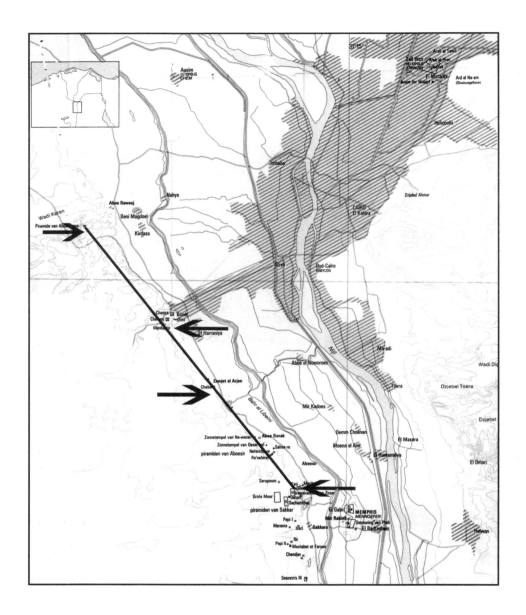

Fig. 27, showing the line of vision between Abu Rawash and the Djoser complex. This line runs at an angle of approximately 52° relative to east-west and is divided up in accordance with the Golden Section. The distance from Abu Rawash to Zawyet el Aryan (the southern pyramid of Chaba) and the distance from the Djoser complex to Giza (Menkaure pyramid) in turn divide the line of vision according to a mean and extreme ratio, i.e. in the proportion Phi =1.618033 as explained in Section 4.11

offer a twofold representation of the Golden Section. The location of the pyramid of Menkaure divides this line of sight from the Djoser complex up to Abu Rawash in the proportion Phi, just as the location of the pyramid of Chaba divides the line from Abu Rawash to the Djoser complex in the same ratio (see fig. 27). These segments represent the "sacred proportion" within a pentagram, i.e. a figure with five points. As a hieroglyph, this figure symbolises a star. The five-pointed star with the circumscribed circle was written as follows: (see hieroglyph N 15, *Egyptian Grammar*) and means "netherworld". For the Egyptians, writing and pictographic signs were incorporated into a form of visual art. In hieroglyphic script, the word and the image form a unity, a principle that this necropolis could not possibly have manifested more clearly.

Consequently, we divide this line of sight into two equal parts, thereby determining its mid-point, and set up a perpendicular at that spot. This perpendicular points towards the Nile meter on the southern end of Gezireth el-Roda, close to ancient Cairo. The perpendicular could be said to point in the direction of the north-eastern tip of the star. We suggest that this Nile meter, which served to measure the water level of the river, once belonged to the Pyramid Field.

For the time being, this may serve to prove that over and above their exploitation of the specific qualities of the territory, they also determined and plotted the locations of the aforementioned pyramids along a line of sight before actual building work began. This line of sight served to emphasise the direction in which observations of the stars were made. The line fulfilled an essential function in the design of the Pyramid Field. Its purpose was twofold, since the line of sight also possessed an *iconographic* function: it portrayed the basic outline of the awe-inspiring posture of the god Horus, the image of Orion, whose militant bearing, known as "smiting the enemy", was frequently depicted in images of the Egyptian pharaohs; it was even adopted by the Roman emperors (cf. fig. 28), as well as the Phoenicians and other nations from the Near East. Its concept was the stylistic icon of eternal Egypt and was displayed to establish a link between the heavens and the Earth.

Is it conceivable that hieroglyph N 15 (see Survey Hieroglyphs of *Egyptian Grammar*) presents us with a literal image of the design of the netherworld? Could the five-pointed star with the circumscribed circle and its centre, bearing the meaning of "netherworld", be used to track down the centre of the circle of this netherworld in the Pyramid Field? The concept might seem far-fetched, but we need to ask whether they did determine the specific point that marked the centre of the circle of the netherworld? It is significant that §151 of the Pyramid Texts describes how "Orion, i.e. Horus is *encircled* by the Netherworld". Figure 29 shows the plan of the necropolis, consisting of the five-pointed star which was drawn up by the proportional division of the line of sight between the pyramid of Abu Rawash and the Djoser complex. In conjunction with the location of the Nile meter on the island of Roda, at least three points were marked by buildings. Research and excavations need to be carried out in search of the two remaining points in order to test our hypothesis that the Egyptians did in fact design the netherworld according to their

Fig. 28. In the course of thousands of years, this specific posture has been depicted on numerous occasions. The earliest example known to us is found on the palette of Pharaoh Narmer, followed by that of Pharaohs Den, Sekhemkhet, Snofru (pictured above), Khufu, Sahuré, Neuserrê, Pepi, Amenemhet III, Thutmosis III, Thutmosis IV, Nefertiti and Seti I, Ramses II; seen in variations of this posture are Pharaoh Ramses II who is shown kicking his opponent against the knee (cf. Pyramid Text, esp. §959), Ptolemy XII and some depictions of female Meroitic rulers. One depiction shows the god Horus in this posture together with Ptolemy VIII (see www.zitman.org or Egypt image of Heaven, ch. 8a- 8y). The basic pattern of this specific bearing

pictographic script. It would enable us to ascertain that at the very beginning of the Egyptian culture, the plan of the necropolis, i.e. the outline of the various building components, was specifically designed according to the basic rules of the Golden Section.

4.13 The Hidden Circles of Rostau

The centre of these circles should lie on the line of sight as shown in figure 27, somewhere between the Djoser complex and the pyramid of Menkaure or between the Djoser complex and the pyramid of Abu Rawash. The mid-point on the line of sight, halfway between the Djoser complex and the pyramid of Menkaure, is easily determined. The mid-point on the line of sight between the Djoser complex and the pyramid of Abu Rawash is located exactly halfway between the southern pyramid of Zawyet el Aryan and the pyramid of Menkaure (see fig. 30). The two centres do not coincide.

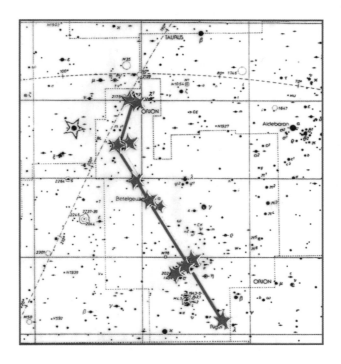

was shaped and immortalised by means of ten pyramids, plus a Pyramid city (black dots) between Abu Rawash and Dahshur. This shape was based on eleven stars of the constellation of Orion, i.e. Horus (cf. star chart). The basic pattern is shown in accordance with the ancient Egyptian custom of viewing from north to south. When the Egyptian calendar was installed on 19th July 4242 BCE, the battle-axe in the right hand was marked by the planet Mars. This particular event is related to the myth known to us from Edfu as the Triumph of Horus. Obviously, this specific posture is shown on the pylon of this Horus temple.

However, a topographic map of the entire area on a scale of 1:50,000 provided a surprising conclusion. South of Saqqara, the first pharaoh of the Fourth Dynasty, Snofru, built two pyramids in the vicinity of Dahshur. The distance between both these pyramids is relatively small (approximately 1850 metres). The northern pyramid is known as the Red Pyramid, the southern one as the Bent Pyramid. What was least expected now proved to be true: the distance between the Bent Pyramid and the assumed centre turned out to be equal to the distance between the pyramid of Abu Rawash and that same point. This central point was therefore determined by the Egyptians as the centre of two circumscribed circles, with differing radii.

One of these circumscribed circles runs through the Djoser complex and the pyramid of Menkaure, the other runs through the Bent Pyramid of Dahshur and the pyramid of Abu Rawash. Both circles point to the common centre of the hidden circles of Rostau, and this centre is located near a little lake at a crossroads, about a kilometre and a half south-east of the southern pyramid of Zawyet el Aryan. One road leads across the Bahr el Libeini canal to the village

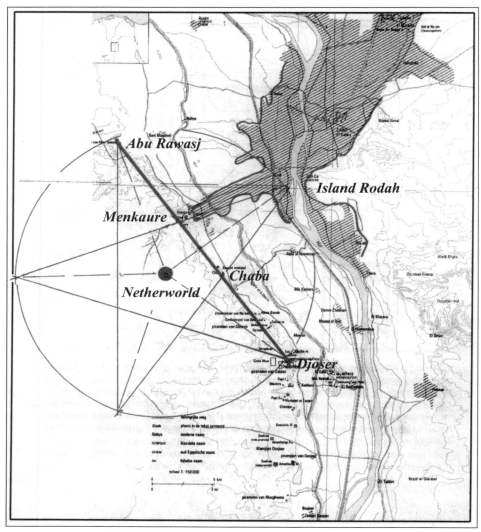

Fig. 29 shows the overall plan of the necropolis as a five-pointed star corresponding with hieroglyph N15, denoting the netherworld. The centre of the five-pointed star, i.e. the netherworld, correlates with the star Bellatrix in the constellation of Orion. It would be interesting to find out whether this site bears any markings of remains of a building.

of Abu el Numrus, the other runs from Giza to Saqqara, as shown on figure 30. Hence, during the Third to the Sixth Dynasties, the region of the necropolis was limited in the south by the southern pyramid of Dahshur and in the north by the pyramid of Abu Rawash. This was the region that was called Rostau. Towards the end of the Fourth Dynasty, Queen Mother Khentkawes, was still alive. A memorial tomb had been built for her at the end of the wadi east of Giza. Maybe this Queen Mother fulfilled the role of precursor at the beginning of the new, Fifth Dynasty; maybe she rounded off the ancestral line of the pharaohs of the Fourth Dynasty. During the reign of pharaohs Sahure,

Neferirkare, Shepseskare, Raneferef, and Niuserre from the Fifth Dynasty, pyramids were built on a territory which they had chosen to the south-east of Abu Gorab and to the north-west of Abusir, near the lake of the same name. Here, an agglomeration of five large and three small pyramids rises skywards, the latter group including a pyramid for the Queen Mother Khentkawes. Lehner writes that "this site points to a relationship between these pharaohs and their pyramids, and the role of the Queen Mother who conveys the royal ka [vitalizing life force] from one generation to the next".[40] Since the consort of Pharaoh Neferirkare was also called Khentkawes, it is uncertain as to which of the two that the name stands for. In any case, the site where the agglomeration of pyramids north-west of Abusir was built appears to specify yet another centre, pertaining to a fourth circumscribed circle (for correlation, see appendix VIII).

Both the pyramid of Neferirkare and the small pyramid of Khentkawes were built on the centre of this fourth circumscribed circle that is located between the pyramid of Menkaure at Giza and the southern Bent Pyramid of Dahshur. It may be that the pharaohs of the Fifth Dynasty chose a new location for their pyramids because Queen Mother Khentkawes was their ancestress. Somewhat further to the north, the first pharaoh of the Fifth Dynasty, Userkaf, built the first sun temple. At a later stage, Pharaoh Niuserre was to erect a similar temple where astronomical observations were carried out (cf. fig. 31).

In *The Praises of Ra,* hymns stemming from the New Kingdom, there are references to these hidden circles. More than fifteen hundred years after the Pyramid Era, the Egyptians compiled this book to articulate the age-old traditions of their ancestors. One of these hymns, number 11, clearly mentions the circles of Ament: "Praise be to thee, O Ra, exalted Sekhem (power), support (cf. Hieroglyphs) of the Circles of Ament; thou art indeed the body of Temu."[41] This **Book of the Underworld** consists of a description of the twelve hours of the night. It is known as the **Book of Amduat** and can be admired on the walls of the magnificent tomb of Pharaoh Thutmosis III (1485-1430 BCE) in the Valley of the Kings at Thebes (Luxor). The hours of the night are not periods of time; they are to be considered as distances to be covered in the netherworld. But since the netherworld was built on the surface of the Earth, the descriptions of the hours of the night can actually be experienced on Earth. The Egyptians accurately specified the distances mentioned in the descriptions of the first, second, third and seventh hours. Unfortunately this book does not allow room for an extensive elaboration on this particular subject, no matter how interesting it may be.

The traveller had to cross the water and journey overland to reach the fourth hour of the night, and somewhat later, he arrived at the fifth hour, located in the region of Sokar, also called Rostau. The name of the town Saqqara is derived from Sokar. At that fourth hour of the night, one arrives at the necropolis of Memphis, of which Dahshur is also a part, subsequently to continue the voyage over land.

The description tells us: "The majesty of this great god next arriveth in the hidden Circle of Ament[et], and he performeth the designs of the gods, who are therein, by means of his voice without seeing them. The name of this Circle is

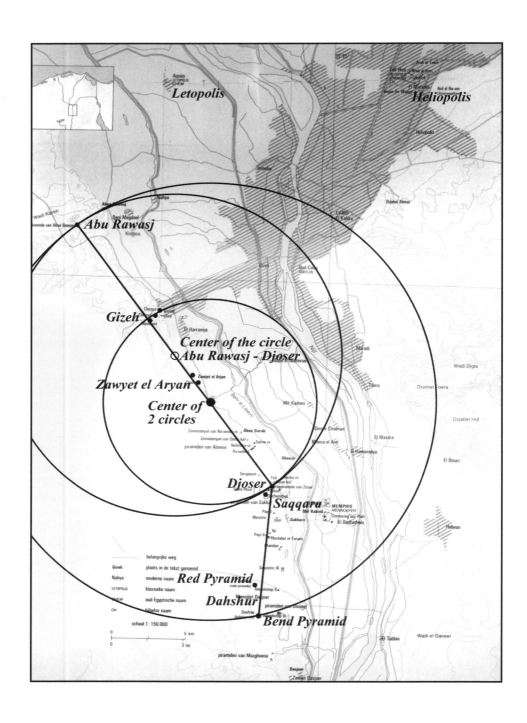

Fig. 30, showing the three hidden circles of Rostau.

Ankhet-kheperu, and the name of the pylon of this Circle is Ament-sthau."[42] The fifth and the sixth hours are the crucial hours of the night. In the burial chamber, these hours were singled out from their sequence and brought to the fore on the south-eastern wall of the tomb of Thutmosis III. This was an intentional act on the part of the Egyptians because once a year, precisely above that south-eastern horizon, the heliacal rising of the stars of the great central celestial circle Jauzah and the appearance of the star Sirius could both be perceived.

At the fifth hour of the night, the traveller reached the gate that opened up to the "Stopping place of the Gods"[43]. He then continues "westward". Actually, the journey went on in a north-westerly direction, towards the pyramids of Giza and the Sphinx, where the netherworld, Rostau, the domains of Sokar, was located. This is where one enters the netherworld, the habitat of Orion, which is illustrated in the following Pyramid Text: "The Netherworld has grasped your hand at the place where Orion is, the Bull of the Sky has given you his hand, and you eat of the food of the gods whereof they eat, the savour of *Ddwn* is on you [...]."[44]

4.14 Bent and Aligned

Between the northernmost pyramid at Abu Rawash and the Djoser complex, the pyramids were built on the local rock formation. It forms the line of sight that runs diagonally to the south-east. Close to the Djoser complex, the rock formation veers off to the south. Within this bend, we find an agglomeration of six pyramids. Lehner describes this bend as: "When Teti, the first pharaoh of the Sixth Dynasty, built his pyramid to the north-east of the pyramid of Userkaf (first pharaoh of the Fifth Dynasty), a chain of pyramids from the Third, Fifth, and Sixth Dynasties extended diagonally from the north-east to the south-west across the Saqqara plateau. A line can be drawn from the north-western corner of the pyramid of Sekhemkhet via the pyramid of Unas (off-centre), the south-eastern corner of Djoser, and the south-eastern corner of Userkaf, to the centre of Teti. The line can be extended to a small, comparatively ruined pyramid (by Merikare also called Menkauhor) east of Teti and runs on north-eastward towards the edge of the slope [rock formation]"[45] (cf. fig. 32). According to Lehner, this bend is caused by the rock formation bearing off to the south. We stipulate that the Egyptians integrated this natural bend into their plans when they erected their pyramids, this to emphasise the powerful forearm of the god Horus as it appears in the Orion image. This is known as the "strong arm", which we re-encounter in the name Djoser (cf. appendix VII).

The bend with the concentration of pyramids at Saqqara marked the elbow, where the forearm began and subsequently ended at the hand in Dahshur. From the Djoser complex onward, the forearm is highlighted by the Mastaba el Faru'un, which was built by Pharaoh Shepseskaf, and is aligned from the Djoser complex onward with the Bent Pyramid of Snofru at Dahshur. The hand at the end of this forearm derives its shape from the two pyramids of Dahshur.

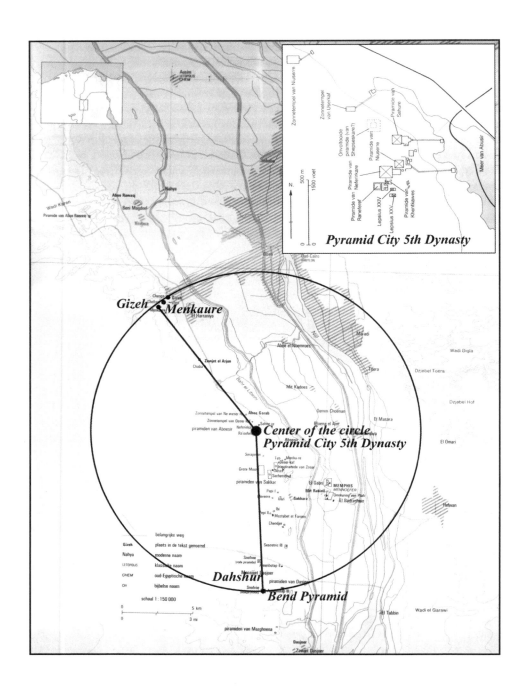

Fig. 31, showing the fourth hidden circle of Rostau and its centre, on which the pyramids of the Fifth Dynasty were built (Pyramid-city of Abusir). The inset is an enlargement of the dotted centre of the Pyramid city.

This posture is how Orion was depicted and personified when these pyramids were built. The basic pattern of the entire figure stands out in the domain as a throw-stick or boomerang (see fig. 28 and 34; cf. hieroglyph T 15 and T 14, see www.zitman. org, chapter 5 or **Egyptian Grammar**). Nowadays, this figure would be compared to a golf club. The Egyptians roughly outlined this basic pattern by means of ten pyramids and a pyramid city. Primarily, it depicts the ritual pose of Horus, known as the Orion image. Utterance 477 in the Pyramid Texts expresses this ritual pose with its long stride in well-chosen words: "[...] there came into being this his name of 'Earth-attacker'; when you said, O Seth; 'It was he who kicked me', when there came into being this his name of origin, long of leg and lengthy of stride, who presides over Upper Egypt."[46]

4.15 The Pyramid Field and the Meridians

Before the Egyptians began to construct the Pyramid Field, they first determined the north-south meridian. They did this at the occurrence of a specific astronomical phenomenon that they considered important, namely the disappearance from view (for a period of approximately 70 days) of the star Sirius, prior to their New Year festivities.[47] The date corresponds with II SMW 26 on their civil calendar and with May 10th of the Julian calendar. Counting from this date onwards, the Osiris festival, which began on IV Achet 26, still lay half a year ahead. The latter date coincides with November 11th on the Julian calendar. Both dates divide the solar year into two halves.[48]

We have already explained how the pyramids of Zawyet el Aryan and the neighbouring crossroads form the centre of two circumscribed circles. The pyramids of Zawyet el Aryan are situated at 31°09' E. This point is the centre and the core of the Pyramid Field. The pyramid-annex-observatory tower of Meidum is located around 62 kilometres (approximately 118,000 royal cubits) to the south of the pyramids of Zawyet el Aryan and also lies at 31°09' E.[49] Thus, both the pyramid of Meidum and the one at Zawyet el Aryan were built on the same meridian.

Due to the considerable distance between the Pyramid Field of Abu Rawash/ Dahshur and the pyramid-annex-observatory tower of Meidum with the small, neighbouring Step Pyramid of Seila, these two areas are normally considered to be separate fields. However, the pyramids of Meidum and of Seila definitely belong to the entire Pyramid Field. Not only were they built or completed by Pharaoh Snofru, along with the pyramids of Dahshur, the location of the Step Pyramid of Seila also displays a link with the northernmost pyramid of Abu Rawash. The position of the pyramid of Abu Rawash is 31°04' E., while the Step Pyramid of Seila is located at 31°03' E.[50] Consequently, these two pyramids were built on practically the same meridian. They are located approximately 72 kilometres (around 137,500 royal cubits) from one another.

In many respects, the precision of the meridians confronts us with an enigma. After having completed the Djoser complex, Pharaoh Snofru built the pyramid-annex-observatory tower of Meidum and the Step Pyramid of Seila in three stages. Hence, the work force of Pharaoh Snofru began their work on the Pyramid Field about 50 kilometres south of the Djoser complex, then interrupted their routine to return to Dahshur, where they built two enormous pyramids and after fifteen years, returned to finish the last stage of the pyra-

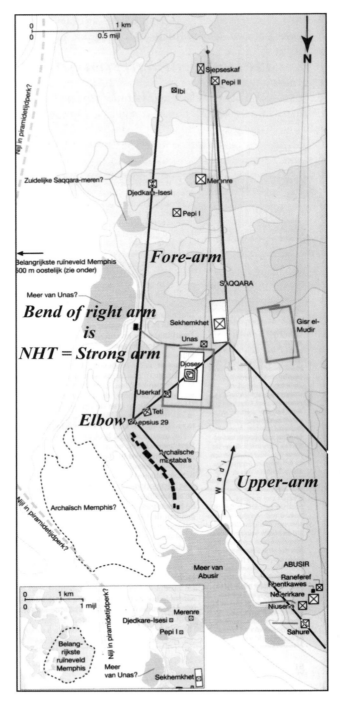

*Fig. 32 shows the stylistic bend near the pyramids of Saqqara and represents the elbow between the upper arm and the forearm. It expresses the power of "the Strong Arm" that holds the battle-axe (Nht or Nekhet= hieroglyph D40. see www.zitman.org or **Egyptian Grammar**). The activities which led Egypt becoming a state started in Saqqara.*

114

mid-annex-observatory tower of Meidum.

This hardly seems logical, unless these buildings, apart from serving as tombs, fulfilled additional functions which may for instance have been of a geodetic or astro-geodetic nature. Actually, the geodetic function of the pyramid-annex-observation tower of Meidum has already been established due to its location on the same meridian as the pyramids near Zawyet el Aryan, known to be the heart of the central circle of the netherworld.

The shape of the pyramid-annex-observation tower, a three-stage-tower with a height of some ninety metres, does make it look like an enormous observatory. In 1899, Robert discovered an opening in the centre of the top platform, approximately 30 centimetres deep, which could have been intended to hold some type of instrument.[51]

Meidum was built in stages. During the first phase, a stepped pyramid was built (phase E1). Lehner remarks: "Before the builders completed the fourth or the fifth stages, the king expanded the project and increased the pyramid to a total of eight steps (E2), which was accomplished during the first fourteen years of Snofru's reign." He adds: "Yet [the German Egyptologist] Stadelmann claims that he sent his labourers back to Meidum during the last fifteen years of his rulership, in order to enlarge the original step pyramid and shape it into a genuine pyramid (E3)." All the same, a step pyramid with an astronomical-geodetic function may already have existed in Meidum before Pharaoh Snofru rebuilt it as a pyramid during that last stage. This hypothesis should definitely be examined, since the meridian that runs across Meidum and Zawyet el Aryan had a function which is related to the 0 hour 00 minutes of Right Ascension on 11th May 3701 BCE (data: cf. note 49. See Appendix VIII for explanation of Right Ascension). In the subsequent century, this 0 hour 00 minutes of Right Ascension ran from Thuban, the Pole Star at that time, through the star Menkalinan in the constellation of Auriga and coincided exactly with the meridian of Meidum (cf. fig. 33). The star Menkalinan will be shown to correlate with the pyramid-annex-observatory tower of Meidum.

In Chapter 2, the date of the founding of the State of Egypt in 5300 BCE and the meridian of Memphis were linked up with the "Osiris meridian". In 5300 BCE, the 0hr.00m. of Right Ascension was in conjunction with the star Alhena. A correlation of that kind occurs only about once every 26,000 years.

The meridian across the step pyramid of Seila acquired a similar function. On 11th May 3101 BCE, the 0hr.00m. of Right Ascension ran from the Pole Star Thuban through the star Capella in the constellation Auriga; this star will subsequently prove to correlate with the Step Pyramid of Seila.

4.16 The Lost Observatory of Cercasorus

Was the lost observatory located on the same meridian (31°09' E) as the pyramid-annex-observatory tower of Meidum and the pyramids of Zawyet el Aryan? Did the observatory of Cercasorus (Kher-aha) form part of the Pyramid Field many centuries later?

Herodotus pointed to the existence of the town of Cercasorus.[52] The distinguished 4th century BCE Greek mathematician Eudoxus of Cnidos is known to

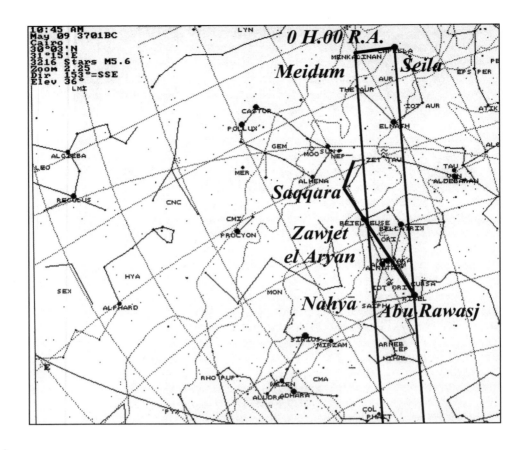

Fig. 33. Star chart set for 3701 BCE showing that the 0h.00m. of Right Ascension runs exactly across the star Menkalinan. The correlation of the star Menkalinan with the pyramid-annex-observation tower of Meidum indicates that observations were already being made on this site around 3701 BCE. In our opinion, the location of Meidum in the immediate vicinity of the prehistoric settlements of Girza and Tarkhan (Nagada II) alludes to observations made at that time in order to plot a meridian. This meridian served to determine the location of Zawyet el Aryan, from which the Pyramid Field was then marked off and measured. Meidum furthermore served to determine the location of Seila. The meridians that run through Seila - Abu Rawash and through Meidum - Zawyet el Aryan form a matrix. It is not inconceivable that the meridian from Meidum to Zawyet el Aryan continued on towards a location between Cairo-west and the village of Nahya. Hypothetical remains of a location on that spot would correlate with the star El Saiph.

have made repeated visits to this observatory. Eudoxus dwelt in Egypt before 360 BCE, during the rule of Pharaohs Nectanebo I and II, whose names were encountered repeatedly on stelae in the town of Aussim-el Zeidiyeh. For several years, Eudoxus dwelt in Heliopolis, where he studied in the company of Plato. Eudoxus is also said to have studied philosophy in Athens and astronomy in Egypt, to have learnt the Egyptian language and to have drawn up reports together with an Egyptian prophet from Memphis, called Chnoufis - also known by the name of Chenouphis or Ichnouphis. According to Pliny (**Hist. Nat.** II, 47), Eudoxus made a highly accurate count of the length of the year, namely 365 days, to which a quarter of a day had to be added, a length of time which was subsequently adopted when the Julian calendar was introduced. Eudoxus died in 356 BCE. His work and scientific thoughts irrefutably dominated the fourth century BCE.[53]

What kind of observatory was this, and where was Cercasorus located? What do the sources tell us? The traveller, historian and geographer Strabo (64/63 - circa 25 BCE) was an Asiatic Greek from Amasia in Pontus. His geographical notes were incorporated into seventeen books that bore the title **The Geography of Strabo**, in which he describes the location of Cercasorus: "From Heliopolis, one comes to the Nile above the Delta. Of this, the parts on the right, as one sails up [from the north], are called Libya, as also the parts round Alexandria and Lake Mareotis, whereas those on the left are called Arabia. Now Heliopolis is in Arabia, but the city Cercesura, which lies near the observatories of Eudoxus, is in Libya; a type of watch-tower is to be seen in front of [the town] of Heliopolis, as also in front of Cnidus [36th parallel, which is highly important], with reference to which Eudoxus would note his observations of certain movements of the heavenly bodies. Here the Nome is the Letopolite."[54] According to other ancient sources, the location of Cercasorus is indeed intertwined with the location where the Nile branches off and the Delta begins. Pomponius Mela also stated that "Cercasorus was located on the spot where the Nile splits into three branches".[55]

The number of branches kept on changing throughout the centuries. Herodotus mentioned five, Ptolemy recorded six, whereas Strabo and Diodorus even spoke of seven branches. And Herodotus adds: "When the Nile covers the land, only the towns are visible above the water, and they look like nothing so much as the Aegean islands. The rest of Egypt becomes an open sea, with only the towns rising out of it. So under these conditions people take ferries not just along the course of the river, but right across the plain! The journey by boat from Naucratis to Memphis becomes one that goes past the pyramids, instead of the normal route via the apex of the Delta and the city of Cercasorus."[56] Thus, Herodotus also locates the town of Cercasorus at the top of the Delta. Former Letopolis developed into the present town of Ausim, which is located about three kilometres west of the branches of the river Nile. Letopolis used to rise on an elevation named "Kom" and hence served as a local refuge during the flooding period.

The meridian of Letopolis is 31°08' E. Accordingly, the location where the Nile branches off and the location of the lost observatory of Cercasorus lie between 31°09' and 31°10' E. We therefore conclude that the observatory of Cercasorus must have been located on the same meridian: from Meidum, via

Zawyet el Aryan to the observatory of Cercasorus. Since Strabo mentioned that Cercasorus was situated opposite Heliopolis, it can be assumed that the tower of Cercasorus lay on the same latitude as Heliopolis, namely 30°08' N.

This meridian allowed for astronomical measurements and observations. If this observation tower, from where Eudoxus performed his observations, had not been positioned on an extremely notable location or had not possessed the aforementioned importance, then he could just as well have made these observations on the pylons of the temple of Heliopolis. Instead, he preferred to carry out his investigations here. The observation tower Cercasorus was called Kher-aha and is mentioned in *The Ancient Egyptian Coffin Texts*, Vol. I, p.115,118,122,123,164,272; Vol.II, 87; Vol.III, p.108,128,174.

4.17 Orion and the iconography of the Pyramid Field

The basic pattern of the Pyramid Field between Abu Rawash, via the bend near the Djoser complex, and on to the southern pyramid of Dahshur, is outlined in the grounds as a colossal throw-stick, a pattern which is mainly determined by ten pyramids and a pyramid city. (cf. fig. 34 and hieroglyph T15 and T14, supplemented by its variant T13 note 5, see Survey Hieroglyphs *Egyptian Grammar*). These ten pyramids and a pyramid city fulfilled a primary function. Two other pyramids, built in Meidum and Seila during the Third and Fourth Dynasties, played a meaningful role in the design of the plan of the Pyramid Field as a whole.

The basic pattern (the prime line) in the design of the Pyramid Field between Abu Rawash and Dahshur corresponds exactly with hieroglyph T15, though in reverse (cf. fig. 34 for hieroglyph T15). In his book *Egyptian Grammar*, Gardiner calls this hieroglyph a "throw-stick", a weapon that was used during the Old Kingdom.[57] Notice how the shape changed after the Old Kingdom (cf. fig. 34 for hieroglyph T14), so that it ceased to correspond with the pattern of the Pyramid Field. In their design, the Egyptians apparently made use of the traditional shape of the throw-stick, which was based on the main diagonal in the constellation Orion. This enabled them to introduce a system in the overall plan which would remain recognisable throughout the ages.

Their dominant nature manifests itself fully in the ritual pose known as "smiting the enemy". The most well-known image of this pose is that of Pharaoh Narmer, whose palette is sometimes referred to as the icon of ancient Egypt. Pharaoh Narmer's militant posture on the palette depicts this conqueror as a veritable giant. Is this huge figure supposed to represent the Giant, a name often used to identify Orion? Orion is also called the Hunter or the Warrior.[58] We have already explained that Giza means Orion and that the middle of the central celestial circle is located in Zawyet el Aryan. Fig. 28 shows the lesser known image of Pharaoh Snofru also with this typical bearing.

The diagonal connection between the left foot and the right shoulder is known as "the main outline" of the constellation of Orion (see 4.18). May we assume that the Egyptians had this imposing stature in mind when they built the pyramids along this diagonal in the Pyramid Field? On the other hand, referring to the theory forwarded by Bauval in *The Orion Mystery* that "the diagonal through [the pyramids of] Giza is inspired by the stars in the belt of the constellation Orion, which the Egyptians saw as a symbol of Osiris"[59], but Lehner points out: "Yet when Orion is projected onto the map of Giza and the pyramids, then Orion appears to contain stars that lack the corresponding pyramid and vice versa, certain pyramids lack their corresponding stars in Orion or other constellations." Lehner emphasises that Orion consists of many stars, and implies that Bauval's correlation theory is incomplete. Still, the Egyptians demonstrably emphasised the diagonal "main outline" of the constellation Orion when they used it as the basic diagonal pattern in their design of the Pyramid Field. In turn, this basic pattern corresponds with the typical posture of numerous pharaohs (cf. fig.28). The fact is that Bauval erred when he projected the stars Saiph and Bellatrix, instead of Rigel and Betelgeux, onto the pyramids of Abu Rawash and Zawyet el Aryan respectively (see *The Orion Mystery*, p.124). It will be clear by now that we consider this point of view to be incorrect. However, this complicated matter is highly fascinating and therefore worth further examination.

4.18 The Main Outline and the Diagonal Pattern

Every constellation consists of stars of varying magnitudes, i.e. their luminosity to the naked eye, the predominant stars form an outline that gave rise to the name of the constellation. In astronomy, the diagonal in Orion is called the "main outline".[60] This diagonal is determined by the two bright stars of Betelgeux and Rigel (cf. fig. 34).[61] Betelgeux marks the right armpit, while the star Rigel pinpoints the left foot of this constellation,[62] the footstar Sah.[63]

One Coffin Text provides a splendid description of Rigel's significance as the "navigator", the star that precedes the rising of other stars of Orion and also, at its rising, marks the point on the horizon where the star Sirius around 2000 BC will appear one hundred minutes later. "I am Orion [the toe-star Rigel] who treads his Two Lands, who navigates in front of the stars of the sky on the belly of my mother Nut."[64] Both stars, Betelgeux and Rigel, define the diagonal in the body of the Giant.

The pattern of the Pyramid Field consists mainly of a similar diagonal that runs from Abu Rawash via Zawyet el Aryan to the Djoser complex. This diagonal corresponds with the principal line that is portrayed in the pose of "smiting the enemy". In many versions of this ritual posture, the right upper arm is depicted as an extension of the diagonal posture of the body, such as in the renderings of Pharaoh Den, Sekhemkhet, Snofru, Khufu, Amenemhet III, Thutmosis III, Thutmosis IV, Nefertiti, Seti I and Ramses II. The bend is located exactly at the elbow. If we reduce the bodily posture to a diagonal and a short upright segment that corresponds with the right forearm of the pharaoh (cf. fig. 34), then the essence of the ritual pose becomes clearly recognisable as the basic design of the Pyramid Field between Abu Rawash and - via the bend at the Djoser complex – to the southern pyramid of Dahshur. This shape resembles the throw-stick, and was also represented in the battle array of Egyptian troops.

It seems incontestable that the Pyramid Field is based on the diagonal of Orion which stretches out from, amongst others, the star Rigel (footstar Sah)

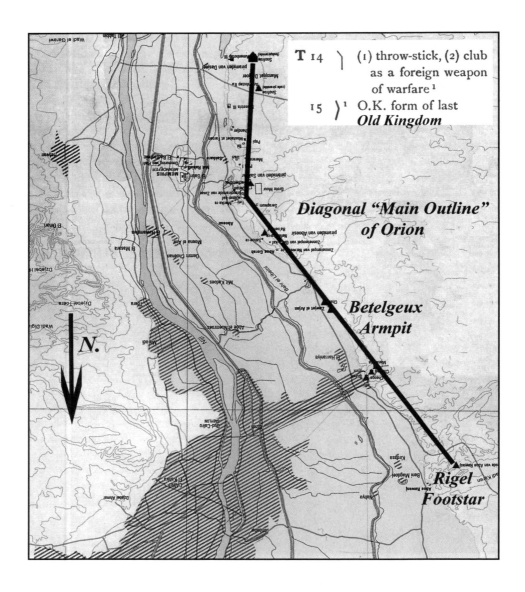

Fig. 34. Map of the Pyramid Field between Abu Rawash and Dahshur, looking from north to south in accordance with the ancient Egyptian manner of viewing. The stylistic personification of the constellation Orion was shaped by building ten pyramids and a pyramid city. The overall figure was based on the throw-stick (T15). The basic pattern is founded on what is known in astronomy as the "Main Outline" of Orion. This essential feature became the fundamental principle in all iconographic renderings of the ritual Horus posture.

to the star Betelgeux (northern pyramid of Zawyet el Aryan, Pharaoh Baka), i.e. from the left foot to the right armpit. The diagonal continues its way via the right shoulder to the elbow, where it merges with the forearm and subsequently with the hand holding a battle-axe or another type of hand-weapon. The star Bellatrix marks the left shoulder of the Orion constellation;[65] Saiph accordingly marks the right foot.

Thus, Orion the Giant gazes westward to the stars Aldebaran and the Pleiades. Orion the Giant presents himself with his back turned and his face in profile, his right arm lifted and holding a sword or battle-axe in his hand.[66] This battle-axe is rendered by the star Propus (eta Gemini) and was known as such by the Chinese.[67] It is also identical with the very important decans 26 and 27, *rmn hry* (signify above the Arm), on the Coffin Lid of the official Nakht from the Middle Kingdom, 11th Dynasty.

So far, we have established theoretically and provisionally that the basic pattern of the ten pyramids plus a pyramid city, built on a natural rock formation and extending from Abu Rawash, via the bend near the Djoser complex to Dahshur of the Third, Fourth and Fifth Dynasties, was based entirely on the militant ritual posture of the pharaohs, known as "smiting the enemy". The basic pattern portrayed in this posture corresponds with a natural, clearly visible feature in the landscape, which was subsequently provided with majestic architectural constructions.

This natural "diagonal" forcefully characterises the basic bearing that the ritual pose expresses. The basic diagonal pattern of the Pyramid Field corresponds perfectly with the principal line within the constellation of Orion and with the small-scale replica of the "throw-stick': hieroglyph T15. The various locations of the pyramids could be said to delineate a horizontal statue of their god Horus on earth. In section 4.25 *"An Image of Heaven"*, we will point out which stars of this constellation correlate with each of these ten pyramids and the pyramid city. Ultimately, a total of twelve main pyramids, one pyramid city and three temple cities correspond with the sixteen parts of Osiris.

4.19 The regional Step Pyramids as the Latitude, and the Uas Sceptre, an ancient theodolite

In order to complete the overview of the building activities of the Third and Fourth Dynasties, a number of small step pyramids must still be accounted for. These lie spread about along the Nile, as is shown in the figure 35. The relatively small pyramids were all built without a burial chamber, which points to a function other than that of a tomb.

Until now, the purpose of these step pyramids has remained a mystery. Lehner states that the southern pyramids differ from the northern ones, yet that their similarity leads to the assumption that they all belong to one single building programme.[68] They are assumed to have been built by Pharaoh Huni, the father of Pharaoh Snofru and the last ruling pharaoh of the Third Dynasty. The surface area of some of these pyramids is practically identical at approximately 18.5 x 18.5 metres. Their height varies from four to eight metres.

The step pyramid of Elephantine is situated on the island of the same name, while the others were built on the customary western bank of the Nile - the step pyramid of Zawyet el Amwat forming the exception, as it was erected on the eastern bank. This area was known as the "Horizon of Horus".[69] This is where the "Way of Horus" started, which ran from Men at Khufu (El Minja) to the north.

The locations of these pyramids and of settlements point to a methodology in which the territory was partitioned:

Buhen (fortress)	21°55' N. equals	22th parallel
Sayala (settlement)	22°57' N. equals	23th parallel
Elephantine (step pyramid)	24°05' N. equals	24th parallel
Edfu (step pyramid)	24°59' N. equals	25th parallel
Ombos (step pyramid)	**25°56' N. equals**	**26th parallel**
El Badari (settlement)	27°00' N. equals	27th parallel
Zawyet el Amwat (step pyramid)	**28°03' N. equals**	**28th parallel**
Heracleopolis Magna (settlement)	29°05' N. equals	29th parallel
Giza (pyramids)	29°58' N. equals	30th parallel
Abusir (settlement)	30°55' N. equals	31st parallel

This survey points to the use of the Jacob's staff (the uas-sceptre S40, a sceptre with a straight shaft and the head of an animal - possibly associated with Seth – otherwise known as a djam-sceptre), which enabled the user to determine a specific location (i.e. the Latitude) by measuring the altitude of stars and/or planets. Various readings of celestial bodies, made at a certain time and place with reference to the horizon, will produce an intersection that approximates the true position (i.e. latitude) of the observer at the average time of the readings. Jacob's Staff was the alternative name for the "Orion Belt". This is a curious and most remarkable association, since the Pyramids of Giza actually represent the Orion Belt.

The significant prehistoric settlements El Badari and Giza were added to this overview, in order to complete the sequence from Upper Egypt to Lower Egypt. The four above-mentioned step pyramids fulfilled a surveying and/or observational function. It is not known what function the step pyramids of El Kula and those of Abydos (Sinki) had. The step pyramid of Zawyet el Amwat ranks as the most important of its kind, as it lies at the beginning or end of the "Horizon of Horus", which also bears the Sumerian name Way of ENLIL.

4.20 A Remarkable Emphasis?

The pyramids of Pharaoh Userkaf and Pharaoh Unas, both of the Fifth Dynasty, were built in the immediate vicinity of the Djoser complex. The pyramid of

Unas harbours the earliest Pyramid Texts. The chambers inside the pyramid "merely contain 283 of the more than 700 known formulae, some of which were already very old in Unas' time".[70] The first pharaoh of the Fifth Dynasty, Userkaf, and its last pharaoh, Unas, each built their pyramid on the north-eastern, and the south-western corners respectively of the Djoser complex. These two pyramids could be said to "embrace" the monumental cornerstone of the Pyramid Field of their ancestor Djoser. Is it mere coincidence that the first and the last pharaoh of the Fifth Dynasty had their tombs built here? Lehner comments: "Unas thereby accomplished a historical and an architectural symmetry."[71] Yet the symmetry could also be chronological, maybe even genealogical. It might mean that Pharaoh Unas knew that he was to be the last pharaoh of the Fifth Dynasty. The closing line in the Turin papyrus under the rule of Unas could imply as much. In fact, Syncellus mentioned this juncture when he wrote that for the first time, the king who succeeded Unas was a pharaoh of Egyptian descent (see section 4.7).

Both pyramids emphasise the bend between the right upper arm and forearm. The same applies to the pyramid of Pharaoh Teti of the Sixth Dynasty. Due to their specific location, the pyramid of Djedkare Izezi of the Fifth Dynasty and those of Pepi I, Pepi II and Merenre of the Sixth Dynasty lend support to the "strong" right forearm which was meant to express "striking power". This is also the region where Shepseskaf, a pharaoh of the Fourth Dynasty, had already engaged in building activity, which resulted in the Mastaba el Faru'un.

The right forearm is located between the southern pyramid of Zawyet el Aryan, the pyramid of Chaba, and the Djoser complex. This continuously recurring diagonal was also strongly emphasised by the construction of five pyramids and two sun temples of the Fifth Dynasty and the pyramid city between Abu Gorab and Abusir. The pyramid of Pharaoh Neferirkare and that of Queen Mother Khentkawes are also situated on that site, right in the centre of the fourth circumscribed circle, that of Giza-Dahshur. The sun temples served to make astronomical observations.

4.21 The Necropolis turns into a Hennu Boat

The 12th Dynasty, which ruled for 213 years and the best part of two months, belonged to the Middle Kingdom (circa 1996-1783 BCE).[72] From the Middle Kingdom onward, the private tombs were adorned with the image of a two-fold boat journey. Captions in these tombs mention pilgrimages from Abydos to Busiris, which were also made in the opposite direction. The journey upstream to Abydos was made with the help of a sail that was hoisted on board.

These journeys are known by the name "Abydos voyage".[73] Abydos (the Osireion) coincided with the rear end of the constellation of the Scorpio: "This is where Osiris was worshipped and where one kissed the Earth in honour of the great god Osiris, the lord of the West, during the great exodus."[74] Around 5300 BCE, in the aftermath of "the great exodus", the "Followers of Horus" moved from the west to the east, in order to settle permanently in Egypt. The ritual boat journey that was referred to, was related to the mysteries and festivities dedicated to Osiris, which were held for five days - corresponding with

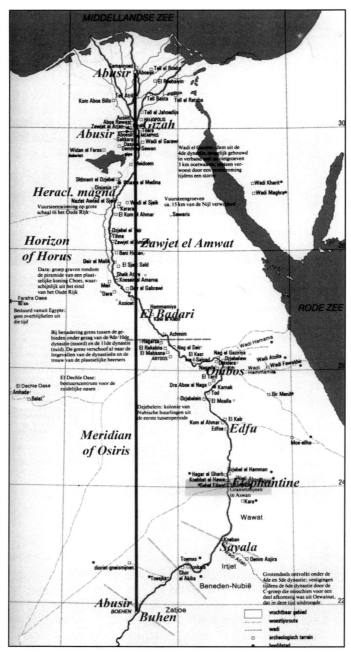

Fig. 35. Map of Egypt showing the area between the 22ⁿᵈ and the 31ˢᵗ parallel from Abusir to Abusir. These parallels are indicated by small step pyramids as well as by settlements and fortresses. The locations on the parallels point to the partitioning of the territory. The 28ᵗʰ parallel (Men at Khufu, with the step pyramid of Zawyet el Amwat) was already known in ancient times as the "Horizon of Horus". This 28ᵗʰ parallel divided the territory according to the sacred proportion of 1/3 (28ᵗʰ – 31ᵗʰ parallel) to 2/3 (22ⁿᵈ – 28ᵗʰ parallel), known as rwy.

the five epagomene days - from IV Achet 26 until I Peret 1 (beginning on November 13th by the Julian calendar) and which preceded the celebration of the second New Year's Day. Depictions offer a clearer notion of the circumstances under which these boat-journeys occurred during the kingship of Hatshepsut/Thutmosis III. From the New Kingdom onward, these pilgrimages set off from Thebes and followed the Nile downstream to Abydos.

The pharaohs of the Middle Kingdom enlarged the initial design of the Pyramid Field which they had inherited from their ancestors of the Third, Fourth and Fifth Dynasties. Six pyramids were built, which extended the borders of the Pyramid Field and changed the necropolis into a huge depiction of a boat. The name given to the boat during the Old Kingdom was the Sokar-boat, which was subsequently changed during the Middle Kingdom into "Hnw-boat".

The pharaohs of the 12th Dynasty set out to enlarge the plan of the Pyramid Field by building two pyramids in El Lisht. Pharaoh Amenemhet I, the first pharaoh of the 12th Dynasty, founded a new capital near El Lisht and named it Iti-tawi. He built the northern pyramid around a core of crude limestone blocks and a loose filling of sand, debris and loam. Near this pyramid, various blocks were found that had once been part of the ceremonial causeways of Pharaoh Khufu and Khafre (Fourth Dynasty). Very little has remained of the local temple of the Dead.

The southern pyramid of Pharaoh Sesostris I is located about two kilometres to the south-south-west. Once a medium-sized pyramid, it fell into ruin and has now deteriorated into an almost shapeless mound. Within the outer enclosure around this pyramid, nine small pyramids were built, which are called queen's pyramids. Both pyramids at El Lisht were built on the "Osiris meridian" (31°13' E.), the meridian that runs from Busiris via the Djoser complex to the far south, up to the second cataract in the Nile near the stronghold of Buhen.

The Royal Turin papyrus (fragment 67) states that Pharaoh Amenemhet I united the "Two Countries" under his sceptre and that he built a pyramid, that of El Lisht, on that location. The foundation slabs of the pyramid of Pharaoh Sesostris bear the following inscription: "Sesostris beholds the Two Countries." This proves that at the start of the 12th Dynasty, the border between Upper and Lower Egypt ran close to El Lisht, and not near Dahshur. This border was moved back to Mazghuna towards the end of the 12th Dynasty. The border strip that ran between the pyramids of Dahshur and those of Mazghuna marked the area where the ecliptic, i.e. the solar, lunar and planetary orbits, were projected onto the earth. This was where the gods (planets) sometimes came to a halt in the heavens.

Highlighting this strip that had existed ever since the beginning of the Fourth Dynasty, Mazghuna was emphasised by building two pyramids that were positioned symmetrically in relation to Snofru's pyramids near Dahshur. These two pyramids near the settlement of Mazghuna were both left unfinished and are located on the "Osiris meridian". Together with the five pyramids near Dahshur, they mark the border between Upper and Lower Egypt. They are located about five kilometres south of the concentration of pyramids near Dahshur. These unfinished pyramids of Mazghuna are tentatively attributed to Pharaoh Amenemhet IV and his successor Sobekneferu, yet their names were never found on this site. In conclusion, it is clear that the pharaohs of the 12th Dynasty built a total of *seven* pyramids on the "Osiris meridian".

The choice of the sites of the two remaining pyramids, namely in Lahun and Hawara, appears to indicate that the Fayum oasis at that time experienced an increased importance. This seems particularly true in the development of the pyramid and temple city of Lahun. Yet more is at stake: while the locations of the pyramids of El Lisht are functionally explicable, those of Meidum, Seila, Lahun and Hawara appear to be much harder to understand. After all, the locations of this latter group of pyramids show no apparent signs of connection with the Pyramid Field in its entirety.

But let us not be deceived: admittedly, it is most remarkable that during the rule of a small number of pharaohs, extraordinary building works were undertaken at sites that were far removed from the main Pyramid Field. Pharaoh Snofru (Fourth Dynasty) displayed this kind of fervent zeal when he built no less than four pyramids on three apparently arbitrarily chosen sites. The distance from Meidum to Dahshur amounts to no less than 50 kilometres.

A similar exceptional vigour was shown by Pharaoh Amenemhet III (12th Dynasty), who not only built a pyramid in Dahshur but also in Hawara, the latter even including a labyrinth. The distance between those two sites, measured along a straight line, amounts to approximately 70 kilometres. Due to the particular spatial relationship between the site of the pyramid of Meidum/ Seila and the three pyramids near Giza, these locations jointly form a rigid reference grid that allows the star chart to be accurately projected onto the Pyramid Field (cf. section 4.25 for further details). Apart from serving as tombs and fulfilling, as we saw, "iconographic" purposes, we may well query whether the pyramids performed additional functions, which are mentioned in the Pyramid and Coffin Texts, a function that might be depicted in the emblem of the Nome, known as the Mansion of the Mace (cf. section 3.9).

4.22 Dahshur, Mansion of the Mace (battle-axe)

Close to Dahshur, to the east on the "Osiris meridian", in the direct neighbourhood of the two pyramids of Pharaoh Snofru from the Fourth Dynasty, three pyramids were built by Pharaoh Amenemhet II, Sesostris III and Amenemhet III. The erection of these three pyramids completed the image of the "smiting the enemy". In all, five pyramids were built in this area. These appear to form the five fingers which completed the hand and turned it into a fist that holds the mace or a battle-axe, thereby enhancing the iconographic image of the ritual pose.

This mace or battle-axe coincided with the star Propus (eta Gemini). This region of the Mounds of Horus and Seth (see also section 4.29) is described in the Pyramid and Coffin Texts as the "Mansion of the Mace" (cf. Pyramid Text §598, 948, 949 and in Coffin Texts I 294g; V 140b; VI 99b and 154a; VII 285a). The Chinese were also familiar with this hand-weapon under the name Yüe.[75]

This battle-axe marks certain points on the Ecliptic, where the Sun, Moon and planets would, at specific times, appear in conjunction with this star and thereby emphasise the mace or axe. The Egyptians interpreted this as an assurance of their invincible power. One of these "specific times" at which a

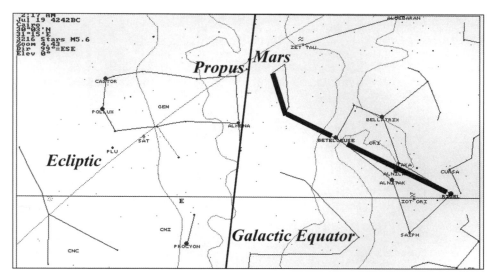

Fig. 36. Star chart set for New Year's Day on 19th July 4242 BCE, the beginning of the Egyptian calendar; the planet Mars is shown to be in conjunction with the mace or battle-axe (the star Propus).

conjunction occurred between the planet Mars (ancient Egyptian name Hor Dshr = the Red Horus; Dahshur is derived from Dshr), the veritable hallmark of combat, and the star Propus (cf. fig. 36), happened to coincide with the beginning of the Egyptian civil calendar (19th July 4242 BCE, New Moon-day, JD. 172,232). The fact that this phenomenon occurred on the same day that marked the start of their calendar emphasised their invincibility and the militancy of their vigorous culture. This planetary emphasis underlined the link between heaven and earth. At the same time, this exceptional celestial scene at that specific calendrical moment was laid down forever by the conception of the Pyramid Field, in which the ritual pose of the pharaoh was portrayed (cf. section 4.29 and Chronology, the periods of 363 years of the Triumph of Horus, celebrating the 'Unification of the Two Lands').

4.23 Two Images in one?

Further deep-reaching investigations into the system behind the plan do indeed show that the complicated design of the entire Pyramid Field was based on two images. The first image dates back to the Old Kingdom and is the rendering of the ritual pose of the "smiting the enemy". The second image dates from the Middle Kingdom and represents the "Hennu boat". Due to the many boat pits that were found (e.g. near the tomb of Pharaoh Khasekhemwy and near the pyramids of Giza), we may even consider the alternative possibility that work was undertaken during the Old Kingdom to create this image of the boat, a design that was completed during the Middle Kingdom and adapted to the style of this subsequent period. Still, the two images complement each other and jointly make up the completed "Hennu boat" (cf. fig. 37).

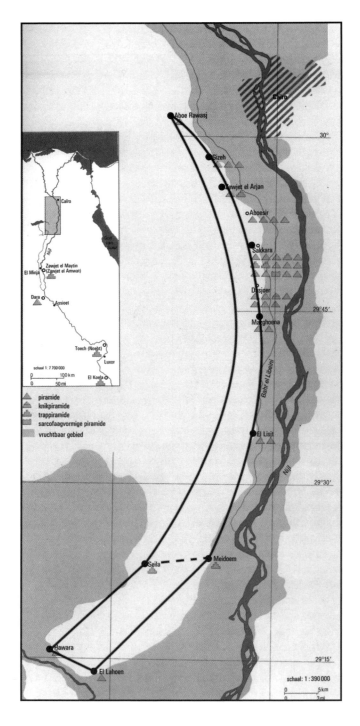

Fig. 37. Various Pyramid Texts interpret the image of Horus as the Sokar boat or Hennu boat. This illustration shows that this boat was shaped by the locations of the various pyramids. The outline of this boat - in other words, the combined sites of the pyramids - was mainly determined by Orion, i.e. Horus.

128

The outline of this Hennu boat, harbouring Osiris, is formed by the pyramids in Abu Rawash, Giza, Zawyet el Aryan, Saqqara, Dahshur, Mazghuna, El Lisht, Meidum and Seila respectively. The raised stern is marked out separately by the pyramids of Lahun and Hawara (cf. fig. 37). The pyramids of Mazghuna and El Lisht form the belly of the ship. The location of the southern pyramid of El Lisht catches the eye because of its rather south-westerly position. It is striking how these two images complement each other to form a unity, in which the first image (from the Old Kingdom) serves as the prow while the second one (from the Middle Kingdom) contributes the belly and the stern.

The stern had, to a large extent, already acquired its shape during the Old Kingdom by the pyramids of Meidum and Seila. This boat was imagined to sail on the Nile, the river Hapi, which is synomymous with Osiris. The Nile renders the stylistic principle of the god Osiris, who reminded them of their distant ancestors and the territory from where they had once come.

Various Pyramid Texts (e.g. §138; §619-620-621; §1824 and 1826) endorse the striking image of this region that was ruled from Sokar (i.e. Saqqara): "But you shall bathe in the starry firmament, you shall descend upon the iron bands on the arms of Horus in his name of Him [Osiris] who is in the *Hnw* [Hennu]-barque." And: "O, Osiris the King, you are a mighty god, and there is no god like you. Horus has given you his children that they may bear you up; he has given you all the gods that they may serve you, and that you may have power over them; Horus has lifted you up in his name of *Hnw*-barque; he bears you up in your name of Sokar." "O Osiris the King, Horus has lifted you into the *Hnw*-barque, he raises you into the Barque of Sokar, for he is a son who raises up his father." These Pyramid Texts show that, in the region of Sokar, Horus carried his father Osiris into the Sokar boat or Hennu boat.

Plutarch wrote that Seth tore the god Osiris into fourteen pieces.[76] There is also frequent mention of Osiris' body consisting of either fourteen or sixteen members.[77] We now know that the constellation of Osiris (Scorpio) consists of sixteen stars (cf. chapter 2). The entire necropolis of the Old Kingdom, of which the design was largely based on the star constellation Orion, comprised ten main temples with annexes and one pyramid city (Abusir). With the inclusion of the three temple cities of Letopolis, Heliopolis and Memphis, they amount to a total of fourteen parts (see fig. 38). The further addition of the pyramids of Meidum and Seila makes for sixteen parts.

4.24 Necropolis, the Antechamber to the Netherworld

"Amazing precision" is a phrase that is often used by those who have studied the Egyptian culture. They express our admiration and our respect for the technical abilities of that nation. How did they ever reach such precision? This question keeps on haunting our minds. Where do we start our search to retrieve their knowledge that seems lost to us?

Obviously, these abilities seem to be based on their everyday activities. Yet this presumption cannot explain their knowledge of the universe on which their religion was based, not to mention their methods of orientation. Astronomer P. Moore claims that "the Egyptians had no real concept of the na-

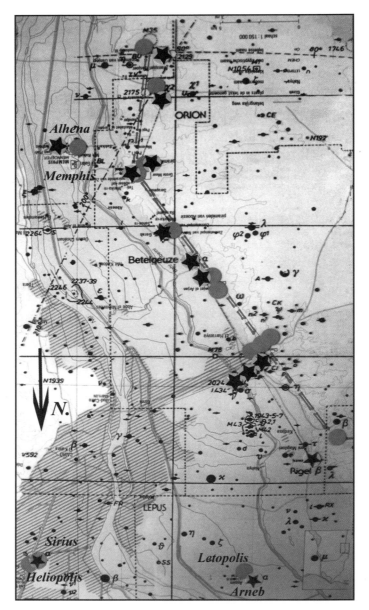

Fig. 38, showing the map of the region south-west of Cairo, the area where the pyramids were built. The map is presented in accordance with the ancient Egyptian standpoint, i.e. viewing from north to south. The dots accurately pinpoint the locations of ten pyramids, a pyramid city, and three temple-cities. The pertaining star chart, taken from Uranometria 2000.0, was projected onto this map in the corresponding scale. A star that correlates with a pyramid or a temple city is shown as such next to the pertaining dot. The positions of the stars on the star chart for the year 2000 CE hardly differ from the locations which the Egyptians, 5,000 years ago, determined for the pyramids from their observations of the stellar sky. The Ecliptic crosses the Bent Pyramid of Dahshur.

ture of the universe",[78] yet research in that direction shows just the opposite. On the other hand, he observes that "their precision was amazing by any standards, and there is no doubt that the pyramids were astronomically aligned."[79] The aforementioned facts make it more than clear that what we are actually dealing with is a mixture of astronomy and religion, combined with their building projects.

The Egyptians built a necropolis in the shape of the Hennu boat, with which they symbolically transported their dead to the netherworld, since this netherworld, which lay in the far west, could only be reached by boat. Were they familiar with the location on Earth of this netherworld? They actually did have knowledge of a region that shows great stylistic similarity with Egypt's geography, a topic we will discuss in part 2.

Without overestimating or underestimating their knowledge, we may safely state that they showed a particular preference for the star Deneb. Deneb had been the Pole Star between approximately 17,500 and 14,000 BCE. Numerous texts prove that the Egyptians displayed a marked preference for what they called "immortal stars", the stars around the northern pole star which never set. But does that also apply to the star Deneb as it appeared in those ancient times? If so, then why? Could this possibly be related to some method of orientation and navigation they had acquired in those prehistoric times? Various explanations (Chapter 1) have already shown that they had aligned their buildings or annexes with the rise of this star.

Later on, they showed a similar preference for the Pole Star Thuban. Around 3000 BCE, the position of Thuban lay precisely on the celestial North Pole. This also explains why the pyramids of Giza, Dahshur and Meidum, which were under construction at that time, were accurately aligned to this celestial North Pole. Moreover, it explains their preference for the "immortal stars" that always remain visible and hence make them ideal candidates for orientation and navigation.

Astronomy is the "mother" of all sciences, yet her knowledge can only be acquired after hundreds of years of observations, in which data is constantly recorded and compared. Could people in prehistoric times have performed such tasks? A prehistoric rock painting, dating from approximately 6500 BCE, has substantiated that this is indeed the case. The painting represents an astronomical constellation and resembles the depiction of an ancient Egyptian star-clock. The similarity is striking. It was created at an intersection close to a very ancient caravan route as a guidepost to help the traveller. This level of astronomical knowledge could only have been collected after many observations of the night skies.

This means that we need to search for the origin of an archaic era that the Egyptians and the Sumerians brought to the forefront. When these tribes moved to the rivers of Egypt and Sumeria around 5300 BCE and introduced civilisation to those countries, they already possessed vast knowledge of astronomy. This knowledge allowed them to choose their locations and to attune their architectural projects to fundamental laws.

It should not therefore come as a surprise that boats and boat pits were found near the tombs of the pharaohs. They served the dead to sail to the netherworld (the West), the domain from where the Egyptians claimed they had originally come. On their imaginary journey, they would take their bearings from the immortal stars. The discovery of "a phantom fleet", as Lehner describes it, "enhances the comparison between these enclosing walls and pyramid temples, which were meant as harbours (porches) that preceded the netherworld". Here, Lehner is referring to the discovery of a row of twelve buried boats. "Each wooden boat is enclosed in a plastered, limewashed casing made of loam. The length of these boats varies between 19 and 29 metres."[80] This highly spectacular discovery occurred in 1954, when south of the Cheops pyramid a boat was found lying in a boat pit, buried under enormous limestone slabs. The boat had been completely taken apart and its 1,224 components, including 656 large ones, lay arranged in the boat pit according to their position in the original boat. Various components had been made out of one piece, such as the remarkably well-preserved cedar planks, about 23 metres long, 50 centimetres broad and 11 centimetres thick. This points to the use of large trees, which needed to be hacked down, transported and sawn up, followed by fine tooling before they could be used.

The boat, including its superstructure, has a displacement of 45 tons, is 43.32 metres long and 5.90 metres wide, and draws 1.48 metres. The loose parts were originally connected by means of rows of mortise-and-tenon joints and ropes.[81] The boat is a wooden replica of the ships that were made of papyrus in prehistoric times.

Thor Heyerdahl proved experimentally on his Ra expedition that these papyrus boats were indeed seaworthy. The boat of Pharaoh Khufu was artfully re-assembled thanks to the particular enthusiasm of the restorer Ahmed Youssef and can now be admired in a separate museum near the pyramids of Giza. Various boats and boat pits have been found elsewhere, for instance near the tomb of Queen Mother Khentkawes, of Pharaoh Hor Aha of the First Dynasty and of Pharaoh Sesostris I and III.[82]

4.25 An "Image of Heaven"

The Followers of Horus instilled a deeper meaning into the land of Egypt by superimposing depictions of human activity onto the natural layout of the territory. The final accomplishment of the Pyramid Field led to the Sokar or Hennu boat and was in all respects a multifunctional design. The ingredients of this master plan were astronomy, religion, navigation, orientation and architectural knowledge. At the same time, they used the design as a means to uphold the memory of their former habitat. In all its aspects, the project reveals how this contemplative nation combined ingenuity, efficiency, accuracy and tenacity in its pursuit to make Egypt into an Image of Heaven.

The twelve pyramids and their annexes from the Third and Fourth Dynasties and the pyramid city from the Fifth Dynasty were fitted into the landscape, and the inclining grounds were used to give the complexes a royal dignity. The principal feature of the completed plan (ten pyramids and one pyramid city) is located in the vicinity of the triangle formed by the towns of Memphis, Letopolis and Heliopolis. The Mokattam plateau was divided up according to the Golden Section and includes the centre of the circles of Rostau (cf. fig. 30), located in close proximity to the crossroads near the southern pyramid of Zawyet el Aryan (of Pharaoh Chaba from the Third Dynasty). This centre near Zawyet el Aryan is crosscut by the meridian which runs from the pyramid of Meidum to the no-longer extant observatory of Cercasorus. Hence, the location of the pyramid of Meidum is in any case aligned to the centre of the circle of Rostau, which was determined during the Third Dynasty. The location of the pyramid of Seila is related to the location of the pyramid of Meidum as well as to the pyramid of Abu Rawash (cf. fig. 39 or www.zitman.org).

As to the twelve pyramids that were built during the Third and the Fourth Dynasties, the underlying plan shows a number of remarkable facts.

In four different locations, the infrastructural plan of the Pyramid Field shows remarkable discontinuities and inconsistencies, which cannot be merely put down to some condition of the building site or to possible constructional problems. These singularities concern:

1) the characteristic positioning of the three pyramids of Giza (cf. fig. 4);
2) the intentional bend at the location of the Djoser complex (cf. fig. 32);
3) the characteristic positioning of the pyramids of Dahshur (cf. fig. 34);
4) the characteristic positioning of the pyramids of Meidum and Seila (cf. fig. 39).

These four remarkable singularities guarantee the transposition of the celestial chart onto the Pyramid Field. Thus, the correlation of the celestial chart with the Pyramid Field is immutable!
The line known as the great diagonal of Giza points north-east (Azimuth 45°-46°). The diagonal was aimed at the rising of the star Deneb in 3000 BCE (cf. chapter 1.4). The design of the Pyramid Field of Giza shows that the diagonal, which runs through the two major pyramids, does not transect the smaller pyramid of Menkaure (cf. fig. 4). This noticeably smaller pyramid is about 65 metres high. To the eye, it seems even smaller next to these two colossal pyramids, each approximately 145 metres high. The pyramid of Abu Rawash was erected on top of a hill, at approximately 80 metres above sea-level.

The pyramids of Giza are set on a substantially lower plateau. The small pyramid of Menkaure is located precisely on the line of sight from Abu Rawash to the Djoser complex. One can, as it were, look "downhill" towards the Nile valley in a south-easterly direction, over the top of the pyramid of Menkaure. Hence, the latter forms no optical hindrance; on the contrary, it serves as an intermediary bearing to pinpoint the Djoser complex.

The intentional bend near the Djoser complex and its particular iconographic meaning have been adequately described above. As to the pyramids of Dahshur, they also have a number of mysterious aspects to their name. The northern pyramid of Dahshur was made of red rock and possesses a deviating slope of 43°22'. The Bent Pyramid of Dahshur deviates completely from the normal pyramid design. It slopes up to the bend at 54°28', then declines to 43°22'. The identical angle of inclination of the two pyramids of Dahshur undoubtedly points towards a preliminary decision to abide by a specific angle throughout the entire design.

Egyptological dogma states that the decision to discontinue the slope of approximately 54° at a height of 49.40 metres and to carry on at an angle of 43°22' was due to technical problems. We do not share this view. On the winter solstice (on January 16th or 17th, Julian Calendar, the Sun is directly over the tropic of Capricorn) around 3100-3000 BCE, at precisely 12h:00 PM, noon, the Sun reached an altitude of approximately 43° above the horizon at Philae/Aswan, the site where the Egyptians had projected the tropic of Cancer (cf. chapter 1.4) In short, the *Bent Pyramid* of Dahshur is the world's first and oldest *Sundial*.

Hence, both the design and the shape of these pyramids had been settled on before work began. In other words, this planned deviation points to a particular feature that was to be recognisable to everyone, i.e. the border between Lower and Upper Egypt. This border, highlighted by the Red Pyramid and the Bent Pyramid, separated the "Two Lands", Lower and Upper Egypt. The red-coloured crown of Lower Egypt comprised the area of the Delta and corresponded with the colour of the Red Pyramid in the north. The Bent Pyramid was built in white Tura limestone and hence corresponded with the white crown of Upper Egypt. The pictogram representing the name of the pyramid contains the hieroglyphs "*swt*-plant", referring to Upper Egypt, and "strong arm", which points to power and victory.

The deviating incline of the Red Pyramid and the shape of the Bent Pyramid point to this particular location between the "Two Lands" near Memphis/Dahshur. It had once been the scene of the battle between Horus and Seth, which was decided by dividing the land of Egypt. This battle is described in Memphite theology. This was once the site of the "Balance of the Two Lands in which Upper Egypt and Lower Egypt have been weighed. Horus and Seth were united in the temple of Ptah in Memphis."[83] In addition, this border area correlates to the Ecliptic (the Ecliptic is defined as the apparent path of the sun, moon and planets), determining the border between Lower and Upper Egypt (cf. fig. 38). The sun above the horizon, on that winter solstice exactly at noon, indicates the precise angle of the Ecliptic. This fact, combined with the corresponding slope of the Red and the Bent Pyramid of approximately 43° (equal with the altitude of the Sun) as described above, proves that the Egyptians projected the angle of the Ecliptic at the winter solstice onto this location.

The characteristic positioning of the pyramids of Meidum and Seila is extraordinarily significant and endorses the correlation with the two main stars in the constellation of Auriga (cf. fig. 39 and 40). The visible correspondence is just as incontestable as Bauval's theory (*however, read my critical of his stereographic projection, p. 119!*) concerning the correlation of the three pyramids of Giza with the three stars in Orion's Belt (cf. Appendix VIII for further details). The constellation of Orion was visible at night in the southern celestial sphere during the Osirian festival period around 3000 BCE.

The inspiration to insert twelve pyramids into this area during the Third and Fourth Dynasties, plus a single pyramid city (Abusir) during the Fifth Dynasty,

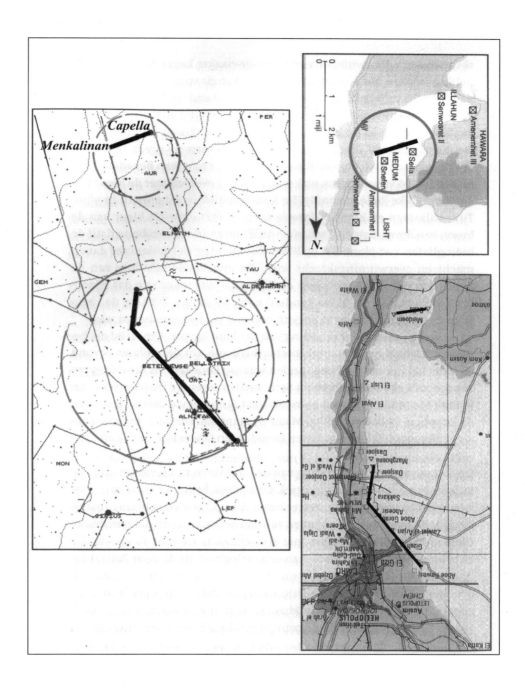

Fig. 39 shows four remarkable details in the design of the Pyramid Field, which cannot merely be put down to some condition of the building-site or to possible constructional problems.

135

was undoubtedly linked with the position of thirteen stars within the "great central celestial circle". Eleven of these stars belong to that central celestial circle that bore the name Jauzah. Two of them do not, since they belong to the constellation of Auriga, which nowadays is called the Charioteer. In classical poetry, the name of that constellation stood for "Steersman".[84] As we know, the steersman's place is generally at the stern of the boat, in this case the aforementioned Sokar boat or Hennu boat.

The insertion of the pyramids and solar temples between Abu Gorab and Abusir (central point) was also based on the position of one specific star (mu Orionis), which also belongs to that same central celestial circle of Jauzah.

4.26 Memphis, Letopolis, Heliopolis and their correlation

Not only do the locations of the twelve pyramids of the Third and Fourth Dynasties and the single pyramid city (Abu Gorab) of the Fifth Dynasty correlate with thirteen stars, each of the temple cities that form the triangle of Memphis, Letopolis and Heliopolis also correlate with a star. The geographical locations of the temple cities of Memphis (31°15' E.), Letopolis (31°08' E.) and Heliopolis (31°18' E.) contribute to the correlation theory which is hereby postulated. Heliopolis and Letopolis are equidistant from the "Osiris meridian" (31°13' E.) to the east and the west respectively. The geodetic distance between Heliopolis and Letopolis, measured horizontally on the same parallel, amounts to 30,000 royal cubits. The "Osiris meridian" of archaic Egypt runs exactly equidistant - in other words at a distance of 15,000 royal cubits - from each of these towns (cf. fig. 11).

The Egyptian name for Memphis (31°15' E.), which is Ineb-Hedj, the White Wall, came into existence towards the end of the second Dynasty. The name and its hieroglyph suggest that the temple city was a fortification. The British Memphis Project discovered that the archaic settlement was built near the slope of North Saqqara (13°13' E.). Immediately across the Nile, thousands of archaic tombs in Helwan (31°22' E.) point to a settlement that is no longer in existence on the east bank. It would seem that the twin towns served as stanchions (buttresses) of the "gate to the Delta", as Memphis was to be called later on.[85] This twin town, better known as Memphis, was spread out across an extremely large territory and correlated with the star Alhena. Memphis was the town that was linked up with the Sokar sanctuary.[86] This may well point to the Djoser complex in Saqqara. Memphis correlates both with the star Alhena (cf. fig. 38) and with the star Antares of the constellation of Scorpio (stratigraphically, cf. chapter 8).

The town Chem (*Gem*) or Letopolis is located on practically the same meridian geographically as the Great Pyramid of Khufu. This meridian marks the transition of (*Gem*)ini (Twins) to Taurus (Bull). During the reign of the Ptolemies (332-31 BCE), the Egyptian town names were translated into Greek, and Chem became Letopolis. This name mirrors an astronomical quality that derives from the Greek goddess Leto. The area immediately west of Letopolis correlates with the star Arneb in the constellation Lepus. The name of this main star is derived from the Greek *Arnebeschènis* meaning "Horus, the foremost of Letopolis".[87] The constellation Lepus is the throne of Orion (cf. fig.38).

The Greek name Heliopolis corresponds with the Egyptian Iunu and mirrors certain astronomical qualities. The names An, On (biblical name), Ana (Hethitic) and Unu (Assyrian) are equivalent denominations for Heliopolis and mean "town of the sun", a term that was introduced at the beginning of the Fifth Dynasty. Previously, this had been the town of Atum, the star Sirius, the great creator, who merged with Re (cf. section 1.4). It so happened that Sirius correlated with the temple of Heliopolis (cf. fig. 38). The above astronomical correlations in the names of the towns Letopolis and Heliopolis point to an astronomical relationship between the locations of the pyramids and the two local cult centres.

4.27 Hawara and the Labyrinth, and the Demon Star Algol

Off the beaten tourist track, near the pyramid of Hawara in the Fayum oasis, lies the labyrinth that Herodotus described in his book **Histories,** Book II-148: "Now, they decided to build monuments together to leave for posterity, and having reached this decision they constructed a labyrinth just beyond the lake of Moeris, very close to the place called Crocodilopolis. I have personally seen it, and it defies description." Herodotus ends his last sentence with the words: "By the corner where the labyrinth ends there is a pyramid forty fathoms in height, with huge figures carved on its surface. The approach to the pyramid has been built underground."[88] Crocodilopolis is now known as Medinet el Fayum, and immediately to the south-east of this town is the pyramid of Hawara.

The German Egyptologist Lepsius (1810-1884) studied archaeology and then went to Paris to take up Egyptology. "Lepsius' contributions to Egyptology are numerous, yet his greatest is undoubtedly the **Denkmäler**, his elaborate work on the monuments of Egypt, consisting of twelve volumes containing 894 folio plates, which was published after his death."[89] Prior to this work, a series of books had appeared in France bearing the title of **Description de l'Egypte**, which contained 3,000 illustrations. Lepsius had taken note of Herodotus' description and travelled with a team of scholars to the pyramid of Hawara and the neighbouring labyrinth in 1843.

He expected to encounter something that exceeded the pyramids of Giza as one of the Wonders of the World, yet it turned out to be a disappointment. The labyrinth had, to a large extent, become a ruin, its blocks of stone exploited for the benefit of other buildings. Since Roman times, only its foundations remained. In the end, it was Sir William Matthew Flinders Petrie (1853-1942) who finished Lepsius' work at the labyrinth, by carrying out further research on Hawara. The structure next to the pyramid of Hawara had functioned as a "temple of the dead", yet its architectural design was so utterly uncommon that it became known as "the labyrinth" and since Antiquity, it had become associated with the Knossos labyrinth on Crete. This Cretan labyrinth was the prison of the monster or demon Minotaur (constellation Bull), begotten by Pasiphae, queen of the semi-legendary king Minos. In Homer (Od. 11, 568), Plato (*Gorgias,* 523, 524, 526) and others, Minos appears as a judge of the dead in the netherworld.[90]

In Antiquity, the labyrinth was linked inextricably with the dwelling of a *demon*. For this reason, only one star exists that qualifies for a correlation with the pyramid and the labyrinth of Hawara, namely Algol. This star is called the "Demon Star". "Algol, the Demon, the Demon Star, and the Blinking Demon ...".[91] The astronomical position of Algol, beta Persei, is 01°24' Bull. Herodotus mentioned the constellation Perseus in a different context: "What brought Perseus to Egypt, according to the Chemmitans, is the same as in the Greek story: it was to collect the Gorgon's head [as a rule, this alludes only to Medusa] from Libya."[92] Alpha Perseus, Mirfak, is the main star of this constellation and probably correlates with the pyramid of Lahun.

The correlation of the pyramid and the labyrinth of Hawara with the star Algol is based on the fact that this star is known as the Demon Star, not on a mathematical calculation. The exact correlation point for Hawara ought to be 30°40' E. instead of 30°54' E., whilst that of Lahun should be 30°44' E. instead of 30°58' E.

In his **Geography**, Strabo records that the number of halls of the labyrinth corresponded to the number of Nomes, or provinces, into which Egypt had been divided.[93] He mentions 36 Nomes altogether: ten for the area of the Delta, ten for the region below Thebes, and sixteen for the intermediate area. The division of the land into 36 Nomes was probably imposed by the Greeks during the reign of the Ptolemies and is based on the division of a circle into 36 equal parts (decans). The Egyptians, however, divided their land into 42 Nomes.[94] They allocated 20 Nomes to Lower Egypt and 22 Nomes to Upper Egypt, corresponding to the 42 assessors (Judges of the Dead). Before one enters the inner court of the Djoser complex, one passes along an arcade with 21 alcoves on each side, 42 in total. This number was sacred, and they indicated the size (42°) of the central celestial image from the first and the second cultural periods.

4.28 The Pyramid Field points to the Firmament during the Osiris Festival

The ten pyramids from the Third and the Fourth Dynasties plus the single pyramid city from the Fifth Dynasty form the pose "smiting the enemy". This image symbolised the power and dominion of Egyptian kingship (Horus) over the world. The ground plan, i.e. the plan of the Pyramid Field, points to the constellation of Orion that was visible in the southern hemisphere (SSE, about 52° from the exact east) in the evening hours between approximately 09h50 and 11h00 PM, during the nights on which the Osiris festival was held (cf. fig. 40).

On the last day of the Osiris festival and the flooding season, IV Achet 30, the "Interment of Osiris" was performed. From this date onward, the waters of the Nile that had inundated the land began to recede. After a few days, the land was ready to be worked upon. The waters receded and Osiris disappeared into the earth. In Pyramid Texts §1044, Osiris appears as a personification of water: the god of the Nile. In a hymn to Osiris, Pharaoh Ramses IV utters: "You are the Nile ... gods and human beings live from your emanations...." Pyramid

Text §848 states: "The canals are filled, the waterways are flooded by means of the purification which issued from Osiris". Osiris is identified with water and the ocean, amongst other things.[95]

On the evenings of the Osiris festival, the starry sky showed the constellation of Orion (Jauzah) and Orion appeared in the heavens in full splendour. Again, two images merge, that of Osiris (Scorpio, the sign of water) and Orion-Sahu (Bull/Taurus, the sign of earth). Water fertilises the Earth. Osiris, the god of grain, makes the corn sprout on what is known as the Osiris beds.[96] Through water, Osiris bequeaths life to the earth. Pyramid Text §819-820 gives a poetic rendition of this merging process: "Behold, he has come as Orion, Osiris has come as Orion, Lord of the Wine in the Wag-festival."[97] Hence, Osiris is simultaneously life and death. The tenor of the festivities at the festival was a detailed symbolic rendering of an "eternal relationship between heavens and earth".

The average Egyptian's philosophy of life focused on an existence that pleased the gods in order to fend off a catastrophe and to guarantee the continuation of creation. That is why they chose a site close to the Nile, where they built the Pyramid Field according to the constellation Orion (Horus) to depict the image of Osiris. Horus belonged to the temple city of Letopolis, while Osiris had his origin in the temple city of Memphis (cf. chapter 8), and Isis in Heliopolis. This typifies their family relationship in a mythological context.

The Pyramid Field was built "for all eternity", i.e. in a temporal, chronological sense. The annual celebration of the Osiris festival and the extremely important Sed feast (once every thirty years) were held in order to shape the notion "for all eternity", in other words: it counted the years. The function of the Pyramid Field including its temples of the dead actually bears an immediate relationship with the rituals that were enacted during both festivities, in which the eternal rule of the pharaoh, even after his death, played an essential role. It explains why the sepulchral offerings reflect their daily life.

Osiris was called "the Bull of the West" or "the Bull of Abydos".[98] In Abydos, "Osiris was worshipped and there, one kissed the earth in honour of the great god Osiris, the lord of the West during the great exodus".[99] According to the compass, the Nile basin runs from south to north. And yet the text tells us that Osiris is Lord of the West. What did the Egyptians mean by that? Are they supposed to have sailed from the north to the south in order to worship Osiris as Lord of the West? If the Egyptians considered Osiris to be Lord of the West, then that is where he will be found. After all, Osiris was their principal god. Did the Egyptians or their ancestors, the Followers of Horus, happen to be familiar with that region in the west?

4.29 The Planet Mars and the 363-year Cycle of the Myth of the Triumph of Horus

From early dynastic times onward, the Egyptians had already divided their country into Nomes or provinces, showing their proficiency in land surveying techniques. Each province possessed an individual insignia or emblem. One example of its application might be on the heads of persons depicted on walls, so that they personified a province. This reveals intentional structuring, which contained a religious function.

The emblem of the first province of Lower Egypt is shown in figure 11, in the lower left part. It represents a ground plan of a building, with a battle-axe on its right-hand side. This province extends from the pyramids close to Dahshur, the border between Upper and Lower Egypt, to approximately the pyramids of Giza. The temple city of Letopolis was located in Nome 2 and that of Heliopolis in Nome 13 of Lower Egypt. Close to Dahshur, we find the Red and the Bent Pyramids. According to a very ancient tradition, this is also the site where the gods Horus and Seth fought against each other, yet also rose again after their disastrous battle. It is also the site of reconciliation after that battle and furthermore that of the "Unification of the Two Lands", where the treaty concerning the alliance was concluded. The moment of these battles and the corresponding reconciliations is described in the "Myth of the Triumph of Horus".

Millennia afterwards, the commemorative festivities were held in the Horus-temple of Edfu. Written historical data about these battles and reconciliations are known, amongst others, from the Second and Eighth Dynasties, and from the Graeco-Roman period. The cycle that is mentioned in the "Myth of the Triumph of Horus" amounts to 363 years. This matches the cycle of the planet Mars, which, after completing this period, starts a new cycle of 363 years from the Arm of Orion (the planet Mars at the maximum distance from the Earth). The planet Mars, including its cycle, was and remains extremely important to determine the Egyptian chronology and was definitely known and important to the ancient Egyptians from the fourth millennium BCE onwards (cf. Chronology in the Appendix). In the past, the exact cycle of the planet Mars was difficult to determine due to its eccentric orbit. Kepler needed no less than five years to calculate the cycle and finally, at the beginning of the 17th century, he filled 900 sheets with calculations in order to determine the correct cycle. How the Egyptians resolved this problem thousands of years earlier is still unclear.

Never before have astronomers or Egyptologists noticed that the Egyptians were familiar with this cycle of the planet Mars. Even less correspondence was found with the various myths such as the one about the battle and the reconciliation between Horus and Seth, known as "The Horus and Seth Myth", (also "The Conflict of Horus and Seth", and the "Unification of the Two Lands") and the one about the festivities around the "Triumph of Horus", which were held much later.

Figure 36 shows the planet Mars above the right arm of Orion near the star Propus, known as the "Battle-axe", on New Year's Day (cf. sections 4.18 and 4.22). At that moment, Mars is seen near the intersection of the Ecliptic and the Galactic Equator. This day, 19th July 4242 BCE, the New Year's Day of ancient Egypt, is the oldest calendar day known to Mankind. From a mythological perspective, Mars is a god of war, a symbol of battle; he is also the deity who signified power and invincibility. The *Constellation of Horus,* Orion with the planet Mars, is the expression of their cosmic iconography, the personification of the Pharaoh with the battle-axe in his right hand, his ritual regal bearing denoting "I shall maintain". This was the emblem of prehistoric Egypt as a world power. It is probably very ancient and also ranks as the emblem of their ancestors, the Followers of Horus. Illustrations of this emblem, which were rendered in Egypt from 3516 BCE onward, are found on the website www.zitman.org in chapter 8) The people of Mesopotamia adopted this image after 1500 BCE. It is also found amongst other cultures such as the Phoenicians, the Romans and those of Meru up to approximately 300 CE; for illustrations, see chapter 10 on the above website.

The story that has gradually unfolded in this book has now reached the summit of perfection. The location of the Red and the Bent Pyramids near Dahshur indicates the site that the Egyptians used to carry out their astronomical observations. Standing on the Osiris meridian, they turned their eyes towards the south and gazed at the spot in the sky above these pyramids in order to determine the cycles of the planets. This is where one of the intersections of the Ecliptic with the Galactic Equator, the Perihelium, the "Gateway to the Cosmos", the "Stopping-place of the Gods" is located. It is important to know whether this location is mentioned in ancient Egyptian texts, where its function is also expressed. In my opinion, the following twenty Pyramid Texts (§135; 218; 222; 480; 487; 598; 770; 915-916; 943; 948; 949; 961; 994; 1295; 1475; 1735; 1904; 1928 and 2099) mention the pyramids of Dahshur as the "High Mounds" or the "Mounds of Horus and Seth". Pyramid Texts §948-949, with the "Mounds of Horus and Seth" as the Red and the Bent Pyramids, clearly refer to the Mansion of the Mace, where, via the Gateway to the Cosmos, the ferryman carried the deceased across the Milky Way, which the Egyptians believed to be the dwelling place of the souls. Equipped with this new knowledge, their religion, which was founded on the principle of resurrection, acquires a new countenance. The pyramids of Dahshur represent the "Gateway to the Cosmos". Thus, the Egyptians built the Aphelium of the cosmos on earth.

The various illustrations in this book, such as figures 38, 39 and 40, show all too clearly the diagrammatic rendering of the constellation of Orion as the Egyptians projected it stereographically onto the face of the Earth and subsequently built it. Even now, scholars consider this to be pure speculation, yet "there is more to explore". A theory has to be well-founded, or it should be borne out by texts or corresponding evidence, for instance by means of a ground plan of the very ancient enclosing wall of the Temple of Heliopolis. The correspondence between the shape of the western part of the wall (cf. fig. 39A) and the stylistic shape of the plan of the Pyramid Field is striking (see hieroglyph T15). A similar stylistic model of the "Arm" is also found in the design of the corridor of Sphinxes in combination with the ground plan of the temple at Luxor (see website, chapter 8, fig. 8y). These are the only temples in Egypt (Heliopolis and Luxor) that were based on such a ground plan. The constellation Orion is the image in the starry sky of the god Horus; at certain moments, the planet Mars - representing the battle-axe - hovers above his right "Arm". The "Arm" was the exceedingly sacrosanct symbol of Creation and of their ancestors. They applied this symbol *in situ*, not only in the Pyramid Field but also in the ground plan of the enclosing wall, to wit in the façade of that wall surrounding the temple of Heliopolis, as well as in the corridor of Sphinxes in

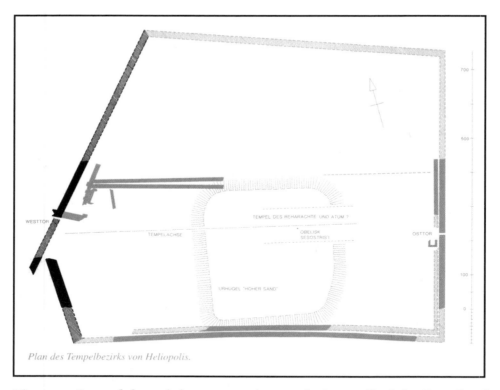

Plan des Tempelbezirks von Heliopolis.

Fig. 39a. Groundplan of the very ancient enclosing wall of the Temple of Heliopolis. The correspondence between the shape of the western wall and the stylistic shape of the plan of the Pyramid field is striking (cf. also hieroglyph T15).

combination with the temple of Luxor. The Edfu Texts state that the *in situ* presence of this prehistoric symbol raises the place to a cult centre of the Creator.

The Pyramid Field was universal and it functioned as the Perihelium on Earth, as a "temple" for the benefit of their religion of death and resurrection, as an observatory to detect the movements in the heavens (*the "Egyptian" system*), as a netherworld for the deceased, as an iconographic image on behalf of Creation, as an icon for the purpose of the pharaoh in his preservation of that Creation, as an eternal calendar, as a means to calibrate their general chronology that was based on the 363-year cycle of the planet Mars and was known to them as the moments when the "Unification of the Two Lands" occurred. This list is probably incomplete... The theory described in this book is the first step on the way to a more encompassing a far wider domain, covering the Cosmological Empires of Mesopotamia and Egypt.

142

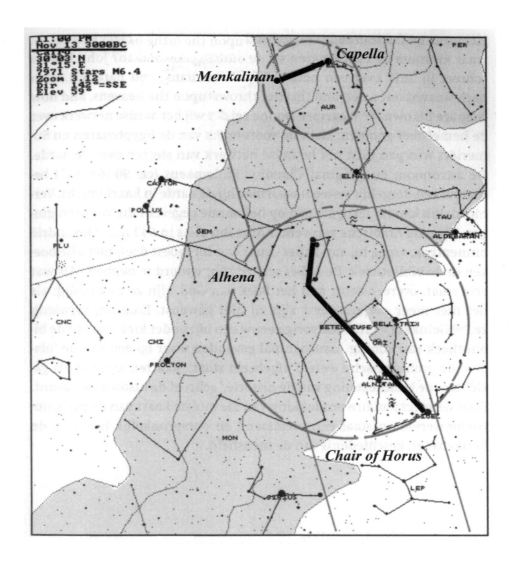

Fig. 40. The star chart shows the southern starry sky in the evening (between 09h50 and 11h00 PM) during the Osiris festival around 3000 BCE. The design of the Pyramid Field is based on this part of the starry sky; the line of sight between the pyramid of Abu Rawash and the Djoser complex runs at an angle of approximately 52° to true east. At the top, a circle is drawn around the stars Menkalinan and Capella of the constellation Auriga. The direction of the line connecting the two stars corresponds with the line running through the centre of the pyramids Meidum and Seila. A further circle is drawn around the typical image of Orion.

4.30 Where did they originate?

Until roughly 1980, Egyptologists, with the exception of a few pioneers such as Wallis Budge and Frankfort, were convinced that the ancestors of the Egyptians originally came to Egypt from Asia. Since then, investigators have turned their attention to the south, and now re-subscribe to the theory that these ancestors reached Egypt by drifting along the Nile from Nubia and its neighbouring areas. Archaeological discoveries in the vicinity of Nabta Playa near the 22nd parallel corroborate this opinion.[100] However, the subject has many facets and is based on an ethnic difference that has been observed between the people in Upper and Lower Egypt. The original population of Egypt consisted of at least two tribes that merged after centuries of battle. One of these tribes, the Followers of Horus, came from the West, while the other, the Children of Seth, who, since the eighteenth Dynasty, were also known as the Followers of Seth, had their origin in the southeast.

Nubia (modern Sudan) currently prides itself on an increasing archaeological interest, which even resulted in an exhibition, under the management of the German Egyptologist Professor Wildung, that opened its doors in 1997 at the *Institut du Monde Arabe* in Paris and bore the appealing title *Soudan, Royaume sur le Nil.*

The formidable and fascinating question, which has already existed for two hundred years, is the following: where did the Egyptians and the Sumerians originally come from? In 1611, John Donne wrote about a network "of meridians, and parallels, man hath weaved out a net, and this net thrown upon the heavens, and now they are his own."[101] Donne meant that man cast the terrestrial network across the celestial sphere. Yet the ancestors of the Egyptians and Sumerians did the opposite and cast the celestial stellar network across the Earth. The astronomer and geographer Claudius Ptolemy (circa 90-168 CE) described a similar system, which he used to map the Earth. He was presumably able to refer to existing data, which were subsequently lost. When the Arabian conqueror Amr ibn al-As marched into Alexandria, he asked Caliph Omar what he should do with all the books in the library. The caliph is said to have replied: "If their contents agree with the Book of God, they are redundant; if they no longer agree, they are undesired. Therefore, destroy them."[102] Fortunately, a unique clay tablet was found during the 19th century in the library of King Assurbanipal. One of its "pages" shows an image of the prehistoric world. To quote the words of the historian Durant: "Maps are like faces, [they contain] the signature of history." The spectacular discovery of that earliest map of the prehistoric world enables us to obtain a surprising and original view on the source and history of Mankind.

Part II

The Planisphere and the Lost Cradle

Explorations always bear a touch of madness, and they will therefore
tarnish the territory of existing circumstances.
(*National Geographic*, Vol. 193, No. 22, Exploration)

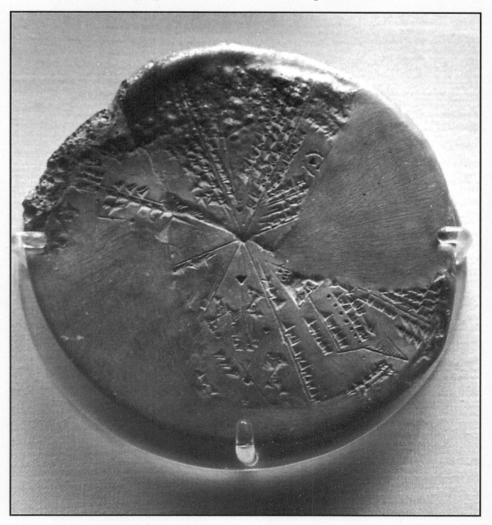

*Fig. 41. Planisphere K 8538, permanently on display in the British Museum,
London*

Chapter 5

The Divine Network

In the millennia long development of civilisation, a great deal of knowledge has been lost. This loss often happened gradually and naturally, yet sometimes it occurred abruptly, by accident or even wilfully. Entire libraries have gone up in flames. These sad acts of destruction have occurred in every age. The ancient world possessed many libraries and witnessed an equal amount of fatal fires, with that of the library of Alexandria being the most notorious. That library once possessed 700,000 papyrus scrolls.

Alexandria was reputed to be the capital of all sciences of the ancient world and became the target of various conquerors on three occasions. The Alexandrian library was partly housed in the Museum and partly in the Serapeum. The Museum was located near the harbour, opposite to the famous lighthouse on the island of Pharos. This is where Eratosthenes once worked as a librarian, and in all probability so did Hipparchus. Later, Claudius Ptolemy would also work in Alexandria.

The first time that part of the library was set on fire happened when the Roman Emperor Julius Caesar conquered Alexandria in 48 BCE. It was his "punishment" for the resistance offered by the population. In 391 CE, a second destruction (the destruction of the Serapeum) was caused by a Christian mob, headed by a fanatical patriarch who believed that the knowledge contained in the library would undermine Christianity. In the end, the final blow to the Alexandrian library was dealt by the Arabs in 642 CE. According to an anecdote, the dusty, befouled Arab legions found enormous Roman baths ready for use. Yet they lacked the necessary fuel to heat the water. So they decided to set the library on fire as their method of combustion

A destruction of a similar magnitude hit the town of Carthage, located near modern Tunis, which the Romans destroyed in 146 BCE. This town also possessed a famous library, consisting of 500,000 volumes. A treasury of Phoenician history and knowledge was eradicated on that occasion. After all these major losses, we are only left with the possibility of careful historical reconstructions. This method will, to a certain extent, provide us with an insight into the early scientific knowledge of the Egyptians, Sumerians and Phoenicians on astronomy, geometry, geography and of navigational skills.

The Phoenicians moved away from the west and east coast of the Red Sea to the Sinai peninsula and the coast of Canaan in approximately 2200 BCE. Before they lived in Asir, a mountainous range on the Saudi Arabian Peninsula and in Ethiopia (Punt). They maintained contact with the Egyptians and acquired part of their knowledge.[1] After approximately 2350 BCE, the Akkadians acquired their knowledge in a similar manner from the Sumerians, which they, in turn, then passed on to the Assyrians after approximately 2000 BCE.

The technical skill and scientific knowledge of the Egyptians are expressed in the construction of the Pyramid Field and the geodetic capabilities on which it was based. Their knowledge of astronomy and geometry, on which they founded their iconographic-religious notions, has already been discussed. Their earliest development reached a peak during the rule of the pharaohs of the Third and Fourth Dynasties of Egypt, a period of nearly 300 years. The building activities prove that the Egyptians were capable of realising a large-scale celestial map on Earth by means of pyramids, which they located on appropriate, geodetically determined sites.

Their exceptional achievements have frequently given rise to the assumption that some unknown, lost civilisation must once have existed on Earth, of whom the Egyptians were the descendants. It has often been suggested that "it may be, as some indeed suspect, that the science we see at the dawn of re-corded history was not science at its dawn, but represents the remnants of the science of some great and as yet untraced civilisation."[2] But until now, even after many centuries of searching for that lost civilisation, hardly any tangible results have turned up.

The fascinating question is: where is that grey area on the map where the mystery of this civilisation originated? Was it in the vicinity of Nabta Playa and the Gilf Kébir plateau in the extreme south-west of Egypt? Or elsewhere? The actual whereabouts on the African continent can only be discovered if we happen to find a map which they themselves manufactured and on which they marked their former dwelling place. After all, Africa is the continent where Mankind experienced its beginning.

5.1 Maps and Geographers

The oldest map of the world, on display in the British Museum, is a clay tablet showing a circular motif. It dates back to approximately 500 BCE and shows Babylon as a rectangle, transected by two vertical lines that represent the river Euphrates. Small circles mark neighbouring towns and the flat, round world is surrounded by an ocean.

It would be interesting to know whether clay tablets on which a map has been drawn are generally round, as is the case in the depiction of the Earth on an Egyptian sarcophagus from the 30th Dynasty (approximately 380-343 BCE). This image in relief shows the celestial goddess Nut, bending her body across the world. The outer rim of the circle bears the names of "foreign" countries, the middle circle shows the Nomes of Egypt, and the netherworld is pictured within the inner circle. The first Greek geographer Hecataeus (circa 550-475 BCE) also drew a round map of the world on which the world was completely surrounded by an ocean.

Attempts to calculate the circumference of the Earth, which the Greek geo-grapher Eratosthenes (circa 276-195 BCE) did, prove that he assumed that the Earth was spherical. Plato was the first to substantiate this assumption in his book **Phaedo**: "First of all, should it be true that the Earth exists in the centre of the heavens and is spherical, then it would require neither air nor any other form of suspension to stop it from falling."[3] Aristotle would later repeat this. Plato quoted Socrates again from the latter's description to Simmias of the

Earth as seen from outer space: "First of all, the real Earth, seen from above, would more or less resemble one of those balls made of twelve pieces of leather, multicoloured, with strips of various colours of which our colours down here, such as the ones painters use, are like specimen. Seen from up there, the entire Earth is made up of colours of that kind, yet of a far greater brilliance and purity than ours."[4]

In this description, Socrates talks to Simmias about *"balls"* and *"strips"*, referring to the spherical shape of the Earth. Could these words have given Mercator (1512-1594 CE), the most original and most influential geographer of the Renaissance, the initial idea which resulted in his famous Mercator projection? He simulated the meridians by making twelve incisions in the rind of an orange, pealing the twelve sections off and then laying them next to each other on a table. He then stretched the top and bottom ends to shape them into rectangles that fitted in with the neighbouring pieces along their entire length. Thus, the whole rind of this spherical object, representing the Earth, turned into a single rectangle on which the meridians ran parallel from the North Pole to the South Pole. By stretching them carefully, the surface shapes remained intact, even though their size increased. Hence, the Mercator projection is a method of drawing a map on which the meridians and parallels are represented as straight lines. Thus, the spherical shape of the Earth is conceived as a flat rectangle, subdivided by a coordinate grid of parallel lines representing the fixed meridians and parallels.

5.2 Ancient Mapmakers

One of the oldest geographers known to us from Antiquity is the Greek Eratosthenes who, in addition to having calculated the circumference of the Earth, also manufactured a map of the world. The Greek geographer Hipparchus (circa 165-127 BCE), an astronomer and the founder of systematic astronomy, (re)discovered plane and spherical trigonometry. It is not known whether he ever drew any maps, or whether he used his mathematical knowledge to do so.

The ability to apply this knowledge requires the calculation and/or the use of co-ordinates. This proved to be the specific weakness of Greek cartography, since mathematics depended on a set of instruments that could, by simple means, determine the meridian.[5] Hipparchus advocated the use of astronomical observations in cartography.[6] The Greek philosopher Posidonius (circa 135-51 BCE) pictured the Earth as an ellipsoid, the cosmic egg, a shape which, in the original Sumerian pictorial script, denotes land or earth (pronounced *ki*). A similar shape also exists in Egyptian pictography, pronounced Ro, which is claimed to mean *mouth*.[7]

The Greek historian and geographer Strabo (circa 64 BCE - 25 CE) created a body of work consisting of either 43 or 47 volumes on general history. He described how the parallel of Alexandria (31° N.) and that of the Gulf of Sirte, especially the seaport of Charax, were identical.[8]

Pomponius Mela (approximately 50 CE) originally came from Tingentera in Spain (near Gibraltar) and created a geographic work consisting of three volumes. The map contained in that work depicts a typical "periplus", a cruise along all the coasts of the world.

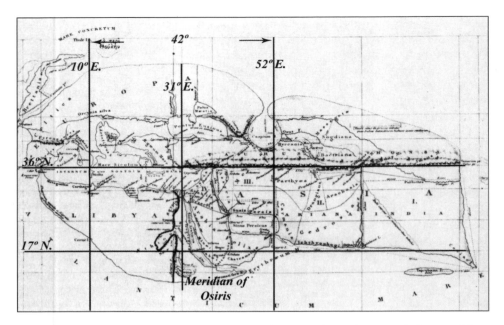

Fig. 42. A 19th century reconstruction of Eratosthenes' map of the world as he knew it. This reconstruction was based on information from other authors in Antiquity and on some fragments of his own writings.

Marinus of Tyrus (approximately 110 CE) wrote **Revision of the Geographical Map.** This work had a considerable impact on the geographic handbook of the famous Greek mathematician, astronomer, astrologer, geographer and physicist Claudius Ptolemy (circa 90-168 CE). He occupied himself with the use of mathematics in astronomy, geography and physics. He laid down the results of his studies in a vast number of books and treatises. His enunciations ranked as standard works for nearly 1,500 years and as such, they dominated astronomical and geographical thinking.[9]

5.3 Hipparchus versus Eratosthenes

Hipparchus is known as the inventor of plane and spherical trigonometry. Trigonometry was still unknown during Eratosthenes' lifetime. However, Hipparchus lashed out at Eratosthenes and wrote books entitled **Against Eratosthenes.** He accepted the calculations that Eratosthenes had made concerning the circumference of the Earth, but he criticised the latter for having made his map without calculations. Strangely, Hipparchus opposed Eratosthenes even though he himself claims to have invented mathematical science. Could Hipparchus have known of alternative geodetic methods of calculation that Eratosthenes had omitted, methods which may have been based on lost geometric techniques known to the Egyptians?

Further investigation shows that Eratosthenes did indeed make use of very ancient knowledge of the Earth's dimensions when he prepared his atlas of the

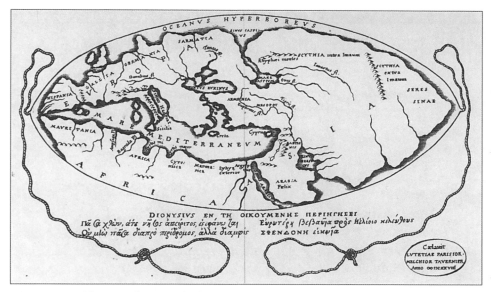

Fig. 43. Posidonius the Greek drew the earth in the shape of an ellipsoid.

world, a knowledge that he derived from Egyptian/Sumerian geographic material. However, his map was not drawn to scale. He used, albeit without painstaking precision, two meridians: the western meridian through Carthage/Agadez (approximately 10° E.) and the eastern meridian through the Elburz mountain range/Straits of Hormuz (approximately 52° E.). Both meridians play a *decisive role* in the disclosure of the former cradle of the Egyptians and the Sumerians. Eratosthenes drew the Nile in the centre at equidistant (approximately 31° E.) from the two meridians. He moreover used the parallel of Agadez/Meroe (17° N.) and that of the Gulf of Sirte/Alexandria (31° N.), and the 36th parallel through Gibraltar/Malta/Rhodes/the Elburz mountain range. Hence, this map is based on a rectangle (cf. fig. 42). Where did Eratosthenes obtain this intriguing knowledge from?

5.4 Posidonius and the 'Centre' of the World

Posidonius is known as one of the most universally-minded practitioners of science in Antiquity. He applied a synthesis of Hellenistic science and in his cosmology he returned to the views of that ancient philosophical school, the Stoa. His philosophical attitude to life was founded on harmony and particularly on the coherence of all phenomena.

In his contribution to geography, he drew Egypt in the "centre" of the world, where it coincided with the Alexandrian meridian (30° E.). The left half of the ellipsoid shows the Pillars of Hercules (Gibraltar, 6° W.); the right half ends at the estuary of the Indus river, close to 66° E. The left and the right half of the ellipsoid both measure 36°. Apparently, Posidonius assumed the world to be harmonious, and its shape to be based on an ellipsoid with a maximum size of 72°, one fifth of the circumference of the circle and of the Earth (cf. fig. 43). The

151

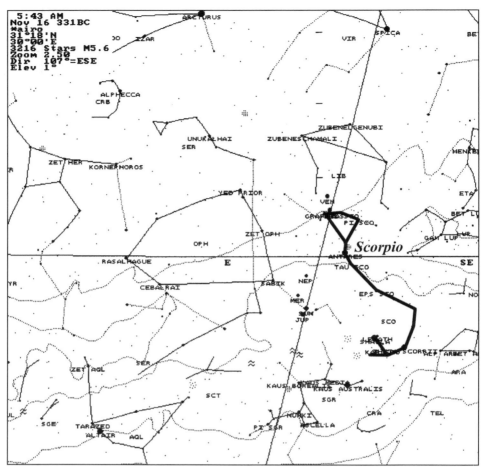

Fig. 44. Star chart of the eastern horizon observed during the Osiris festival, approximately one hour before sunrise in Alexandria, the town that was founded on this occasion by Alexander the Great.

shape corresponds with the Egyptian hieroglyph Ro (cf. D21, Survey hieroglyphs **Egyptian Grammar**). Posidonius was therefore the first to apply a scale. Up to now, Ptolemy was assumed to deserve this credit. In Posidonius' days, Egypt was still the heart of the ancient world, yet that notion had changed by Ptolemy's days.

5.5 Claudius Ptolemy

Claudius Ptolemy was born in Ptolemais and worked in Alexandria. The official foundation of the latter town took place on I Peret 1 of the civil calendar (November 16th, Julian calendar, JD 1,600,845), the day after the festivities around the "Interment of Osiris" in the year 331 BCE. The foundation was carried out by Alexander the Great, on the day of the Full Moon. About an hour before sunrise, the constellation Scorpio (Osiris) became visible on the

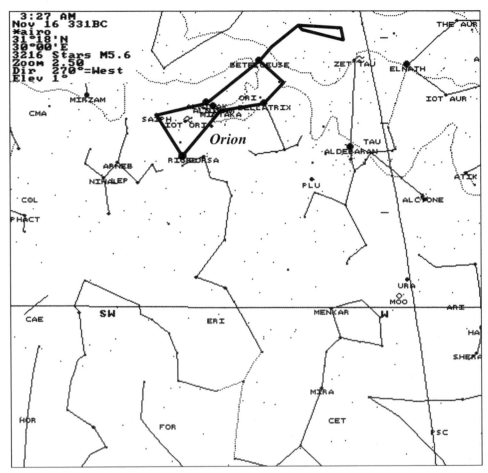

Fig. 45. On the western horizon, the Full Moon was visible, while the constellation Orion was about to set under the horizon. The stars Rigel, Aldebaran and Mirfak were also about to set (cf. Fig. 44 and 45).

eastern horizon. The planets Venus and Mars were in conjunction with the star Graffias just above this eastern horizon. At sunset, on the eastern horizon the Full Moon was visible, while the constellation Orion was about to rise above the horizon. In addition, the stars Rigel, Aldebaran and Mirfak were also about to rise above the eastern horizon (cf. fig. 44 and 45). The Egyptians attached extreme importance to the Osiris festival and by founding this important town, Alexander the Great paid tribute to Osiris. This raised him even higher in the esteem of the Egyptian population.

It was also the town where Ptolemy worked on his **Geographia**, which comprised eight volumes. Book I contains the general theory of cartography on an astronomical basis, while books II to VII consist of lists with a total of 8,000 names of towns. These are arranged in books II to V in accordance with the provinces of the Roman Empire. Books VI and VII deal with Arabia, Central Asia, China and India. All the names of these towns have been provided with

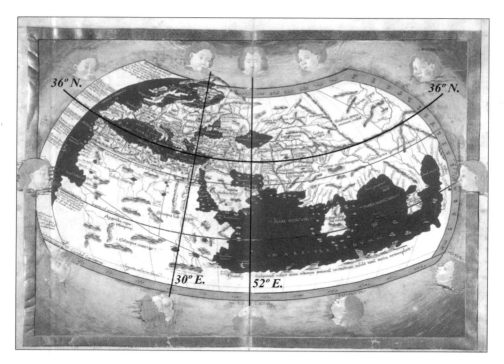

Fig. 46. World map by Claudius Ptolemy showing the 36° N. parallel as the dividing line between the northern and southern regions around the Mediterranean. It also shows the meridian of Alexandria and the revised location of the "Centre" of the world, which he adapted to the prevailing notion of the world.

their calculated geographic longitude and latitude, which he obtained with the help of the work of Martinus of Tyrus and a number of travel accounts.[10] He formulated a definition of geography, and made one of the most important remarks: *"In Geography one must contemplate the extent of the entire Earth, as well as its shape, and its position under the heavens, in order that one may rightly state what are the peculiarities and proportions of the part with which one is dealing, and under what parallel of the celestial sphere it is located..."*[11]

5.6 The Relocation of the 'Centre' of the World

Various Greek geographers based their work on what is called the meridian of Alexandria. The influence of Ptolemy still exists, as he was the one who introduced a system of co-ordinates and placed north at the top and east to the right on the parchment. He also had the ingenuity to draw the spherical shape of the Earth on the map, which he achieved by using a spread-out conical projection with meridians and parallels. The usefulness of meridians and parallels had already proved invaluable. However, in his version, Egypt no longer occupied the centre of the world; he shifted this meridian to the highest mountain in the Elburz mountain range, the Damavand-Qolleh-ye, which reaches a height of 5,670 metres. The geographic co-ordinates of this mountain are 35°56' N. and 52°08' E.[12]

After the victory of the Romans, Egypt lost its supremacy in the world, and the "centre" of the world was transferred to the Empire of the Medes and the Persians. Obviously, the world had increased in size after these exploratory voyages. Yet surprisingly, on his outline map of the "familiar world", Ptolemy drew the pseudo 90° meridian near the Elburz mountain range. He may have used this high, possibly sacred, mountain as a geographic marker. This highest mountain is also notable for yet another reason. The meridian of the Elburz mountain range denoted the eastern border of the ancient world, that of Egypt and Sumeria, a world which is pictured on Planisphere K8538, which we will study shortly.

Ptolemy used this ancient dividing line as the main meridian and gave it its due on the outline map (cf. fig. 46). Following Hipparchus, he divided the circle and the sphere of the Earth into 360°. In this way, starting from this 90° meridian, he deliberately divided the mainland on both sides, including the Canary Islands, into equal parts. Many people believed this to be an inexcusable mistake with far-reaching consequences, yet the scale division that he finally applied to this outline map shows that he knew that the coast of China was actually located in the region of the modern 120° E. He placed the Zero Meridian on the Canary Islands, which we know to be located at about 15° W. Hence, Ptolemy *divided* approximately 135° of "mainland" into 180 parts. On this map, he drew the pseudo 60° meridian near to Alexandria. A simple conversion shows that Ptolemy's map has Alexandria at approximately 45° E., counting from the Zero Meridian near Hierro, the westernmost island. According to the present Zero Meridian of Greenwich, Alexandria is located at approximately 30° E.

5.7 The 36° N. parallel, an ancient Boundary line

Our attention is drawn once again to the highest peak of the Elburz mountain range by the additional fact that the island of Rhodes, with its observatory of Eudoxus at Cnidos, and the island of Malta, as well as the Pillars of Hercules (Gibraltar) are also located exactly on that 36° N. parallel. Eratosthenes made use of this parallel to draw up his map of the world. Ptolemy elaborated on Eratosthenes' principle and used this parallel to divide the world into what is known as the northern and the southern part of the Earth, which he described in the **Tetrabiblos**. In Antiquity, this 36° N. parallel evidently divided the northern from the southern region around the Mediterranean Sea.

5.8 The Ancient Zero Meridian

Of all the islands belonging to the Fortunate Insulae, Hierro is one of the smallest and westernmost of the Canary Islands. Formerly also known as the "Islands of the Blessed" (remarkable, the creation of the first land of the ancestors of the Egyptians was a domain with the name *Blessed Island*, the ancestors greeted the Falcon as their Lord, see Edfu texts VI.182,10-15, translation in

The Mythical Origin of the Egyptian Temple, p.17 of E.A.E. Reymond).
It was exactly across Punta Orcilla, on the extreme west of the island, that
Ptolemy drew the Zero Meridian. The island is located at 18° W. within the
Atlantic Ocean. He used this meridian to determine the beginning and the end
of the sea. For nearly 1,500 years, Hierro remained the beginning and the end
of the "known world". In 1492, Columbus set sail from the island of Gomera,
also belonging to the Canary Islands, and headed for the far west. The line that
divided the old from the new world ran through Hierro. Columbus' voyage
began at the end of the old world in order to explore terra incognita.

5.9 A mysterious Planisphere

A planisphere is an image of a terrestrial or celestial hemisphere on a level
surface (cf. fig.41 and 47). The Planisphere offers us a fascinating insight into
the knowledge and the technical ingenuity of a lost culture. It allows us to
penetrate a world that is no longer ours. The clay tablet shows a prototype of
the layout of the old world - a matrix - on which regions and places were
connected with and classified under certain stars and/or constellations. Hence,
certain areas on Earth were considered to be "subject to" the stars.

In Antiquity, geographers had cast a celestial network of stars over the
Earth in order to create a terrestrial grid, which would serve to chart the world.
They were obviously looking to relate regions or places to a certain celestial
meridian, which in turn was linked with certain stars. To that end, they invented a matrix that possessed the characteristics of an *alignment system*, as
depicted on the Planisphere, which enabled them to classify the old world.

One of the most mysterious planispheres ever found is a round Babylonian
clay tablet, flat on top and spherical underneath, with a diameter of approximately 15 centimetres. Found before 1880, this tablet once belonged to the
Library of King Assurbanipal of Assyria and is at present on display in the
British Museum in London, catalogued as number K8538. Sayce and Bosanquet
published the first article on the mysterious clay tablet in ***Monthly Notices
of the Royal Astronomical Society***; XL, 3, January 1880.[13] Until now, the
Planisphere has managed to retain practically all of its secrets.

The third investigation into the Planisphere and its history begins with
Weidner, who quotes the aforementioned magazine in his research: "[...] the
picture between page 118 and 119 shows a copied illustration of the object; the
cuneiform script has meanwhile been translated. The translation has been replaced by Greek letters. These were published by von Hommel in the magazine
Das Ausland, 1891, page 224, who added a few remarks. Some time later, an
excellent photo, numbered 1627, appeared in the ***Sammlung Mansell***. Subsequently, Weidner copied the text and published part of it in ***Babyloniaca***
VI, p.157. The complete text has now been published by King in CTXXXIII, l.
10."[14] (cf. fig. 41, photo by P.Coppens).

In 1912, King, who was then curator of the department of Assyrian and
Babylonian Antiquities of the British Museum, made an exact copy of this
Planisphere[15] (cf. fig. 47). The Royal Astronomical Society published a
drawing of the original object, to which Oppert and Jensen added a few interpretations. Prior to this, Sayce and Bosanquet had already come to the pre-

liminary conclusion that this Planisphere bore an astronomical connotation. What intrigued them were "seven" dots in one of the sectors alongside a line, next to the names Dilgan and Apin. Though they were unable to offer a conclusive interpretation, they were convinced that the round clay tablet was a Babylonian map of the heavens.

5.10 Assurbanipal

King Assurbanipal ruled over Assyria from approximately 668-631 BCE, during the final golden age of this empire. He is best known for his Library and as a collector of Chaldean antiquities. He ordered that old texts throughout his entire empire were meticulously copied and subsequently had them stored in Nineveh, in his palatial library that did not come to light until Layard excavated it in the middle of the 19th century.[16]

A closer examination brought to light that he had collected the principal products of earlier Akkadian literature in this library. On a small clay tablet the following words recall how Assurbanipal praises himself when he utters: "I ordain that the artfully written tables shall remain in Sumerian, a language which is difficult to understand, and in obscure *Akkadian*, which is hard to decipher. I rejoice in reading these tablets, which date back to the *time before the Deluge*."[17]

His words tell us unmistakably that the Sumerian clay tablets should in any case be dated back to before the Deluge. This means that the period of prosperity of dynastic Sumeria must be dated to *before* the Flood of approximately 2520 BCE. After the Deluge, the Akkadian Empire of Sargon I ruled around 2355 BCE.

5.11 Peculiar, unrecognizable Star Constellations

Weidner was the first scholar who in *Handbuch der Babylonischen Astronomie* (1912) expressed doubts as to whether the texts on the Planisphere could ever be properly understood. He claimed: "In reality, we are confronted with a document that served to perform sorcery and fortune telling with the help of astrology."[18] Evidently, Weidner believed he was dealing with a magic spell. Somewhat further on, he remarked: "Apart from these phrasings, the object mentions a number of constellations. Although the positions they occupy in relation to one another are not entirely accurate, the correct sequence has nonetheless been maintained. It merely mentions a few important stars, which refutes the assumption of a complete 'Celestial Map'."[19]

Hence, Weidner concludes that the sequence of the constellations on the celestial map does not correspond with reality, and then adds a few sentences in which he deals with the division of the Planisphere into eight sectors. He then begins his analysis of each of those sectors, to conclude his research with: "I will round off my explanation of the text, although I am well aware how little I have actually 'explained'. Yet who is momentarily able to decipher this peculiar text in its entirety which, due to its peculiarities, presents such extreme difficulties? If no other similar texts are found that are in a better state of

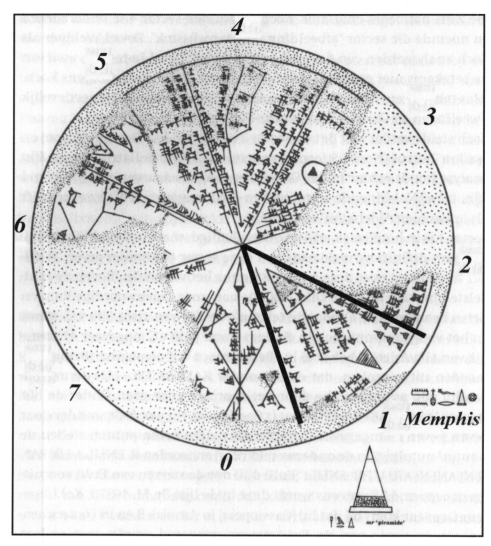

Fig. 47. An exact copy of planisphere K 8538, manufactured in 1912 by King, curator of the British Museum. It shows an adapted version of the numeration and division of the sectors. Our research focuses on sector 1. Compare the isosceles triangle (the Pyramid) below the Planisphere with the isosceles triangle in sector 1.

conservation, then all future endeavours to achieve a precise and complete explanation are bound to fail."[20]

The latest research into the Planisphere dates from 1989. It was carried out by Koch, who made it public in **Neue Untersuchungen zur Topographie des babylonischen Fixsternhimmels**.[21] Koch also shares Weidner's opinion that we are dealing with a unique document on which certain constellations are indicated. However, these constellations have been specified in a

158

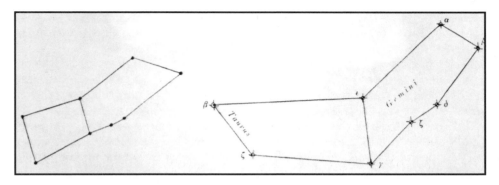

Fig. 48. The outline in sector 4, adapted and distorted according to Weidner's own interpretation. He presented this in an attempt to find an acceptable solution for the enigma in sector 4.

manner which has never yet been encountered; it is known as the *"alignment system"*. Koch states in his introduction that this Planisphere withstood all exploratory efforts and that its constellations remained practically unrecognisable. A comparison between the research of Weidner and that of Koch reveals an minor discrepancy. Koch labels Weidner's Sector 8 as sector 0. All other sectors retain the same numbering.

5.12 A Proto-classification of the World

Weidner personally changed the image of sector 4. He revised it according to his own insight by extending two lines, so that the drawing on sector 4 more or less corresponds with the outline of the constellation Gemini.[22] Yet not all lines in the figure on sector 4 are continuous (cf. fig. 47, sector 4, and compare these with fig. 48). Apparently, Weidner did not attribute any particular value to these interrupted lines and changed the drawing of sector 4 in such a way that it corresponds to a certain extent to the constellation Gemini mentioned earlier, although this intervention distorted the original image. Koch failed to examine sector 4 and called that sector "picture with pointer". Weidner as well as Koch analysed the part of sector 4 that contains "Lu-lal La-ta-rak", which lacks a clear meaning. Furthermore, Koch claims that sector 4 contains the words "Mas-tab-ba" and "Sipa-zi-an-na", and that they stand respectively for Gemini and Orion[23] (appendix IX, table III of Koch).

Moreover, Koch specified that sector 3 contains the stars éta Taurus (Alcyon), epsilon Taurus (Northern Eye of the Bull) and gamma Orion (Bellatrix). Yet his analysis implies that Orion or some of its parts are not mentioned, whereas Weidner combines the sectors 3 and 4 and mentions these as "maybe Aldebaran" and Orion.[24]

On the whole, sector 1 has remained practically undamaged, yet even in that condition, Weidner appears to be unable to offer a definitive explanation for that sector. He describes its figure as follows: "The line in the centre has KAKKAB DIL-GAN above it, which complies with our present-day constellations Aries and Cetus. Since the text dates back to approximately 700 BCE, and the vernal equinox was in Aries at that time (approximately 4° east of alpha Arietis in 700 BCE), I already expressed my assumption in "**Babyloniaca** VII", page 18, that the line underneath KAKKAB DIL-GAN appears to represent the meridian line which runs through the vernal equinox. Below the line we read: KAKKAB APIN, known to us as Cassiopeia and represented further down by seven dots [comment Zitman: these seven dots represent the Anunnaki or Igigi in the netherworld], which are called IL ENLIL A-LIK PAN KAKKABANI SU-UT IL ENLIL: 'Enlil who precedes the stars of Enlil'. Enlil is also mentioned in the list Br.M.86378, column I.1. What is more, it [Cassiopeia] is mentioned in **Astrolab B** and in **Fixsternkommentar** as the first of the Enlil stars; in other words: it is, amongst the Enlil stars, the group of stars that lies closest to the meridian line that runs through the vernal equinox. Whatever purpose the two triangles in our picture might serve is hard to explain."[25]

As to sector 1 of the Planisphere, Koch states that the sequence of the stars in this sector is incorrect. Epsilon Pegasus (Enif) precedes alpha Pegasus (Markab) and is subsequently followed by Epsilon Pegasus (Enif) at the end of table III. Koch comments on this with the words: "Nevertheless, this remarkable conclusion will not be followed up."[26] He states that this image also includes a pair of triangles, yet without offering any further explanation for this curious depiction.[27]

Sector 6 has the name Assur inscribed on it, which is pointed out by Weidner and Koch. Weidner's comments: "One corner of the drawing contains the word Assur. Subsequently, in list II R 48, 55-59ab (=CT XIX, pl.19, K4386, RII, 58-62), a row of constellations are linked up with dwelling places, and amongst these dwelling places we also find Assur."[28] Sectors 2, 3, 6, and 7 have suffered various extents of damage.

Unfortunately, the analyses of the Planisphere do not deal with the language that is used on the clay tablet. Consequently, it remains unknown whether the inscriptions were made in the Sumerian or the Akkadian language. Whether this also applies to the images on the various sectors of this Planisphere will be discussed later on. Weidner and Koch evidently assume that the clay tablet was created around 700 BCE, a rather doubtful assumption, as we will see further on. Furthermore, Koch states that the star epsilon Pegasus appears twice on the Planisphere. As a matter of even greater importance, the Planisphere demonstrates that either the city or the country Assur (Assyria) is related to the star alpha Bootes (Arcturus, in transition from the sign Virgo to Libra).

5.13 Ptolemy's classification of the World

In **Tetrabiblos** II:3, Claudius Ptolemy dedicated an entire chapter to "*the Alliance of the regions on Earth with the Trinity and the Planets*". He divided the Earth into four quadrants, which he achieved with the use of the aforementioned 36° northern parallel and the 35° eastern meridian. In doing so, he provided each quadrant and the regions (countries) it contained with a Trinity: three constellations, i.e. zodiacal signs. The country Assur (Assyria) and the town of that name were contained within the south-eastern quadrant and fell under the same zodiacal sign as Babylonia, namely Virgo. Lower Egypt lay in the south-western quadrant and obviously came under the zodiacal sign of Gemini, as Memphis correlates with the star Alhena (15° Gemini).

Further analysis of the Planisphere will show that the technique that Ptolemy used was definitely no less than 800 years old at that time. In Antiquity, it was not just regions or countries that were considered to be under the influence of stars and zodiacal signs; this clearly also held true for towns. However, the "alignment system" that applied to the Planisphere, did not serve Ptolemy as a basis for his classification of the world, which therefore deviates from the former.

5.14 Diagrammatic Cartography

Koch's remark, stating that the Planisphere is a unique document as the star constellations are indicated in what Weidner already called the "alignment system", is of inestimable value. This method of imaging has never yet been encountered. Did Koch realise that the round Planisphere has the qualities of an astronomical matrix? This makes the Planisphere the first known expression of diagrammatic cartography with which the celestial sky was embedded onto a matrix model.

Cartography developed from diagrammatic images. In Antiquity, no drawings had ever been made of the Earth or of the landscape representing them as geographic shapes. The diagrammatic images were both simple and comprehensive and are difficult to recognise as cartography. In **De Stenen Spreken**, the archaeologists De Jonge and IJzereef cast new light on the meaning of inscriptions that are found on the Western European megalithic monuments, such as "The Thing" (see **The Megalithic Art of Western Europe**, E.Shee Twohig), which they hypothesise to be an inscription representing the coastal line of Great Britain.[29] Furthermore, they claim that various inscriptions are an image of coastal routes and sea voyages, which were undertaken from about 6000 BCE onwards.

A different sample shows a diagrammatic image that was originally made by seafaring inhabitants of the Marshall Islands in the 19th century (cf. fig. 49). These stylised diagrams, simple in appearance, turned out to be cartographic images. "The oldest one, of which unfortunately no illustration exists, was made in 3800 BCE and shows the Euphrates as it flows through the north of Mesopotamia, with double rows of scalloped incisions, representing the mountain ranges in the east and the west."[30] These people tried to give shape to their knowledge of the landscape by means of diagrammatic, sometimes even geometric images.

InEgypt:"Image of Heaven", section 4.25, remnants of this geographic knowledge were amply demonstrated. At the same time, the Egyptians also made use of their "Osiris meridian", which served as the Zero Meridian of the archaic world. They also used parallels of latitude (cf. section 4.19) which offer just as

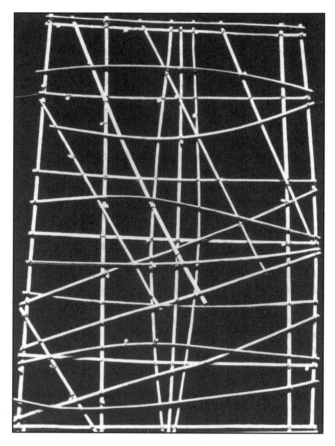

Fig. 49. Diagrammatic map consisting of filaments from a palm leaf and small shells, manufactured in the 19th century by seafaring inhabitants of the Marshall Islands. The secret method was passed on from father to son. The curved lines indicate the prevailing direction of the waves in relation to the islands, which are represented by the shells. This primitive nautical chart shows how man tried to find his bearings. Diagrammatic images of this kind serve as an example of how abstract cartography was practised in primitive societies.

much evidence of their edifying knowledge of how to "order" the world.

Such evidence is not restricted to their own territory, as the following text of Egyptian origin shows: "The most sacred land of our ancestors is located in the centre of the world".[31] This text shows that they had a certain geographic notion of the surrounding parts of the Earth with which they were acquainted. In addition, they knew exactly where their country was located on the Earth, and we will therefore revert to the notion Ro, in particular to rwy, the meaning of which is 2/3 (cf. Survey hieroglyphs D22, **Egyptian Grammar**). Its shape corresponds with Posidonius' ellipsoid.

5.15 An ideal Apportionment of the ancient World

The general map of the world as drawn up by Claudius Ptolemy shows that Alexandria is located on the 60° meridian and that he divided the whole world, from west to east, into 180 degrees. Ptolemy no longer placed Egypt in the "centre" of the world; he divided it as he knew it according to a different system, which the ancient Egyptians with their enhanced knowledge of the world had developed on the basis of the "sacred" proportion 2:3.

He used the meridian that runs through Alexandria to divide the world into two sectors: one sector, encompassing 1/3 of the world to the west of Alexandria and the other, covering 2/3 of the world to the east of this Ptolemaic metropolis from the Graeco-Roman period. By doing so, he paid tribute to the knowledge of the Egyptians (cf. fig. 46). By the same token, the Egyptians built the pyramids of Giza on the "ideal" 30° N. parallel, thereby dividing the northern hemisphere into the proportion of 1/3 to 2/3.

The Pyramid Field of Giza, with the three majestic pyramids on 29°58' N., is still manifest on this parallel as the centre of the legendary State of Egypt. Yet their craving for precision and rigid structure remains a mystery, although this northern parallel does reveal a number of peculiarities. Counting from the far west to the east, the Atlantic Ocean confronts us with an enormous volcano in the shape of a table mountain on an island, the size of which coincides more or less with the volcano *de Teide* on the island of Tenerife in the Canary Islands. The marine mountain and the island bear the name *Great Meteor*, the peak of which now lies at 238 metres below sea-level. This marine mountain is located at exactly 30° N. and 28°30' W., as a kind of Omphalos Thalasses, also known as the "Navel of the Sea". At what moment did this mountain tower above sea-level? Furthermore, could its recollection have inspired Homer when he wrote his Odyssey?

The next station on our journey eastward is the Pyramid Field of Giza. Following that, we encounter an enormous territory covered with ruins on the border between Iran and Afghanistan, known as the Ruins of Tarakun, of Rämrod and of Godari Shah. We then travel on, across the "roof of the world", to Lhasa in Tibet, which was founded in 746 CE by the legendary magus Padmasambhava, before arriving near Zhenhai, a town on the Yellow Sea. At some time, this parallel was apparently subdivided by ideal locations that coincide with a sequence of meridians that are each spaced apart by 30°, this along the entire area of the known world. The mysterious division of this ideal parallel lies hidden in the relationship between this parallel and the Golden Section (cf. appendix X).

Outline from west to east:
(The co-ordinates are based on the present Zero Greenwich Meridian and have been rounded off).

Great Meteor (unknown)		Giza	Tarakun	Lhasa	Zhenhai
Atlantic Ocean		Egypt	Iran/Afghan.	Tibet	China
29° W.	1°E.	31° E.	61° E.	91° E.	121° E.

This outline shows that the ideal Zero Meridian was at one time located at 1° or 2° E, in other words, through Dieppe in France. (This was one of the reasons why the French were so keen to have the Zero Meridian running through Paris) The five earliest town states of Sumeria were located precisely in the "centre" of that world at approximately 46° E., between the Zero Meridian and the town that built subsequently at Lhasa at 91° E.

As Mankind discovered more regions of the Earth, the "centre" of the world was relocated. In mediaeval Islamic astronomy (after 800 CE), there is the *Cupola of Arin*, mentioned in the ***Journal for the History of Arabic Science and in Vistas in Astronomy***. In those days, it had been established that merely half of the Earth was habitable. According to the maps, the place between the western and the eastern limits where the Earth was divided into two equal halves lay on the equator and was known as the "Cupola of the Earth". Both parts measured 90 degrees. Portuguese and Spanish charts from around the end of the 10th century, show that a western meridian existed in the Atlantic Ocean, called the *"Meridian of Water"*. The location of this westernmost meridian was around 30° to 32° W., as deduced from the *Tables of Toledo*. Hence, the legendary land of Arin, which has never been found and is thought to lie in what was then considered to be the "centre" of the world, ought to be searched for in a region somewhere between 58° and 60° E. We presume that the ruins of Tarakun/Rämrod, on the border between Iran and Afghanistan and situated on the "ideal" 30° N. parallel, are in fact this legendary, long-sought Arin.

Thus it should not come as a surprise that Persepolis, the residence of the Persian king Darius I (approximately 518 BCE), was also built on this "ideal" parallel. His palace compound (29°57' N. and 52°59' E.) was built on a plain, 1,570 metres above sea-level, with an artificially constructed terrace which was reached via a monumental flight of steps that led to the entrance.

All these scattered pieces of evidence remind us of the diagrammatic development of cartography in times long gone. Similar developments in cartography are also discernible on the Planisphere. The eight sectors show a precise astronomical arrangement. The way the Planisphere was apportioned according to the *"alignment system"* enables us to develop an astronomical matrix that can be spread out over the Earth. In Antiquity, geographers used the same method to project the celestial network of stars onto the Earth, in order to determine specific locations. We find relics of that knowledge in Claudius Ptolemy's works.

5.16 "Paradise rediscovered"

The image on sector 1 of the Planisphere with the two triangles ranks as one of the most intriguing figures on the clay tablet (cf. fig. 47). It shows a closed isosceles triangle, which is connected to an open isosceles triangle. The first one shows a remarkable and conspicuous correspondence, yet an equally conspicuous contrast with "the complete, descriptive hieroglyph for "pyramid"[32] (cf. fig. 47). The text (cf. hieroglyphs O24, *Egyptian Grammar*) is claimed to point to the pyramid city of Saqqara, opposite Memphis, the capital of Egypt.[33] The image of the line at the bottom with an empty Egyptian pyramid shows a red centrefield and a pyramidion. Its meaning is not quite clear. The red zone might indicate Lower Egypt, while the empty centrefield might symbolise Upper Egypt. In contrast, the image of the pyramid on the Planisphere shows an empty bottom zone with translated cuneiform, a shaded centrefield and a pyramidion with four dots that, taking the top of the pyramidion into account, would add up to five dots in total.

Weidner and Koch offer no explanation for the meaning of the image on sector 1 of the Planisphere. The two triangles are a mystery to them. We postulate that the "open" isosceles triangle symbolises either *the beginning of Creation, or unfinished Creation*. The open isosceles triangle was, after all, the sign for the Creator Atum, thereby symbolising that the One (Atum) brought forth Two (Shu and Tefnut) (cf. fig. 16). Furthermore, a line connects the open isosceles triangle to the closed isosceles triangle. In our opinion, this closed isosceles triangle is the iconographical symbol for the "Land of Sopdet" *brought to completion, the "land of God"*. Hence, this image shows two successive creations, whereby the open isosceles triangle stands for the unaccomplished, "lost" cradle that was abandoned in 5300 BCE.

The closed isosceles triangle symbolises the subsequent foundation of the states of Egypt and Sumeria, after 5300 BCE. Hence, the image on sector 1 of the Planisphere appears to render a diagrammatic outline of the unfinished Creation and the foundation of the states of Egypt and Sumeria. The stars on this sector, alpha Pegasus (Markab) and epsilon Pegasus (Enif), as well as the connecting line with the seven dots between the two triangles, will contribute to further disentanglements. Next to this line, we read "Enlil, who precedes the stars of Enlil", which is a reference to the "Way of Enlil" (cf. fig. 50).

Enlil was an important Sumerian god. Together with Anu and Ea, he divided the globe into three parts, which to some extent can be compared to the land on either side of the two tropics and the land in between, including the Equator. Enlil ruled over the northern hemisphere, Anu over the region around the Equator, while Ea reigned over the southern hemisphere.

The text alongside the seven dots along the "Way of Enlil" refers to "mul AS-iku", the Pegasus square, the I-Iku, which is formed by stars of the zodiacal signs Aquarius and Pisces (cf. fig. 51). This Pegasus square, known as "Paradise rediscovered", was extremely important, as shown by a passage from one of the Babylonian New Year festival ritual texts: "He [the Urigalla-priest] shall (then) go out to the Exalted Courtyard, turn to the north and bless the temple Esagil three times with the blessing: 'Iku-star, Esagil, image of *heaven and Earth*'."[34][italics by the author]

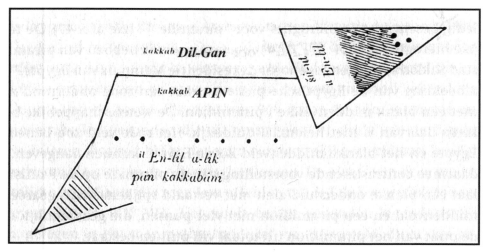

Fig. 50. Enlarged image of the main part of sector 1 on the Planisphere

This blessing unmistakably mentions heaven as well as Earth. The Sumerians attached extraordinary importance to this Pegasus square, in which the star Markab ranks as the main star. The fact is that the Sumerians considered the "I-Iku", i.e. the Pegasus square, to represent "Paradise rediscovered", as the German scholar A.Ungnad understood it.[35] The star alpha Pegasus, Markab of the sign Pisces, marks the beginning of the Pegasus square, which consists of alpha Pegasi, beta Pegasi, gamma Pegasi and alpha Andromedae: the I-Iku, the Apsu.[36] Accordingly, this square forms part of the celestial network. By transforming this part of the network into a matrix and spreading it across the Earth, the location of the "lost" cradle can be rediscovered. This solves the problem of sector 1. The Planisphere was there to lead us on the way to explore the geographic horizon of the ancestors of the Egyptians and the Sumerians. But where was the Way of Enlil?

5.17 Where was the Way of Enlil?

It appears that attempts were made to shape geographic knowledge by means of diagrammatic or trigonometric figures. The image on sector 1 of the Planisphere is a case in point (cf. fig. 47). It is apparent that the line that links both triangles is connected to the middle of the base of the closed isosceles triangle. Further examination of the Planisphere proved that this detail, as well as the angle between the base of the isosceles triangle and the connecting line, is of extreme importance to the solution of the problem.

This angle is reminiscent of the observation track of the star Sirius between the two prehistoric capitals of Hieraconpolis and Buto, respectively in Upper Egypt and Lower Egypt, with the step pyramid of Zawyet el Amwat precisely halfway on that track, close to the settlements of Hebenu and Men at Khufu (also known as El Minja), an area known as the "Horizon of Horus".[37]

166

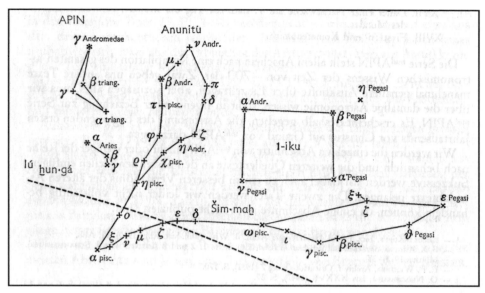

*Fig. 51. Star map of I-Iku, from **Anfänge der Astronomie**, showing the stars of Pegasus and Andromeda.*

Men at Khufu, near the step pyramid of Zawyet el Amwat, marked the beginning of the "Way of Horus". The term "Way of Horus" dates back to Antiquity and is already listed in Pyramid Text §607, with a reference to Pharaoh Weneg of the Second Dynasty. It ran from Zawyet el Amwat via Heliopolis in a northerly direction, to the fortified town of Sile in the eastern Delta. Sile was located on the border of the province that bore the name "Front of the East", where the "Way of Horus" continued along the coast in an easterly direction towards Raphia (now called Rafah), on the border of the Gaza strip.[38]

Could the "Horizon of Horus" and the "Way of Horus" have intersected at the step pyramid of Zawyet el Amwat? Indeed; from this junction, the "Way of Horus" does run to the north, while the "Horizon of Horus" leads westward, along the 28° N. parallel. The Sumerians called the parallel the "Way of Enlil".

The different designations could have been made to avoid confusion. The "Horizon of Horus" in Men at Khufu and its surroundings evidently ran westward and continued along the 28° N. parallel. Therefore, the connecting line between the two triangles on the Planisphere stands for the "Horizon of Horus" as well as the "Way of Enlil" (cf. fig. 50). The explanatory text alongside, stating "Enlil, who precedes the stars of Enlil" ratifies this.

5.18 The 'Horizon of Horus' changes into 'Horus of the Horizon'

The pyramids of Giza marked the 30° N. parallel, which correlated with the celestial equator (boundary line between the Northern and the Southern Hemisphere). As the "Horizon of Horus", the "Way of Enlil" was located on the 28° N. parallel. Since the site of the three pyramids at Giza was chosen to mark the projection of the celestial equator onto the surface of the Earth, the "Way of Enlil", the "Horizon of Horus", had to be relocated to the 30° N. parallel. Ingeniously, the name was changed into "Horizon of Horus", so that the memory of the previous 28° N. parallel was retained in the new name. The Great Sphinx was built on this site in order to mark its significance permanently.[39]

The name of the Great Sphinx became Horakhti, "Horus, Dweller of the Horizon". After the star cult had merged with the sun cult (the end of the Fourth Dynasty), the combined Atum-Re cult was installed at Heliopolis. The Sphinx is manifest testimony to this event, and it was subsequently given the name Atum-Re-Horakhti. Iconographically, the Sphinx represents the entwined zodiacal signs of Leo and Aquarius. The countenance of the human being (Aquarius) deli-berately faces to the east as a tribute to the gods, i.e. the stars, which always rise from that direction. Hence, the relocation of the "Way of Enlil" and the "Horizon of Horus" to Giza occured around 3000 BCE, which means that the image on sector 1 of the Planisphere dates back to the fourth millennium BCE.

5.19 Once again, Sirius is the Geographic Guide

The fact that the isosceles triangle on the Planisphere is reminiscent of the hieroglyph denoting the star Sirius is obvious. However, the correspondence of the angle between the connecting line and the perpendicular to the base of the isosceles triangle on the one hand, with the angle between the observation track from Hieraconpolis to Buto and the compass-bearing true north on the other, is an astounding discovery. This angle measures approximately 17°. This congruence, combined with the identical angle, made us project the entire isosceles triangle, and subsequently the entire figure, onto the map of Africa and the Near East. To that end, we used two maps, one of the Middle East and one of North Africa, from the National Geographic Society's **Atlas of the World**, on a scale of 1:8,250,000.[40]

The intriguing thing about the isosceles triangle on the Planisphere is its evocation of the star Sirius. The slanting base of this triangle was reminiscent of the observation track between Hieraconpolis and Buto. Another striking feature was the manner in which the Way of Enlil, i.e. the Horizon of Horus (the line in the centre), divides the base of the isosceles triangle into two equal parts, whereby the intersection might well correspond with the middle of the observation track (junction Men at Khufu/Zawyet el Amwat), and could coincide with the site where the pyramid of Zawyet el Amwat was built on the 28° N. parallel. The angle of 17° also ought to be taken into account. These singularities allowed us to make a transparent enlargement of the entire figure on sector 1 of the Planisphere, which we then superimposed on the maps.

At this point, the recent excavations of Buto took on new significance, as they had revealed layers attesting to local dwelling places dating from approximately 3650 to approximately 3000 BCE, immediately followed by layers dating from around 300 BCE.[41] These exceptional stratigraphic details prove that the depiction on sector 1 of the Planisphere dates back to ancient Antiquity, It also shows that the Planisphere could never have been created around 700 BCE.

This stratigraphic discovery offers convincing and decisive proof that the depiction on sector 1 of the Planisphere dates back to the fourth millennium, when Buto served as an administrative centre for overseas connections.[42] Findings of a specific type of decorative nail, known as the "Grubenkopfnagel", have confirmed that this was once the location of an important building frequented by Sumerian merchants.[43] Accordingly, trading relations must have existed with the Uruk culture of Sumeria. The "Horizon of Horus", running westward, and its connection with the "Way of Horus" at the junction of Men at Khufu show that these roads were trade routes between territories in the far west and the far east.

The projection of the isosceles triangle on the maps of Africa and the Middle East led to the conclusion that the locations of the five town states of Sumeria bore a geodetic relationship to Buto in Egypt. Buto (31°12' N.) and the Sumerian towns Uruk (31°18' N.) and Larsa (31°14' N.) are all located on almost precisely the same parallel, while the meridian of Buto is separated from the meridian of the five town states by a distance of almost 15°, which means that they have a time difference of exactly one hour. Furthermore, the top of the isosceles triangle coincided with the respective locations of the five town states.

The top part of the isosceles triangle contains four dots, and with the inclusion of the top, this could point to the five town states of Sumeria (cf. fig. 50): Uruk, Larsa, Ubaid, Ur and Eridu. The foundation of Uruk dates back to approximately 4000 BCE, maybe even earlier; Larsa around 3500 BCE, Ubaid between 5300 BCE and 3500 BCE, Ur approximately 4000 BCE, while the foundation of Eridu occurred during the First Dynasty of the Sumerian Kinglist (date unknown).

The next step was to calculate the distance between Buto and the five town states, and between Hieraconpolis and these town states; it was also necessary to determine whether two equal distances could be found that would then qualify as the sides of the isosceles triangle. The co-ordinates of the five Sumerian towns are as follows:

Uruk	31°18' N. - 45°40' E.	
Larsa	31°14' N. - 45°51' E.	
Ubaid	30°58' N. - 46°05' E.	Buto 31°12' N. - 30°45' E.
Ur	30°56' N. - 46°08' E.	
Eridu	30°50' N. - 46°02' E.	

The distances between the Sumerian towns and Buto, respectively Hieraconpolis are:

Uruk to Buto	1416 kilometres
Larsa to Buto	1437 kilometres
Ubaid to Buto	1461 kilometres *
Ur to Buto	1464 kilometres *
Eridu to Buto	1455 kilometres *

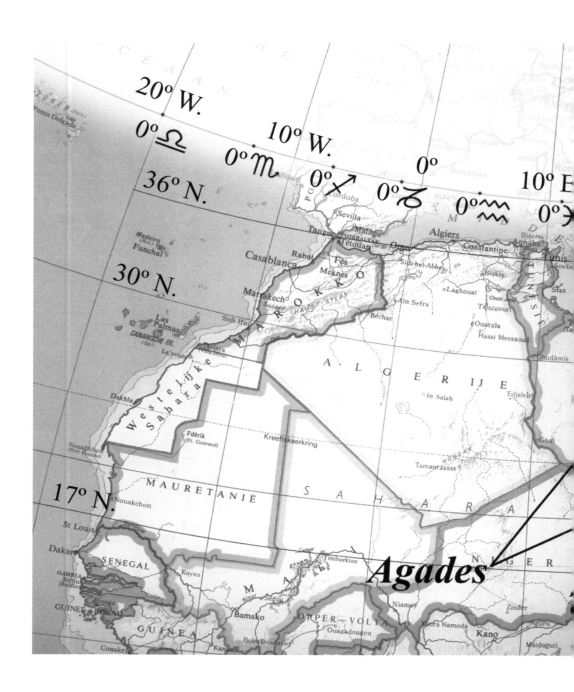

Fig. 52. Map of North Africa and the Middle East, extending to the Caspian Sea. The celestial network, consisting of constellations with stars (matrix), is spread out across the map.Upon the map, the complete image of Sector 1 of the Planisphere (cf. fig. 50) is precisely projected. The observation track between the prehistoric towns Hieraconpolis and Buto served as one of the

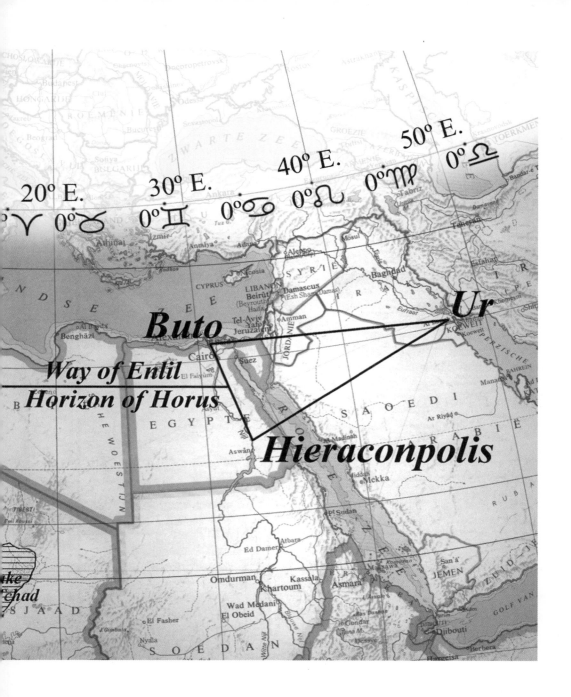

reference markings. The top of the closed isosceles triangle corresponds with Sumeria (five town-states). The 28° N. parallel was identical with the Horizon of Horus as well as with the Way of Enlil. The top of the open triangle coincides with Agadez. The meaning of the word Agade is meeting-place, to gather.

Uruk to Hieraconpolis	1436 kilometres
Larsa to Hieraconpolis	1451 kilometres
Ubaid to Hieraconpolis	1460 kilometres *
Ur to Hieraconpolis	1460 kilometres *
Eridu to Hieraconpolis	1447 kilometres

"By chance", the length of the sides, marked by *, of the isosceles triangle (in kilometres) corresponds with the duration of the Sirius year, namely 1,460 years. Was this their way of underlining the phrase *"Time is equal to Distance"*? Irrelevantly, the length of both sides proved to be identical, which confirmed the existence of an isosceles triangle. The distance between Hieraconpolis and Ubaid, respectively Ur, and also between Buto and Ubaid are indeed optimal. The remaining differences are clearly negligible.

Overview in royal cubits:

Distance between the co-ordinates of Buto/Larsa	=	ca. 2,759,000 r.cubits
Distance between the co-ordinates of Hieraconpolis/Larsa	=	ca. 2,759,000 r.cubits
Distance between the co-ordinates of Hieraconpolis/Buto	=	ca. 1,350,500 r.cubits

The circumference of the isosceles triangle is ca. 6,870,000 royal cubits

Remarkably, the circumference of this isosceles triangle equals 10,000 x 687, with 687 corresponding to the sidereal orbit of the planet Mars. This is not a coincidence. Figure 36 shows the beginning of the authorised Egyptian calendar. On that date, the planet Mars crossed the stopping-place of the Gods, the Perihelium, where the star Propus (the battle-axe) is located. Mars returns to this celestial position after having completed one sidereal period of 686.98 days around the Sun. (The sidereal period is the period between one conjunction of the planet with a particular star and the next one.) Since the Egyptians considered one sidereal period to be a circle of 360 degrees, and 360 degrees equals 0.524 x 686.98, a numerical unit is obtained which coincides with the length of the Egyptian Royal Cubit, measured in centimetres (0.524 centimetres). In this context, it should be pointed out that Mars' synodic orbit (the period between one conjunction of the planet with the Sun and the next one – in the case of Mars: 779.94 days) results in the following correspondence: 360 degrees equals 0.4616 x 779.94. This unit coincides with the length of the Egyptian Standard Cubit (0.4618 centimetre, the Nilometer), measured in centimetres. They may have been unfamiliar with the ellipse.

Amongst all the pictographic signs of the Egyptians, the hieroglyph of the star Sirius sits in a unique position. The linguistic meaning that Egyptologists nowadays attribute to this sign is: "thorn, sharp",[44] but also "Triangle of the Deity".[45] This triangle, Sopdet, specified by the locations of Hieraconpolis and Buto in Egypt and Larsa in Sumeria, was literally projected onto the surface of the Earth, thereby imaging it as a virtual, imperceptible depiction (cf. fig. 52). Together, these three towns formed the sacred locations of God, since the sides of this isosceles triangle enclosed the "Land of God". 1,500 years later, this was also communicated to the patriarch Abraham. "In the same day the Lord made a covenant with Abram, saying, Unto thy seed have I given this land, from the river of Egypt [the Nile] unto the great river, the river Euphrates."

This explains why the Jewish people went in search of the "Land of God" and why they moved into the Sinai after their exodus from Egypt. They did so because the Sinai peninsula belonged to the promised land, which, from the beginning of the second millennium, was inhabited by the ancestors of the Phoenicians, who originated from the southern land of Punt (the Ethiopian Highlands and the Asir mountain range of Saudi Arabia).

An interesting etymological and linguistic similarity exists between Buto and Larsa. In Buto, the snake goddess was called Uto, while Utu was the Sumerian name for the Sun, which was primarily worshipped in the temple town of Larsa.

Uto, the Egyptian snake goddess of Buto, was referred to as: "Uto, Egyptian snake goddess of Pe and Dep" (Buto = transcription of pr-w3dj.t = location of the Eye of Horus) "temple of Uto", i.e. "the papyrus-coloured one", "the green one". This cobra and its town Buto symbolise the Delta (Lower Egypt), in contrast to the vulture of Hieraconpolis, which represents Upper Egypt. The former personifies the red crown, while the latter relates to the white crown. They appear in the royal forms of address as nb.ty, "the two mistresses". Furthermore, Uto is embodied in the uraeus on the forehead of the king [from the Middle Kingdom onward] and the gods, whom she protects with her magical power.

The link with the papyrus plant that is inherent in her name also causes Uto to signify viability, freshness and fertility.[46] "Utu" or "Shamash" (*Samas*; cf. sapsu in Ugaritian; sémés in Hebrew), was the Babylonian name for the Sun god, called Utu by the Sumerians. His worship was centred in his temples in Larsa [a Sumerian centre during the Djemdet Nsr-period] in the south and Sippar in North Babylonia, both called E-babbar, "Shining House". In addition, he had important temples in Mari (from the early dynastic period onward) and Assur (a double temple with Sin). During the Parthian period, Hatra was an important cult centre.

Shamash counts as the son of the Moongod, brother of Ishtar and Adad; his spouse is Aja, while Bunene is his vizir. At night, after he sets, he journeys through the netherworld, to rise again in the east, between two mountains. This scene is often pictured on ancient Akkadian cylinder seals, where Shamash can be distinguished by his symbol, the saw [cf. the Egyptian palm-stalk with its kerfs to denote time and the Year].

Elsewhere, e.g. on the relief on the Hammurabi Codex, he is characterised by the sunbeams that emanate from his shoulders. As the god of light, he is a benevolent deity whose appearance causes joy; he dispels and challenges the darkness and those who work in favour of the dark, e.g. demons and malefactors. As such, he is the unsurpassed god of justice, "the great judge of heavens and earth, of the living and the dead" and a refuge for the outlawed and the weak, for widows and orphans. "Law and justice" (kittu and mesaru) are his essence; they are sometimes personified as his sons. One of the facts that clearly illustrate his judicial function is his role in inspiring Hammurabi to issue the code of laws.

To fend off demons and evil powers, he is often appealed to in prayers that are called ki-itu-kam, literally "where Utu is", which are based on the notion that he can summon these evil powers to appear before his seat of justice in order to pass sentence on them. He also exercises his judicial function as a god of omens, by writing his "sentence", together with Adad, on the intestines of the sacrificial animal. He also administers justice in the netherworld. The exclamation "Oh, Utu!", i-Utu, even became a famous outcry for justice.

Babylonian literature contains a great number of prayers that are directed at Shamash. In addition to the ki-itu-kam prayers, numerous su-illas or prayer-like incantations are known to have been addressed to him, which play an important role in the magic rituals surrounding the king, and the great "Shamash hymn", which ranks amongst the best-known literary creations. This god plays no dominant role in mythology, even though he is mentioned in the Gilgamesh Epic and other texts. There are indications that Shamash was considered to be a goddess amongst the Semitic population of the third millennium, which was also the case in Ugarit and amongst the Arabs in later times.[47]

UTO (Buto) and UTU (Larsa) are etymologically/linguistically analogous and were linked to each other due to the reverence for Sirius in relation to the Sun. In Egypt, Buto fulfilled an important role as it was the town where the "freshness" of the New Year began, marked by the festivities of New Year's Day. These rites may also have been performed in Sumerian Larsa.

5.20 Archaic Meridians

After having established that the isosceles triangle of sector 1 of the Planisphere was geodetically drawn between the above mentioned towns, we possess convincing evidence that this sector was designed on cartographic principles. But there is more: the use of the map of North Africa and the Near East, superimposed by the transparent projection of the isosceles triangle, also shows that the top of the open triangle points to the town of Agadez (modern Niger) (cf. fig. 52).

By means of simple measuring and extrapolation of the data obtained so far, the remaining parts of the sector can be accurately projected onto the map of North Africa (cf. fig. 52). Exact measurements shows that the geodetic line connecting the point of attachment to the bend has the same length as the sides of the isosceles triangle. This projection also shows that Ar Ramlah al Kabirah (15°45' E., with Sabha to its southwest) in Libya is located exactly 15° west of the meridian of Buto. Remarkably, Men at Khufu (30°45' E.) is also located on the same meridian as Buto. Hence, the meridians of Larsa, Buto and Ar Ramlah al Kabirah in Libya are separated from each other by 15 degrees. At the last town, the geodetic line on the 28° N. parallel (Way of Enlil) veers off and slants downward over a distance of approximately 500 kilometres, subsequently to end at the Murzuk Sandsea at what was then the Tropic of Cancer, on 24° N. Here, the line veers off to the south-west, at an angle of approximately

25 degrees and ends at the top of the open triangle near the town of Agadez (17°00' N. and 07°58' E.) in Niger, at the edge of the Central Mountain Range of North Africa.

5.21 Prehistoric Cultures between the Air Massif and the Paleo-Lake Chad

The oldest ceramics in the world (circa 7500 BCE) have been found in the Air Mountains, near Bagzane and in the Adrar Bous, which will be dealt with in detail later on. From the top of the open triangle, the other side runs at an angle of approximately 42 degrees, in the direction of the towns Tozeur and Faya-Largeau (17°58' N. and 19°06' E.) in Chad, so that the southern foothills of the Tibesti mountain range seem to be embraced by the two sides of this open triangle. This side ends near the northern bank of the former gigantic Paleo-Lake Chad. In those surroundings, the ancient pebble culture (the first primitive tools made of pebblestone were made approximately 700,000 BCE) of Zouar is located. To the north-east of the Paleo-Lake Chad, the Yoa-lake once existed, where flint tools were found in Ounianga-Kébir, which date back to 160,000 BCE. In 1965, the palaeontologist Professor Coppens discovered fossilised fragments of the countenance of the *Tchadanthropus Uxoris* in the falaise d'Angamma, which are claimed to date back to that same period. In addition, the prehistoric settlements of Bilma and Bardaïs, dating from approximately 30,000 BCE are situated in this region.[48]

Between 6500 and 5300 BCE, the Paleo-Lake Chad was an inland sea with a surface area of approximately 330,000 square kilometres. Around 30,000 square kilometres of this area consisted of papyrus lakes and marshes. During the extreme draught from 5300 until 4900 BCE, this vast lake was reduced to approximately 25,000 square kilometres. This illustrates the extreme climate conditions of that time. After 4900 BCE, the lake developed once again into an inland sea, retaining its maximum size until approximately 3400 BCE.[49] Subsequently, its proportions gradually decreased until approximately 2600 BCE, followed by a rapid further reduction until approximately 1500 BCE. From 2600 BCE onwards, the water-level sank some 25 metres, and went down a further 18 metres after 2000 BCE. During that period, the water-level sank no less than 43 metres.[50]

5.22 The Planisphere and shifting climatological borders

The diagrammatic image on sector 1 of the Planisphere seems to point to the Central Mountains of North Africa as the area that played a major role in the history of the ancestors of the Egyptians and the Sumerians. Do the Central Mountains of North Africa harbour the mysterious region known as the "lost paradise", from the era between approximately 8400 and 5300 BCE? The Egyptians called this "lost" paradise in the Central Mountains of North Africa a half-way house, a Wtst-Neter-place, on the way to what was later termed the "hinterland" of Egypt. The Sumerians spoke of a paradise that was under the authority of the constellation I-Iku (the Pegasus square), part of the constellation of Pisces.

They called themselves very appropriately "Black Heads", thereby typifying their racial origin. According to geneticists, this epithet might allow for the identification of the ultimate cradle of man, which, as followers of a specific theory stipulate, stems from the Bushmen, whereas a different theory considers him to originate from the Pygmies.[51] Could this explain the outspoken preference of Egyptian kings and royalty of the Mediaeval European courts for dwarfs and Pygmies? Various illustrations, such as the Narmer Palette, offer evidence in that direction.

Between 8400 and 5300 BCE, this region in the Central Mountains of North Africa fulfilled all the climatological, topographic and geographic conditions to serve as the centre of the subsequent "Big Bang" of civilisation that occurred after 5300 BCE. Prior to 5300 BCE, the 17° N. parallel formed an ecological barrier. This view is supported by fieldwork carried out by the French archaeologist Roset. His findings show that prehistoric man gradually moved northward because of climatological conditions. In ancient times, the ecological barrier consequently extended from Agadez in the Central Mountains of North Africa to Meru on the Red Sea.

At present, the 22° N. parallel counts as that boundary. This applies to the period after 4900 BCE, since the profound climatological regression that prevailed at that time shifted the ecological boundary to the 22° N. parallel. The gateway to Egypt also lay on this parallel, while the "Osiris meridian" of Egypt ended there, near the fortification of Buhen, built many millennia later.[52] Almost a thousand years after Buhen was built, Pharaoh Ramses II built Abu Simbel on this site, to commemorate the glorious period marking the birth of the State of Egypt.

In those times, the climate was clearly the ultimate, determining factor in the life of man. Data, gathered from paleo-climatological research gives the following overview:
- from 8500 BCE onward: the climatological conditions of the Sahara improved and lead to a period of "Great Humidity";
- from 6500 BCE onward: a climatological optimum, marked by "Great Humidity", prevailed on the entire subcontinent and stimulated the development of the Neolithicum; its dating varies per region. This period is characterised by a maximum expansion of extensive humid, tropical forests;
- from 5500 BCE onward: the start of a short period of aridity; middle Holocene, with irregular consequences, absent in certain regions, yet causing dehydration of Paleo-Lake Chad;
- from 4500 BCE onward: the start of a period of humidity that cannot be compared with the continuation of the period of "Great Humidity"; less intense. This enables cattle breeding;
- from 2500 BCE onward: aridity at the time of the post-Neolithicum.[53]

The data concerning paleo-vegetation of the northern part of Africa stem from **Quaternary Environments Network**, 1997, Jonathan Adams. This range of data, obtained through paleo-climatological research, shows that from 8500 until 5300 BCE, the principal climatological border coincided with the 17° N.

parallel, whereas from 4900 until 2500 BCE, it had settled on the 22° N. parallel.

The 17° N. parallel of Africa appears to have been an ethnical borderline, in contrast to a spreading opinion that this role was fulfilled by the 22° N. parallel, based amongst others on the findings of Wendorf near Nabta Playa.[54] However, data extracted from the diagrammatic image on sector 1 of the Planisphere and from the World Map of Eratosthenes clearly point to the 17° N. parallel as the former definitive borderline.

5.23 The Planisphere and the World Map of Eratosthenes

The information offered by the World Map of Eratosthenes is remarkable and fascinating. He used the western meridian through Carthage/Agadez on approximately 10° E. and the eastern meridian across the Elburz mountain range/Strait of Hormuz on approximately 52° E. The distance between the two meridians amounts to 42 degrees, a figure we have encountered in Egypt (Pyramid Field, assessors and nomes). The "Osiris meridian" (31° E.) ran in between and at an equal distance from these two meridians. At the same time, he used the parallel through Agadez/Meru on 17° N. and the parallel across Gibraltar/Malta/Rhodes/Elburz mountain range on 36° N., so that he based his map on the main meridians and parallels from very ancient times. He used these lines to construct a rectangular matrix (cf. fig. 42).

Apparently in imitation of Eratosthenes, Ptolemy no longer placed Egypt in the "Centre" of the world and shifted that dividing meridian to the highest peak of the Elburz mountain range, the Damavand-Qolleh-ye. This mountain marks the intersection of the 52° E. meridian with the 36° N. parallel and forms the northernmost and easternmost corner of the rectangle.

This astronomical data of the Planisphere can be used to place the stars that are listed on it, onto the matrix of the rectangle, according to the *"alignment system"*. These stars could be considered to form the meshes of the celestial network that is cast across the Earth. Ptolemy states "that stars which can be observed on every [vertical] line that is drawn from one zodiacal pole to the other through parts of the zodiac [12 constellations] are connected with a country. The star in question, or the part of the zodiac concerned [one of the twelve constellations], is then in alliance with that specific country." He called this simply *"the Alliance between the regions on Earth and the stars."*[55]

5.24 The Heavenly Network falls into place

The Planisphere was drawn up according to the *"alignment system"*, in which sectors 1 and 5, containing the names of stars that are found in opposite sectors of the zodiac, accordingly face each other from opposite sides. The stars concerned are epsilon Pegasus (7° Aquarius) on sector 1 and the star Regulus (5° Leo) on sector 5, in the zodiac, these stars are practically 180 degrees apart. Furthermore, sector 1 contains the star alpha Pegasus (29° Aquarius), while on sector 5 the star alpha Virginis (29° Virgo) is depicted immediately next to the star alpha Boötes (0° Libra) on sector 6. The stars alpha Virginis and alpha Boötes are both on the border of the zodiacal sign Virgo and in transition to the sign of Libra. On sector 6, which contains the name alpha Boötes, we also find the term Assur, which is the country Assyria (cf. appendix IX, table III by Koch). Hence, the region of Assyria was related to the constellation Virgo, a conclusion adopted by Ptolemy in his *"Alliance of the regions on earth."*[56] This means that the Planisphere is not merely an image of a hemisphere: Planisphere K 8538 is an image of a terrestrial *as well as* a celestial hemisphere.

The distance in degrees of longitude between the stars alpha Pegasus (Markab) of sector 1 and alpha Virginis (Spica) and alpha Boötes (Arcturus) of sectors 5 and 6 amounts to 210 degrees, since the stars are located on 0° Pisces and 30° Virgo respectively. The "centre" between 0° Pisces and 30° Virgo, lies at 15° Gemini and thus coincides with the zodiacal position of the star Alhena (which correlates with Memphis). This explains why Egypt supposedly lay in the "Centre of the World". The "Centre of the World" correlated with the "Osiris meridian". Ptolemy postulated in his overview that Assyria, Babylonia and Mesopotamia belonged to the sign of Virgo. Casperia, the country of the Medes (south of the Caspian Gulf), ranked under the sign of Libra, while Lower Egypt belonged to Gemini. In conclusion, Phazania, Nasamonitis and Garamantic (Fezzan and West Libya) came under the sign of Pisces[57] (cf. fig. 52, notably the signs of the zodiac).

The range of scale of the Planisphere can thus be determined: the difference in zodiacal length (positions) between the stars alpha Pegasus and alpha Virginis is 210 degrees. The length of the 17° N. parallel or 36° N. parallel (cf. fig.42) between the 10° E. meridian and the 52° E. meridian is 42 degrees, so that the geographic scale and the astronomical scale are in the proportion of 1:5 (42° : 210°).

5.25 The Planisphere and the Epic of Creation

At this point, the celestial network of stars, ranging from west to east, can be spread out across the Earth, enabling us to specify the alliance between the regions on Earth and those of heaven. Assuming each sign of the zodiac covered 6° of longitude, the meridian of 8°/10° E. correlated with the 0° of the sign Pisces, while the remaining geographic meridians correlated with respectively the sign of 0° Aries (16° E.), 0° Taurus (22° E.), 0° Gemini (28° E.), 0° Cancer (34° E.), 0° Leo (40° E.) and 0° Virgo (46° E.), terminating at 0° of Libra, with which the area near the meridian on 52° E. correlated.

On sector 1, the Planisphere also mentions the star epsilon Pegasus (Enif) as mul Anuni, while sector 6 shows the star alpha Librae, its Southern Scale, with respective positions of longitude at 7° of Aquarius and 21° of Libra. In that order, their pertaining geographic meridians are approximately 5° E. (near the former banks of Lake Triton (Tunisia) and the western foothills of the Hoggar mountain range) and 56° E. (near the foothills of the Elburz mountain range and the Strait of Hormuz, the estuary of the present Arabian Gulf) (cf. fig. 52).

Why should the Sumerians have paid so much attention to the part of the zodiac where I-Iku is located, as is clear from the fact that on New Year's Day, they performed certain rituals, which were related to I-Iku? The I-Iku, the Pegasus square, is a constellation that to Sumerians represented "Paradise" and the original "homeland" – at least that is how Ungnad interpreted it in his study **Das Wiedergefundene Paradies**.[58] This is most remarkable, especially because Sumeria resides under Virgo and *not* under Pisces, signs that are diametrically opposed.

The Sumerians were convinced that they came from the area that belonged to the sign of Pisces. According to the Planisphere, that area is to be found in the Central Mountains of North Africa. This is the region in Africa where the Sumerians had their roots. Later on, they called their original country the "APSU", their "lower world", where the *seven* gods-cum-judges of the netherworld, the Anunnaki, dwelt. As it is, the Central Mountains of North Africa are indeed located below Sumeria. The APSU dwelt under the signs of Pisces and Aquarius.[59]

Yet what do those *seven* dots along the "Way of Enlil" represent? Their explanation can be found on a tablet that deals with the Epic of Creation. This epic describes a battle between cosmic order and chaos. In Mesopotamia, this was solemnly enacted every year on the *fourth* day of the New Year festival.[60]

On tablet VI of the Akkadian Epic of Creation, the *Enuma elish*, mention is made of the Anunnaki, the *seven* gods-cum-judges of the netherworld. [61] Apparently, the Anun(nak)i are linked up with the star epsilon Pegasus, called "Mul Anuni" in Koch's table III. This would explain why the "Way of Enlil" with the seven dots running westward leads to the netherworld, the Apsu. This means that the depiction on sector 1 of the Planisphere is an image of the Akkadian Epic of Creation, *Enuma elish*.

In **Kingship and the Gods**, Professor Frankfort points out a remarkable fact: "The New Year's festival [in Mesopotamia] could be held in the autumn and also in the spring. We translate the Sumerian *zagmuk*, which means 'beginning of the year', and the Akkadian *akitu*, which has an uncertain meaning, as 'New Year's festival', because these feasts are essentially what the modern term indicates, [namely] festive celebrations of a new beginning in the annual cycle."[62] This could indicate that the Sumerians celebrated their New Year festival twice, just as the Egyptians did.

The fall of the Sumerian Kingdom meant a great loss of historically relevant material, so that data concerning their festivities is lacking. Consequently, sources of the Akkadian Kingdom are commonly used to clarify prevailing customs in the Mesopotamian culture. The rituals around the New Year festival in the Mesopotamian as well as in the Egyptian culture appear to have been typical for an atmosphere in which a fatal and dramatic event was commemorated. This is explained by the fact that in the Mesopotamian as well as in the Egyptian culture, special days were observed that preceded their New Year celebration. These were solemn days, days on which the people commemorated a natural catastrophe that had once occurred on Earth. The Egyptians called these days the "ill-fated days", with the exception of the *fourth* day. To them, the *fourth* day was the day of the "beautiful festival of heaven and earth".[63]

Its meaning is evident: instead of chaos, heaven and earth were in harmony and cosmic order prevailed.

On the corresponding *fourth* day of the New Year festival, the Akkadians recited the *Enuma elish*, the Epic of Creation. "The epic which deals with these events was therefore the most significant expression of the religious literature of Mesopotamia."[64] The sixth tablet of the Epic of Creation adds a few important elucidations, especially concerning the function of the Anunnaki (also called Igigi), and the role of the star Sirius as the Bowstar in the process of Creation (the Chinese also knew Sirius as Bowstar). The meaning of the "Triangle of the Deity" should also be borne in mind:[65] "The fifty great gods took their seats. The seven gods of destiny [seven Anunnaki, the dots along the Way of Enlil] set up the three hundred [in heaven]. Enlil raised the bow, his weapon, and laid (it) before them. The gods, his fathers, saw the net he had made. When they beheld the bow, how skilful its shape, his fathers praised the work he had wrought. Raising (it), Anu spoke up in the Assembly of the gods, as he kissed the bow: 'This is my daughter!' He named the names of the bow as follows: 'Longwood is the first, the second is Accurate; Its third name is Bowstar [Atum and Sirius], in heaven I have made it shine.' He determined a place with the gods, his brothers. After Anu had decreed the fate of the Bow, and had placed the exalted royal throne before the gods, Anu seated it in the Assembly of the gods."[66]

The star Sirius is Atum, who, as the First Deity and Creator, was included in the ranks of the gods by Anu. In another conversation between Atum and Osiris, Atum says: "I will destroy everything I created. The earth will once again become a primaeval ocean, like the waters in the beginning."[67]

5.26 The Geography of the Gods

In 1564, the Venetian mapmaker Jacopa Gastaldi based his large-scale map of Africa on maps made by Martin Waldseemüller and information from Arabian sources. In 1507, Waldseemüller had drawn up a map of the world that included details of the African coast which the Portuguese seafarers Diaz and Da Gama had provided. The map by Gastaldi consisted of eight loose folios, printed from copper plates. "Gastaldi calls this map, which modern geographers considered to be the most beautiful and most important map of the 16th century, a modern geographic map of Africa in its entirety. Gastaldi depicted the continent with a network of mountain ranges. He extracted the names of places, including some inland towns, from Portuguese and Arab sources."[68] The upper left corner of the second folio shows a lake, into which the river Niger is seen to flow. Immediately above, one reads "Regno de Agadez", and, somewhat higher to the right, it says "Deserto de Ighidi". This name is reminiscent of the Igigi and confirms the location of the territory of the Igigi (i.e. the Anunnaki), namely above and to the right of Agadez.

Research into the diagrammatic image of sector 1 of the Planisphere can rightfully be called an exploration of the geography of the gods. From the link between the geography of the stars and the Akkadian Epic of Creation, it was possible to rediscover the "lost" cradle. It enabled us to transform an abstract diagram into a graphic interpretation of the site where circa 8400 BCE, the "Primeval Era", Mankind began to explore the world. Yet, were the Central Mountains of North Africa really the setting where it all started? What do Egyptian and Sumerian sources tell us about the whereabouts of their roots and ancestors?

The Great Sphinx is a focal point of magical powers. With its red complexion and gracious features, it reveals its quality as a paragon of the secret wisdom with which the ancestors of Egyptians and Sumerians were endowed; ancestors who, in the case of the Egyptians, were to be found amongst the Followers of Horus, as well as amongst the Children of Seth. This image of eternity, "Horus of the Horizon", marks the 30° N. parallel that was named after them. The Sphinx symbolises the cosmic powers that were attributed to the constellations of Aquarius and Leo. The Planisphere points to the corresponding territory between the foothills of the Hoggar mountain range and the Straits of Hormuz as the cradle of both cultures.

The cosmic powers of the constellations of Taurus and Scorpio are manifest in the Pyramid Field and in the Nile basin. It is an expression of the astronomical iconography that is inherent in the words that Hermes Trismegistus spoke to Asclepius: *"Or are you ignorant, Asclepius, that Egypt is (the) image of heaven? If it is proper for us to speak the truth, our land is the temple of the world."* Hence, the creation of Rostau represents the cosmic power of these four zodiacal signs and thus guaranteed their stability, invincibility and perseverance.

The Sumerians boldly called their cradle the "lost" paradise, which we now know lies in the Central Mountains of North Africa. The Egyptians called that area a point of assembly, a halfway-house, a Wtst-Neter-place (The Sacred Domains), where the gods dwelt. They claimed to have come originally from an island that was surrounded by the sea, a magical place on the edge of the world. The search for their cradle has evidently not yet come to an end.

The resurrection of Osiris took place after 5300 BCE, yet Osiris' cradle lay somewhere else, amidst the waters: "The gods are said 'to give an island' to the justified Osiris and [an] Egyptian legend spoke of 'Middle Island', an unknown, distant locality that was reached by the boat of Anty, the ferryman..."[69] According to the Egyptians, Osiris was the ruler of Amenti, the West.[70] The matrix of the Planisphere, the Geography of the Gods, will enable us to retrace the lost location of the "Primeval Place" of Osiris in the Zep Tepi, the genuine "First Era" of Osiris.

Chapter 6

The Origins of the Followers of Horus

The barren, endless Sahara with its desolate emptiness and stirring silence has conquered what was once a paradise for man, flora and fauna. The desert extends from west to east and covers almost the entire African continent. It is interrupted by the Central Mountains of North Africa, consisting of the Hoggar, the Tassili n'Ajjer, the Adrar de Ifornas, the Air massif, the Tibesti and Ennedi mountains. Roughly speaking, these Central Mountains are located between 5° E. - 24° E. and between 17° N. - 28° N. Some of these mountain tops rise to more than three thousand metres.

These mountains are bordered by various sandseas, including the largest one on earth, the eastern Erg. The continuous wind erodes the mountains and keeps the sand in perpetual motion. Before the encroachment of the sand, lakes of water existed in this colossal area. They were fed by rivers that branched out in a network that now resembles a dried-up skeleton. 650 kilometres east from the Tibesti mountains, we find the Gilf Kébir plains and also, in the extreme south-west of Egypt, the Nabta Playa. At one time, these plains and the lake of Nabta Playa used to be staging posts between the Central Mountains of North Africa and the Nile valley. In the south, the Central Mountains bordered on the prehistoric Paleo-Lake Chad and in the south-west on the Hoggar mountains, from where the branches of rivers fed the river Niger. In the north, 650 kilometres from the Tassili n'Ajjer mountains, was the legendary Lake Triton, an inlet of the Mediterranean Sea. Only a few small salt marshes now remain of this once gigantic lake. Vast lakes probably also existed in various other places, for instance in the area around the present Murzuk Sandsea.

This enormous area was a breeding-ground for a budding civilisation. On the southside of the foothills of the Atlas mountains, near Lake Triton, was Gafsa, where an important cultural group (Capsien) developed between approximately 8400 and 5300 BCE, with a link to eastern Spain, of which firestone artifacts have also been found in the vicinity of Kom Ombo in Upper Egypt.

In the north-west, we find the Maghreb with the Atlas Mountains, covering parts of Morocco, Algeria and Tunisia. The Central Mountains of North Africa were opened up by the caravan routes. One of those routes ran from the centre of Egypt via the Siwa oasis to Sabha and Germa, the ancient capital of the Garamants. In Sabha, this route joined the caravan route that ran from Abrotonum, which was located in the north (Tripoli) and bordering on the Mediterranean Sea, to the south via Ghat, Djado and Bilma, ending up at Lake Chad. At a much later date, Phoenician Carthage also became connected with Ghat by a caravan route. At Bilma, a different route ran westward via Agadez and Gao to Timbuktu on the Niger. Agadez is a historical Tuareg town, capital of the Air, and it is claimed to have been founded in 1430 CE. These surroun-

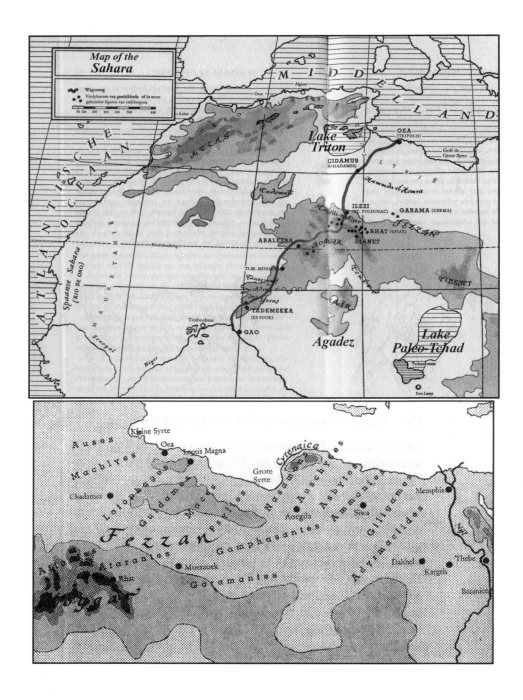

Fig. 53. Map of the Central Mountains of North Africa showing the Tibesti and the Paleo-Lake Chad, Ténéré, Air, Hoggar, Tassili-n'-Ajjer (Akakus) and Lake Triton in the north.

Fig. 53a. This figure shows the names of the tribes inhabiting this area according to Herodotus.

dings have been known for many centuries as a "gathering-place for travellers", from which the name Agadez is derived. From Agadez, a caravan route runs further south.

The earliest source mentioning the tribes that once populated North Africa is Herodotus. His inventory of these tribes dates from approximately 450 BCE and was illustrated in detail on a map, allowing an immediate and clear overview.[1] Whether all these tribes dwelt here from times immemorial is entirely unknown (cf. fig. 53 and 53a).

6.1 A Paradise of Lakes, Rivers, Flora and Fauna

Between 18,000 and 11,000 BCE,[2] the Sahara experienced an extremely dry period. These extreme meteorological conditions are comparable to the climate that has prevailed since 2500 BCE, which resulted in the enormous deserts we see today. Around 9000 BCE, the Sahara began to experience a humid period. After detailed climatological research by Dansgaard et al, "the transition from the Pleistocene to the Holocene was highly accurately determined to have occurred in 8770 BCE (+/- 150 years). This dating has also been acknowledged as the end of the last Glacial Period."[3]

Therefore, before 9000 BCE, living conditions in this region were difficult. However, during the humid period between 9000 and 5300 BCE, an ideal climate developed that could be called subtropical. Because of the weather conditions during that period, there were hardly any signs of a desert.[4] Around 5300 BCE, the climate in the Central Mountains of North Africa differed considerably from present circumstances, with annual inundations occurring in the region.

The Central Mountains of North Africa were surrounded by a conglomeration of lakes, big rivers and marshes where Atlas cedars, wild fig trees, ash trees, lime trees and willows grew. On the banks, roses and papyrus flourished. The waters were the habitat of crocodiles, hippopotami and tortoises. Elephants, rhinoceros, buffalo, wild oxen and great antelopes found a favourable habitat within this paradisiacal area. In this region, a Palaeolithic "industry" developed over a period of about a million years. Developments around 25,000 BCE prove that the inhabitants subsequently moved in a northerly direction towards Djado, de Ténéré, and Bilma and to the eastern valley of the Air Mountains, down to Agadez.[5] After 8500 BCE, the Central Mountains of North Africa also became populated. The eastern foothills of the Air, including the Bagzane mountain, down to the plains of Adrar Bous, harbour rich archaeological material. A few decades ago, ancient pottery was found in that area by the French archaeologist J.P.Roset. In the meantime, we may presume that the region around the Paleo-Lake Chad, including such as the Ténéré, was once one of the centres of the form of civilisation that unfolded much later and stretched from the Paleo-Lake Chad via Agadez to Ghat, Djanet near the settlements of Sefar and Ti-n-Tazarift, and in particular the Akakus, the eastern foothill of the Tassili n'Ajjer mountains and to Lake Triton (cf. fig. 53).

6.2 The Discovery of Very Ancient Pottery

Roset's spectacular discovery of pottery in the Air Mountains, north of Agadez, was announced thus: "To the utter amazement of a certain number of members of the *Académie des Inscriptions et des Belles Lettres* in Paris, an announcement was made on October 15th 1982, which proved highly unusual and contained revolutionary conclusions. Jean-Pierre Roset, a young archaeologist from l'ORSTOM who had been investigating the north-east of the Republic of Niger for ten years, spoke neither of inscriptions nor of philology. In sober words, he spoke about the circumstances surrounding an extraordinary discovery, which he made in December 1978 in the town of Tagalagal, where he found pottery that dated back 10,000 years. This site is located in the mountains of Bagzanes, in the north-eastern part of the Air Massif [approximately 90 kilometres north-east of Agadez]. Roset addressed an audience who were very convinced of the priority [the precedence in time] during the transition to the Neolithic of all aspects concerning the Near East - such as the choice of a fixed dwelling-place, stock breeding, agriculture etc, and also pottery - so that he used moderate terms to 'explain the existence of a centre in the Sahara, where a method had been invented to fabricate pottery that might be even older than the centre of the Near East'." [6]

The discovery and the subsequent investigation of Tagalagal in 1978 occurred under extremely difficult circumstances. The site is located in the open air, at a height of approximately 1,850 metres. It covers an area of roughly 20 by 40 metres, in the vicinity of an enormous rock in the shape of a cinnamon loaf, and is surrounded by large fragments of granite. The site can only be entered with considerable difficulty and the journey requires various hours on the back of a camel before one reaches the plateau. It took two days to get to the rock of Tagalagal; this was followed by two hours of climbing with a load that consisted of research material and camping utensils. But once on site, the archaeologist discovered objects that made him forget all prior exertion. The ground was covered with potsherds, broken as well as undamaged millstones and various stone tools. Moreover – and this was the substantial trump card that underpinned the reliability of the dating - the area included a kind of shelter in the southern part, underneath an overhanging rock with an old garbage dump that erosion had not touched. Nevertheless, there was no water. After he had taken an immediate sondage, Roset was forced to return to Tagalagal to clear the shelter and to make systematic collections from this open-air site in the three following years (1983).

In 1982, these investigations produced three essential results: two Carbon 14 datings, calculated in 1979 and 1980 in the Laboratory for Hydrology and isotopic Geochemistry in Orsay, under the supervision of Jean-Charles Fontes, indicated an age of 9,300 years. This result was linked with two datings, namely one of 9,200 years, which had been published in 1976 by J.P.Maître, concerning the place where pottery had been found near Tiltekin (the site of Launay) in the Hoggar Massif, and with another, of 9,000 years, which was mentioned by Barbara Barich, pertaining to the oldest pottery of Ti-n-Torha in the Akakus in Libya.

The datings of the Tagalagal allowed Roset to determine that "tribes, which had inhabited certain mountainous regions of the central and southern part of the Sahara, produced pottery in the second half of the tenth millennium before our time". Quite often, the potsherds were large enough to reconstruct the shape of the vases. Those from Tagalagal show an amazing diversity in the decorations, which are in the shape of furrows, either straight or circular, made by means of a comb-like object. Such technical skills would point to an even older form of "industry", which is more likely to date back to the beginning rather than to the end of the 10th millennium BCE.

A third characteristic feature of the site is the abundance of ground material, possibly corn. Certain authors have suggested that the necessity to increase the digestibility of corn by boiling it to porridge or soup could have triggered off the invention of the terracotta dish. Alternatively, a utensil made to contain water has always fulfilled an even greater functional need in the African countryside.

6.3 The Star Constellation Nekhet and a Prehistoric Rock Painting

The famous professor of Egyptology Sir William Matthew Flinders Petrie (1853-1942) gained an interest in archaeology at an early age. He became obsessed by the pyramids and was the first to draw up precise surveys of the Giza pyramids. In 1892, he became the first Edwards professor in Egyptology at London University. Two years later, he excavated the pre-dynastic tombs of Naqada and Diospolis Parva. He worked fanatically to trace the origin of pharaonic Egypt, which he was convinced was linked with pre-dynastic cultures. His views still colour the descriptions of the earliest phase of Egyptian civilisation.

In his yearning to find the roots of pharaonic Egypt, he advanced the theory that the eastern region of Naqada, in particular the Wadi Hammamat near Thebes between the Nile and the Red Sea, provided the breeding ground for dynastic Egypt. He believed that people had sailed from the Gulf of Arabia via the Red Sea and the Wadi Hammamat and had entered Egypt. Furthermore, he presumed that they had originally come from Elam. His theory was partially based on the depiction on the handle of the "Gebel el Arak" knife. Petrie was even convinced that the Sumerians and the Egyptians had a common origin, an idea that has frequently been discussed, and still is. Recent findings of specific Sumerian objects, such as the "Grubenkopfnagel" in Buto, have recently contributed to this issue. Despite his eastward focus, he unwittingly provided evidence that one tribe of the Egyptians, the Followers of Horus, had its origin in the west.

Petrie, an extraordinarily gifted man, made a reconstruction of the star constellations in the northern hemisphere, based on the Ramessidian Starclock, which dates back to approximately 1190 BCE. Around 1940, Flinders Petrie concluded that during the period from the first to the sixth hour of the night, a number of stars make up the giant star constellation of *Nekhet*. According to the **Lexicon der Ägyptologie**, Nekhet signifies "threatening with the arm, strong arm, invincible and courageous".[7] The image of Nekhet by Flinders Petrie is shown in figure 54.[8] It was taken from Clagett's **Ancient Egyptian**

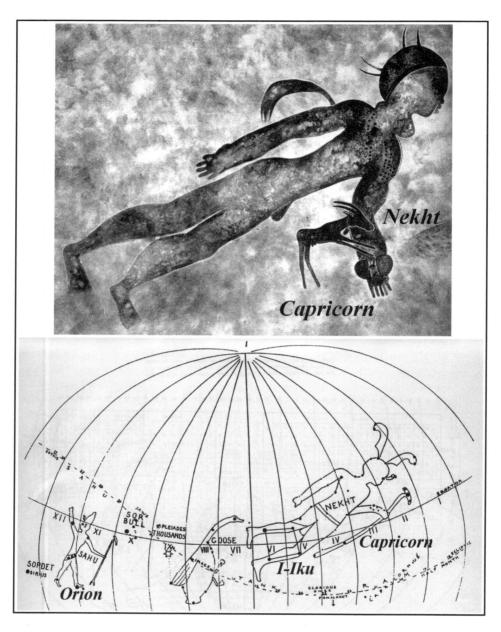

Fig. 54. Prehistoric rock painting called "The Swimmer" by its discoverer Lhote. Compare the figure with the one of the Egyptian Starclock. The image of "The Swimmer" is based on the star constellations of Pisces, Aquarius and Capricorn. On the rock painting, we see a stone that is attached to the wrist of the left arm (pointing to the strong arm = Nht); at a later date, a capricorn (alluding to the constellation Capricorn) was superimposed. The figure Nht on the Star Clock has a staff (Jacob's staff, §4.19) in his left hand, which signifies eminence and/or leadership. This man probably belonged to the tribe of the Nekht-Iberians, who also inhabited the surroundings of modern Marrakesh in Morocco, and were called Nectiberes by Ptolemy.

Science (Vol. II). The image of Nekhet is composed of star constellations within the Pegasus square and of stars in the constellation Aquarius, e.g. Enif and Sadalsuud.

These constellations were present in our study of the Planisphere. Furthermore, the Nekhet figure consists of stars of the Dolphin (Delphinus delphis) and the constellation of Capricorn, such as the star Altair (cf. fig. 54). In Antiquity, this part of the firmament was called "the water and the sea", as Hinckley Allen mentions in his introduction to the sign of Aquarius. "Capricornus, Cetus, Delphinus, Eridanus, Hydra, Pisces and Pisces Australis, all the watery shapes in the early heavens, with Argo and Crater, are to be found in this neighbourhood; as to some of those stars, Aratos said 'that these are called the Water'; indeed, in Euphratean astronomy this region of the sky was 'the Sea', and was thought to be under the control of Aquarius."[9]

6.4 Lhote's Discovery of the Prehistoric Rock Painting, called Nekhet

In the Central Mountains of North Africa, between Djanet and Ghat on the east side of the Tassili n'Ajjer, a conglomeration of prehistoric settlements remain. This centre is known for its magnificent rock paintings, such as the "Great God of Sefar" and "the Swimmer" of Ti-n-Tazarift (cf. fig. 54). Ti-n-Tazarift is located in the surroundings of the caravan route from Djanet to Ghat in the Tassili n'Ajjer, on approximately 24°40' N and 09°30' E.

It was the famous French archaeologist and ethnologist Henri Lhote who discovered "the Swimmer" during an expedition in the 1950s. He gave it that name due to the floating, slanting position of the figure on the face of the rock. Lhote described Ti-n-Tazarift as a "prehistoric town that extends in both directions for about two kilometres". This is also true for Sefar.[10]

The depiction of "the Swimmer" dates back to the prime time of the so-called Round Head Period. Lhote has the following to say about his discovery: "These two figures with round heads were discovered within the cavity of an overhanging rock. The 'swimming' figure, pictured on the left in the original, seems to be moving about in the water. His Negroid profile is roughly outlined, which is quite rare in the case of Round Head figures. The headdress consists of four tapered horns. There are some remarkable stippled tattoo marks on the left shoulder and the breast. The ornament on the right arm looks like a feather... Both figures are coloured bright yellow, with white borders. They belong to the prime time of the *Round Head Period* [approximately 6500-6000 BCE]. The small antelope, drawn across the arm of the 'swimmer', dates from a later period."[11]

An exact comparison of the rock painting of "the Swimmer" in Ti-n-Tazarift with the image of Nekhet on the Ramessidian Starclock shows two almost identical figures. The painting of "the Swimmer", i.e. the star constellation Nekhet, was carried out by Round Head people more than 8,000 years ago. This figure is practically identical to the image of Nekhet, which Flinders Petrie reconstructed on the basis of the Ramessidian Starclock from approximately 1190 BCE. Hence, Lhote unwittingly yet very discerningly specified the *"watery"* quality of the aforementioned area in the sky when he named this figure "the Swimmer".

The figure shows a stone attached to the wrist of the left arm, which points to the ancient Egyptian notion of "strong arm" (cf. hieroglyph D40, **Egyptian Grammar**, is Nht = "strong") and invincibility, a notion that the reader will recall from the Pyramid Field and the Horus pose. At the same time, this rock painting shows convincingly that man's awareness of star constellations was thousands of years older than science had, until now, assumed it to be. This prehistoric image of a section of the stellar firmament is unique. According to the present scientific status quo, familiarity of this kind with star constellations was non-existent before 419 BCE and even then, could only be attributed to the Babylonians.[12]

The fact that Nekhet is rendered in a "swimming" position shows that prehistoric man had actually already built himself an image of the star-spangled firmament, a star map that remained unchanged in ancient Egypt for at least 5,000 years. Yet above all, this heritage proves that part of the ancestors of the Egyptians originated in the Central Mountains of North Africa.

6.5 The Pegasus Square and the Tablet of Pharaoh Djer

The Pegasus square, I-Iku, is indeed rendered as an actual square (cf. fig. 51). To the Sumerians, it represented a standard field measure. This standard field amounted to "approximately 3,600 square metres".[13] They divided this up into *nine* equal parts. The Egyptians recognised *nine* gods, as is apparent from the original *Ennead* of Heliopolis: Shu, Tefnut, Geb, Nut, Osiris, Horus, Seth, Isis and Nephtys, with Atum as the supreme creator.

The museum of the University of Pennsylvania possesses a tablet from the reign of Pharaoh Djer of the First Dynasty (cf. fig. 55). On the left, the tablet shows the Serekh, the "coat of arms" of Pharaoh Djer, surmounted by the Horus falcon. Below the Serekh, we see the hieroglyph for "strong arm" (Nht), signifying invincibility and victory, followed underneath by a square subdivided into *nine* sections. The hieroglyph at the bottom is the sign for "village, location or region". The square with the *nine* sections stands for the Pegasus square and the *nine* gods, the Neters, who will grant invincibility to Pharaoh Djer and for the I-Iku of the Sumerians. No square that is subdivided into *nine* sections is known to exist in the Egyptian hieroglyphic script. Therefore, this exceptional hieroglyph points to familiarity with the I-Iku of the Sumerians and the *nine* gods, the Neters. In addition, the tablet may well contain a reference to the dwelling-place of the gods in the Central Mountains of North Africa, the Wetjeset-Neter place. Did Pharaoh Djer originate from that area? Perhaps, but we also need to note that prehistoric man believed that the gods dwelt up on the mountains.

6.6 A Prototype of Orion?

Could the rock engraving of a theranthrope (half human, half animal, with the head of a hyena - Lycaon pictus) from Ti-n-Sharuma in the Messak Plateau, located between Ghat and the Murzuk Sandsea, dating back to 4500 BCE, possibly be a prototype of the iconographic image of Orion?[14] Was this gigantic

Fig. 55. Tablet of Pharaoh Djer (Museum of the University of Pennsylvania) showing the Serekh surmounted by the Horus falcon; underneath, in that order, we see the strong arm (= Nht), the square with nine sections (I-Iku), and the hieroglyph for "region". A bludgeon or staff is shown in the centre; the goddess Sekhet-Hor is pictured on the right, above a set of plants.

figure possibly meant to depict a ritual posture of the "Giant", a name often used to indicate Orion? Orion was also named Hunter and Warrior, a typical god for prehistoric man.[15] The bearing of the theranthrope does indeed show similarities with the iconographic image of Orion (cf. fig. 56). The rock painting of Nekhet from the Tassili (6500 BCE) and the rock engraving of the theranthrope from the Messak (4500 BCE) are prototypes of the characteristic posture of Horus, i.e. invincibility and power.

6.7 The Goddess Neith and Lake Triton

The goddess Neith is one of the most ancient goddesses of Egypt, appearing in the Egyptian predynastic and the early dynastic period. She is the goddess of the primal beginning and the tutelary deity of soldiers and the army. She was the goddess of the town of Sais that, at the beginning of the third millennium, served as one of the capitals of the Old Kingdom. At that time, Sais lay at the end of the observation track of the star Sirius, with Edfu marking the beginning. This explains why the great annual festival in honour of Isis-Neith was held in Sais.

During the 26th Dynasty (after 666 BCE), Neith was "reborn". The Egyptians recognised a period of 3,000 years that must pass before a person or god was born again.[16] In due course, this also happened to the goddess Neith and this recurring notion also caused Sais to regain its importance. Pharaoh Psametik I initiated this revival and founded the residence of this dynasty in Sais, which is why it is also called the Saite Dynasty. Edfu also regained its previous importance during this period. It was probably due to the pressure caused by Egypt's numerous hostile occupations from 525 to 332 BCE, that the notion of "rebirth" only slowly and sparsely gained recognition. It received a new impulse during the Ptolemaic period after 300 BCE, when work began on the famous Temple of Horus in Edfu. This was mainly dedicated to the ancestors of the Egyptians, the Shemsu Hor, the Followers of Horus.

Various important figures from a distant past re-entered the scene during the Ptolemaic period, such as Pharaoh Djoser and his Famine Stele, and Imhotep, his vizier and the architect of the Pyramid Field. Neith was not only linked to the Egyptian town of Sais, she had an initial bond with Lake Triton, as she originated from an island in this lake.[17] She was the goddess of the "far west" and the Three-fold Goddess of Libya. Robert Graves, in **Greek Myths**, mentions how the Pelagians, ancestors of the Greeks, report that the goddess Athena, tutelary goddess of the town of Athens, was born in Libya, on the borders of Lake Triton. Plato identified Athena with the Libyan goddess Neith.[18] She was also the forerunner of the Roman Minerva. Neith wore the crown of Lower Egypt at all times. This is clearly expressed in Utterances 220 and 221, part of the ritual accorded to the crown of Lower Egypt, Pyramid Texts §194-198: "O Neith-crown, Neith was the queen of the gods and actually stood at the head of the Followers of Horus".[19]

North of Lake Triton, the Capsien culture, known for its snail farms, developed around the modern Gafsa in Tunisia, from approximately 8400 BCE onward. They are said to be the authors of the engraved images and rock paintings in the Atlas Mountains of the Sahara Desert and differed greatly from the Iberomaurusians and African Cro-Magnon. These images definitely date back to the same period as that of the "ancient buffalo", the bubalu, which died out long before 5300 BCE. We might ponder whether the ability to produce these images and paintings, and their habit of eating snails could point to their possible origin: the Dordogne (the Perigordinian-Aurignacian period of 30,000-12,000 BCE) in France. Engravings discovered in the Atlas Mountains show a ram adorned with a decorated headdress and are characteristic and exclusive to this culture. It is believed that this headdress represented a "sun-disc".

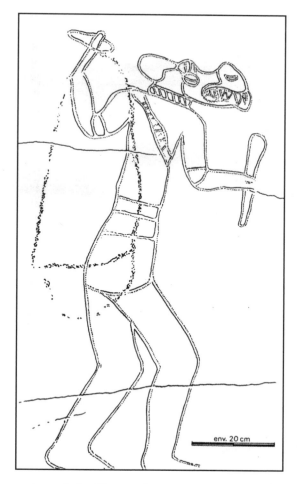

Fig. 56. Rock engraving of the Theranthrope. A prototype of the ritual Horus posture?

In graves of the oldest settlements at El Badari in Egypt, people were buried wrapped in goatskins.[20] In **Predynastic Egypt**, Adams describes this form of burial from the El Badari period: "During the Badarian period, graves were oval or circular and the bodies were often wrapped in goatskins or mats."[21] This form of interment was a ritual gesture to favour the goddess Neith. Goat-skins were also worn by Libyan (North African) women, who covered their clothing with bare goatskins, adorned with fringe, and dyed red by madder. These aprons, called "aigis", were also called Amalthea, after the goat that once fed Zeus.[22] The "aegis" was originally a protective goatskin shield carried both by Zeus and Athena.

It appears that the Egyptians, Greeks and Romans jointly worshipped the same goddess that inhabited an island in Lake Triton. The names of this goddess were respectively Neith, Pallas Athena and Minerva and she was identified with the primeval ocean.[23] According to a Ptolemaic text, she was "Mistress of the Sea"[24] and also the goddess of the "Great Flood", which refers to the catastrophe known as Irra or Era. The Great Flood is also mentioned repeatedly in the Pyramid Texts.[25] In §507-510, Neith is explicitly connected with this catastrophe, the "Great Inundation". She is the cow goddess who once again rises from the floods and who had merged with Mht-wrt during the Old Kingdom.[26] Mht-wrt (pronounced Mehetweret) was depicted in the shape of a cow that raises itself out of the waters.

As the beginning of the annual flooding of the Nile coincided with the heliacal rising of the star Sirius (the New Year celebration), this combined event reminded the Egyptians of the "great Flooding" from a distant past. That is why this cow goddess bore a conspicuous yet understandable epithet, "Cow that bore life unto the Sun".[27] Hence, the celebration of New Year had always marked a new beginning. Neith, goddess of the west and especially of the former Lake Triton was therefore of great importance and does indeed date back to times immemorial. She was seen by Egyptians as the culmination of "That which is"; she was eternal and personified the creative power of heavens, earth, the netherworld and of all creatures, and was also considered the prototype of virginal procreation.[28] Neith was the goddess of the beginning and the end, of life and death. An ancient Egyptian image shows how the sun and its moment of setting are worshipped on behalf of the Souls of Pe (Buto) and Nekhen (Hieraconpolis), the baboons and the dead. "Apart from the rising and setting of the sun, the image also shows [...] the falcon with the sun disk, which, though representing the sun-god as 'Horus of the Horizon', at the same time forms with his support the hieroglyph for West. The Goddess of the West [Neith] offering water with her hands, is also depicted."[29] The offering of water is the symbol of the constellation of Aquarius.

6.8 The Mythical Religion and Lake Triton

According to the high priests of the Dogon tribe in Mali, the gods descended to the north-east of their territory. The present-day members of the Dogon tribe claim that this landing took place in Lake Debo.[30] The Dogon called their gods the Nommos (cf. fig. 57) DA, "the masters of the water", who had landed in an Ark. It is possible that the high priests of the Dogon meant that the gods had descended in Lake Triton, instead of in Lake Debo. Lake Triton is indeed located to the north-east of Mali in Tunisia.

According to the Sumerians, their gods were half-human and half-fish, who were also called "Tritons".[31] The Dogon tribe have images of the Nommos, which they render as a Silurian fish, slightly resembling the European catfish. We also encounter the Silurian fish on the Serekh of Pharaoh Narmer (Nar-fish) of Egypt's First Dynasty (cf. fig. 57). Both the Egyptians and the Sumerians used this image as a hieroglyph. The Sumerians and the Akkadians - though somewhat later - were familiar with the same image of this fish that the Dogon tribe is still acquainted with, for instance on the collar of the silver vase of the priest-king Entemena of Lagash, approximately 2500 BCE (ligature of the signs Gir-su; however, according to the prevailing opinion amongst Assyriologists, this is a case of phonetics, see fig. 57).

Fig. 57. Four comparable stylistic images of a fish (Silurian fish as a European catfish?). From left to right: the Gir-su on the collar of the silver vase of the priest-king Entemena of Lagash, the Sumerian specimen (a god with large eyes) and the Egyptian Nar-fish (Palette of pharaoh Narmer). Below: the Nommo of the Dogon.

The Sumerians, the Dogon, and also the Phoenicians - the latter at a much later stage - recognised a deity that was half-human and half-fish. They named him respectively Oannes, Nommo and Dagan, while the Greeks called him Triton, a name which is derived etymologically from Lake Triton, the place where these mythical Fish-people (I-Iku-square = Pegasus) originally appeared on Earth. The assumption that the origin of this mythical religion is to be found in this region is substantiated by Lhote's archaeological work in Sefar, located in the eastern foothills of the Tassili n'Ajjer. In this prehistoric settlement, Lhote identified "lanes", "streets" and "squares" which he then gave names.

He derived these names from the depictions that were found in that specific location and from people who had witnessed how the frescoes had been discovered. Thus, Lhote named an open space the "square of the Fish-God",[32] a Fish-God who is at the same time identical with the fishtailed amphibious god Dagon, or the Dagan of the Phoenicians; "Dagon, the god of wheat, whose origin is very remote"[33] and who is identical with the Nommo of the Dogon. The ***"Statenbijbel"*** (the version of the Bible that is authenticated by the Dutch Reformed Church) states: "A Philistine (Phoenician) idol, bearing this name because he resembled a fish with his lower part and a human being with his upper."[34] This Fish-God is identical with the Nommos of the Dogon and the

Sumerian Oannes, who in turn is identical with the Fish-God Triton, who is claimed to have given birth to civilisation. It is quite evident that there is a religious component to some of these rock paintings.

6.9 Catastrophes hit Lake Triton

Lake Triton (cf. fig. 53) was once an enormous inlet or inland sea with a surface area of approximately 90,000 square kilometres. It was devastated by a catastrophe around 2520 BCE. This was accompanied by violent earthquakes, causing the lake to drain into the Mediterranean Sea. The Greek historian Diodorus Siculus (1st century BCE) stated in Book 3.55: "And it is said that due to the earthquakes, those parts of Libya that lay between the [Atlantic] Ocean and Lake Triton were flooded, causing [most of] the lake to disappear."

According to the Roman poet Ovid (43 BCE), the position of Earth in the solar system was altered. He reported that the Earth subsided, causing the climate to change. Following this catastrophic change of the Earth's orbit, the geography and the climate was drastically altered at these latitudes, with the remains of Lake Triton gradually decreasing in size. Its dimensions were still considerable in classical antiquity. In his time, the Greek geographer Skylax estimated its size to be around 2,000 square kilometres. At present, no more than a few saltmarshes remain, e.g. the Chott el Jerid and Chott Melrhir. The presence of cliffs at the former mouth of the River Triton makes the Gulf of Gabès on the Tunisian east coast still extremely dangerous and embraced, as it were, by two peninsulae. The northern one bears the name "Kerkenah", while the southern one is called "Jerba", after the goddess Ker.

The geographic appearance of this region had already undergone a drastic change around 5500 BCE, after the natural land connection between the continents of Africa and Europe had disappeared. Prior to this date, the Mediterranean Sea consisted of two inland seas. The remains of that overland connection still exist in the shape of three islands: Pantelleria, Gozo and Malta. In the early 20th century, Gozo harboured a small colony of original pharaonic dogs, living in isolation. This is most remarkable, because this peculiar type of dog (Anubis) should be considered a living fossil.[35]

To the south-west of Gozo, we find the Pelagian Islands Lampedusa, Lampione and Linosa. Etymologically, the name of these islands contains the name of the ancestors of the Greeks: the Pelagians, who were known as a "primitive man or seafarers".[36] After the land bridge submerged, the remaining Pelagians moved to the islands of Crete, Rhodes and Ionia. After the catastrophe of circa 2520 BCE, they returned to Libya where they, as a tribe, were given the name Garamantes, which is derived from the name of the goddess Ker (Gar), who in turn points to Crete and Caria. According to Pausanius, these Pelagians were the first human beings[37] and lived to the north-east of what was once Lake Triton. At the same time, a possible link may exist between the name Pelagians and Pallas (Pelas), and therefore also with the goddess Neith. These same Pelagians, described as unsurpassed "seafarers", were the same people who would later be known by the Egyptians as the Keftiu, outstanding sailors, extremely well versed in building boats and in navigation.

An additional similarity can be found between the ancestors of the Egyptians and the Pelagians, namely the bee culture, which existed around Lake Triton and subsequently on the island of Crete. On the Minoan island of Crete, professional bee-keepers had a bee-glove as their trademark. The Greek word for bee-bread, kerinthos, is Cretan. This bee-culture is related to the goddess Kar, Ker and similarly sounding names. Over time, Ker generally acquired the meaning of "fate" or "destiny".[38]

Strangely enough, the Pharaohs from the First Dynasty onward bore a nesubit-name (insibya), which in their pictographic script is rendered by a hieroglyph in the shape of a bee (hieroglyph L2, *Egyptian Grammar*). In Lower Egypt, the pharaohs possessed the title "biti"-man, i.e. "man of the bee"; the town of Sais (Neith) possessed a "House of the Bee".[39] Egyptologists have been unable to offer a unanimous explanation for this "third" title of the pharaoh. Various experts believe that the pharaoh did not acquire this "third" title or name until after his death. This theory may be correct, as death is our natural "destiny". In that case, this hieroglyph would point to Lake Triton, the place in the "far west", a region which the Egyptians linked with the netherworld.

In ancient cultures, "life" itself was also related to that Lake Triton, and therefore with Neith. Later on, she became the ruler over Sais, where the "House of the Bee" stood.[40] Neith, the bearer of the crown of Lower Egypt, is known as a guide and a leader. She headed the Followers of Horus, whose standard bore the Horus falcon.

6.10 The Horus Falcon and the West

Do ancient Egyptian sources offer any clear indications that their people actually originated from the West? The answer is that they do, but not to the same astonishing extent as the Sumerians. Nevertheless, the Followers of Horus, the original primeval tribe known as the Shemsu Hor, were known by a characteristic symbol: the Horus falcon (Survey hieroglyphs, R13, *Egyptian Grammar*). Before the catastrophe of 2520 BCE, that ancient Egyptian symbol stood for the West.[41] After 2000 BCE, the Egyptians determined a new symbol for the west. By their standards, such a change was quite radical as their attitude to life was highly traditional.

For the Egyptians, the west lay to their right, and in their depictions of a human being, the right side of the body is emphasised. This means that they faced south. To the Egyptians, the Horus falcon represented the prime principle of this specific quarter of the compass, the direction where they came from and where they would return to after death. It was the Egyptologist Sethe who discovered that the symbol of the Horus falcon incorporated the primeval emblem of the Egyptians. The Horus falcon encompassed and represented the prehistoric notion of the entire Horus culture.[42] It is clear that one tribe of the Egyptian ancestors, i.e. the Followers of Horus, exchanged the Lake Triton area and the Central Mountains of North Africa for Egypt's Delta. This move occurred in approximately 5300 BCE and was the result of a climatological catastrophe.

6.11 Triton, the Son of Delphinus delphis

When Sirius rises on the eastern horizon, the group of stars that form Delphinus delphis sets on the western horizon. This group of stars, which can be found exactly opposite Sirius at 19°30' of the constellation Sagittarius, was known as Amphitrite, the goddess of the sea, and also the mother of Triton. The dolphin persuaded her to become the wife of Neptune, and as recompense, as the Roman poet Manilius (author of the **Astronomica**) states, she "rose up from out of the Seas [...] to become the glory of the Flood and the stars". Neptune and Amphitrite begot a son with the tail of a fish, who bore the name Triton.[43] The star chart compiled by Sydow shows the constellation Delphinus delphis in the northern heavens as a human embryo with the tail of a fish.[44]

Probably, Amphitrite (the pre-Grecian goddess of the sea)[45] was the forerunner of the subsequent goddess Pallas Athena, just as Neith was a forerunner of Pallas Athena. Hence, Amphitrite or Neith was not only the goddess of Lake Triton and "Mistress [Lady] of the Sea"; after her marriage to Neptune, she also ruled over the Atlantic Ocean and the Mediterranean Sea, which is in complete agreement with a Ptolemaic text in which Neith is called the "Goddess of the Sea".[46] Tritons were also depicted on tombstones as escorts of the dead on their way to the islands of the blessed.[47]

It is more than obvious that the very ancient religion of those tribes that introduced civilisation leads us to Lake Triton, west of Egypt. The Egyptians worshipped their goddess Neith who emerged from out of Lake Triton, while in the Sumerian culture, the Triton was a half-human and half-fish being, to whom they attributed the origin of their civilisation. The Greeks and Romans had their Pallas Athena and Minerva. To the Dogon, the Nommos were gods in the shape of the Silurian fish. The Phoenicians had their Dagan who was depicted in the shape of a being that was half-human, half-fish, in other words: the Triton of the Sumerians.

6.12 Neith and Anubis

Neith is linked with the constellation Aquarius, but she also possessed the same epithet as Anubis, the "Opener of the Way", whose banner with the jackal or dog's head accompanied her at all times (cf. fig. 58).[48]

Anubis is pictured as a dog of a breed that closely resembles that of the wild dog, wolfhound and jackal. Its insignia are the club, the bow and the boomerang. Neith's crossed pieces of weaponry and the weapons of Anubis show that both fulfilled a protective function. Apart from that, their alert and keen demeanour guaranteed their effectiveness as guardians. Anubis was also the keeper at the gate that gave entrance to Osiris' realm of the dead, typified by the recumbent posture of Anubis.

The Anubis-cult can be identified from the very beginning of the First Dynasty in Abydos in the shape of the recumbent black dog Chontamenti or Khentiamentiu, who alludes unmistakably to the characteristics of "warden or guardian of the dead" (cf. fig. 58). Epitaphs show that from the Sixth Dynasty onward, its identity became merged with Osiris in Abydos and thus changed into Osiris-Khentiamentiu.[49]

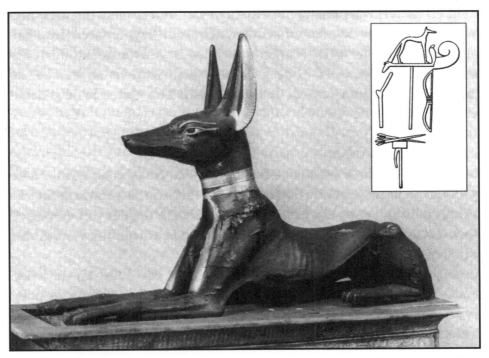

Fig. 58. A recumbent Anubis as the keeper; the inset shows him in a standing position together with a boomerang and an arrow, above the crossed pieces of weaponry of the goddess Neith.

Khentiamentiu was known as the "Sheepdog of the westerners".[50] What does this intriguing utterance conceal? The plaque of Denderah already proved its good services in the search for the true identity of Osiris and it does so once again in our research on Anubis. Anubis is pictured at the edge of the plaque as a cynocephales, a human being with the head of a dog. Next to Anubis, a goat is depicted, bearing a "sun-disk" between its horns. Both belong to the constellation of Aquarius. Before Aquarius lies the Goat-Fish, the constellation Capricorn (cf. fig. 6).

A search through **Star Names** for references on the constellation Aquarius produced another surprising discovery, which explained the as yet unknown identity of the giant Chumbaba (Humbaba), an important character in the **Gilgamesh Epic**. Consequently, this would pinpoint definitively the location of the "Westland", where Gilgamesh journeyed to.

The constellation Nekhet contains the star Sadalsuud, from the constellation Aquarius, known in Coptic by the name of Upuineuti.[51] Various words in various languages are in circulation to label Anubis, the Egyptian god Inpw, or the wolf-god Upuat. In German, the word Upuat is used, in English it is Upwuat and Wepwawet. Sadalsuud marks the beginning of the sign of Aquarius, when the entire zodiac is divided into twelve equal parts each containing 30 degrees (the star Fomalhaut, 9° Aquarius, has also a similarity with Anubis, the English astronomer W.H.Smyth (1788-1865) called this star Fom Alhout *Algenubi*

199

and has therefore an etymological resemblance with Anubis). In the terrestrial mapping of the stars, a longitude of 0° of Aquarius corresponds with 2°-4° E., placing it close to the former banks of Lake Triton (Tunisia) and the western foothills of the Hoggar Mountains. This was the region of Anubis, the guard at the gate to the region of Osiris, where the "Pure Land" was found. This leads us to the borders of the old world, during the period from 8500 to 5300 BCE.

This historical data has given rise to many mythical topics, which can even be encountered in China, in the Ceylonese *Mahâvamsa*, in the Indian *Petavatthu* or with medieval western authors who had the borderlands of the world, the "mappae mundi", peopled by the cynocephales, human beings with the head of a dog.[52] But now, myths no longer exist because the analysis of the Sumerian Planisphere has identified a terrestrial mapping of the celestial network.

6.13 The Link with Neighbouring Languages

The Egyptian and Sumerian languages are related, as far as the method of notation is concerned. "The Babylonian cuneiform, which developed as an adaptation of an originally hieroglyphic notation to the writing material in use, was invented by the Sumerians and originally served to write in Sumerian; here too, as in Egyptian, ideographic sense-signs and phonographic sound-signs (**Egyptian Grammar** §6) are found side by side. However, the aspect of pure pronunciation of the syllable is entirely lacking."[53]

Only at a much later stage, around 2700 BCE, are Semitic elements encountered in the Sumerian language. At the beginning of Akkad, around 2400 BCE, the Semitic language had become totally integrated into the Sumerian language. This allows us to determine that the original Sumerian language, as far as it deserves that name, is not related to the Semitic language.

There has been much controversy about the origin of the Egyptian language, especially as to whether it belongs to the Semitic or the Hamitic language group. The Semitic language group comprises Akkadian, Hebrew, Aramic and Arabic, while the Hamitic language group comprises the Berber languages of North Africa and the Cushitic languages of Ethiopia. Ever since the relationship between the Berber languages and the Nigero-Chadic languages, including Haussa, was discovered, the problem had to be redefined, with the new consensus that "a Hamitic group is no longer recognised, and the following languages are placed on a level next to one another: (1) Semitic, (2) Egyptian, (3) Berber, (4) Cushitic and (5) Nigero-Chadic.

In addition, some scholars discard the idea that the Berber languages could have come about under the influence of an African substratum (breeding ground). They claim that these are more likely to have developed independently out of a Semitic basic language. It seems that this theory is also presumed to apply to the Egyptian language."[54]

The language of the population of Niger and Chad and that of the ancestors of the Egyptians and Sumerians belong to the Hamitic language group, from countries that border on the Central Mountains of North Africa. This is the original dwelling-place of the ancestors of the Egyptians and the Sumerians, where the development of their technical skills and language came about. The ancestors of the people of the Central Mountains chose this area as their new home; they themselves were immigrants from an island in the sea, inhabited by hawks and, as the Egyptians claimed, located at the edge of the world. This hawk culture which was the forerunner of the later Horus culture, is probably to be found further west. When the first European seafarers arrived on the Azores, they named this group of islands the Açores meaning hawk.

The Central Mountains of North Africa were also the homeland of the ancestors of the Dogon tribe that now lives on the banks of the river Niger in Mali. They still claim that they came from the northeast. This was where the rebirth of humanity occurred, as the Dogon high priests told the French anthropologists Griaule and Dieterlen. It would also explain how the Sirius tradition still partially exists amongst the Dogon. It implies that the Egyptians did not hand down their knowledge to the Dogon, although the origin of the Dogon people does bear a certain kinship with the ancestors of the Egyptians and Sumerians.

6.14 Tuareg or Imushar

The Tuaregs are one of the peoples presently inhabiting the area around Agadez, although they wander about in the Sahara between the south of Algeria and Libya, up to the bay of the Niger and North Nigeria.[55]. Their name is derived from the Arabic "Tawariq", singular: Tarqi, although they call themselves "Imushar". Could the last syllable *shar* possibly stem from the Sumerian language where *shar* means "first name, foremost".[56] Shar (exalted ruler) also means "perfect circle", an "accomplished cycle". Their territory of the Central Mountains of North Africa belonged under the constellation Pisces, which also encompasses the Pegasus square. Hence, a possible link may exist between Imushar and the Pegasus square.

The Tuareg belong to the Berber people. The surroundings of Ghat, on the border between Libya and Algeria, and the area up to the Ahaggar mountains form the dwelling-place of the Khel-Azdjer; to the north-west of that area, we find the dwelling-place of the Kel-Ahaggar. Both are located near the Air mountains, the Kel-Air to the south-east and the Kel-Aovelimids to the south-west.

Originally, their tribal division was based on a segregation between "slaves" (imrhad) and "nobility" (ihaggars). The first group practised agriculture as their main means of existence, while the "nobility" would occupy themselves primarily with caravan trading and slave-trade, robbery and nomadic stock-breeding.[57] However, the French government opposed the slave-trade, which forced them to look for a "steady" source of income. Since then, this caste-system has faded due to their merging with Blacks and Arabs. The drought after 1970 has caused the Tuaregs to renounce their nomadic way of life almost completely. In recent times, they have shown an increasing tendency to settle in and around towns or in camps. The continued existence of their characteristic way of life is under great pressure.

Remarkably, the colour of their skin at birth is white. This matches their eyes, which are more bluish than black and quite noticeably, their skin gradually turns brown under the influence of the sun. A typical Tuareg garment is the veil, generally coloured indigo-blue, which covers their nose and mouth. The colour of this veil has caused the tribe to be nicknamed "the Blue Men", especially since indigo makes the skin appear bluish. This veil, called tidjelmoust, is the hallmark of the "noble", prominent (shar) Tuareg; the "commoner" wears a white veil. This veil, which is only worn by men, is never taken off, except in the company of intimate male acquaintances or one's wife.

The veil distinguishes these Tuaregs from all other tribes in North Africa. Nowhere else does a tribe exist where the man is known to wear a veil. Thus, the Arabs call the Tuaregs "Ahn el Lithan", the tribe of the veiled. Initially, it was thought that the veil was worn to protect the wearer from dust and sand. But the actual reason is the Tuareg's deep-rooted feeling of shame. That is why they will never show themselves unveiled to a stranger. The Tuareg society is dominated by its unveiled women. In many aspects of life, a woman's social position is superior to that of a man. She cannot pay greater tribute to her husband than by acquiring a high reputation in the tribe's social life and to surround herself with a host of admirers. Jealousy does not occur; such behaviour would be unworthy of a Tuareg. Tuareg society is also monogamous.[58]

The Tuareg are an oddity within the African culture; and it is even more bizarre to learn that their origins are unknown. The Tuaregs themselves claim that their descent goes back to Queen Tin-Hinan, whose grave was found in Abalessa, approximately 100 kilometres west of Tamanghasset (Algeria). In 1925, "on the presumed site, [archaeologists] found a round tumulus, four metres high, with a diameter of 25 metres. As excavations proceeded, an extremely solid stone construction appeared that bore the marks of an architecture that was unique in the entire country and obviously dated back to a time before Islam was founded. The monument consisted of various chambers. In the rear chamber the skeleton of a tall woman (1.75 metres), belonging to the white race was found. She was neither European nor Mediterranean, yet her features were reminiscent of ancient Egypt. She wore a leather dress and was adorned with seven gold bracelets around her right arm and seven silver ones around her left arm. Placed nearby was a little wooden box containing small pieces of gold foil bearing the stamp of Roman coins, and a statuette of a woman with staetopygy [an overdeveloped posterior] from the Aurignacian period during the Young Palaeolithic Age, in other words from very early prehistoric times [corresponding with the Palaeolithic female idol of Lespugue (Haute-Garonne) and the Venus of Willendsdorf]. The main building was surrounded by fourteen small sepulchral annexes, destined for the slaves. The entire complex did not have the appearance of a mausoleum, as the burial chamber would then have been placed in the centre. It looked more like a kind of fortress, yet who built it? Maybe the Romans? According to Pliny, they actually visited Abalessa in 19 BCE."[59] Her sepulchral gifts can be admired in the museum of Algiers.[60]

6.15 Mysterious Dilmun and the "Westland"

At this point, we will turn to an analysis of various myths and religious utterances, which we believe to be related to the accounts presented so far. The mythology of the Sumerians contains a description of an island called Dilmun. It depicts a fertile island, the cradle of their culture, described as a mysterious place where the primeval form of an earthly paradise was created. Contextually, Dilmun, the "Land of the Living", also plays an important role in other Sumerian literary texts. Another region is also mentioned, which is called "The Land of the Felled Cedar".

No-one knows with any certainty where Dilmun or the "Land of the Felled Cedar" is located. In the 1960s, the Danish archaeologist Bibby went in search of this paradisiacal island. In imitation of the legendary 19th century researcher Sir Henry Creswick Rawlinson, he believed that the islands of Bahrain and Qatar could be the mythical Dilmun. In *Looking for Dilmun* (1969), Bibby pointed out emphatically that he was searching for Dilmun, but did not claim to have found it. He was following up the assumptions of the officer, politician and pioneer Rawlinson. Bibby stated: "Rawlinson claimed that Bahrain was identical to Dilmun" and "Rawlinson's identification of Dilmun with Bahrain is a guess which comes closest to the facts."[61] Since then, it has become generally accepted that Bahrain is indeed the legendary Dilmun.[62]

Nevertheless, written evidence is still lacking. Of course, Bibby found reed and clay remnants that proved that there had once been villages there, dating back to the fourth millennium BCE, with links to Sumeria. Steatite cylinder seals and pottery were also found that cemented this conclusion. However, the remarkable presence of "merely" four temples and around 175,000 tumuli appear to indicate that this island was a gigantic necropolis.

The idea has been put forward (e.g. in *Bahrain through the Ages, the Archaeology*) that the number of graves is quite impressive, yet that the amount of funerary gifts is meagre. In addition, there was nothing in the tumuli to indicate that this island might have been a booming depository of gold, copper, lapis lazuli, ivory objects, intarsia and pearls, although this is exactly what written sources identify with Dilmun.[63]

Nevertheless, Bahrain can justifiably be assumed to have played a special role during and after the Akkadian Kingdom. When this kingdom emerged around 2400 BCE, Bahrain became their necropolis, their island of the dead. The archaeologist Rice shows appropriate hesitation when he sums up his opinion about Dilmun: "Later, without doubt, Bahrain was Dilmun and was celebrated throughout Sumer for its sanctity and for its numinous character."[64] After 2400 BCE, Bahrain became an artificially created paradise for the Akkadians. And at a later stage, the same held true for the Babylonians and Assyrians who wished to be buried there in memory of the paradisiacal island Dilmun, which was lost after a catastrophe. As such, it can be concluded that Bahrain was Dilmun, but that it was not the original Dilmun.

The era in which both Egypt and Sumeria established their civilisation was already more than a millennium old by then, so that it was no longer known where the original Dilmun had been located. Rice specifies explicitly that the chronology of the Gulf of Arabia and Egypt have nothing whatsoever in common.[65] Therefore, Bahrain, this artificially created Dilmun, cannot possibly ever claim to be the cradle of either Egypt or Sumeria. Accordingly, Rice remarks carefully: "It would be foolish to assert that all references to islands in Egyptian religious or mythological texts must refer to Dilmun; indeed it may be that none refers specifically to it."[66]

It has become clear that this cradle must be looked for in the west, not the east. The description in the **Gilgamesh Epic** and its narration of the journey to the "Westland" leave no room for misinterpretations about the location of Dilmun and the "Land of the Felled Cedar". According to this epic, the giant Humbaba (Chumbaba) dwelt in a cedar forest in the far West.[67]

But who is Humbaba? "A former generation of scholars considered the name *Chumbaba* to be Elamitic and therefore believed that the cedar hill ought to be searched for in the highlands to the east of Babylonia. All we have is some knowledge of a cedar forest and a cedar hill in the "Westland", for instance from the inscriptions of King Sargon I of Akkad [dating back to 2335 BCE, at the foundation of the state Agade, or Akkad, as the case may be] (cf. A.Poebel, UMBS IV/1, p.224)." In his magnificent adaptation of the **Gilgamesh Epic**, the Dutch scholar De Liagre Böhl expresses his belief that the Amanus Mountains near the Gulf of Alexandretta or the Lebanon mountains with the Antilibanus (Hermon) could qualify.

De Liagre Böhl's adaptation of the **Gilgamesh Epic** (p.166) leads us to a solution: "Three items are particularly noteworthy: the hero of the flood (Zisutra or Xisoutros) is presented as a king and a priest; after the tidal storm has subsided, the Sungod appears as the saviour, who accepts the people's worship and oblation as tokens of gratitude for their deliverance; furthermore, the "distant country" where this Xisoutros goes to live as keeper of the "seed of humanity", is mentioned as Dilmun ..."

This region can be located by establishing the identity of Uta-napishtim: "The search for the identity of Zisutra [Uta-napishtim= zodiacal sign Capricorn] comes within closer reach in the following excerpt from the **Gilgamesh Epic** (p.166): 'This Sumerian name is abbreviated to Zisutra [Uta-napishtim] (KAR Nr. 434, cf. JEOL Nr.7, 1940, p.414), and this is where the Greek name Xisoutros stems from: the name of the hero of the Deluge in the Book of Berossos." The next passage (p. 95) offers additional information: "Before this [tempestuous flood and the blessing of Enlil], Uta-napishtim was a mortal human being; henceforth, Uta-napishtim and his spouse will be equal to our gods, and Uta-napishtim will dwell faraway, near the mouth of the streams."

Before the catastrophe, Uta-napishtim lived somewhere faraway in the "Westland", i.e. in the far west. Uta-napishtim is Suchur.Mash.KU6, which corresponds with the zodiacal sign of Capricorn; Uta-napisjtim was the builder of the Ark MA.GUR 8.[68] Meanwhile, we know from an analysis of the astronomical matrix that the sign of Capricorn is indeed located in the far West, between the zero meridian and the High Atlas Mountains. This excludes Bahrain as a candidate.

At this point, the correct identity of Humbaba needs to be established to ensure that the "Land of the Felled Cedar" really does lie in the west. Could Humbaba possibly be Anubis? In **Star Names**, the general description of Aquarius contains the following phrase: "On the Ganghes, as in China, it began the circle of the zodiacal signs [with four of the minor stars of Aquarius]; and Al Biruni (973 CE) said that at one time in India it was Khumba, or Kumbaba, which recalls the Elamite divinity of that name, or Storm God, of Hesychios."[69] This clearly shows where Humbaba or Kumbaba ought to be looked for: in the sign Aquarius.

The general description of Aquarius ends with the following quote: "La Lande, citing Firmicus and the Egyptian sphere of Petosiris, wrote in *L'Astronomie*: Aquarius rises together with another constellation, which he calls Aquarius Minor, with la Faulx, the wolf, the hare and the altar."[70] Here, we again encounter an important link with Aquarius, and even the head of a dog or a wolf is involved. This head, belonging either to a dog or a wolf, is Anubis, the Keeper of the Netherworld, the Judge in the Realm of the Dead, who is also related to Khenti Amentiu, the great God in the West.[71]

Consequently, we can now determine that the area of Humbaba or Anubis, the Judge of the Dead was located around the Zero Meridian. Humbaba was the keeper of Enlil, which means that the Way of Enlil on the 28° N. parallel leads to the dwelling-place of Humbaba. Within that region around the Zero Meridian, lay the "Land of the Felled Cedar". Seen from the east, Anubis or Humbaba watched over the Realm of the Dead, which was thought to lie in the Canary Islands, the Realm of Osiris. In the coastal region of modern Morocco, the same breed of dogs (the Berber greyhound), resembling the Doberman Pinscher, was held sacred in most of ancient Antiquity. We still find traces of this dog cult in the name of the "Canary Islands", which is derived from the Latin word "canis", i.e. dog. Rice remarked that "the seafarer of Dilmun was always depicted with hunting dogs", a statement that is endorsed by a Pyramid Text (Utterance 437) in which Anubis is the acclaimed ruler of the "Pure Land", the region around the zero meridian: "Anubis who presides over the Pure Land."[72]

This makes it very clear that the original cradle of civilisation is to be found in the west. The original Dilmun, the "Land of the Living", was the first cradle of civilisation, and identical to the "Homeland" of the Egyptians. After the catastrophic destruction of this birthplace, the Canary Islands, the "Primaeval Island", were identified with Dilmun. Millennia later, the second cradle was created in the Central Mountains of North Africa. To the west of these mountains, near the zero meridian, lay the "Land of the Felled Cedar". Finally, many millennia later, the Akkadians gave the name Dilmun to the island of Bahrain in order to commemorate the legendary "Homeland".

6.16 The Dogon and the Constellation of Orion in Sanga

In the course of time, part of the primeval tribe travelled from the melting pot of the North African Central Mountains to the major rivers of Africa and Asia. The Dogon tribe, related to this primeval tribe, journeyed in a south-westerly direction, to the river Niger in Mali.

The Dogon are related to the population and the culture of Egypt and Sumeria. Their relationship does not merely express itself in astronomical knowledge of the Sirius system. The core of the collective Sirius tradition is the "amphibious fish", the fish-tailed amphibious God, who, according to the Dogon, brought forth the human embryo. One of the oldest examples of Egyptian writing shows a similar fish on the Serekh (coat of arms) of the palette of Pharaoh Narmer (cf. fig. 57). According to the Dogon tradition, that Fish-God, the Triton, is one of the gods who caused civilisation to come about.

Something similar was related by the Babylonian priest Berossos: "In the first year there made its appearance, from a part of the Erythraean Sea which

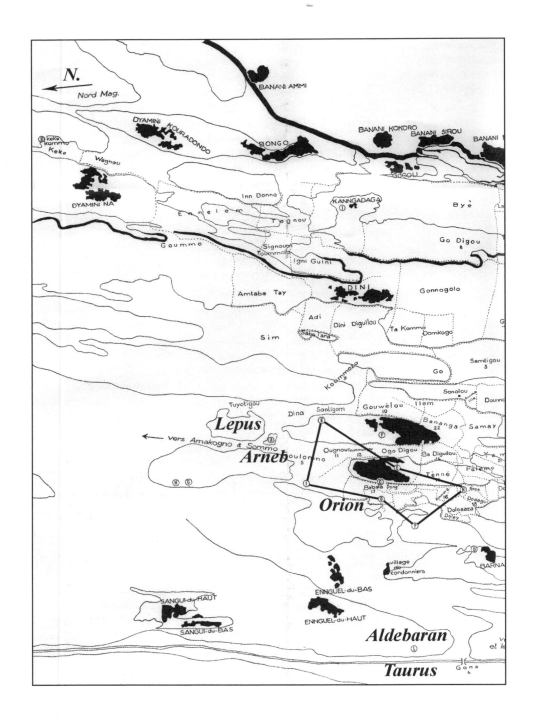

Fig. 59. Topographical map of the region Sanga in Mali, showing the altars. These altars represent stars of Lepus, Orion, and Taurus.

bordered upon Babylonia, an animal endowed with reason, who was called Oannes. According to the account of Apollodorus, the whole body of the animal was like that of a fish; and had under a fish's head another head, and also feet below, similar to those of a man, subjoined to the fish's tail. His voice too, and language, was articulate and human; and a representation of him is preserved even to this day. This Being in the day-time used to converse with men; but took no food at that season; and he gave them an insight into letters and sciences, and every kind of art. He taught them to construct houses, to found temples, to compile laws, and explained to them the principles of geometrical knowledge. He made them distinguish the seeds of the Earth, and shewed them how to collect fruits; in short, he instructed them in everything that could tend to soften manners and humanise mankind."[73]

The Dogon call the manifestation of this Fish-God "Nommo". They claim that the Nommos emanated from Amma, the Great Creator who dwells in the celestial domain where Sirius and Orion are located. That celestial domain, which the Egyptians considered the "central image of the heaven", was projected on Earth between the towns of Dahshur and Letopolis. That same image was also projected and built in the region of Sanga in Mali by the Dogon (cf. fig. 59). The Sanga region, with the village of Ogol, is the centre of the Dogon's spiritual life. The topographical map of that area shows "the altar of Lébé, the object of common worship, located at a square south of the village, and surrounded by a number of consecrated altars - indicated by letters of the alphabet - which are attributed to the principle of binu (totem cult)."

The alphabetical letters on the map point to the names of the altars.[74] The altars indicated by the letters K, I, E, C, D, N and P form the constellation of Orion, with the stars Saiph, Rigel, the Orion belt consisting of the stars Al Nitak, Al Nilam and Mintaka, Betelgeuse and Bellatrix. The letter A correlates with the star Arneb of Lepus, L with Aldebaran. The map shows the God Amma. Undoubtedly, all other letters represent stars too. Fascinating similarities between the Dogon and the ancient Egyptians not only point to a common tradition, they even indicate a common religion.

6.17 The Pyramid of Khufu and its Ritual Function

Isis, the wife of Osiris, was the Mistress of the Pyramid of Khufu,[75] one of the three pyramids of Giza that correlate with the Orion Belt. In the 1940s, Griaule and Dieterlen obtained information from the Dogon priests, which they publicised in **The Pale Fox**: "The three stars in the Orion Belt, bearing east-west, stand respectively for Nommo die, Nommo titiyayne, and the offertory; they are the protectors of the spiritual principles of the corn crop, which are entrusted to them between the harvesting time and the sowing season of the coming year."[76]

The Dogon tribe depicted the two Nommos back to back, as one single statue. The pyramids that are related to the Orion Belt therefore identify Khufu's pyramid as Nommo die, Khafre's pyramid as Nommo titiyayne and the pyramid of Menkaure, the smallest one, as the offertory, the child, the beloved one. In that same sequence, the pyramids represent Isis the woman, Osiris the man and Horus the child. Maybe the inner corridor system in the pyramid of Khufu, including the King's and the Queen's chamber symbolises the female reproductive system.

Pyramid Text §632 describes the stellar copulation between Isis and Osiris, resulting in the birth of Horus: "Your sister Isis comes to you rejoicing for love of you. You have placed her on your phallus and your seed issues into her, she being made ready as Sothis, and Har-Sopd has come forth from you as Horus who is in Sothis." This fertility ritual apparently stems from a single, joint tradition.

In Sefar, rock paintings of similar fertility rituals can be found. A considerable number of paintings of Nommos – identified by some as "Martians" - were rediscovered in the Jabbars, in Adjefu, Ti-n-Tazarift and Sefar, immediately east of Djanet in the Tassili n'Ajjer and north of Agadez. This may also explain the numerous images in the Central Mountains of North Africa of women known as "femmes ouvertes", "open women" – ovulating women – who appear prepared for copulation with the gods.[77]

6.18 The Proto-History of Egypt in a Nutshell

Between 4000 and 3500 BCE, invaders who sailed from Punt in the south to the west coast of the Red Sea explored the Wadi Hammamat. There, they engraved images of their boats onto the rocks. They are the bearded ancestors of the Phoenicians who sailed from the Eritrean coast and the Ethiopean Highland (Punt = To-Nefer) to the north and arrived in the Naqada region via a river or a creak that still existed in those days, and is now known as the Wadi Hammamat.

Here, they founded settlements on the Nile, such as the town of Phoinikon (Lakeita).[78] The Greek name of this town is reminiscent of the origin of these invaders from Punt: Philo of Byblos (circa 60-140 CE) stated that the Phoenicians were the original inhabitants and that the gods and the entire human culture originated from their region. Herodotus (cf. Book I-1 and VII-89) pinpointed the coast of the Eritrean Sea as their territory.[79] The Pyramid Text (§ 802-803) adds further weight to this conclusion: "The Netherworld has grasped your hand at the place where Orion is, the Bull of the Sky has given you his hand, and you eat of the food of the gods whereof they eat, the savour of Ddwn is on you, (even) of the youth of Upper Egypt who came out of Nubia; he gives you the incense wherewith the gods are censed."[80] This Pyramid Text explicitly identifies the cradle of the population of Upper Egypt: they arrived in Egypt from Nubia (Punt = To-Nefer). They developed the Naqada culture, which expanded northward, thereby instigating the end of the El Badari culture.

In the south of Nubia, on a level with Eritrea and north of Khartoum, remnants have been found of settlements from 6000 BCE, whose inhabitants were in close contact with other cultures from northern and central Africa. They are known as the Khartoum Mesolithic culture, marked by hunting, fishing and cattle breeding. The handmade earthenware, which they produced even before they began raising cattle, is characterised by ornamental patterns made up of impressed dots and wavy lines. At the beginning of the fourth millennium BCE, this early form of agriculture moved to the north of Nubia, to the Nile region of Kustul and Sayala, between 22° and 23° N. The objects they made, such as mace heads and slate palettes, show the same high quality as the ones which subsequently the Egyptian pharaohs possessed.[81]

Around 5300 BCE, the Followers of Horus had settled in the Delta after a climatological catastrophe that had driven them from the North African Central Mountains and the surroundings of Lake Triton. In the course of the first half of the fourth millennium BCE, the Children of Seth founded the prehistoric capital Hieraconpolis in Upper Egypt. In their urge to extend their territory to the north, the Children of Seth met in combat with the Followers of Horus in Lower Egypt, as is attested by the Narmer palette.

Pharaoh Narmer, leading the Children of Seth, conquered the Followers of Horus in the Egyptian Delta and founded the State of Egypt by uniting "The Two Lands". Between approximately 3500 and 3150 BCE, the battles between the Followers of Horus and the Children of Seth continued to break out at regular intervals, acquiring a mythical character, the Myth of Horus and Seth. Towards the end of the Second Dynasty both communities engaged in 80 years of warfare (cf. Chronology, especially "Triumph of Horus"), before Egypt was finally united in 3153 BCE, under the rule of the Third Dynasty. Throughout the Old Kingdom, the territory of Egypt was divided into two parts, with the pyramids of Dahshur marking the border between the territory of Horus (Lower Egypt) and that of Seth (Upper Egypt). The Geography of the Gods had taken shape.

Chapter 7

The Chronicles of the Followers of Horus (The Sacred Books of Edfu)

After an almost uninterrupted occupation of 200 years, the Ptolemies felt a need to record the history of Egypt and to restore the past glory by erecting new temples. Pharaoh Ptolemy II Philadelphus assigned the high priest Manetho to write its history. His successor Ptolemy III Euergetes I proceeded to (re)build the temple at Edfu. Edfu had already gained great importance during the Old Kingdom as it was sited on the observation track of Sirius. Its temple was dedicated to Horus, to commemorate the Shemsu Hor, their ancestors. Accordingly, the temple is also called the Temple of Horus. Edfu was the "Place of the Throne" and the "Throne of Horus"[1] and ranks amongst Egypt's best-preserved temples.

Entering the forecourt through the enormous pylon, a row of 16 columns, each with different chapiters, appears to the left and right. Behind the left row, the inner face of the western wall can be seen. This wall, along with the other walls, bears accounts of the "mythical" origin of the Shemsu Hor. They are known as *"The Walls of Records"*, the object of long-pending research:

"From the earliest times the Egyptians seem to have maintained the idea that many of the beliefs and events that characterised their 'culture'- to employ a term which, of course, they would not have recognised – had their origins on a far distant island. The evidence for this belief is contained in various collections of texts and inscriptions, including the Pyramid Texts, some of which certainly date back to Predynastic times, the inscriptions of the Horus Temple at Edfu, which, though Ptolemaic in date, incorporate much earlier material, and the inscriptions of the Thoth Temple at Hermopolis, which may also contain early records or recollections of the Egyptian people."[2]

According to ancient Egyptian standards, the location of the temple at Edfu, with its bearing exactly north-south on the left bank of the Nile, is uncommon. While most temples are orientated east-west, the entrance through the large pylon leads towards the north. This deviant direction emphasises its symbolical function and takes no account of local factors. It is a fact that the river Nile also runs in a south-north direction, yet at this location the river is too far away to have played any significant role for the outline of the building.

On entering the large court, one perceives the entrance to the temple, which at that time was flanked on both sides by two beautiful statues of the Horus falcon, one of which still remains. On entering the hallway of the temple, a Pronaos (a colonnaded hall added to the front of the temple), with three rows of six columns each, leads to the sanctuary, which is straight in front of us. In the rear part of the temple, we find the Naos, or inner chamber, which once housed the cult statue that used to be carried along in processions. After passing through the hallway, one reaches the actual temple court with four rows of three columns each. Ten rooms are grouped around the sanctuary. The Naos that is contained in this sanctuary was made of black granite and dates from the reign of Pharaoh Nektanebo II (approximately 360 BCE). In front of the Naos, the barque of Horus and that of Hathor are each mounted on a base. The cult statue of a sitting falcon holds a flagellum (whip) and was kept in the central space at the far end.

The inner western wall of the inner court bears more than the inscription indicating from where the ancestors of the Egyptians originated; an image, applied where the western wall of the inner court forms a narrow corridor, shows how the gods Khnum, Thoth and Horus assist the king in catching fish. The net contains some birds and also a fish, a deer, two Asian and a few African people. At the end of the corridor, the space between the enclosing wall and the actual temple wall broadens. The continuation of the inner western wall shows reliefs and texts of the battle between Horus and Seth. The western wall is therefore completely dedicated to the "mythical" history of the Egyptian people. Once again, we encounter a clear allusion to the West, from where the Followers of Horus originated, and this explains the orientation of the temple.

The construction of this imposing Temple of Horus started in the early morning of 23rd August 237 BCE (JD 1,635,094) with the ceremony of the "stretching of the cord", which was held by Pharaoh Ptolemy III Euergetes I to mark the foundation. The work started on the sixth Moon-day, favoured for foundation! The Moon fills sacred eye and unites with Osiris (constellation of Scorpio). The foundation ceremony of the temple was held between approximately 04h35 and 05h45. In the north, the temple was aligned with Ursa Minor (especially with the stars Kochab and Pherkad), in the south with Orion (especially with Betelgeuse and Saiph). The temple was completed in the year 142 BCE and inaugurated in an extraordinarily festive manner by Pharaoh Ptolemy VIII Euergetes I and his wife Cleopatra II on 31st August 142 BCE (JD 1,669,800), the twenty-third Moon-day (the planet Jupiter unites with Osiris), 95 years after the foundations had been marked out.[3]

Subsequently, work started on the construction of the Pronaos, which was completed in 125 BCE, followed by the forecourt, the pylon and the surrounding wall, which lasted from 117 until 71 BCE. The entire complex, including the reliefs and decorations, was completed around 58 BCE. Therefore work on the temple lasted for 159 years, not including an interruption of 20 years.

At that time, the Ptolemaic temple formed part of a larger religious complex. The walls of the Temple of Horus bear inscriptions portraying the knowledge of the Egyptians. The west side has an inner and an outer wall that date back to the reign of the Old Kingdom. Remains from that period have also been found in other places. In the Graeco-Roman period, the texts were inscribed in Demotic, which is hard to translate as there were more than a thousand written characters in use at that time. Meanwhile, the texts in and on the temple have been transcribed and now comprise around 3,000 printed pages, which have been bound into 14 giant-sized volumes.

7.1 The Mythical Origin of the Followers of Horus

In addition to translation problems, the vast number of books containing texts and drawings of the Temple of Horus at Edfu present a major obstruction to the formation of a clear overview. Fortunately, the British Egyptologist Dr. Eve Reymond made a special effort during her studies in the 1960s. The title of her book, ***The Mythical Origin of the Egyptian Temple***, is self-explanatory. She based her work on the texts and the facts that the temple of Edfu revealed. These texts have been proved to contain an accurate description of a former "Homeland" and of events in that domain. As such, the Temple of Horus is primarily a *"House of Records"*, transcribing the "mythical" history of the ancient Egyptians.

In ***Egypt's Making***, Rice uses various elements of Reymond's work to prove that Bahrain is identical with this former "Homeland". Since Rice believes that the Edfu texts that Reymond used in her study clearly point to Bahrain, he obviously concentrated on the east in his search for the origin of the Egyptians. Rice argues: "It would appear from these texts that the Egyptians preserved, however faintly, memories of an island, far distant towards the east, on the edge of the world, where the first and most crucial acts of creation occurred and where the first and second generation of gods had their home."[4]

To substantiate his assumption that the island is located in the east, Rice uses Pyramid Text § 353: "That I may be ferried over to the *eastern* side of the sky, to the place where the gods were born."[5] The fact that the ancient peoples saw the stars and the planets as representatives of the gods, which rose on the eastern horizon, cannot be rated as conclusive evidence, since by contrast, numerous Egyptian texts specifically allude to the west as the home of the gods, such as those texts that speak of Osiris, Anubis and Horus, many of which already have been discussed in this book.

The texts on the wall of the temple of Edfu show Memphite influences, which identify the region around Memphis and Saqqara as the source of this mythical history. Reymond commented: "a well-known text on the inner face of the enclosure wall of the temple at Edfu tells us that the temple was built at the dictates of the Ancestors, according to what was written *in this book that descended from the sky to the north of Memphis*."[6] On this evidence, Reymond claims that the Edfu records contain the history of a predynastic religious centre that once existed near Memphis, which the Egyptians looked upon as the *origin* of the Egyptian temple.[7] Some 2,000 years later, after the temple city of Memphis had been founded in 5300 BCE, the Egyptians did in fact build the central star constellation Orion on Earth.

The design of the Pyramid Field represented the Strong Arm and expressed the elementary creative powers of the Creator. That symbol raised the Pyramid Field to the level of a divine domain. The same construct applies to the temple of Heliopolis (cf. Ch.4.29 and fig. 39A), where the outline of the Strong Arm (***Egyptian Grammar***, T15) is repeated in the design of the western section of the enclosing wall. Yet the mythical chronicles refer to periods in their tradition that go back much further in time. This becomes very clear when one reads the description that Reymond gives of the first creation and of the community that lived on that island. Reymond describes this creation as: "The first creation can be regarded, from the point of view of the tradition implicit in our documents, as the history of the *Homeland of the Primaeval Ones*."[8] She describes the birth of a community as: "it is certain that this island was the piece of land where the creation of the world began, and the earliest mansions of the gods were founded."[9] Hence, the *Homeland of the Primaeval Ones* was an island. It becomes apparent from the follow-up that there can be no question of a continent; instead, an island in the ocean seems far more probable.

On the prevailing conditions on that island, she states: "an [...] *island*, which, in part [...] stood in darkness in the midst of the primaeval water [...] which in this tradition bears the name *wa'ret*." Furthermore, she tells us: "It is rather the name of a land lying in the primaeval water."[10] Earlier, she writes: "It seems to describe the primaeval domain of the gods." [11]

In his own book, Rice briefly sums up Reymond's work: "In the Edfu texts, the island itself is called the 'Pool which came into existence at the Beginning'. The island was the nucleus of the world."[12] At this point, Rice adds a Pyramid Text (Utterance 484), intending to produce a definitive answer to the island's location: "I am the primaeval hill of the land in the midst of the sea." Again, it is more than clear that this refers to an island which was located in the primaeval waters. It will become apparent that this pointed specifically to an ocean or a sea. But Rice rounds off the matter resolutely, stating that "the land here is specifically a sea-girt island and not a hillock of mud revealed by the withdrawal of the waters of the inundation [of the Nile] which has so often been described as the first land to appear at the Creation. The Primaeval Place was the Island of Rest, or of Peace."[13]

In one of the Edfu texts, the "Homeland" is given a different name: the "Island of the Egg". The same appellation appears in the Piri Re'is map; furthermore, it is found in its present name: the Atlantic Ocean. The Piri Re'is map, named after a Turkish Fleet Admiral, caused great excitement upon its discovery in the old imperial palace in Istanbul in 1929. Painted on parchment and dated 1513, it caused controversy as the map was the earliest specimen showing America and because its design explicitly differed from all other 16th century maps. In addition, extensive examination by Hapgood et al. proved that the meridians and the coastline of South America and Africa had been charted with relative accuracy. This is most remarkable because in our view the seamen of the 16th century possessed no such knowledge. It was also noted that the bottom of the map showed drawings of bays and islands on the coast of Antarctica, in particular of Queen Maud Land, an area which is at present covered by a 1.5 kilometres thick icecap.

Furthermore, Piri Re'is stated that he used 20 maps and claimed that some of them had been drafted in the time of Alexander the Great, a few of which are based on mathematical principles. His map contains 24 written explanations, the sixth of which states: "This section shows how this map was drawn. In this century there is no map like this map in anyone's possession. The hand of this poor man has drawn it and now it is constructed. From about twenty charts and Mappae Mundi – these are charts drawn in the days of Alexander, Lord of the Two Horns, which show the inhabited quarter of the world; the Arabs name these charts Jaferiye – from eight Jaferiyes of that kind and one Arabic map of Hind, and from the maps recently drawn by four Portuguese that show the countries of Hind, Sind and China geometrically drawn, and also from a map drawn by Colombo in the western region I have extracted it. By reducing all these maps to one scale this final form was arrived at. So that the present map is as correct and reliable for the Seven Seas as the map of these our countries is considered correct and reliable by seamen."[14]

Here, we revert to Reymond's work. She goes a little further in her endeavour to explain the origin of the structure of the Egyptian temple. Reymond mentions the island of the first creation and also gives an account of its increase in size due to the formation of a hill. However, as she herself states, the island that the Edfu texts mention is primarily characterised by a pool, and the powers that had created the island also created the high hill. Reymond states: "This island is described in our Edfu sources as *this Pool that came into existence at the Beginning*, and it is also called the Province of the Beginning, of which an alternative name is the *Island of the Egg*."[15] A few pages further on she continues: "The first world of the gods started on what appeared to the Egyptians as a *sntt, foundation ground*, and which they were wont to describe as the *Island of the Egg*.

The prominent feature of this island was a pool. No tradition seems to be connected with its origin. On the other hand, the island seems to have been extended by the creation of a mound. Both of the translated texts mention the *k3yk3, High Hill*, but they do not explain its origin. Nevertheless, since the island and the hill appear to be closely connected in this drama of creation, we may hazard a guess that perhaps the hill may have been created in the same manner, and that it might have resulted from the creative activities of the same powers that created the island."[16]

Why did the Egyptians call the district or the region of the first creation "the Island of the Egg"? Is this name in any way associated with the term *Atlantic Ocean*, a designation that came about at a much later date? What was the name of the Atlantic Ocean in ancient times? Or was this ocean called the "Sound Egg" and in the 16th century changed into Ovo Sano, implying that the sound of the waves had a tranquillising effect? Did the "Island of the Egg" simply mean "Island in the Atlantic Ocean"?

In item 22 on the Piri Re'is map, we find a more detailed definition, which points in that direction. The explanatory text relating to the former name of the Atlantic Ocean reads: "This sea is called the Western Sea, but the Frank sailors [French sailors] call it the Mare d'Espagna, which means the Sea of Spain. Up to now it was known by these names, but Colombo, who opened up this sea and made these islands known, and also the Portuguese, infidels who have opened up the region of Hind, have agreed together to give this sea a new name. They have given it the name of Ovo Sano [Oceano] that is to say, Sound Egg. Before this it was thought that the sea had no end or limit, that at its other end was darkness. Now they have seen that this sea is girded by a coast and because it is like a lake, they have called it Ovo Sano."[17] Clearly, the name of the Atlantic Ocean was changed due to the discovery of the coasts that surround it, which caused a parallel to be drawn between the Atlantic Ocean and a lake. After the discovery of America by Columbus, the Atlantic Ocean was apparently considered to be an enormous inland sea.

In addition to the "Island of the Egg", Reymond mentions another island called the "Island of Trampling", which also played a role in Creation. Her account states: "We can conclude that the part played by the *Island of Trampling* in the drama of creation was that of a veritable foundation. This may explain why the subsidiary name of the island was the *Foundation Ground (sntt) of the Ruler of the Wing*. This proves that the *Island of the Egg* and the *Island of Trampling* were equal in respect of their primary function in the creation [apparently two volcanic islands]. The close affinities between these two islands can also be proved by the essential features of their configuration. They show a striking resemblance, so that it can justly be claimed that the description of these two islands, as they are known to us from the Edfu texts, was inspired by the same doctrinal ideas.

The second myth, however, shows slightly modified views, such as might have resulted from the traditions of the place in which this second myth was first written down. Another similarity with the *Island of the Egg* can be found in the mention of the primaeval mound. We know from the myth of the *Island of the Egg* that there was created, in a secondary act, a mound, the *k3y k3*, *High Hill*, where the subsidiary phases of creation took place."[18] She then draws a cautious conclusion that "the *Island of Trampling*, too, seems to have been the homeland of the primaeval deities. There is clear evidence of a belief that the island was occupied by some divine beings prior to the time of the creation of land with which our cosmogonic theory is concerned."

Further on, she states that the "Island of Trampling" became submerged due to a battle, and that the island turned into a tomb for its inhabitants. She describes this event thus: "the primaeval water might have submerged the island as a consequence of a fight, and the island become the tomb of the original divine inhabitants; thus the *hbbt-water* became the *w'rt-water*."[19] (cf. Epilogue). It appears that this catastrophic event even changed the name of the primaeval waters from hbbt-water into w'rt-water (pronunciation: hebebet-water into waret-water). On the same page, she continues: "It would appear that the original divine inhabitants of the island, the presumed company of the *Pn-God*, while fighting against the enemy, were killed. If this premise is correct, there may be a link with the idea that the island might become the `tomb´ of its own inhabitants."[20]

The fifth section of the Edfu chronicles (VI, 182, 10-15) tells us that this did not put an end to the islands of creation and their divine inhabitants. The disappearance of these islands beneath the primaeval waters caused the emergence of a new domain. "As a result of this action, it is said that a new domain (*ni'wt*) came into existence, the name of which was the *'Blessed Island'* and *'Hareoty'*."[21] That new territory was called the Blessed Island or Fortune Island.

Yet the first "Homeland" disappeared forever beneath the primaeval waters. According to Reymond, it literally became the underworld into which the soul descended. Reymond summarises her reasoning: "In the history of this domain, the allusions [made] to the fall of the *SOUND EYE [the Eye of Horus]*, the *wa'ret* [the Ocean], the *Underworld of the Soul* and the revelation of the Ancestor Gods, are all valuable pieces of evidence that this *Homeland* ended in darkness and beneath the primaeval waters."[22] Hence, Reymond's analysis of the Edfu chronicles, which she comments on as never yet having been analysed, specifies that the first Homeland was attacked by an enemy, which resulted in its total destruction. Reymond remains cautious and says that an allusion is made to a catastrophe as the cause of the extinction of the Sound Eye. This was followed by total darkness, which ended at the beginning of a new period of creation. She claims emphatically that the Edfu chronicles provide evidence of the Egyptians' knowledge of two separate periods during which the Earth was created. The core of her analysis is based on a war that was followed by a catastrophe. This is a verbatim rendering of the principal item in Plato's **Timaeus** and **Kritias** that gives an account of a disastrous conflict between Athens and Atlantis around 11,400 years ago.

The reason why Reymond translates the term that denotes the place where the soul went as "Eye" is made very clear to us by the oldest and simplest hieroglyphic form of the word Osiris. In the Egyptian religion, no other god but Osiris ever held a position of such prominence. His name was written as (cf. Survey hieroglyphs Q1 and Q2, **Egyptian Grammar**). The first hieroglyph means throne, seat and place. The "eye" stands for the act of looking and seeing. However, the reason why the two hieroglyphs were combined to indicate the name Osiris is unknown. One could suggest that it represents the all-seeing eye of God who, from his throne, judges the human being.

The place where Osiris dwelt is described in a number of Pyramid Texts: "O you of the Abyss, O you of the Abyss, beware of the Great Lake [Atlantic Ocean]! Sit on this your iron throne, give commands to those whose seats are hidden. The doors of the sky are opened for you (the king), the doors of the firmament are thrown open for you, that you may travel by boat to the 'Field of Rushes'."[23] In Pyramid Text Utterance 618 and 619 he commands: "Be silent, O men hear [...] to the Foremost of the Westerners [...] Raise yourself, O King, raise yourself for the Great Adze, raise yourself upon your left side, place yourself upon your right side, wash [your hands in this] fresh [water] which your father Osiris has given to you. I have cultivated barley [...]; take your two oars, the one of w'n-wood and the other of sdd-wood, so that you may cross the waterway to your house the sea and protect yourself from him who would harm you. Oho! Beware of the Great Lake!"[24]

7.2 The "Elysian Fields" of Osiris

Browsing through the complete Pyramid Texts, one will search in vain for a description of the Elysian Fields. They mention the "Field of Rushes", through which one could travel by boat, as was illustrated above in one Pyramid Text. This field is mentioned quite frequently in the Pyramid Texts, more so than the "Field of Offering". The location of the "Field of Rushes" is unknown, apart from the fact that it is presumed to lie in the west. The authentic dwelling-place of Osiris could possibly be determined by means of the astronomical matrix. After all, Osiris is identical with the constellation Scorpio.

Osiris' dwelling-place can indeed be found with the aid of the celestial network, provided that the geographical method which Claudius Ptolemy called *"Of the Familiarities between Countries and the Triplicities and Stars"* is applied. Close to the meridian Almeria-Melilla (2°-4° W), Capricorn passed over

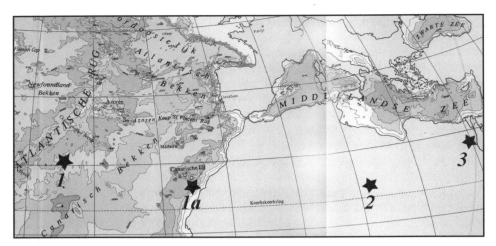

Fig. 60. Map, diagrammatically indicating the four previous dwelling-places of the Followers of Horus.

into the last decanate (20°-30°) of Sagittarius (Hercules), while the first decanate (0°-10°) of Sagittarius ended close to 8°-10° W, near the Phoenician settlement of Mogador (modern Agadir). This proves that the Straits of Gibraltar are indeed what the classics referred to as the Pillars of Hercules (Hèraklès). The precise location of these Pillars has, incidentally, often given rise to long, drawn-out discussions. It can now be determined that Scorpio (Osiris) extended across the region from 8°-10° W to 14°-16°W, and encompassed the location of seven Canary Islands (cf. fig. 52). This corresponds with what Reymond states: that after the "Homeland" of the original people had disappeared into the primaeval waters, the survivors seem to have settled on Seven Islands.

In the Edfu chronicles, this entire period is known as the "First Era of the Primaeval Age", which began (cf. Part I) in 14,213 BCE and lasted for 5,813 years, followed by the "Second Era of the Primaeval Age", which began in circa 8400 BCE in the "Sacred Domains" of the Egyptians. The history of the Shemsu Hor ended simultaneously with the "Hinterland". Reymond presented these periods, as extracted from the Edfu chronicles and are linked to the various dwelling-places of the Shemsu Hor. A summary of the cultural centres shows where the Shemsu Hor established themselves (cf. fig. 60):

First cradle: "Homeland"   = Atlantis
and

Transitional Period "Primaeval Island"   = Canary Islands
                                              Seven Islands

Second cradle: "Sacred Domains"   = Central Mountains of North
                                              Africa   (WTST-Neter-land)

Third cradle: "Hinterland"   = Egypt / Sumeria

218

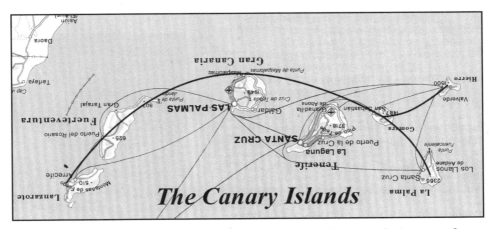

Fig. 61. Map of the Canary Islands seen from north to south, in accordance with the ancient Egyptian custom. The location of these islands corresponds stylistically with the constellation of Scorpio. As explained in chapter 5, the Canary Islands fall under the constellation of Scorpio. The Canary Islands are the Archipelago of the Scorpio, where Osiris originally dwelt.

Thus, evidence that the imposing Edfu chronicles present a rough outline of the origin of the cradle of civilisation and that this must be sought in the surroundings of the Canary Islands, mounts. By a remarkable coincidence, the physiography of the Canary Islands corresponds with the shape of the constellation Scorpio. A map of these islands makes this apparent.

The Egyptians positioned the south above the north, contrary to modern convention. If we observe the map of the Canary Islands, looking from the north to the south, "a curious curved line" ending in a fork is visible (cf. fig. 61 and 62). The correspondence in style between the physiography of the seven Canary Islands and the shape of the constellation Scorpio is striking. It is powerful evidence to claim that the Canary Islands are the Islands where Osiris originally dwelt. The diagrammatic, physiographic image of the constellation Scorpio is also congruent with the basin of the Nile, which reminded the Egyptians of their distant ancestors, Osiris, and the former Islands in the Ocean from where they had come.

By now, it will be evident that Utterance 484 of Pyramid Texts should be taken literally, especially the phrasing in §1022: "the 'primaeval hill' on the land in the middle of the sea."[25] It provides an example of how ancient texts may contain geographical information. In **Myth and Symbol in Ancient Egypt**, Rundle Clark remarks that "Osiris dwells in the Primaeval Place; his throne is placed upon the creation mound, which the deceased now reaches in what he [Osiris] calls 'this city'. I have come to this city, the region of the 'First Time'."[26] The Golden First Time of Osiris was the Period around circa 15,500 BCE. All this points to the fact that the dwelling-place of Osiris was indeed surrounded by water.

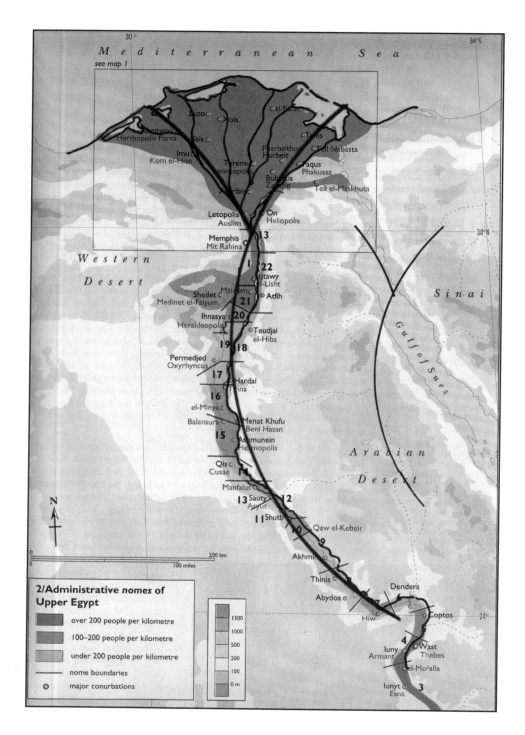

Fig. 62. *Map of Egypt showing the river basin of the Nile. In chapter 2, this basin was shown to correspond with the constellation Scorpio. The basin has a striking resemblance with the diagrammatic outline of Scorpio and consequently also with Osiris.*

220

Osiris resided on a volcano, the mountain of creation, identified as the volcano Pico de Teide (3,718 m) on the island of Tenerife "[...] great and round in (your name of) 'Ocean'."[27] The lava that the volcano poured forth was the seed of Osiris. In the past, Tenerife was sometimes called the Island of Hell, a meaningful expression in our re-interpretation of the island's former glory. In classic times, the Canary Islands were the Islands of the Dead or, in the Graeco-Roman period, the Elysian Fields.[28]

The island of Tenerife takes up a central position amongst the seven islands that remain. "The gods are said 'to have given an island' to Osiris, the rightful owner, and an Egyptian legend mentions the 'Middle Island', an unknown, distant locality that was reached by the boat piloted by Anty, the ferryman, who brought his passengers over to the island."[29] Indeed, these Canary Islands lay at the edge of the World.

The present name of the Canary Islands derives from the word "Canaria". An explanation of this name is given: "Taking these considerations into account, we could suppose that the name of the island Gran Canaria derives from the inhabitants' custom in former days of keeping dogs, or from a religious dog cult that they may have observed, or both. The fact that Galino mentions the devil, who appeared as a dog on Gran Canaria as well as on La Palma, while Marin y Cubas utters a simple statement of facts concerning Tenerife, may indicate that the dog cult developed into a subsequent form of adoration. Redundant saints, similar to fallen angels, often turned into devils. It is interesting to notice how Anubis, the jackal god, was in Egypt particularly linked with the cult of the dead and [also] with embalming, a special act that typified the ancient Canarian culture."[30] In the necropolis of Llano de Maja on Tenerife, graves were found of sacrificial dogs. Similar graves, dating back to the middle of the third millennium, were also discovered in the Kerma culture (Nubia); in addition, similar findings were located in the subsequent Meru culture of Sudan.[31] Anubis was, after all, the keeper of the gate of Osiris, which justifies the existence of his cult on the Canary Islands. (Gran Canaria – Canis Major – Sirius, the Dog Star.)

7.3 Confirmation of a Legend

The Roman author Pliny the Elder (circa 23-79 CE) mentioned the location of the island "Atlantis" in his works: "There is also reported to be another island off Mount Atlas, itself also called Atlantis, from which a two-days' voyage along the coast reaches the desert district in the neighbourhood of the Western Ethiopians and the cape mentioned above named the Horn of the West [Cape Juby], the point at which the coastline begins to curve westward in the direction of the Atlantic."[32] In this work, Pliny assumed that Atlantis still existed, yet this must be based on a misunderstanding on his part, unless he was describing a quite different, unknown island. At that time, Atlantis may have been the name of the Canary Islands. As far as we know, Plato (circa 427-348 BCE) was the first to have mentioned Atlantis when he quoted information that Solon the Greek (circa 638-558 BCE) had received from an unidentified Egyptian priest.

On the other hand, three quarters of a century prior to Plato's account, Herodotus had already given a description in his **Histories** of a race called the Atlants, who apparently lived to the northwest of the Hoggar mountain range.[33]

The Edfu chronicles present an account of the legendary destruction of the "Homeland" of the Shemsu Hor, the result of a war between two superpowers. In the **Timaeus** and the **Kritias**, Plato described a similar legendary war between two superpowers and the ensuing destruction of an island he named Atlantis, which he portrayed as having disappeared into the waves.

The scientific world has never taken Plato's description of this event seriously, witness for example Professor Emeritus J.Gwyn Griffiths' in his study **Atlantis and Egypt with other selected Essays**: "When Plato introduced Atlantis [**Timaeus** 24-25] for the first time, he did so in an endeavour to convey an impression of grandeur, power and arrogance."[34] Increasing knowledge, gained from the tectonic flow theory, has broadened the gap between the possible reality of Atlantis, which, since 1984, has resulted in the study of Atlantis becoming classified as pseudo-archaeology.

However, archaeological documents ought first to be thoroughly examined before they are criticised and discarded; all the more so, as the Ptolemaic Dynasty, in imitation of Alexander the Great, wished to revive the glory and knowledge of the entire original culture of ancient Egypt. For that reason, the remnants of the data from the Ptolemaic and the classical period are of inestimable value as a source that enables us to retrieve authentic sources of knowledge about ancient Egypt.

Plato bore witness to this knowledge when he said "that sea [...] surrounded an island, located in front of the strait which you, Greeks, [...] call the Pillars of Heracles [Gibraltar]. From that island, which excelled the size of Libya and Asia put together, a voyager in those days could cross over to the other islands [the Bahamas and the Antilles], and from those islands he could reach the entire continent [America] that lay opposite and bordered this sea that truly merited its name."[35] This statement is as direct as a statement can be. Plato gave a geographical description of that part of the Earth that we know as the Atlantic Ocean, and while he is on the subject, he casually tells us about the existence of certain other islands in the ocean, and even appears to have knowledge of the American continent. Hence, no location other than the Atlantic Ocean qualifies. Atlantis was either situated in the Atlantic Ocean, or it never existed at all.

Plato's **Timaeus** 24 and 25, as told to the Greek Solon by an Egyptian priest, states that during the reign of Pharaoh Amasis (circa 570 BCE), the Greek philosopher Solon visited the town of Sais, the capital of Egypt at that time. This now totally ruined town was also the city of the goddess Neith, the goddess of the West.

Pharaoh Amasis was the first ruler to open up the borders of his country to the Greeks. Solon is therefore presumed to have been one of the very first scholars to whom the Egyptians, after thousands of years of secrecy, disclosed the contents of their archives. Solon elicited a reaction from the Egyptian priests during his visit when he told them about the history of his country from times immemorial. The priests responded that Solon and his people could not be acquainted with facts in relation to traditions that dated back to a distant past. The reason for this, they explained to Solon, lay in the many natural catastrophes caused by fire and water. Solon knew of only one catastrophe, namely a tidal wave.

The priests told him that their sacred books contained information that specified that Egypt had existed for 8,000 years, which meant that it must date back to *before* 8570 BCE. They also told him about the armed conflict and the heroic deeds of Solon's nation, and the simultaneous destruction of Atlantis, which occurred in a period dating back 9,000 years.

Factually, Plato's authentically documented text on Atlantis is the only one in existence. The words he put down on paper around 350 BCE read: "According to what our sacred books tell us, the foundation of our [Egyptian] state occurred even more than 8,000 years ago. Hence, those to whom I am now referring are your [Hellenistic] fellow citizens who lived more than 9,000 years ago. I will briefly reveal their laws to you and also show you the most illustrious amongst the heroic deeds they performed." Somewhat further on, Plato continues: "On this island of Atlantis, kings had established a grand and marvellous power that governed the entire island, and many other islands and parts of the mainland too. Yet there was even more: on this side of the strait, their rule extended from Libya to Egypt, and from Europe to Tyrrhenia [Italy]. And it came to pass that this power assembled all its forces and endeavoured to subject your country and ours and all the land on this side of the strait in one single throw. And in those days too, Solon, your city openly showed its power to all mankind and distinguished itself in bravery and strength." The narrative ends: "Yet in time, tremendous earthquakes and floods occurred and within one single disastrous day and night, your entire military power disappeared beneath the surface of the earth, whilst the island of Atlantis was devoured by the sea and also vanished."

Reymond's translation of the Edfu chronicles not only show such a remarkable and exact correspondence with Plato's description, they also verify it. Still, the history of the world as we officially know it today does not mention any incidents that occurred 11,400 years ago. Admittedly, we are not familiar with literary epics from ancient Egypt that match the Babylonian accounts. But nearly 5,000 years after Solon received his information, the Egyptians recorded their legendary historical events by hewing reliefs and hieroglyphs into the walls of the Temple of Horus at Edfu. Thus, 2,000 years after Aristotle's critique (384-322 BCE) on Plato's work on Atlantis, it now appears in a different light. Apparently, neither Plutarch (50-125 CE) nor Proclus (412-480 CE) were aware of the fact that the Egyptians had recorded their history in the temple at Edfu. Had they known, they would not have levelled such criticism towards Plato. At the same time, Plato's dialogue on Atlantis will never stand alone again.

Nevertheless, since 1984, the geophysicists' standpoint has taken on ever greater weight. After having examined the bottom of the Atlantic Ocean, they claim that Atlantis cannot possibly be located there. With scientific accuracy, the Czech geologist Kukal collected all available material about Atlantis and

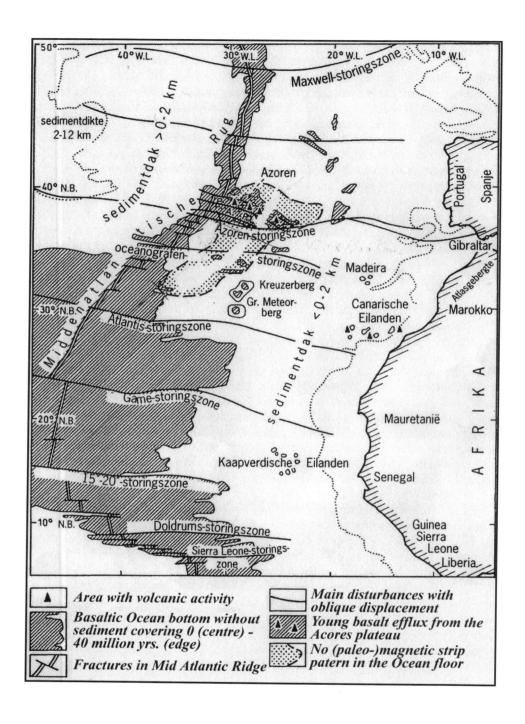

Fig. 63 Map of the bottom of the Atlantic Ocean including the Middle Atlantic Ridge. The map shows a dotted area where the regular paleo-magnetic strip pattern is absent, causing the outline of a large island to appear.

carried out a thorough search.[36] He came to the conclusion that no evidence exists of any submerged terrestrial mass in the Atlantic Ocean. According to Kukal, this ocean has existed in its present shape for at least one million years. Contemporary oceanographers have charted the entire ocean floor and claim that they found nothing that could point to a catastrophe.

However, Kukal's conclusions do not apparently correspond with other facts. Not only do the chronicles of Edfu fully substantiate Plato's version mentioning a war and a subsequent disaster, the doubts which Kukal raised sceptically against it, including the supposedly dubious location of the Pillars of Hercules, prove to be totally unfounded. Kukal also paid special attention to geological aspects. In the end, he considered the possibility that Atlantis might be located somewhere in the Mediterranean Sea, maybe at Thera (following the suggestions of Galanopoulos and Marinatos). But "in those days, the sea was still navigable, it encircled an island located in front of the strait which you, Greeks, call the Pillars of Heracles." Those words point irrevocably to the Atlantic Ocean.

Emery and Uchupi's ***The Geology of the Atlantic Ocean*** describes not only the former exploration of this ocean by Celts and Phoenicians; above all, it mentions each and every cartographic aspect of the bottom of the Atlantic Ocean. Around the Azores, "hot spots" exist where gushes of magma are driven upward out of the depths of the Earth's crust. In that precise area, known to be volcanically active and extremely unstable, a disturbance has been observed hadh in what is called the regular magnetic strip pattern. Here, the regularity in the strip pattern, which has been shown to exist everywhere else on the bottom of the northern and middle Atlantic Ocean, is *lacking*.

To the northwest of the Great Meteor, within an expansive area stretching from the south-west to the north-east (from approximately 30°N. and 35°W. to approximately 41°N. and 22°W.), the regular sedimental covering on the basaltic crust of the oceanic bed is absent. In addition, this area to the south of the Azores completely lacks the regular paleo-magnetic strip pattern that exists everywhere else in the Atlantic Ocean.[37] Almost unbesought, it delineates the *outline* of a large island measuring approximately 400 by 1300 kilometres (cf. fig. 63). The northern side (of the former island) was once crowned by a precipitous mountain range (nowadays the Azores), while the southern coastline bordered on a lowland plain.

The present classification of Atlantis as pseudo-archaeology is not only refuted by geological facts; written evidence from ancient times such as the Edfu chronicles, various vigorous references in the Pyramid Texts, the curious twofold New Year celebration of the Egyptians, all serve to substantiate the existence of a former cradle that has since been obliterated. After a period of 11,400 years, all traces of a catastrophe of said dimensions, along with enormous volcanic eruptions and tidal waves, may well have been erased. Masses of volcanic ashes, pumice and sand have covered the submerged island, now at an average depth of 3,000 metres. The extent of this inferno was enough to raise the temperature by an average of five degrees. This is substantiated by ice-core borings that were carried out at the North Pole (research by Hammer et al).

Towards the end of the last glacial period, the position of the centre of the Keewatin-ice cap of North America was eccentric in comparison with the present North Pole, lying noticeably more towards the Great Bear Lake and the Great Slave Lake. Consequently, the northern part of the American continent, beyond Chicago and down to approximately 41° N., lay hidden beneath the tail ends of the antediluvian ice cap. I argue that the antediluvian North Pole moved from about 120° W. and 66° N. to its present location, a distance of about 2,600 kilometres. A major part of Siberia, as well as parts of the Northern Ice Sea, were not covered by ice. At the South Pole, the ice cap lay more in the direction of Australia and New Zealand, so that part of Antarctica, especially Queen Maud Land, was not covered under an ice cap.

The 16th century Piri Re'is map shows Queen Maud Land without such an ice cap. Seismographic research has proved that the geography of this coastline shows significant correspondence with that map. This is one of the reasons why Hapgood concludes that Piri Re'is map must be based on knowledge of the existence of an ancient civilisation.

Due to a possible shift of the Earth's poles, the North Pole and the South Pole suddenly changed places, causing a world-encompassing catastrophe. A geological period (labelled the Quaternary) came to its end, and the Holocene Period began. It seems that the physiography of the Earth changed drastically, and unrelentingly erased all traces of an archaic civilisation. That is why the Edfu chronicles of the Followers of Horus, the inheritance of a distant past, together with the **Codex Tro-Cortesianus** of the Mayas, the **Codex Boturini** (published in part 1 of **Mexican Antiquities** by Lord Kingsborough) and the Aztecs' **Historia Mexicana** (1576) are the sole historical sources we possess. These sources confirm this atrocious catastrophe and the annihilation of a civilisation. It confirms the existence of two cultural periods, one archaic and lost forever, the other one known to us as the historical cultural period that rose in the fourth millennium BCE.

7.4 The Basis of ancient Egyptian Dualism

Hence, two Creations and two Worlds lived on in the collective memory of the Egyptians. To them, two creations existed, one of a prehistoric world, the other of the existing world in which they lived. And last but not least, Egypt was ruled by the constellation of Gemini, by which belongs duality. This is the profound and fundamental motive behind their dualistic principles. The Egyptian culture was saturated with a dualism that can be found in various settings, such as in the "Two Countries" of Horus and Seth and the prehistoric twin towns of Nekhen/Nekheb (Hieraconpolis) and Pe/Dep (Buto) as the capitals of Upper and Lower Egypt, in the dualistic monarchy with its white crown and its red crown, in the two New Year days and their respective celebrations, and in their hieroglyphic writing in which word and image go together. Their highly regulated structure was full of dualism and symbolism that enabled them to immortalise the memory of their previous existence. Last but not least, the ancient name of Egypt was Khemi, etymologically related to the constellation Gemi(ni), see Chapter 5.24 and fig. 52.

In the 16th century, this dualistic structure of two kingdoms still existed on a few Canary Islands, such as Fuerteventura, Gran Canaria and Tenerife. This was recorded by the Italian architect and engineer Torriani, who dwelt on those islands by order of the Spanish king Philip II. Torriani's work was translated and later re-published by the German author Wölfel.

Chapter 8

Egypt, a Gift of Osiris

"Osiris is raised from the dead. The sky reels, the Earth quakes, Horus comes, Thoth appears, they raise Osiris from upon his side and make him stand in front of the Two Enneads. Remember, Seth, and put in your heart this word which Geb spoke, this threat that the gods made against you in the Mansion of the Prince in On [Heliopolis], because you threw Osiris to the Earth, when you said, O Seth: 'I have never done this to him', so that you might have power thereby, having been saved, and that you might prevail over Horus; when you said, O Seth: 'It was he who attacked me', when there came into being his name of 'Earth-attacker' when you said, O Seth: 'It was he who kicked me', when there came into being his name of Orion, long of leg and lengthy of stride, who presides over Upper Egypt. Raise yourself, O Osiris, for Seth has raised himself, he has heard the threat of the gods who spoke about the god's father. Isis has your arm, O Osiris; Nephthys has your hand, so go between them. The sky is given to you, the Earth is given to you, and the Field of Rushes, the Mounds of Horus and the Mounds of Seth; the towns are given to you and the nomes assembled for you by Atum, and he who speaks about it is Geb."[1]

This Pyramid Text is an account of the catastrophe that once dealt destruction to the Earth, and it points to Seth as the one who caused it. After the catastrophe, Osiris rose from the dead and regained dominion over the Earth and Egypt in particular. In an earlier setting, Seth had smitten Osiris to the ground and even killed him, though this is not mentioned explicitly in the Pyramid Text. Horus and Thoth put him back on his feet again and the gods cautioned Seth never to cause a fatal catastrophe again, whereupon Seth placed the blame for this event on Horus. Not only did he accuse Horus of this deed, Seth even charged Horus with having attacked the Earth. From that moment on, Horus was identified permanently with the constellation of Orion. The entire creation was returned to Osiris, including his first and former dwelling-place, the "Field of Rushes" (the Elysian Fields), which we now know to be the Canary Islands, the Islands of Scorpio. In addition, after his rebirth, Osiris acquired dominion over Egypt.

8.1 Osiris' Arrival and his Rebirth in Memphis

The text known as the "Memphite Theology" includes the mythical origin of Egyptian kingship. It is a cosmological description of the structure of Creation and the foundation of Egypt.

Part 1 of the text describes how the creation of the Earth began with the formation of a hill, the so-called Primaeval Hill, which emerged from the pri-

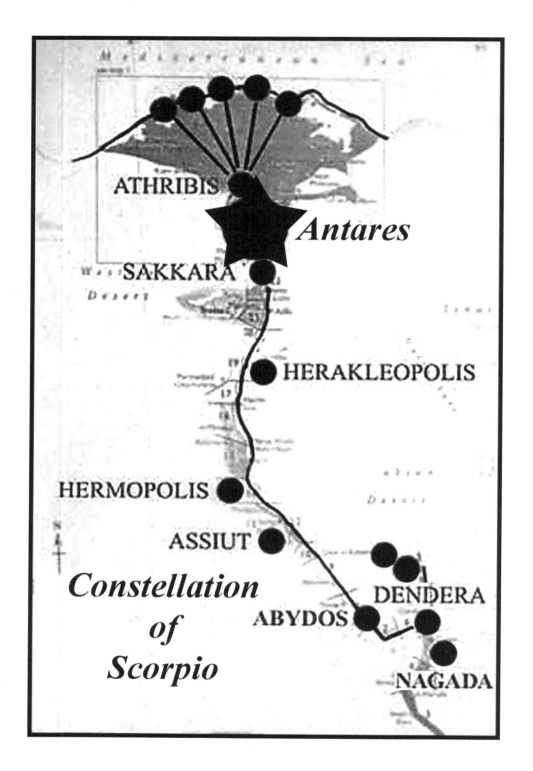

Fig. 64. Map of Egypt showing the star constellation Scorpio, with its main star Antares on the spot where the Golden Triangle Rostau took shape.

maeval waters. Part 2 deals with the end of the conflict that preceded the final stabilisation of the Universe and the Earth. Horus and Seth are separated from one another and Geb, the god of the Earth, addresses them, whereupon dominion over Egypt is divided between them. Hence, the quoted Pyramid Text is entirely consistent with this part of the "Memphite Theology".

Although various other parts of the text, inscribed on what is known as the Shabaka stone, have been seriously damaged, Part 3 is legible enough to inform us that Memphis derived its significance for Egypt from the fact that it harboured the burial-place of Osiris. This fact is repeated in Part 6, which is also in good condition.

Here, we find a detailed account of the significance that Memphis had for Egypt as the country's royal residence and as the site of the Temple of Ptah. The text also mentions that the link between Osiris and Memphis had not always existed. Osiris is said to have reached Memphis via the waters of the Nile. After all, the Nile basin was Hapi, and so it was also the constellation Scorpio and Osiris. He allegedly drowned in this river, and Isis and Nephtys are presumed to have pulled his body on land in Memphis. Osiris' body was committed to the Earth in the immediate surroundings of Memphis, where the semen of Osiris is imagined to have sprouted and created a new state, with Memphis as its capital.[2]

The special role that the Memphis-Letopolis-Heliopolis region acquired in the Egyptian religion is related to the position of the main star Antares (magnitude -0.98) in the constellation of Scorpio. A projection of this constellation onto the surface of the Earth puts Antares on the apex of the Delta (cf. fig. 64). Fictitiously, the star Antares is, as it were, located on a layer (stratigraphically) below the star Alhena in Gemini, with which the capital Memphis also correlates. The star Antares was known as the "Lord of the Seed" and "the creator of prosperity and well-being".[3] In the Egyptians' thinking, the twofold energy of these gods (stars) caused the grain to sprout, but above all it caused life to be reborn. This explains why the Pyramid Field, the necropolis, was built in this region.

Another brilliant example of this mental image is found in what are known as the "Osiris beds". Osiris fulfilled an additional role as the god of fertility. The Egyptians mixed sludge from the Nile with grains of corn and shaped this into small effigies of Osiris. They placed these figures on a bed, and a few days later the corn would begin to shoot. Thus, the small overgrowth that appeared would outline the figure of Osiris. These small figures were then sold as fertility charms.[4]

The unique location of the region around Memphis on the apex of the Delta and the relationship with the position of the star Antares in the constellation of Scorpio provided the ultimate reason why Memphis was founded on that location. Antares was known as the Heart of Scorpio and also governs the degree of the Golden Section (222°30') within the Zodiac. This is identical with the angle (bend) in the basic pattern of the Pyramid Field near the Djoser complex (cf. fig. 34).

Because of its correlation with Antares, Memphis was proclaimed the capital of Egypt. Upon Osiris' arrival in Memphis, the world was reborn, after the impact of the catastrophe. The Egyptians sensed the emergence of a new "Homeland" under the rule of Osiris. The region of Memphis-Letopolis-Heliopolis (Rostau), including the Pyramid Field as its necropolis, formed the "Golden Triangle" where death as well as rebirth prevailed. Accordingly, "Each king, at death, becomes Osiris, just as each king, in life, appears 'on the throne of Horus'; each king *is* Horus."[5] That is the reason why the pharaohs were immortalised in countless iconographic images, which displayed them with a belligerent bearing as Horus: the quintessence of the constellation Orion, namely the Warrior, whose militant posture was rendered symbolically by the construction of pyramids that formed the Pyramid Field around Memphis.

8.2 Shifting Seasons

The Egyptian calendar as we know it began on the first day of the first month of the flooding season, I Achet 1. Originally, this day corresponded with the time when the waters of the Nile began to rise. This was the first New Year Day of the calendrical year. Prior to that day, five additional days existed, known as the epagomene days. Subsequently, exactly four months later, another new beginning occurred, I Peret 1, and it was duly celebrated throughout the country as a second New Year Day. It marked the ending of the flood season, and the waters of the Nile now returned to the riverbed. This was followed by the sowing of new crops. The festivities preceding this New Year Day also lasted for five days.

All three seasons consisted of four months of thirty days each. The Sowing season was followed by the Harvesting season, which started on I Shemu 1. No New Year's celebrations were held on this day.

So we see how the Egyptian year counted two New Year Days, which were both preceded by five special days. What was this calendar based on? The obvious answer would appear to lie in the nature-bound aspect of this predominantly agricultural society. Yet there are more exceptional circumstances to consider, such as IV Achet 26, the day of the Sokar festivities, which began by drawing the Sokar barque around the White Walls of Memphis.

This procession may have been intended as a symbolical boat journey to the residence of their new homeland, i.e. Egypt. Furthermore, IV Achet 30, the last day of the Flood season, marked the interment of Osiris.

The second New Year's Day (I Peret 1) was considered to have been the day on which Horus ascended the throne as Osiris' successor. Hence, on various occasions it served as the day on which, following the death of a pharaoh, his successor ascended to the throne. What is more, this day was claimed to have marked the mythical beginning of the existing world structure, which is therefore linked up with the celebration of the Sed-festival (a festival during which the power of the pharaoh was ritually tested).[6]

In one of the Pyramid Texts, this second New Year's day (I Peret 1) is connected with the ceremony around the Jubilee festival of Heb-Sed: "Osiris appears, the Sceptre is pure, the Lord of Right is exalted at the First of the Year, (even he) the Lord of the Year."[7, 8] These facts do not point to a celebration that might be governed by some agricultural aspect in connection with the flooding of the Nile. The truth is that the Egyptians possessed a collective memory of the "First Era of Osiris", and this New Year festival was held entirely under the patronage of Osiris, which increases the probability that around 15,570 BCE the autumn season, with its characteristic constellation of Osiris, had shifted towards the summer season. This theory is verified by a star map showing that at sunrise on 19th July 15,570 BCE, Scorpio rises on the eastern horizon. A different star map, set for sunrise on 18th March of that same year (the previous season), shows the constellations of the summer season, i.e. Gemini and Orion, at the beginning of spring. This proves that I Peret 1 was considered to be the original *"first"* New Year Day during the pre-historic cultural period of the Egyptians (cf. fig. 65 and 66).

Precise calculations show that according to the "adjustable" Egyptian calendar, I Peret 1 occurred on 19th July 15,442 BCE. Due to a possible correspondence between the constellations and the calendar month, I Achet 1 became the following New Year Day when the Egyptian calendar was re-introduced, which happened on 19th July 4242 BCE. This serves as additional proof that the Egyptians knew of the existence of a prehistoric cultural period through their ancestors, the Followers of Horus.

8.3 Seth who murdered Horus, and the Big Dipper

There are numerous legends about major catastrophes. The Dogon speak of a "Pale Fox", that wreaked havoc upon the Earth: "The fourth Nommo, who bore the name Nommo Anagonno, or Ogo, did not show himself as a fish [Nommo Anagonno is a Silurian fish]. When he was created, he rebelled against his creator and brought chaos upon the universe. In the end, he is claimed to have taken on the shape of the 'Pale Fox', Vulpes pallida, as a token of his decline."[9] What does this mean?

The star that is believed to be synonymous with the fox is Alcor, the accompanying small star gamma Ursa Major, next to zeta Ursa Major in the Big Dipper.[10] The explanatory text tells us that this star is responsible for the first catastrophe, known by the name of Era or Irra.[11] That same star is also considered to have caused the next catastrophe.[12]

Some dramatic versions of this legend exist amongst various tribes. The Laps, the Siberian Kirghiz and the Pawnee Red-Indians each have their own interpretation.[13] And although the Greeks are claimed to have had no knowledge of the star Alcor, an ancient story nonetheless relates how "Electra, the lost Pleiade" wandered away from her companions and subsequently turned into a fox. In the end, the different versions all lead to the principle of cause and effect, as described by Proclus: "the fox-star continuously nibbles at the thong of the yoke which holds heaven and Earth together. German folklore adds that when the fox succeeds, the world will come to its end."[14] Hence, Alcor of the Big Dipper or the 'Pale Fox' of the Dogon, is presumed to have caused the catastrophe from which Uta-napishtim managed to escape. This catastrophe is indeed described in the Era Epic (or Irra Epic). Significantly enough, the Roman poet Ovid named this star *Atlantis*.[15]

A description of the constellation Ursa Major in **Star Names, Their Lore and Meaning**, not only includes the fox, but also a gazelle. The Egyptians

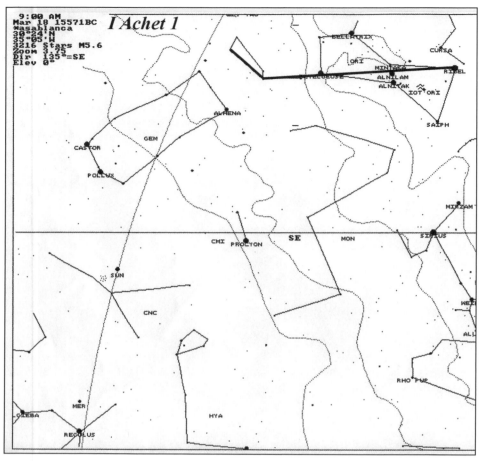

Fig. 65. Star chart set for 18th March 15,571 BCE, the traditional New Year Day, I Achat 1 on the Egyptian calendar. It shows the heliacal rising of the star Sirius. Orion above the star Sirius.

saw the Big Dipper as the foreleg of Mshtyw, the Ox.[16] The present translation of this hieroglyph is erroneous. Instead of construing it as the "foreleg of the Ox', the hieroglyph in question ought to be understood as a representation of one of the hindlegs, i.e. the shank of the gazelle. Two hindlegs occur in hieroglyphic writing (F23 and F24, *Egyptian Grammar*). *Star Names* also mentions two legs of an animal that are each related to two different pairs of stars. One pair denotes the "first jump", the other pair refers to the "second jump". The two stars of the "first jump" are named Tania borealis and Tania australis and mark the "foot" of the right hindleg of Ursa Major. The two stars of the "second jump" are named Alula borealis and Alula australis and mark the "foot" of the left hindleg of Ursa the Bear.[17]

The painting on the ceiling of the tomb of Senmut, vizir during the reign of Pharaoh Hatshepsut (18th Dynasty) shows the northern celestial sphere. The centre of the northern sky is occupied by an obelisk. The point of the obelisk is directed at eta Ursa Major, which appears as a foothold for the Bull's body.[18]

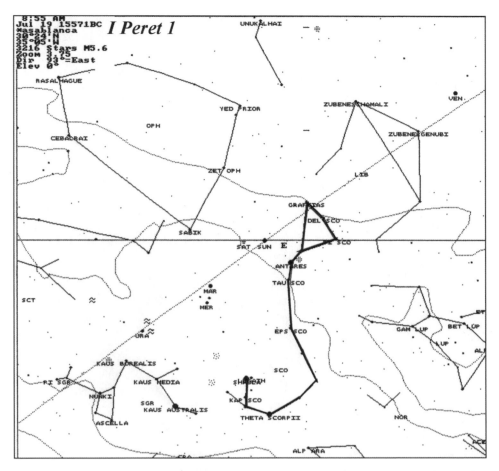

Fig. 66. Star chart for 19th July 15,571 BCE, the traditional Osiris festival, I Peret 1 on the Egyptian calendar. It shows the rising of the star constellation Scorpio.

Behind that body, known as the Big Dipper, we find Selqet, the Scorpion goddess, with a Silurian fish above her head. This fish is identical to the fish in the cartouche (Serekh) of Pharaoh Narmer and to the Nommo Anagonno of the Dogon. Evidently, the gazelle alludes to a star or to stars in the Big Dipper. The Egyptologist Wallis Budge appropriately qualifies the gazelle as the "incarnation of evil"[19].The Horus falcon, drove out, pursued, and conquered those evil powers, which are portrayed by the gazelle.[20] Sethe has even pointed out that this ritual persisted in Tunis [Carthage], in the way falcons hunted gazelles and antelopes.[21]

According to the Mesopotamian chronicles, the monster Tiamat was responsible for the catastrophe. Tiamat, who was sometimes depicted as a snake, personified the "first" chaos and showed hostility towards the gods, opposing law and order. Tiamat is associated with the constellation Draco.[22] At that time, the stars of Draco belonged partly to the Big Dipper, partly to the Hippopotamus and to the variation of the latter, the Crocodile. They are jointly depicted on the walls of the Ramesseum in Thebes and on the plaque of Denderah (cf. fig. 6). In its claws, the creature held an object that resembles a plough-share. The German Hebraic specialist Franz Delitsch (1813-1890) remarked that this creature was Hes-mut, thereby alluding to the Raving Mother. A rather fanciful presumption suggests that this resulted in the name of the neigh-bouring Plough (*Mr*). In time, this shape may have evolved into the knife with which the Hippopotamus was subsequently equipped. The Hippopotamus was identified with Seth. It holds the knife of Seth in its claws.[23]

Thus, we see that the Myth of Horus and Seth is based on the Era or Irra catastrophe and also on stars that had formerly been identified and were pointed out by the ancient cultures as the "Pale Fox", as both shanks of the Big Dipper, and as Tiamat.

Egypt's second New Year festival brought back a notable recollection of the catastrophic end of its former civilisation, the first cultural period. At the same time, a new world was created out of chaos. This sequence of events was described in the Epic of Creation. The first day on the Egyptian calendar, New Year's Day, was an everlasting annual reminder of the destruction of their "Homeland". Besides that, the five days that were added onto the year (the epagomene days) also played an important role. The meaning attributed to each of these days was: Osiris day, a day of misfortune; Horus day, no specific meaning; Seth day, a day of misfortune; Isis day, a beautiful festival of heaven and earth; Nephtys day, a day of misfortune. On the whole, these were indeed evil days. In addition, a threatening incantation was invoked against these gods:

"Then, the heavens will no longer exist.
Then, the earth will no longer exist.
Then, the five epagomene days will no longer exist.
Then, the offering to the gods and to the Lords of Heliopolis will no longer exist." [24]

In this context, the Egyptian Apophis in the shape of a long-drawn-out serpent is similar to Tiamat. Apophis was a demon that was constantly at war with Re (the Sun). This Apophis was the dragon that had to be held at bay. To the Egyptians, Apophis was the disturber of cosmic harmony and order,[25] while Tiamat was its Babylonian counterpart. On the morning of New Year's Day, Apophis was ritually killed throughout the country.[26] An Assyrian proverb poses the following question: "Whither can the fox flee from the sun?"[27]

Both the Dogon and the Assyrians were familiar with a star bearing the name fox; the Egyptians used the name Apophis, which is synonymous with the stars of Draco, the celestial dragon, partially ranked under the Big Dipper. In former eras, Seth was granted the dubious honour of killing Apophis (i.e. committing suicide), but in the end the Egyptian deity Seth became the equal of Apophis.

During the Late Period (approximately. 721 - 332 BCE), this is emphasised even further.[28] Seth created chaos and disorder, which is hinted at repeatedly in the Pyramid Texts.[29] All this reveals the fear that the Egyptians felt for this period around the New Year festival, a fear which even their belief in resurrec-tion was unable to dispel. It resulted in a series of rituals and sacrifices so that the existing cosmic order was maintained. The same fear is also manifest in numerous details that were typical of the Mesopotamian New Year festival, a festival they were at liberty to celebrate during the spring as well as during the autumn.

New Year's Day was the day on which the victory over the demonical powers and the chaos of destruction was celebrated. Joy prevailed, since cosmic order had been maintained. In both the Mesopotamian and the Egyptian cultures, the New Year rituals possessed a quality that typified the commemoration of a fatal and dramatic event. This is explicable, since prior to the New Year celebration, both cultures observed special days that were held in remembrance of a natural catastrophe that had once occurred (cf. appendix XI). These days were known to the Egyptians as the "days of misfortune", with the exception of one day, namely the *fourth*. To the Egyptians, that was the day of the "beautiful festival of heaven and earth".[30] Its meaning is evident: heaven and earth were in harmony, cosmic order prevailed, instead of chaos.

By analogy, the Akkadians celebrated the corresponding fourth day of their New Year festival by solemnly reciting the "Enuma elish", the Epic of Creation. "It was the most significant expression of the religious literature of Mesopotamia."[31] Even though no equivalent ritual text has yet been found in Egypt, the sensitivity that characterised the fourth day nonetheless tells its own tale.

8.4 Egypt, a Gift of Osiris

Herodotus called Egypt "a gift of the Nile".[32] Over the past centuries, these words have taken on a proverbial meaning. In this book, they have acquired an entirely new focus. The idea behind Herodotus' words enables its meaning to create a deeper impact on our imagination. After all, the Nile represented Osiris. Existence itself became manifest in Osiris, since all vegetation in Egypt found its source in the Nile. Osiris therefore stood for vitality, power and sprouting and hence for the rebirth of the crops. The fresh water of the flooding (the melted snow from the mountains of the Ethiopian highlands) was conveyed by the Nile (Osiris). This is described in the Pyramid Texts: "Horus comes and recognises his father in you, you [the Nile] being young in your name of 'Fresh Water'."[33] The Egyptians saw Osiris as the power on the Earth and the ruler of the Netherworld, the realm where the transformation from life to death occurred.

Professor Henri Frankfort in **Kingship and the Gods** wrote: "Osiris, as ruler of the Netherworld, appears sometimes as a true Pluto."[34] Pluto is indeed known in religious astronomy as the ruler of the zodiacal constellation of Scorpio, to which the power of life and death was attributed. In prehistoric times, namely during the first cultural period of the Egyptians, this constellation truly ranked as the predominant zodiacal sign. Due to its former significance, Osiris became the bearer of the notion of "kingship" during the second cultural period. That is why Osiris plays a major role in the texts and regal rituals pertaining to the succession and coronation of the pharaohs.

The Myth of Horus and Seth describes how after the death of Osiris, Isis nevertheless managed to become pregnant by her deceased husband. She then gives birth to a son who is named Horus. Following Osiris' death, Seth claimed

Fig. 67. Osiris, bearing the heka-sceptre and flail, the traditional symbols of this god. The figure originates from the burial chamber of Pharaoh Ramses I in the Valley of the Kings at Thebes (Luxor).

the entire territory of Egypt for himself. However, the birth of Horus forced him to share the country with him. After a battle that lasted for eighty years, Egypt was finally divided between the two. The Delta (Lower Egypt) was given to Horus and Upper Egypt to Seth. The border between the two lands ran south of Memphis, marked by the Red and the Bent Pyramids near Dahshur.

The Egyptians believed that they had received their land from Osiris and the gods. In gratitude, they built a residential necropolis for their supreme god Osiris in the "Golden Triangle" (Rostau), after the image of his son Horus. The gods looked down from heaven on this Pyramid Field... and beheld that it was good.

Once again, we see a preponderance of dualities. The river Nile was Osiris, and the Delta, the native region of Horus, was the site where the Pyramid Field was to be built to create the image of Horus (Orion). In this manner, they connected the world of Osiris to the world of Horus. Duality was also displayed in their calendar system, by their celebration of two New Year days: one for Osiris (I Peret 1), the other for Horus (I Achet 1). One dated from prehistoric times, specifically their first cultural period of Osiris, while the other, that of Horus, originated in the second cultural period. These are the "two heavens" described earlier. Star charts, set for the New Year Day of both cultural periods, illustrate and substantiate this point of view without further need for words (cf. fig. 22 and 23):

First cultural period:
19th July 15,000 BCE   Osiris (Scorpio) rises on the eastern horizon.

Second cultural period:
19th July 3000 BCE   Horus (Orion) rises on the eastern horizon.
                                 Era of Re (the Sun-cult is established)

The celebration of the New Year Day of the first cultural period (the Osiris festival) was thereby laid down for all eternity and maintained as the day on which the First Creation occurred.

"Osiris arose from the Dead" at the beginning of the second cultural period. Horus (Orion) subsequently replaced Osiris (cf. fig. 67) as his "visible manifestation". Osiris descended as the "celestial way" and became the terrestrial Nile, thereby turning Egypt into the gift of Osiris. We are back at the beginning of this book; the circle has been closed.

Epilogue

Egyptians have at all times claimed that they originally came from one or three island(s) in the middle of the ocean (*hbbt* or *wa'ret*, the primaeval waters). Statements that bear witness to this allegation have been kept intact in various collections of texts and inscriptions, such as the Pyramid Texts, some of which date back to the predynastic period. Old factual material can be found amongst the inscriptions of the Temple of Thoth at Hermapolis and the Temple of Horus at Edfu, though the latter dates from the Ptolemaic era. The location of this specific island is described explicitly as "marine". **Pyramid Text** Utterance 484, to mention just one example, states this very clearly: *"[...] the primaeval hill of the land in the midst of the sea"*, in other words: on one of these islands.

"The Edfu accounts clearly set out that according to the Egyptians the Earth was not believed to have been created in a single event. On the contrary, there seem to have been two distinct periods of creation; at first, the substance was created by a properly organic and physical act; then, in a second period, a further action brought substance to the surface of the primaeval waters. The nature of the creative activity completed during the second period seems to vary according to the places in which the myth of creation was elaborated, adopted or adapted. Descriptions of the creation of the Earth, as completed in the second period, may explain why the majority of the Egyptian texts describe the origin of Earth as an *"emergence of the Earth from the water."*[1] What is more, the nature of this creative process points specifically to the typically volcanic features of their land of origin.

In simple terms, these ancient Egyptian texts describe how land was brought forth in the ocean due to volcanic activity, a process that was made known to us in 1960 as the theory of *"Sea-Floor Spreading"*. A million years ago, Iceland was formed on the mid-Atlantic mountain chain according to the laws of that same spread system.

In the 1960s, the American geophysicist H.H. Hess put forward a theory that, supplemented by the *"Vine-Matthews Hypotheses"* on the alterations within the Earth's magnetic field, changed the science of geology. The validity of this theory was proved during the last quarter of the 20th century. Hess' theory is called the *"Sea-Floor Spreading hypothesis"*, which he bases on the assumption that molten substance surges up through the mantle of the Earth along the crests of the mid-Atlantic mountain chain. The magma cools down and subsequently forces the flanks of the mountain chain apart, resulting in a separation of the continents.

In the course of hundreds of thousands of years, this process brought forth islands such as Iceland and presumably even Atlantis, which is thought to be

located on the mid-Atlantic mountain chain. Iceland possesses 140 volca-
noes, and thirty of these are active. Around 9419 BCE, during violent volcanic
activity lasting for three consecutive months, the volcanic archipelago on the
mid-Atlantic chain belched fire, lava and gas (**Troana Codex** of the Mayas),
causing a terrible catastrophe (possibly a shift in the earth's crust) whereby
the island of Atlantis became submerged. A new geological era, called the
Quintar, had begun.

Do we still have reason to misinterpret the Egyptian texts? Their age-old
"Homeland" was located in the middle of the Atlantic Ocean with the distinctive features of an original, mountainous island, of which the Great Meteor, the
Cruiserberg and the Azores are today's remnants. The Egyptians called their
original dwelling place *"Ges-wa'ret"*, translated as *"this location, halfway
across the primaeval waters"*. They also used an alternative name for this
area, "region of the primaeval water", or dwelling place "on the edge of the
primaeval water".[2] Even texts from the Middle Kingdom express their fascina-
tion for these magic islands in distant waters.

Plato called this dwelling place Atlantis. Its name and description, "in the middle of the sea", is very concise. This former island took up a central position.
The Egyptians spoke of "an island that rose up out of the primaeval waters" as
"being the original nucleus of the world". This island is described in the Edfu
sources as *"this Pool which came into existence at the Beginning"*, and was
also called *"Province of the Beginning"*, of which the alternative name was
"Island of the Egg". This island was surmounted by the *"High Hill"*, which was
formed afterwards and consisted of the substance that rose out of the earth
whilst the island was entirely surrounded by the *hbbt* - the primaeval waters.
This description conforms to that well-known ancient image of the world: a flat
circular disc surrounded on all sides by the Oceanus, similar to the yolk of an
Egg or the pupil of an eye. It seems that the Egyptians alluded to a region in the
ocean that they considered to be the centre of the surrounding world, the
"nucleus of the radiance".[3] Were the Egyptians referring to possible connections, radiating from the geographical position of this island with other
ancient centres?

Our hypothesis is that the ancient cultures built their exceptional projects
on unique locations, deliberately chosen, in order to pass on to future generations the geographic position of the archaic nucleus where civilisation was
created. They built and/or marked out the following centres of civilisation on
the circumference of an imaginary circle with a radius of approximately 6350
kilometres and the island of Atlantis as its centre:

Egypt (Giza) :	29°59' N. and 31°07' E.
Mexico (Teotihuacan and surroundings) :	19°42' N. and 98°51' W.
Zaire (Loango and surroundings) :	04°38' S. and 11°50' E.
Bolivia (Tiahuanaco and surroundings) :	16°30' S. and 68°41' W.

The distance between Egypt (Giza) and Mexico (Teotihuacan) is 12,733 kilometres, which is almost equal to the earth's diameter (12,756 kilometres),
measured along the equator. If we draw a circle around the centre (Atlantis -
30°30' N. and 35°07' W.) with the radius of 6,350 kilometres, the circumfer-

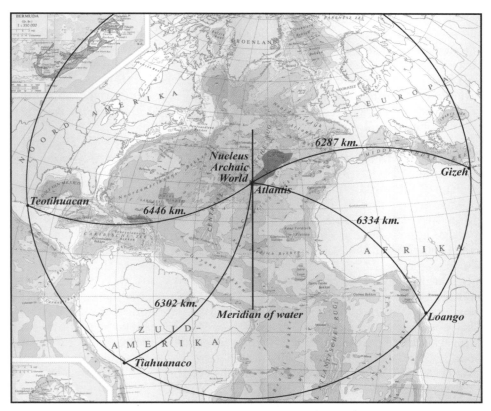

Fig. 68. Geographical representation of the Hermetic text: "The sacrosanct land of our ancestors (Followers of Horus) lies in the centre of the earth."

ence of this circle cuts across Egypt (Giza), Zaïre (Loango), Bolivia (Tiahuanaco) and Mexico (Teotihuacan). The respective distances from former Atlantis to Egypt, to Loango and to the ancient centres of civilisation of Mexico and Peru/ Bolivia in each case amount to 6,350 kilometres (see fig. 68 for distances).

The circumference of this circle equals 2 x Pi (3.1416) x R (radius, approximately 6,350 kilometres) = 40,000 kilometres, or the circumference of the earth measured at the equator. Atlantis can justifiably be considered as the archaic nucleus of the subsequent ancient centres of civilisation, a phrase that expresses accurately and concisely the significance of the following Hermetic text: *"The sacrosanct land of our ancestors lies in the centre of the earth."*[4] It also matches the official opinion in Plato's days. Long afterwards, this significant fact was frequently recognised and adopted by other civilisations as a fundamental principle of great consequence (e.g. Akkadia, its seals bearing the four quarters of the world with Egypt as the Centre, and then Mecca at an even later stage).

In 1907, a German expedition explored Loango, near the mouth of the river Congo, on the west coast of Africa, south of the equator. Loango is well-known as the region where the Moon-calendar is also based on the heliacal rising of the star Sirius. For them, a new cycle of twelve months per year begins when the first New Moon coincides with the rising of Sirius in the east. At present, this calendar, showing an Egyptian influence, is presumed to have been handed down as a cultural relic from the ancient Hamitic substratum, or that it was brought there from East Africa.[5] However, just like those other ancient centres of civilisation, Loango may be said to pride itself on an illustrious past, which is still completely unknown to us.

Incontestably, the now-submerged Atlantis was once the heart of an archaic civilisation. The Egyptians had enough reason to call their 'Homeland' the nucleus of the world. Remnants of that knowledge of the geographical location of Atlantis was known to Arab scientists. Both medieval Islamic mapmakers (from approximately 800 CE onwards) and the scientists from Cordoba (Andalusia, approximately 1300 CE) are known to have used its position. They called this place in the Atlantic Ocean the *"Meridian of Water"*.[6] This meridian, which was believed by the Andalusian scientists to indicate the "prime western meridian", was located approximately 17°30' west of the Canary Islands, in other words past the island of Hierro (18° W.), on approximately 35° W. The map of the Turkish admiral Piri Re'is shows the portolan at 24° N. and 35° W. This portolan also marks the *"Meridian of Water"*. Hapgood requested his good friend and mathematician Strachan to calculate the co-ordinates of that point, which resulted in a portolan located at 35°25' W,[7] or exactly 66° west of Giza and surroundings, and 66° south of the North Pole.

After the worldwide catastrophe, the survivors moved away to, amongst other places, the Canary Islands, where one island resembles a *"mountain in the middle of the sea"*, namely Tenerife (island Inferno) with its volcano Pico de Teide (3715m). Stylistically, these seven islands (*the Greek Elysian Fields*) form the constellation Scorpio (Osiris), and remain located on the edge of the world as it was formerly known. Later on, the primaeval race moved to the Central Mountains of North Africa. Other members from that primaeval race arrived in Loango on the West Coast of Africa, while some survivors sailed to Middle and South America. Part of the information the Mayas gave in the **Troana Codex** (*Troano MS*, part 11, pl. VI and VII) was that originally, they came from the islands of the Scorpion.

The Followers of Horus spread civilisation on our planet. They gave it shape in Egypt and Sumeria. More detailed research will reveal when civilisation began in Middle and South America. This development of Meso-America seems to have started with the Olmecs in approximately 1360 BCE, around 8,060 years after the Atlantis catastrophe (in accordance with the period mentioned in the **Troano Codex**).

The civilisation of Atlantis seems lost forever. The source of our second "lost civilisation" and its "unexplored territory" in the Central Mountains of North Africa has not disappeared yet. An urgent task awaits us...

Appendix

General remarks

Thinking, language and the rituals of ancient cultures were pervaded with the use of astrology. Plutarch wrote in **Moralia** about "the Oracles of Delphi", line 403 on page 306-307, that *"Thales [of Milete, sixth century BCE] did truly compile the Astrology [translated as Astronomy] which is attributed to him"*. In ancient cultures, the cosmos held a central position, in contrast to our modern world, where we have little or no awareness of this knowledge. Furthermore, modern notions of the true meaning of astrology are irrelevant and we would be well-advised to bear this in mind constantly in our efforts to investigate and interpret Antiquity.

Horoscopy for "the man in the street" did not develop until around 500 BCE. This, along with the discovery of horoscopes from that era, led to the assumption that astrology was then developed by the Babylonians. Before that time, the use of this skill was restricted to the high priest or the vizir, who advised the king or the pharaoh on, for example, religious or secular issues. Only towards the end of the Renaissance did modern astronomy develop from mathematical astrology.

In the Egyptian culture, the focal position of the cosmos is made evident in an extraordinarily forceful manner. They not only used pyramids as a means to create a reproduction on the face of the Earth of the star constellation they identified with their god Horus, but an important part of this Pyramid Field has furthermore proved to be a projection of a 'central image of the heaven' or 'centre of the heaven', in which the Egyptians buried their dead in mastabas in the belief that their ancestors were to be reborn after 3,000 years. According to Van der Waerden, the migration of the soul touches upon the deepest religious roots of astrology (horoscopy).[1] Undoubtedly so, but in particular upon those of the Egyptians and their notions of the immortality of the soul, and consequently upon the most profound essence of Egyptian religion. Herodotus wrote: *"The Egyptians were also the first to proclaim the doctrine that the human soul is immortal, and when the body dies, it takes its abode in another living being that is born at that moment; after the soul has accomplished the cycle through all animals on the earth and in the sea and in the sky, it will return into the body of a human being who is born at that time, and this cycle is completed in 3,000 years."* [2]

The Pyramid Field between Memphis and Hawara is a projection of the aforementioned *"centre of the heaven"* (size of the celestial sector of 42 degrees, corresponding with the 42 assessors (are Judges of the Dead) from **The Book**

of the Dead, Proverb 125) in which the dead dwelt and were reborn after 3,000 years. The size of this celestial sector (42 degrees) corresponds with the backwards motion of the precession over a period of 3,000 years (one degree in 71.4285 years, thus 42 degrees x 71.4285 years equalling 3,000 years). This clearly proves that the Egyptians of the Old Kingdom were acquainted with Precession and that they expressed this in the Pyramid Field and in their religion. Thus, the soul is an integral part in the cycle of the stars including that of Precession.

Van der Waerden goes even further in his conclusions, after briefly calling attention to the Egyptologists' insistence that Herodotus was mistaken about this version of the Migration of the Soul.[3] Furthermore, he states that the Pythagorean philosopher Iamblichus (circa 400 CE) reported that the Egyptians considered geometry and astronomy to be interrelated.[4] It is a fact that the Pyramid Field was plotted out geometrically in correspondence with the 'centre of the heaven'. In addition, Van der Waerden states "that these 3,000 years should be considered as a cosmic period and that this period is on the same level as *"Planetenperioden der Astronome und die Weltperioden der Kosmologen"*[5] (Planetary periods of the Astronomers and the World Eras of the Cosmologists). Undoubtedly, many examples exist to support this view, such as the celebration of the Sed festival, which was held every thirty years, and the intemperate concern of Pharaoh Ramses II about the *"Sense of History"* and the *"Lists of Royal Ancestors"*.[6] During the reign of Ramses II, 3,000 years had passed since the Egyptian calendar system had been introduced in 4242 BCE. This led, amongst other things, to a Kinglist being drawn up, which is known as the Kinglist of the Turin papyrus.

APPENDIX I : The *Chronicle of World History*, and its mutual link with the Biblical and with the Egyptian Chronology

One of the main problems in using the garbled and hardly accessible work of the Egyptian high priest Manetho as a chronological source and traditional Kinglist is caused by the fact that his original book has been lost, so that we must be satisfied with texts copied by Flavius Josephus, Julius Africanus and especially the **Chronicle of World History** by Eusebius. In the Renaissance, chronologists considered his work to be the most acceptable of all.

Josephus Justus Scaliger (1540-1609) made use of Eusebius' work when he wrote his **Emendatio Temporum** and **Thesaurus Temporum**. During the autumn of 1581, Scaliger came in contact with the tradition of technical chronology, which had, to a considerable degree, drawn the interest of mathematicians during the first half of the 16th century. He researched the chronology of ancient peoples, whilst selecting the Biblical Chronology as his starting-point. He noticed that chronologists had made errors in the past as they had been unable to work accurately enough. He wanted to exclude these imperfections from future investigations. To that end, he devised a long-term cycle which he based upon the 532-year cycle of Dionysius (Easter cycle of 28 x 19 years). He multiplied this Dionysian cycle by the indiction period of 15 years. (The indiction period was a cycle of 15 years introduced by Constantine the Great in 313 CE for chronological and taxation purposes.) This resulted in the Julian Period of 7,980 years,[7] a period he named after his father *Julius Caesar Scaliger*. Intriguingly, Scaliger did not claim this cycle to be a structural novelty. "Indeed, he made it clear to his reader that a [unknown] computist 900 years before his time had devised something comparable."[8] "The 19-year lunar cycle or Golden Number, in particular, proved in Scaliger's hands a multi-application tool that eliminated the need for most others, especially in the time before Christ's birth". He made this cycle start on 1st January 4713 BCE; it will end in 3267 CE.[9]

Jewish chronology offered Scaliger a clear starting date: 1st October 3760 BCE.[10] "However, his opinion of the usability of the Biblical Chronology was ambivalent. Since his thirties, he had argued that the Old and New Testaments could not stand on their own as complete records of human history.[11] [...] On the other hand, he also insisted that Biblical history was useless until it was set into a wider, world-historical context."[12] Subsequently, he declared that "Biblical history and astronomy thus dovetailed as neatly as the mortise and tenon elements in a fine piece of joinery. Without the former, one could attain no certainty about the first two millennia and more of world history. Without the latter, one could derive no absolute dates for Creation itself and the intervals the Bible reckoned from it in whole (but otherwise undefined) years."[13] "In private conversations, in the margins of his books, in personal letters and in one remark in the **Thesaurus**, Scaliger went further, admitting that while the core structure of the Hebrew Bible was sound, it rested in part on shaky foundations."[14] Scaliger was obviously in two minds about the Biblical Chronology.

It is an established fact that on certain issues, the Jewish and the Samaritan Hebrew texts are at variance with the Greek version, which is known as the Septuagint (texts of the Old Testament compiled between 250-100 BCE). "Considered in that light, Professor Grafton remarked that 'the difference between the Hebrew and Septuagint computations of the period between the Creation and the Flood [are] 1,236 years'". [15] This number of years will play an important role in our explanation.

In the **Thesaurus Temporum**, Scaliger wrote that he thought that it was a reasonable conclusion, if such was considered necessary and usable, "to extend the same cycles backwards by another 7,980 years".[16] He knew that the Byzantine Era (beginning 5509 BCE) existed before the start of the Julian period in 4713 BCE. "He defined the time into which Manetho's first dynasties fell as *tempus mythicon*"; it went back into a very far past. In order to explain his thinking, he resorted once again to his favourite fragment by the famous Roman Varro (116-27 CE), who specified *three distinct periods of time*.[17] What did Varro mean by that?

In the 12th century, Europe (i.e. or via Spain) became acquainted with the theory of the *Great Conjunctions* through the Arabs. It claimed that the conjunctions of the planets Jupiter and Saturn marked transformational moments in human history. The great Arab astronomer, mathematician, music theorist and philosopher Al Kindi (circa 800 CE) is considered to be the father of Arabian astrology. He corroborated this point of view when he drew up a treatise about the *"Principle and the Influence of the Great Conjunction between Jupiter and Saturn on the rise and fall of World Empires and World Religions"*.

On 7th December of the year 7 BCE, the great conjunction was visible. Could there possibly be a link between this conjunction of the planets Jupiter and Saturn and Biblical Chronology, when we note that at the birth of Christ, the three kings hastened to Bethlehem from the east (Matthew 2:2)?

Survey of the Biblical Chronology:

Genesis 5:3, 130 years; Gen. 5:6, 105 years; Gen. 5:9, 90 years; Gen. 5:12, 70 years; Gen. 5:15, 65 years; Gen. 5:18, 162 years; Gen. 5:21, 65 years; Gen. 5:25, 187 years; Gen. 5:28, 182 years; this results in a sub-total of 1056 years until the birth of Noah.

From the birth of Noah until the Deluge:

Gen. 7:11, 600 years + 2 months + 17 days.

A total of 1,656 years + 2 months + 17 days until the Deluge.

Gen. 8:13 and 14, l year + 2 months + 27 days from the Deluge until the draught.

After the Deluge:

Genesis 11:10, 2 years; Gen. 11:12, 35 years; Gen. 11:14, 30 years; Gen. 11:16, 34 years; Gen. 11:18, 30 years; Gen. 11:20, 32 years; Gen. 11:22, 30 years; Gen. 11:24. 29 years; Gen. 11:26, 70 years; this results in a total of 292 years until the birth of Abraham.

Subsequently:

Gen. 21:5, 100 years until the birth of Isaac.

Subsequently:

Gen. 25:26, 60 years until the birth of Jacob.

Subsequently:

Gen. 47:28, 130 years until the entry into Egypt.

Subsequently:

Exodus 12: 40 and 41, 430 years until the Exodus.

Subsequently:

1 Kings 6:1 and 2 Chron. 3:2, 480 years + 1 month + 2 days until the Temple of Solomon began to be built.

A subtotal of 3,149 years, 6 months and 16 days

*Periods of rule of the **Kings of Judah**:*

1 Kings 11:42,	Solomon 40-4 years =	36 years
1 Kings 14:21,	Rehoboam	17 years
2 Kings 13:1,2 and 3,	Abijah	3 years
1 Kings 15:9,	Asa	41 years
1 Kings 22:41 and 42,	Jehoshaphat 25-4 yrs.=	21 years
2 Kings 3:1,	Jehoram	8 years
2 Kings 8:25 and 26,	Ahazia	1 year
2 Kings 11:1 until 4,	Athaliah	7 years
2 Kings 12:1,	Jehoash	40 years
2 Kings 14:1 and 2,	Amaziah	29 years
Interregnum		11 years
2 Kings 15:2,	Azariah	52 years
2 Kings 15:32,	Jotham	16 years
2 Kings 16:1 and 2,	Ahaz	16 years
2 Kings 18:1 and 2,	Hezekiah 29-2 yrs.=	27 years
2 Kings 21:1,	Manasseh	55 years
2 Kings 21:19,	Amon	2 years
2 Kings 21:26,	Josiah	31 years
2 Kings 23:31,	Jehoahaz	3 months
2 Kings 23:36 and 2 Kings 36:8,9,	Eljakim/Jehoiakim	11 years
2 Kings 24:8,	Jehoiachin	3 months
2 Kings 24:18 and 2 Kings 36:11,	Zedekiah	11 years

A Subtotal of the years of rulership of the Kings of Judah: 435.5 years.

Biblical Chronology, a total of 3,149 years, 6 months and 16 days + 435 years and 6 months = 3,585 years and 16 days

The fall of Zedekiah and the destruction of the Temple are presumed to have occurred in 589 BCE.[18] This occurred after a siege that lasted one year and six months. However, other sources place this event in 587 BCE.[19] According to these calculations, the Biblical Chronology comprises around 4,174 or 4,172 years up to the year 1. Our hypothesis is based on the assumption that the translation of the Latin word Genesis, namely "constellation under which something is born", has a deeper meaning: for example birth under a planetary cycle. The title of the first book of the Bible and the meaning it has could refer to a comparable beginning of a planetary cycle, for example the conjunction of the planets Jupiter and Saturn. Such a conjunction occurred on 3rd December 4177 BCE (JD 196,111) and on 7th December 7 BCE (JD 1,719,208).

Starting-point: 3rd December 4177 BCE =	4,177.923 years
Minus: total of the Biblical Chronology:	3,585.004 years
Remainder	592.919 years up to the year 1

This results in a slight chronological difference of approximately 3 years, compared with the assumed fall of Zedekiah, a chronological difference that may have come about due to the revision of the Biblical books.

On the above grounds, it can be cautiously concluded that the beginning and the end of the Biblical Chronology may have been based on the astronomical cycle of the planets Jupiter and Saturn. Between 3rd December 4177 BCE and 7th December 7 BCE, a total of 1,523,097 days elapsed, during which 210 conjunctions occur between these planets, every 7,252.842857 days (19.8572 years).

Based on this planetary cycle, the beginning of the Biblical Chronology could be determined historically and scientifically and hence become practicable for use in long chronological counts for ancient cultures.

There is more corroborating evidence of this nature. The date on which the Jewish Era began (corresponding with Scaliger's notions) was 26th September 3760 BCE (JD 348,352). This era began on the day of the New Moon, coinciding with a conjunction of the planets Jupiter and Saturn, which would be a remarkable astronomical event. Certain arguments by Rabbi Hillel led Scaliger to revise the date on which the Jewish Era began, changing it to 7th October 3761 BCE.[20] However, we believe that Scaliger's first date was actually the correct one.

Based on this evidence, we can draw the following cautious conclusion:

1. Varro based the *three separate periods of time* on Manetho's work. In doing so, Varro was alluding to the three eras (3 x 7,980 years) that led into a distant past. Based on Manetho's writings, Eusebius calculated a period of approximately 24,575 years from the beginning of the **Chronicles of World History** until the beginning of the rule of the Thinite Kings of Egypt. In addition, our thesis is that the beginning of the Biblical Chronology of Genesis circa 4181 BCE marked the start of the 4th era of 7,980 years (cf. Chronology).

The reason why Scaliger made use of the scientifically unfounded period of 15 years (Indiction period) to draw up his cycle of the Julian Period (28 x 19 x 15 years = 7,980 years) remains a mystery, unless he took the preceding three periods that Varro mentioned into account. If Scaliger had chosen to apply the radix of the sexagesimal chronometric system (i.e. 60), he would then have obtained a cycle of 28 x 19 x 60 years = 31,920 years (known as *The Chou Pei Suan Ching*-period, after which time 'all things come to an end and return to their original state', **Science and Civilisation in China**, Vol. II, Astronomy, p.406, Dr. Joseph Needham) which equals 4 x 7,980 years, in other words: four Julian Periods. This would definitely have made the **Chronicle of World History** of Manetho/Eusebius with a total of 24,575 years fit into the established view of history.

According to Manetho/Eusebius, the beginning of the **Chronicle of World History** began in approximately 28,121 BCE. After the course of *three* Julian Periods of 7,980 years, the chronology of the Bible begins in 28,121 BCE - 3 x 7,980 yrs. = 4181 BCE or approximately 4177/4174 BCE.

According to the chronology of Manetho/Eusebius, another 24,575 years elapsed from the beginning of the **Chronicle of World History** in approximately 28,121 BCE until the earliest phase of the State of Egypt (3540 BCE). This period ended in 3516 BCE, when the State of Egypt was born (Installation of Kingship in 3517 BCE. The Year of the Unification of the Two Lands was 3516 BCE.

2. 4181 BCE (4713 BCE minus 532 years) as the starting date of the 4th Julian Period is in better agreement with the authentic chronological facts. This would place the end of the 4th Julian Period in 3799 CE. The astrologer/mathematician Nostradamus (1503-1566) was, for some years, an intimate friend of Julius Caesar Scaliger, the father of Josephus Justus Scaliger, who even invited Nostradamus to move with his family from Saint-Rémy de Provence to Agen, where the two families lived around 1530. After some years, their friendship ended in animosity. It is probable that Nostradamus was also familiar with the cycle of 7,980 years (maybe through the works of Manetho, Dionysus or Varro), since he wrote in the introduction to his famous Prophecies (published in 1555 and 1558), that his predictions would extend to the year 3797 CE (see Chronology, especially World Chronicle).

3. Based on the fixed start of the Biblical Chronology, calculations provide us with the year in which the Deluge occurred. This event brought the Pyramid Era of the Egyptians to an end:

4177 BCE − 1,656 years = Deluge in 2521 BCE.

4. The Chronology in the Septuagint lists 1,236 years from Creation until the Deluge. If we assume that the Septuagint begins with the Jewish Era in 3760 BCE (Scaliger's dating), this would provide a basis to determine the date of the Deluge anew.

3760 BCE − 1,236 years = Deluge in 2524 BCE.

Accordingly, the Deluge actually occurred around 2520 BCE. We have calculated that the First Dynasty of the Egyptians began in 3516 BCE, with the end of the pyramid era at approximately 2521BCE. The total duration of the rule of the Egyptian First to the Sixth Dynasties undoubtedly amounts to either 995[21] or 955[22] years. Unfortunately, the exact number of years is unknown.

5. The Biblical Chronology of the book of Genesis starts with a new beginning, namely the 4th period of 7,980 years. The start of this 4th period is set at approximately 4177-4174 BCE and will end around 3803-3806 CE. Jupiter and Saturn complete their planetary cycle at the same time (cf. appendix XI).

APPENDIX II: The beginning of the Egyptian calendar system and the "adjustable" calendar

The Egyptian calendar system consisted of three calendars: a "fixed" calendar (astronomical), a civil calendar (adjustable) and a Lunar-Sirius calendar. These calendars were governed by the heliacal rising of the star Sirius.

The beginning of the year, New Year's Day, was characterised by the heliacal rising of the star Sirius which, prior to its heliacal rising, had remained invisible for approximately 70 days.

New Year's Day was the day of the "first brilliant visibility" of Sirius, observed around 3500 BCE in the prehistoric capital Buto in Lower Egypt, about one hour before sunrise. The appearance of the first rays of the sun on that specific day marked the beginning of the Egyptian year, I Achet 1, New Year's Day, which was celebrated throughout Egypt, from Hieraconpolis to Buto on that very day (appendix V).

The three calendars began simultaneously on I Achet 1, New Year's Day, 19th July 4242 BCE (JD 172,232) on the day of the New Moon. This New Moon was named after the goddess Neith. On that special New Year's Day, the planet Mars, the symbol of power and vindicate, was in conjunction with the star Propus, the battle-axe.

The principle of the "adjustable" calendar (365 days) resulted in the notion that every four years, the calendar day I Achet 1 moved ahead by one day; therefore, after exactly 1,460 years, this day would synchronise once again with the New Year's Day on which the heliacal rising of the star Sirius occurred. Around 3500 BCE, the day of the winter solstice fell on January 16th or 17th (Julian calendar). Between 3518 and 3514 BCE, on the "adjustable" calendar, I Achet 1 fell on January 16th or 17th , i.e. winter solstice (4242 BCE - 3518 BCE = 724 years : 4 = 181 days, conform with the difference in days between July 19th and January 16th). This day, 19th July 4242 BCE, ancient Egypt's New Year's Day, is the oldest calendar day known to us (see section 1.4)

APPENDIX III: The Star-cult is replaced by the Sun-cult

The ancient Egyptians experienced the transition from star-cult to sun-cult as a radical event. According to our chronological research, the new cult was gradually introduced between 2930 and 2900 BCE, until around 2825 BCE, i.e. the beginning of the Fifth Dynasty, when it had become definitively installed.

This transition was based on an important astronomical event. The Egyptologist Krauss describes this in *"Sothis- und Monddaten"*, without drawing the slightest conclusion that might point in the above direction. Krauss states: "Until 3000 BCE, the rising of Sothis was seen from all locations to occur *before* the summer solstice." At the beginning of the 19th century, the astronomer Dr. von Gumpach drew up a table ranging from 2700 BCE to 300 CE, in which he published the approximately calculated dates of the Equinoxes and Solstices.[23] Around 2900 BCE, the summer solstice (position of the Sun: 0° Cancer) at Memphis coincided with the heliacal rising of Sothis; since then, the pertinent difference has increased to 40 days."[24] According to the current state of scientific research, "the ancient Egyptians had no knowledge of either goniometry or of means to locate the position of stars. Only during the second century BCE did precession become a known fact through Hipparchus [the Greek]."[25]

In our opinion, the Egyptians actually did observe precession and the measurements they took were made with that knowledge in mind. This is proved not only by the accuracy in their construction of the Pyramid Field between Saqqara and Hawara (grid of meridians from east to west, cf. Appendix VIII), it is also substantiated by their approach in developing various tracks in the course of the millennia to observe the heliacal risings of the star Sirius, as well as by the foundation of settlements along the Nile for the benefit of those observations. The ensuing implications have a far-reaching effect on the general chronology of Egypt and on the history of astronomy in particular (cf. Appendix IV and V).

The following table is an overview of the zodiacal position of the Sun between 19th July 2901 BCE (Julian Calendar) and 19th July 3011 BCE at 02h45 GMT, at sunrise after the heliacal rising of the star Sirius in Heliopolis:

July 19, 2901 BCE	position Sun	01°02 Cancer
July 19, 2906		00°16 Cancer
July 19, 2911		00°28 Cancer
July 19, 2916		00°40 Cancer
July 19, 2921		00°53 Cancer
July 19, 2926		00°06 Cancer
July 19, 2931		00°18 Cancer
July 19, 2936		00°31 Cancer
July 19, 2941		00°43 Cancer
July 19, 2946		29°57 Gemini
July 19, 2951		00°09 Cancer
July 19, 2956		00°22 Cancer
July 19, 2961		00°35 Cancer
July 19, 2966		29°48 Gemini
July 19, 2971		00°00 Cancer
July 19, 2976		00°13 Cancer
July 19, 2981		00°25 Cancer
July 19, 2986		29°39 Gemini
July 19, 2991		29°51 Gemini
July 19, 2996		00°04 Cancer
July 19, 3001		00°16 Cancer
July 19, 3006		29°30 Gemini
July 19, 3011		29°42 Gemini

APPENDIX IV: The heliacal rising of the star Sirius at El Badari

A star chart can be created by means of the Skyglobe 3.6 computer programme to show the heliacal rising of the star Sirius at a given date. We set the star chart for July 13th (Julian cal.) at 04h00 a.m. in 4501 BCE, as observed from the prehistoric settlements Deir Tasa and El Badari. The heliacal rising of the star Sirius occurred on IV SMW 30 (July 13th), approximately 50 minutes before sunrise. The Arcus Visionis and the critical depth of the Sun below the true horizon is 9.40 and was located exactly on the upper limit of the critical depth of the Sun, 8.534 - 8.567 and 9.378 - 9.411 (the range 8.40 to 9.30 will be referred to as the "range of doubt"), so that the "first brilliant visibility" of Sirius was a given. This result confirms the former investigations and the conclusions by Emeritus Prof. G.W van Oosterhout relating to that field of enquiry.[26]

APPENDIX V: Astro-geodetics and the Planological Infrastructure of Egypt

Definition of the subject:
With the help of a basic geodetic line between certain locations in ancient Egypt, calculations of the date of observation of the heliacal rising of the star Sirius are presented (cf. fig. 13, 14 and 15). The significance of observations of this astronomical phenomenon clearly shows that the calculated day of observation at a specific latitude in a certain location (fixed point) underpins the theory that a derived form of triangulation determined the planological infrastructure of pre-, proto- and historical Egypt. In the course of many millennia, this fixed observation point (its co-ordinates specify the intersection of its geographical longitude and latitude) on that specific date was lost as a result of precession and the orbital movement of the star Sirius itself. The significance of certain locations eventually disappeared and as a consequence, new settlements were established along the river Nile, whereupon this process was repeated (specification in co-operation with G.W. van Oosterhout).

In general:
Triangulation is a method of measuring distances by means of a network of triangles with known sides, that is constructed with the help of a basic geodetic line and a number of visible points or locations in the landscape.

The ancient Egyptians used a method that was derived from the one metioned above. They measured distances by measuring time as well as *distance*, with the use of a single geodetic line between specific locations.

We recognise this technique in their pictorial script, e.g. the geometrical hieroglyph denoting the star Sirius (an isosceles triangle). We will subsequently refer to the basic geodetic line as the *observation track*.

One of the puzzling aspects in the field of the astronomical chronology of ancient Egypt still concerns the location of the observation of the *first brilliant visibility* of the heliacal rising of Sirius. This is caused by, amongst others, the loss of source material. Gradually, a firm conviction developed in scientific circles that "Egyptian astronomy had much less influence on the outside world, for the simple reason that it remained through all its history on an exceedingly crude level which bore practically no relationship to the rapidly growing mathematical astronomy of the Hellenistic age." Their calendar and the division of a day into 24 hours are the exception.[27]

Until now, authentic source material and explanatory texts constitute the basis on which scientific analyses are based. Yet should that keep us from adopting alternative possibilities to analyse their astounding precision? All the more so, since texts are known to exist that direct attention to their use of geometry and land-surveying. The Egyptians used this skill in their methods of partitioning their territory, in which observations of the heliacal rising of the star Sirius served as their starting-point. A planological partitioning of the infrastructure based on astronomy (the *first brilliant visibility* of the star Sirius) offered them a cultural context. After all, the heliacal rising of Sirius was linked with the flooding of the Nile, which produced fertile agricultural soil. Its significance is obvious, especially because they based their calendar on that event. In addition, research will vindicate that the "Egyptian tradition [decidedly] [shows] a very beneficial influence, that is, in the use of the Egyptian calendar by the Hellenistic astronomers."[28]

In general, "observation of the heliacal rising of Sirius in the Nile valley from the south to the north advances with a delay of approximately one day per 1° of geographic latitude"[29] (cf. the tables by Baehr). Research does not confirm this conclusion. On the contrary: over time, the interval between the first observation of the heliacal rising in the south and the last observation in the north changed from nine to eight, seven, six and after 1000 BCE (Late Period) to five days. Before 1000 BCE, considerable deviations ought to be taken into account. These various intervals are caused mainly by the changed declination of Sirius, which is due predominantly to precession. This remarkable difference will not have gone unnoticed by the Egyptians.

The beginning of an Egyptian calendar day and the exact moment of transition from one calendar day to the next is mentioned in various texts, with specific reference to the rising of Sirius in the 12th hour of the night. The day was divided into twelve hours of daytime and twelve hours of nighttime. This points to the beginning of a new day at dawn, i.e. at sunrise. Around New Year's Day, the time of observation of the star Sirius lay between 55 minutes and one hour before sunrise on the eastern horizon.

Three periods can be distinguished, each totalling 1,460 years, namely from 4242 BCE to 2782 BCE, from 2782 BCE to 1322 BCE, and from 1322 BCE to 138 CE. The Egyptian calendar system was based on a period of 1,460 years; the extent of precision we apply today has established that the Sirius periods are not all equally long and that 1457-1456 years is a more accurate figure (since 1927, Schoch and Ingmar). Therefore, in order to obtain truly correct results, the Sirius periods ought to be avoided; instead, the date of the heliacal rising of Sirius should be calculated by means of the critical depth of the Sun (Arcus

Visionis) of 9.41 at a specific location, so that the first brilliant visibility becomes a confirmed fact. We based this investigation on the *Observation track* between Hieraconpolis and Buto for the period from 4242 BCE to 2782 BCE.

Overview of the optimal latitude for the following points of observation:
(all calculations in co-operation with Van Oosterhout)

July 9, 4242 BCE	24°48 N
July 10, 4242	25°32 N
July 11, 4242	26°15 N
July 12, 4242	26°57 N (El Badari/Hemamieh)
July 13, 4242	27°38 N
July 14, 4242	28°20 N
July 15, 4242	29°00 N
July 16, 4242	29°40 N
July 17, 4242	30°19 N (Merimde)
July 18, 4242	30°58 N
July 19, 4242	31°36 N

Although the figures in this survey are unnecessarily accurate, they do present us with the latitude of two extremely important prehistoric settlements. Both locations, El Badari/Hemamieh and Merimde, are situated precisely on the parallel in question.

In prehistoric times, a prototype of the observation track between El Badari and Giza may have been developed initially in conjunction with the latitude of the following settlements. The locations are situated precisely on the latitudinal parallel in question.

Table from ca. 4,500 to ca. 3,800 BCE:

Location	Julian date	Arcus Visionis	Coordinate of Latitude
El Badari	July 13	9.40 - 9.20	27°00 N
Sheik Atiya	July 14	9.40 - 9.40	27°31 N
Zawyet el Amwat	July 15	9.80 - 9.40	28°03 N
El Kom el Ahwar Saw.	July 16	10.00 - 9.70	28°34 N
Maiyana	July 17	9.70 - 10.00	29°05 N
Tarchan (Girza)	July 18	10.00 - 9.60	29°30 N
Giza	July 19	9.50 - 10.20	30°00 N

The following observation tables show the three consecutive Sirius periods, specifying location, Julian date, Arcus Visionis, latitude of the specific location and the proportional division of the Observation track.

Obviously, the following three tables are average, static and are merely presented as an introductory guideline.

Table of the first Sirius period:

From 4,242 to 2,782 BCE; Observation track Hieraconpolis/Buto:

Location	Julian date	Arcus Visionis	Latitude	Proportional
Hieraconpolis	July 10, 4242 BCE	09.842	25°06 N	25°06 N
Khizam	July 11, 4242	09.894	25°46 N	25°47 N
Thinis	July 12, 4242	10.030	26°20 N	26°27 N
Assiut	July 13, 4242	09.906	27°11 N	27°08 N
Hermopolis	July 14, 4242	09.989	27°47 N	27°48 N
El Kom Ahmar	July 15, 4242	09.914	28°34 N	28°29 N
Heracleo. M.	July 16, 4242	10.040	29°05 N	29°10 N
Memphis/Djoser	July 17, 4242	09.898	29°50 N	29°50 N
Ternuthis	July 18, 4242	09.995	30°26 N	30°31 N
Buto	July 19, 4242	09.853	31°12 N	31°12 N

Table of the second Sirius period:

From 2,782 to 1,322 BCE; Observation track Philae/Elephantine/Heliopolis:

Location	Julian date	Arcus Visionis	Latitude	Proportional
Philae/Elephan.	July 10, 2782 BCE	09.373	24°03 N	24°03 N
Edfu	July 11, 2782	09.421	24°59 N	24°48 N
Tod	July 12, 2782	09.678	25°35 N	25°32 N
Thinis	July 13, 2782	09.752	26°20 N	26°18 N
Assiut	July 14, 2782	09.768	27°11 N	27°04 N
Hermopolis	July 15, 2782	09.969	27°47 N	27°49 N
El Kom el Ahmar	July 16, 2782	10.027	28°34 N	28°35 N
Atfih	July 17, 2782	09.958	29°25 N	29°21 N
Heliopolis	July 18, 2782	10.051	30°08 N	30°07 N
Busiris	July 19, 2782	09.997	30°55 N	30°52 N

Table of the third Sirius-period:

From 1,322 BCE to 139 CE; Observation track Philae/Elephantine/Heliopolis:

Location	Julian date	Arcus Visionis	Latitude	Proportional
Philae/Elephan.	July 12, 1322 BCE	09.568	24°03 N.	24°03 N.
Hieraconpolis	July 13, 1322	09.641	25°06 N.	25°03 N.
Thebes/Dendera	July 14, 1322	10.139	25°42 N.	25°56/ 26°08 N
Assiut	July 15, 1322	09.559	27°11 N.	27°05 N
Hebenu	July 16, 1322	09.627	28°03 N.	28°06 N
Heracleo. M.	July 17, 1322	09.553	29°05 N.	29°07 N
Heliopolis	July 18, 1322	09.481	30°08 N.	30°08 N
Buto	July 19, 1322	09.309	31°12 N.	31°09 N

Obviously, the latter three surveys are static and merely serve as a means of orientation.

With the help of a computer program (developed by Van Oosterhout for Atari), any desired point in time, location and critical Arcus Visionis can be calculated accurately. The calculation of the first and last visible rising shortly before sunrise hardly presents difficulties, yet the criterion of visibility is extremely subtle: he informs us that an angular accuracy of better than 0.1 degree is required. His calculations are based on the observations made by Borchardt,[30] and on the Canopus Decree and the Censorinus text.

APPENDIX VI: The phenomenon of Precession of the Equinoxes and its transition through the Zodiacal Signs

The Great Year is a novelty to many. We are all familiar with the solar year, a period of approximately 365.25 days, during which the Earth completes one orbit around the Sun. The Earth itself is in three types of motion. It revolves on its axis during a period of 24 hours, which gives us our cycle of day and night. It orbits the Sun every 365.25 days, which gives our yearly cycle. Finally it sways back and forth on its vertical, or polar axis, giving us our cycle of the seasons. During this third cycle, the point at which the North Pole is at its extreme north or south is known as the solstice, i.e. the Sun appears to be standing still at that moment before it starts moving back in the direction from which it has just come. At this point it is either at its nearest or its furthest point from the Sun and gives us our high points of summer or winter, with their differing lengths of day and night. The equinoxes are the half-way points in the cycle when the Earth is standing vertically upright and the lengths of day and night are equal around the globe. These occur in spring and autumn and are known as the vernal and autumnal equinoxes respectively.

There are of course more things than just the Earth moving about within the cosmos. Everything is in motion and one of these things is the point of the vernal equinox during the phenomenon known as the Precession of the Equinoxes. But first a little more about the structure and motion of the cosmos as we see it from here on Earth. As we look out, we see that the sky is full of stars, which over the millennia we have formed into set groups called constellations. For practical purposes, the band of constellations that form the background to the solar ecliptic (i.e. the plane of the sun's equator in which all the planets in the solar system have their orbits) is called the Zodiac, or Circle of Animals and Man, because of the names we have given these groupings. The circle has been divided into 360 degrees and each of these groupings has been allotted 30 degrees, giving a total of 12 constellations. There are more than twelve constellations around the ecliptic, but again for practical purposes only twelve are counted to represent the twelve-fold division of the circle.

In one year the Sun passes through each of the 12 signs of the Zodiac, transiting the Vernal Equinox at 0° Aries (The Ram), the Summer Solstice at 0° Cancer (the Crab), the Autumn Equinox at 0° Libra (The Scales, part of the Serpent), and the Winter Solstice at 0° Capricorn (the Goat).

So, what exactly is precession? The Earth wobbles on its polar axis and as a result of this in combination with its three-fold motion, it spins like a top as it revolves around the sun and its equatorial axis describes a cone shape around the axis of the ecliptic taking approximately 25,920 years to complete one cycle. This is known as a Great Year. Each year, the vernal equinox is seen to move slightly further along the ecliptic in the opposite direction to the annual cycle of the Sun, that is, in the reverse sequence of the zodiacal signs, travelling back 1 degree about every 72 years. So once every 2,160 years, the vernal equinox will be seen against the background of a different sign of the Zodiac. This is the phenomenon known as the precession of the equinoxes or general precession. This means that every 13,000 years or so, the constellations which began as winter constellations are seen in the summer and vice versa. Currently the vernal equinox is thought to be passing through the last degrees of the sign of Pisces into the first degrees of the sign of Aquarius. After about 26,000 years, each constellation will have completed an entire circuit through all four seasons. Thus, the 12 signs of the zodiac are transited in around 25,920 years (known as the Platonic Year, due to an *"obscure wording"* from **"The State"** VIII-546-b), also known as the Great Year. In the 19th century, the astronomer Bell calculated the duration of the Great Year at 25,868 years. Modern computations have established a period varying between 25,657 and 26,367 years (*Astronomy and Astrophysics*, Laska, 1986, p.59-70).

Overview of precessional transitions:

Ca. 27,805 BCE, the vernal equinox is in	0°Taurus
Ca. 25,649 BCE	0°Aries
Ca. 23,493 BCE	0°Pisces
Ca. 21,337 BCE	0°Aquarius
Ca. 19,182 BCE	0°Capricorn
Ca. 17,026 BCE	0°Sagittarius
Ca. 14,870 BCE	0°Scorpio
Ca. 12,714 BCE	0°Libra
Ca. 10,558 BCE	0°Virgo
Ca. 8,402 BCE	0°Leo
Ca. 6,247 BCE	0°Cancer
Ca. 4,091 BCE	0°Gemini
Ca. 1,935 BCE (Start Amun-cult = Aries-cult)	0°Taurus
Ca. 221 CE	0°Aries
Ca. 2,377 CE	0°Pisces

The Greek geographer and astronomer Hipparchus of Nicea (circa 190-125 BCE) is considered to be the founder of systematic astronomy. He worked on Rhodes and presumably also in Alexandria. Hipparchus discovered the Precession of the Equinoxes by comparing his observations of the stellar positions current in his time with those of astronomers in earlier times. Since the precession of the equinoxes is so slow that hundreds of years must pass before differences become noticeable, Hipparchus was forced to make use of written observations of stellar positions that had been recorded before his time. Undoubtedly, the Precession of the Equinoxes had been observed earlier. Since the time of Hipparchus and Ptolemy, the zodiac has been considered to begin at 0° Aries. (See my notes.)

Prior to Hipparchus, the Babylonians used the stars Arcturus and Spica as starting points to determine the Autumn Equinox. Around 2900 BCE, the Egyptians even used the summer solstice as their calibration point to change their star-cult into a sun-cult. However in 3517 BC, they used the winter solstice (January 16th or 17th on the Julian calendar) as their calibration point (correlating with I Achet 1 of their "adjustable" calendar) as the foundation of the Installation of Kingship in the State of Egypt.

Egyptologist Selim Hassan aroused curiosity with his studies on ancient Egyptian cosmology (pLouvre 3292). Hassan found that they recognised two heavens, which were placed "one above the other".[31] These evidently differed in significance, and Herodotus in his **Histories** described what was considered as the principal heaven during the period between 17,500 and 14,500 BCE. He identified the stars Polis and beta Libra accurately as the extreme limits of that celestial sector (42 degrees). Herodotus described the slight movement along the ecliptic in the opposite direction, called the precession of the equinoxes, through the star constellation Hèraklès (Hercules) and the subsequent one through Typhoon (Opiuchus with Serpent) and Hooros (ancient Horus, originally associated with Scorpio,[32] and completely different from the later Horus). Herodotus named the corresponding period and he also mentioned the intermediate period of 3,000 years. In our view - which we base on the precession of the equinoxes and relate to that period - the ancient Horus represents beta Libra, rather than Scorpio.

Overview of the vernal equinox, due to precession, in conjunction with the star mentioned:

Archaic Celestial sector of the First Era,

17,500 BCE, the vernal equinox in 8° Sagittarius, in conjunction with the star Polis.

14,500 BCE, the vernal equinox in 25° Libra, in conjunction with the star beta Libra.

Historical Celestial Sector of the Second Era,

5,300 BCE, the vernal equinox in 15° Gemini, in conjunction with the star Alhena.
(*Horus*-cult in Egypt, cf. plaque of Denderah).

2,200 BCE, the vernal equinox in 2° Taurus, in conjunction with the star Algol.
(End of the *Horus*-cult, approx. 2000 BCE, period of transition to *Amun*-cult, the vernal equinox enters the zodiacal sign of Aries, Amun-cult is introduced under Pharaoh Amenemhat I, the first pharaoh of the 12th Dynasty).

The intermediate period has an equal duration of 3,000 years = the motion of precession in 42 degrees

(42° x 71.428... year per degree equals 3,000 years).

APPENDIX VII: Photographic reproduction (fig. 69) from Ägyptische Chronologie by Eduard Meyer, Berlin 1904

Turiner Papyrus

Die erste Zahl bezeichnet die Nummer in der fortlaufenden Königsliste, die zweite die in der mit Zoser beginnenden Dynastie.

		Name	Regierungszeit	Lebensalter
19.	1.	[hieroglyphs] (Zoser) regierte	J. 19 M. – T. –	. verloren .
		. . . . . .		
		. . . . . .		
20.	2.	[hieroglyphs] (Zoserti) .	» 6 » 0 » 0	. vacat .
21.	3.	[hieroglyphs] (. . . zefa) . .	» 6 » 1 » x	. O .
22.	4.	[hieroglyphs] (Ḥuni) . .	» 24 [Monate und Tage	Bemerkung
		. . . . . .	· von hier an ver- loren]	. . . .
23.	5.	[hieroglyphs] (Snofru) .	» 24	——
24.	6.	[Cheops]	» 23	——
25.	7.	[Dedefreᶜ] . . .	» 8	——
26.	8.	[hieroglyphs] . .	» x . . .	——
27.	9.	[Mykerinos] . .	» x . . .	——
28.	10.	x	» x . . .	——
29.	11.	x	• 18 [oder 28] . .	——
30.	12.	[Šepseskaf] . . .	» 4 . . .	——
31.	13.	x	» 2 . . .	——
32.	14.	[hieroglyphs] (Userkaf)	» 7 . . .	——
33.	15.	[Saḥureᶜ]	» 12 . . .	——
34.	16.	[Nefererkereᶜ] regierte	» x . . .	——
35.	17.	[Šepseskereᶜ] . . .	» 7 . . .	——
36.	18.	[Akeuḥor] . . .	» x . . .	——
37.	19.	[Newoserreᶜ] . . .	» 30 + x[1] . . .	——
38.	20.	[hieroglyphs] (Menkeḥor)	» 8 . . .	——
39.	21.	[hieroglyphs] (Dedkereᶜ) . .	» 28 . . .	——
40.	22.	[hieroglyphs] (Unas) .	» 30 . . .	——
		[hieroglyphs]	»Summe der Könige von Menes bis auf . . .«	

APPENDIX VIII: Technical explanation: Correlation of the Constellation with the Pyramid Field

Right Ascension: Imagine the night sky as we see it to be a celestial sphere decorated on the surface with the constellations and fixed stars. The Sun's equator and the Ecliptic are extended to infinity to become the celestial equator and the celestial ecliptic. The North-South axis extends to the Pole Star, from which the meridians are drawn. These are known as Meridians of Right Ascension, or R.A. They are the equivalent of meridians of terrestrial longitude, and the celestial equivalent of the Zero Meridian is known as the Prime Meridian or the Prime Vertical and is counted as 0hrs 00mins of Right Ascension.

An imaginary matrix of meridians, running from west to east and spaced at intervals of one geographical minute of arc (0° 01'), is drawn across the entire Pyramid Field. Our thesis is that the star Capella (Right Ascension: 05h 16.41) correlates with the Pyramid of Seila (31°03 E.), and likewise, that the star ksi Orionis (R.A.: 06h 11.56) correlates with the Step Pyramid of Djoser (31°13 E.). The difference in Right Ascension (R.A.) amounts to 0h 55.15, which equals 3,315 chronological seconds, a total of 0° 10' (10 minutes of arc) in geographical longitude. A difference of one geographical minute of arc therefore equals 331.5 chronological seconds or 0h 05min. 31.5 sec. of Right Ascension.

Table:

Meridians	Right Ascension correlating with the meridian	Correlating star and the present R.A (epoch 2000 CE)		Pyramid Temple city
31°02 30	05h 13.55	Rigel	05h 14.32	Abu Rawash
31°03	05h 16.41	Capella	05h 16.41	Seila
31°04	05h 22.12			
31°05				
31°06	05h 33.17	Mintaka	05h 32.00	Giza Menkaure
31°07	05h 38.49	Al Nilam	05h 36.12	Giza Khafre
31°07 30		Arneb	05h 36.00	Letopolis
31°08	05h 44.20	Al Nitak	05h 40.45	Giza Khufu
31°09	05h 49.52	Variable star near Betelgeux	05h 50.00	Zawyet North Baka
31°09 30	05h 52.38	Betelgeux	05h 55.10	Zawyet South Chaba
31°10	05h 55.24	Menkalinan	05h 59.31	Meidum
31°11	06h 01.56	mu Orionis	06h 02.22	Abu Gorab
31°12 30	06h 10.14	nu Orionis	06h 07.34	Sekhemkhet (Saqqara)
31°13	06h 13.00	ksi Orionis	06h 11.56	Djoser (Saqqara)
31°13	06h 13.00	64 Orionis	06h 02.30	Dahshur Red Pyr.
31°13	06h 13.00	x2 Orionis	06h 03.55	Dahshur Bent Pyr.

31°14	06h 18.32			
31°15	06h 24.04			
31°16	06h 29.36			
31°17	06h 35.08	Alhena	06h 37.42	Memphis and eastwards
31°18	06h 40.40			
31°18 30	06h 43.26	Sirius	06h 45.00	Heliopolis

The pyramids of Dahshur are located at the intersection of the Ecliptic with the Galactic Equator (Perihelium).

At the beginning of the Egyptian Calendar (19th July 4242 BC), the planet Mars (God of Power and Vindicate) is in conjunction with the star Propus (known as Battle-axe), close to chi Orionis/64 Orionis.
The minor difference between a meridian and the present Right Ascension of the relevant star is attributable to the proper motion of the star. The difference is negligible.

Table of stars correlating with the Pyramids of the Third and Fourth Dynasty, including the necropolis Abu Gorab/Abusir of the Fifth Dynasty:

From north to south:

1.	Pyr. Abu Rawash	Beta Orionis	Djedefre
2.	Pyr. Giza	Zeta Orionis	Khufu
3.	Pyr. Giza	Eps. Orionis	Khafre
4.	Pyr. Giza	Delta Orionis	Menkaure
5.	Pyr. Zawyet el Aryan	Variable star	Baka
6.	Pyr. Zawyet el Aryan	Alpha Orionis	Chaba
7.	Location Abu Gorab	mu Orionis	5th Dynasty
8.	Pyr. Saqqara	Ksi Orionis	Djoser
9.	Pyr. Saqqara	Nu Orionis	Sekhemkhet
10.	Pyr. Dahshur (Red)	64 Orionis	Snofru
11.	Pyr. Dahshur (Bent)	X2 Orionis	Snofru
12.	Pyr. Meidum	Beta Aurigae	Snofru
13.	Pyr. Seila	Alpha Aurigae	Snofru

Each of the three temple cities, i.e. Memphis (star Alhena), Letopolis (star Arneb) and Heliopolis (star Sirius), correlates with the three stars mentioned in brackets. This amounts to a total of 16 parts, as mentioned by Plutarch.

Table of stars correlating with the pyramids of the 12ᵗʰ Dynasty:

Pyr. Mazghuna	Two stars above eta Gemini (Propus) close to the Ecliptic	Amenemhat IV/ Sobekneferoe
Pyr. el Lisht	chi Aurigae	Amenemhat I/ Sesostris I
Pyr. Lahun	Alpha Persei	Sesostris II
Pyr. Hawara	beta Persei	Amenemhat III

General remarks:

The pyramids of the Third and the Fourth Dynasty correlate with stars:

The mastabas of the First and the Second Dynasty at Saqqara underline the bend between the upper arm and the forearm, symbolically marking the beginning of the "strong arm" = Nekhet;

The sun temples and the site of the pyramid city of the Fifth Dynasty between Abu Gorab and Abusir correlate with mu Orionis. The location 31°11' E (various buildings) corresponds with mu Orionis. This could mean that the southern pyramid of Zawyet el Aryan (Chaba, Third Dynasty) was a pyramid-annex-observation tower with the same function as the one at Meidum (on the same meridian). For unknown reasons, this function was apparently passed on to the tower of Cercasorus. Further research in this matter is required;

The pyramids of the Sixth Dynasty also contribute to the design, yet *do not* correlate with stars; they emphasise the "strong arm";

Mazghuna and El Lisht correlate with stars; the three remaining pyramids near Dahshur complete the hand;

One pyramid in El Lisht *does not* correlate with a star;

The pyramids of Lahun and Hawara represent *hypothetical* positions and *do not* show an exact correlation with the stars of Perseus.

The shafts in the Great Pyramid:

The southern wall of the King's chamber in the Great Pyramid contains a shaft (22 x 22 cm), which runs at an angle of 45°. Hypothetically, the stars of the Belt of Orion may have been observed through this shaft (Trimble, Bauval). If this theory is correct, then the Egyptians observed these stars during the night of the Osiris festival. This festival was held from November 13th (Julian calendar) onwards (cf. fig. 40). The measurements of the shaft do not allow an *accurate* observation (margin approximately two degrees). It is precisely this margin which warranted the use of the shaft for centuries.

Theoretical survey of the altitude of a star on the meridian in the following sequence; both outer stars of the Belt of Orion (Mintaka and Al Nitak), Sirius, Kochab and Thuban (Source: Skyglobe 3.6)

mid-November 3001 BCE at   11h17 PM the star Mintaka, alt. 43°12'
                                      11h28 PM the star Al Nitak, alt. 42° 48'

mid-November 2601 BCE at   11h24 PM the star Mintaka, alt. 45°06'
                                      11h34 PM the star Al Nitak, alt. 44° 42'

According to a hypothesis put forward by Bauval, the southern shaft, running at an angle of 39°30', is directed at the star Sirius:

mid-November between approximately 1900-1750 BCE at   01h30 AM

According to that same hypothesis, the lower northern shaft, running at an angle of 39° (its direction fluctuates between 33°18' and 40°06', cf. R.Gantenbrink), is directed to the star Kochab:

mid-November 2500 BCE at   06h30 PM

According to that same hypothesis, the upper northern shaft, running at an angle of 32°36' (Gantenbrink), is directed at the star Thuban (alpha Draconis):

mid-November 3200 BCE at   10h00 PM

Obviously, *no absolute chronological datings* can be deduced from these spread datings.

APPENDIX IX: Photographic reproduction (fig. 70) of Table III by Koch

		mul apin I			Planisphäre K 8538		Modern	
		Sternname/Epitheton	S	Sternname/Epitheton Synonym		Sternfigur	K	W
i	40	mulAŠ-iku šu-bat dÉ-a a-lik pān kakkabē šu-ut dA-nim	1	mulAŠ-iku		Figur zweier Dreiecke	αPeg	20.90°
	1	⌜mulapin dEn-líl a-li⌝k pān kakkabē šu-ut ⌜dEn-líl⌝	1	mulapin dEn-líl a-lik pān kakkabē šu-ut ⌜dEn-líl⌝		Figur zweier Dreiecke		
	41	kakkabu ša ina meḫret mulAŠ-iku izzazuzu mul si-nu-nu-tum					εPeg	22.00
	42	kakkabu ša arki mulAŠ-iku izzazuzu mulA-nu-ni-tum						
	43	kakkabu ša arki-šu iz-zazuzu mul-⌜lu⌝ḫun-gá dDu-muzi						
	44	mulmul Sebettu ilānimeš ra-bûtimeš	3	m⌜ul⌝mul⌝		Ellipse mit eingeschlosse-nen Dreiecken	ηTau	1.33
ii	1	mulgu₄-an-na dis[le-e agù dA-nim]	3	muli[s le-e]		Ellipse mit eingeschlosse-nen Dreiecken	εTau	2.03
	2	mulSipa-zi-an-na dPap-suk-kal suk[kal A-nim dIš-tar]	3	⌜dPap-sukkal⌝ sukkal AN-NA dIš-tar dI-li-ab-rat mulSipa-zi-an-na			γOri	3.11
	3	mulmaš-tab-ba ša ina meḫret mu⌜r⌝ !Sipa-zi-an-na]	4	mulmaš-tab-ba šá ina maḫra-at mulSipa-zi-an-na izzazumeš-zu ⌜d⌝ lú-làl dLA-TA-RAK		Figur mit Zeigerstab		
	4	izzazumeš-zu dlú-làl u dL[A-TA-RAK]						
	5	kakkabu ša arki-šu iz-zazuzu mul[dar-lugal]						
	6	mulgag-si-sá šil-ta-ḫu qar-radu rabu-ú d[Nin-urta]						
	7	mulpan dIš-tar e-la-ma-tum mārat d[En-líl]						
i	9	[kakkabu ša . . . m⌜ul⌝ur-gu-la izzazuzu mul-LUGAL	5	LUGAL		LUGAL LUGAL LUGAL LUGAL		
ii	8	mulmuš dNin-giz-zi-da bēl er-ṣe-tum	5			Kleinfigur (fast abge-brochen)		
	9	muluga mušen a-ri-bu kakkabu dAdad	5	ḪU		Kleinfigur eingeschrieben: mušen mušen mušen mušen		
	10	mulab-sín dŠA-LA šu-bu-ul-tum	5	BAD		Kleinfigur eingeschrieben: BAD BAD[. . .]	αVir	11.16
i	12	mulŠU-PA dEn-líl ša ši-mat māti i-šim-mu	6	Aššur			αBoo	12.23
ii	11	mulzi-ba-an-na	6	⌜mulGI-G]I		Waage-Figur	α²Lib	12.53
			0	dDumuzi ilu rabû		Pfeilfigur		
			0	⌜d-]tar belet mātāti		Pfeilfigur		
			1	mulš[ím-maḫ]			εPeg	22.00
			1	mulA-nu-ni-[tum]				

APPENDIX X: The Geometrical function of the 30th parallel

Egyptian arithmetics afforded an intriguing role to the fraction rwy = 2/3.[33] Further investigation has shown that this fraction possessed a significant geometrical function. Phrases such as "in the centre of the world" expressed the need of the Egyptians for structure and for a diagrammatic, geometrical partitioning of the world.

The 30th parallel divides the northern hemisphere of the world in the proportion of 1/3 to 2/3, as seen from the equator. The site chosen for the three pyramids of Giza shows that around 3000 BCE at the latest, the Egyptians were familiar with this particular location and its parallel on the northern hemisphere.

Claudius Ptolemy also applied the proportion of 2/3 when he drew up his map of the world. In his days, Alexandria was the principal city of Egypt which he located at 1/3 of the distance from what was then the Zero Meridian (Hierro, one of the Canary Islands) and 2/3 of the distance from the Chinese coast. This is clearly shown on Ptolemy's map.

In Antiquity, this parallel was emphasised by means of conspicuous and representative buildings. In addition, characteristic, striking features in the landscape such as high mountain tops, elevations in the landscape, the course of rivers and coastlines, etc. were put to the same use. The Pillars of Hercules (the Straits of Gibraltar), the islands Malta and Rhodes and the highest peak of the Elburz mountain range are cases in point. The name of the town of Antioch (modern Antakya, 36°12' N.) served to indicate its location north of the ancient dividing line (36th parallel).

Amongst the conspicuous features that were built on the 30th parallel, we find the pyramids of Giza, Tarakun (possibly the legendary Arin?) and the formerly forbidden holy town of Lhasa in Tibet. These locations divide the parallel into equal segments of 30 degrees each.
In all cases, the distance between the above locations amounts to approximately 5,500,000 royal cubits (approximately 2,880 km), or 2618 x 2100 royal cubits (21 "rods of cord" equal 2100 royal cubits = 1100 metres). The 30th parallel was divided by these locations into segments that all equal 1000 x 2.618 (the square of Phi) x 2100 royal cubits. This parallel harbours the Golden Section, which is why there appeared to be a preference for it in Antiquity. Furthermore, this parallel was divided into "ideal" proportions by these sacred locations, thereby simultaneously underlining its sacred character.

APPENDIX XI: Doctrine and Influence of the Great Conjunction between Jupiter and Saturn on the rise and fall of Empires and World Religions by the Arabian Astronomer Al Kindi and the day of the catastrophe on which the Holocene Geological Period began.

A factual chronological indication of a world-encompassing catastrophe on Earth, which lived on in the collective consciousness of the Egyptians, is found in Plato's deliberations about the catastrophe involving Atlantis and the time at which this occurred, about 9,000 years before his birth. The Edfu Chronicles (the Sacred Books) offer contemporary accounts about a similar event, without however mentioning a specific time or period.

Modern scientific research has shown that the geological timescale between 10,000 and 9,000 BCE displays a sudden transition towards an improved climate (a climate warming of approximately 5° C), whereby this geological dividing line between the Pleistocene (Quartair) and the Holocene (Quintair) appears to lie closer to 9000 BCE.

This correspondence between the two points in time cannot be coincidental.

The 4th Julian Period of 7,980 years (cf. appendix I) began with the start of the Chronology of the Bible around 4177-4174 BCE and will end approximately 3803-3806 CE.

The actual cause of the catastrophe that resulted in the transition of this geological era (the Pleistocene) to the Holocene is entirely unknown.

Ancient Arabian astronomers mention a "Great Conjunction", a conjunction of all planets, which could possibly have generated a cataclysmic event on Earth. A close accumulation of this type rarely occurs. This singularity was apparently seen as the beginning of a new era, which resulted in a series of calculations and observations.

In addition, all conjunctions between Jupiter and Saturn were observed. The Arabian mathematician Al Kindi (circa 800 CE) specialised in the field of history, especially in the ***Doctrine and Influence of the Great Conjunction between Jupiter and Saturn on the rise and fall of Empires and World Religions***. In the course of time, in particular during the late Middle Ages, the notion of the "Great Conjunction" was demoted to just the conjunctions between the planets Jupiter and Saturn (occurring approximately every 19.86 years). We determined that between the beginning and the end of the period from approximately 9400 BCE to approximately 3800 CE, a total of some 13,200 years (around half a Cosmic Great Year), the number of conjunctions between the planets Jupiter and Saturn will reach the total of 665. Further specification of the limits showed that in the year 3808 CE, a conjunction will occur between the planets Jupiter and Saturn, and a new cycle will begin. This brought the number of conjunctions to 666. We set the start of this cycle to the year 9419 BCE, for these 666 conjunctions to occur in the period of 13,227 years. In "The Revelation of St. John the Divine", this cycle of the planets Jupiter and Saturn is revealed: "Here is wisdom. Let him that hath understanding count the number of the beast: for it is the number of a man; and his number is *Six hundred three-score and six* [666]."[34]

The number 666 intrigued us, but there was more in store. Further research revealed the rare occurrence of a genuine "Great Conjunction". On 15th July 9419 BCE, a New Moon or Eclipse occurred in conjunction with the planets Mercury, Venus, Mars, Jupiter, Saturn and Neptune in the constellation Virgo (Virgo = constellation of Thoth/Hermes), close to the stars Spica and Arcturus (marking a Babylonian autumnal equinox of yore). This happened on the 362nd day of the year, the epagomene day that was allotted to the god Horus.

If we assume that the Arabs acquired their knowledge from the Egyptians in Alexandria, then Al Kindi may have been alluding to a rare configuration such as this "Great Conjunction". This planetary configuration, occurring on one of the epagomene days (known as the unfortunate days) and immediately preceding New Year's Day, could have been considered a crucial moment in the evolution of our civilisation. It explains the title Al Kindi chose: ***Doctrine and Influence of the Great Conjunction between Jupiter and Saturn on the rise and fall of Empires and World Religions***.

We argue that Atlantis was destroyed on one of these epagomene days (16th July 9419 BCE, the day of Seth). Theoretically, this entailed the end of the Paleolithic Period, on 18th July 9419 BCE. Many millennia later, the following day, July 19th (I Achet 1), obviously became the New Year's Day of the Egyptians. It was the day on which they observed the heliacal rising of the star Sirius just before sunrise (for instance in Buto around 3500 BCE). This heliacal rising of Sirius could be said to mark the resurgence of the Earth and Mankind after the catastrophe and the ensuing chaos. They saw New Year's Day as the birthday on which the New Creation began: "New Year's Day is the anniversary of Creation" and "Today is the beginning of thy works, the memorial of the first day".[35]

Chronology

The following chronology does not claim to be "absolute". On occasion, deviations from traditional chronological surveys are considerable.

According to Egyptian chronology as acknowledged at present, the First Dynasty started around 3100/3000 BCE.[1] However, Egyptian chronology of the period before 2000 BCE remains highly speculative. Carbon dating, carried out in 1984 and 1986 on samples taken from pyramids of the Fourth Dynasty, have shown a significant deviation from the current Egyptian chronology. These datings place the age of the pyramids some 400 to 450 years further back in time. This would mean that they were built around 3000 BCE. The ensuing implications carry great weight, especially for the period between approximately 2500 BCE and 2050 BCE. At present, the era known as the First Intermediate Period is presumed to have covered merely 100-120 years.[2] This short interval comprised the rulership of the Seventh up to and including the Tenth Dynasties, which has generally resulted in a choice of "improvised" chronological constructions, as important factual material about that period is lacking.

The absence of texts and other archaeological sources led to the search for other methods of chronological circumscription. This is required as there are neglected texts such as the texts of the *Solar eclipse and the Birth of Kingship* on the Potterswheel, and *fragments of the Turin Royal Canon describing a ruling period of 2,291 years, 4 months and 22 days until the preparation of the Turin papyrus*, and other indications such as the *alignment of the Pyramids to the Polar-star alfa Draconis, i.e. Thuban*, and the *transition from star-cult to sun-cult* in Egypt during the rulership of the Fourth Dynasty and its final introduction at the beginning of the Fifth Dynasty. All mark characteristic chronological points in time that substantiate the carbon dating results of the age of the pyramids. It places the events in the right context and proves that the pyramids of Giza were not built around 2500 BCE. They do indeed date back to circa 3000 BCE. In addition, Syncellus' mention that the first *Egyptian king* took up rulership in the year 2776 of the world (which began around 5500/5508 BCE) acquires its proper value. Syncellus thereby set the beginning of the reign of Egyptian pharaohs at around 2725 BCE. As it is, Pharaoh Djedkare Izezi ruled as the last but one pharaoh of the Fifth Dynasty.

After Unas, the last pharaoh of the Fifth Dynasty, the Turin papyrus ends with a red line under an addition. Unfortunately, the sum of the First Dynasty up to and including the Fifth was lost. The facts are incontestable, as the solar eclipse at the winter solstice on 17th January 3517 BCE at the beginning of Kingship of the State of Egypt (contained in texts which hitherto appeared incomprehensible or were simply overlooked), the chronological fragments of the Turin Royal Canon, the transition from a stellar to a solar cult at the beginning of the Fifth Dynasty in 2825 BCE, the observation tracks, all contribute to an inevitable revision by approximately 400/500 years of the Egyptian Chronology, which in our reconstruction places the start of the First Dynasty and the transition from prehistory to history in 3517 BCE.

The Djemdet-Nasr period (circa 3500-3000 BCE), with Uruk as its primary archaeological site, was until now extremely difficult to fit into the chronology.[3] This period corresponds with the Nagada II and the Nagada III period in Egypt. The Djemdet-Nasr period could not be appropriately integrated into either the Sumerian or the Egyptian chronology. However, the revised chronology for Egypt does away with those difficulties. In Egypt, this cultural period ended around 3000 BCE, through Pharaoh Snofru, the first pharaoh of the Fourth Dynasty, who developed an independent style and architecture that was untouched by influences from Sumeria. The step pyramids and the enclosing walls incorporating the characteristic panelled niches of the Third Dynasty (circa 3153-3010 BCE) still show the typical Djemdet-Nasr style. For centuries afterwards, the influence of the Djemdet-Nasr period remained apparent in Sumeria.

A mysterious and unprecedented chronological coincidence is found in Manetho's **History of Egypt**, specifically in the version of Africanus (*the fact is that 'years' are not solar years*), concerning the period of rulership of the First to the Eleventh Dynasties, excluding the reign of Amenemhat I.

Overview:

1st to 6th Dynasty:	1,492 'years' of rulership x 2/3 =	995 *solar years*
	(Bickerman, 1980, p. 83)	
1st to 8th Dynasty:	1,639 'years' of rulership x 2/3 =	1,092 *solar years*
8th to 11th Dynasty:	783 'years' of rulership x 2/3 =	522 *solar years*

For some unknown reason, Africanus apparently did not convert the recorded number of years of rulership of these dynasties into solar years! However, the number of solar years as deduced from the years of rulership is in accordance with our revised chronology.

Overview:

1st Dynasty	begins	3523 BCE
6th Dynasty	ends	2527 BCE
Interruption by Flood		6 years ("ausgelassen" von Beckenrath, p.149)
8th Dynasty	begins	2521 BCE
8th Dynasty	ends	2424 BCE
11th Dynasty	ends	1999 BCE

The "Triumph of Horus" of Edfu and its chronological significance

According to our research, the 363rd year of the "rulership" of Re, which appears in the "Triumph of Horus" of Edfu, proves the existence of a chronological commemorative period of 363 years. 363 solar years of 365.25 days each contain a total of 132,586 days. This number of days is equal to 193 cycles of the planet Mars (686.9728 days/cycle). One of the cycles of the planet Mars equals 363 years (see *Sterrengids* 2003, p.107, J.Meeus). On the foundation day of the Egyptian calendar, 19th July 4242 BCE. (JD. 172,232), the planet Mars was also in conjunction with the star Propus. This star constitutes an essential part of the constellation of Horus and of the astronomical iconography of the Pyramid Field (cf. chapter 4).

The "Triumph of Horus" marked the commemoration of the *"Year of the Unification of the Two Lands"*, with the intention of maintaining this Year of the Unification of the Two Lands for the following 363 years. This specific text appears in the eighth decree of Pharaoh Neferkauhor, the penultimate pharaoh of the Eighth Dynasty. The last sentences read: "Sealed in the presence of the King. *Year of the Unification of the Two Lands*, second month of the sowing season, day 20."[4] After the decree, Pharaoh Neferkauhor and his successor Neferirkare (II), the last pharaoh of the Eighth Dynasty, ruled for approximately three years.

Overview of the commemorative periods of 363 years:

13-07-5331 BCE		Date of Big Bang of civilisation in Egypt/Sumeria
19-07-4968 BCE		
19-07-4605 BCE		
19-07-4242 BCE		Start of the Egyptian calendar
19-07-3879 BCE	1.	First series of Predynastic Kings of the Palermo Stone
19-07-3516 BCE	2.	Dynastic Egypt, Narmer's Palette, Union of the Two Lands
26-07-3153 BCE	3.	Third Dynasty, Djoser's Union of the Two Lands (Clagett, Vol.I, p.81)
28-07-2790 BCE	4.	Fifth Dynasty, Neferirkare's Union of the Two Lands (Clagett, Vol.I, p.93)
29-07-2427 BCE	5.	Eight Dynasty, Neferkauhor's Union of the Two Lands
30-07-2064 BCE	6.	Eleventh Dynasty, Menthotpe II, yr. 12, Union of the Two Lands
03-08-1701 BCE	7.	
03-08-1338 BCE	8.	Conspiracy against Tutankhamun
06-08- 975 BCE	9.	
08-08- 612 BCE	10.	
08-08- 249 BCE	11.	

Only on these days that occurred on or around New Year's Day was the planet Mars in conjunction with the star Propus in the constellation of Horus. The eleventh period of the "Triumph of Horus" was celebrated in the middle of the third century BCE. It was predicted that in this third century BCE, the god Horus would oppose the enemy symbolically for the *eleventh* time.[5]

Hence, the 363-year period offers a chronological framework and identifies various important events. Prior to the developments of the Third Dynasty, towards the end of the Second Dynasty, warfare and scrummaging between the Followers of Horus from Lower Egypt and the Children of Seth from Upper Egypt occurred over a period of approximately 80 years (from 3232 BCE). This dissension occurred in the rule of Pharaoh Sekhemyeb (Horus-name). He was incapable of solving the problems and forced to change his name to Peribsen (Seth-name). His successor in the kinglist of Manetho was called Seth(enes). However, the actual war between the Followers of Horus and the Children of Seth was fought under the penultimate pharaoh of the Second Dynasty Kha-sechem. His successor Kha-sechemui – the last pharaoh of this dynasty – achieved permanent peace between the two tribes. This is substantiated by the various depictions on the Serekhs of these pharaohs, which sometimes show the Horus falcon on its own, whereas at other times the Horus falcon has its back turned against the Seth animal. The Serekh of Pharaoh Kha-sechemui shows the falcon, while the Horus-falcon kisses Seth. After Kha-sechemui's rule, the Third Dynasty came to power, during which period the cornerstone of the State of Egypt was built under Pharaoh Djoser.

World Chronicle

*(see **Appendix I**; Julian Period 28 x 19 x 15 years = 7,980 years)*

Beginning	28,121 BCE	according to Manetho/Eusebius
-/-	7,980 years	first Julian Period
	20,141 BCE	
-/-	7,980 years	second Julian Period
	12,161 BCE	
-/-	7,980 years	third Julian Period
	4,181 BCE	**Start of Biblical Chronology, Book Genesis**
-/-	7,980 years	fourth Julian Period
	3,800 CE	

Note: the beginning of the *World Chronicle* was in approximately 28,121 BCE according to Manetho/Eusebius. After a total of 942 Jupiter-Saturn cycles of 19.8572 years, the Atlantis catastrophe took place in approximately 9419 BCE. The ascent of Meso-America took place from approximately 1360 BCE onward (Troano Codex mentions 8060 years after the catastrophe). The Maya-cycle with a duration of 5,125.25 years, start from approximately 1360 BCE and will be finished approximately 3797 CE.

After the Atlantis catastrophe in approximately 9419 BCE, until the end of the fourth Julian period in 3805 CE, 666 (number of the beast in Revelations!) Jupiter-Saturn cycles of 19.8572 years will have elapsed (app. XI).

Egyptian Chronology I   according to Manetho/Eusebius.

Beginning	**28,121 BCE**	Precession of the vernal equinox in conjunction with the Pleiades
-/-	13,900 years	Period of the Gods until Bitis (End of the Osiris era)
	14,221 BCE	Beginning of the Horus era
-/-	5,813 years	Period of Empire of Spirits/Demi-gods
	8408 BCE	Precession from Leo to Cancer Period of Sacred Domains, Central Mountains of North Africa
-/-	1,255 years	Period of People of Demi-gods
-/-	1,817 years	Period of Other Kings
	5336 BCE	Big Bang of Civilisation in Egypt: Memphis, Fayum-oasis, Merimda

Sumerian Chronology I

Beginning	**32,910 BCE**	The year after the Flood
-/-	24,510 years	Period of the First Dynasty of Kish
	8400 BCE	Precession from Leo to Cancer
-/-	3,195 years	Period of Second Dynasty of Kish
	5205 BCE	Big Bang of Civilisation in Sumeria: Ur, Erech, Ubaid, Eridu

The historiography of the Phoenicians also dates back to 30,000 BCE (according to Africanus in Syncellus, p. 31)

Egyptian Chronology II

Development towards a State of Egypt from 5331-3516 BCE

Lower Egypt:

Beginning	5331 BCE	Migration of the Followers of Horus from the Central Mountains of North Africa to Lower Egypt and settlement in Merimda, the Fayum-oasis and around Memphis/ Helwan/ Maadi/Omari.

-/-	1,790 years	Hekla 5/ Thjorsa ca. 5470 BCE (catastrophe without a time margin)[6] Period of 30 Kings reigning from Memphis
	3541 BCE	Warfare between Followers of Horus from Lower Egypt and the Children of Seth from Upper Egypt (ca. 24,575 years after the beginning of the World Chronicle).
	3517 BCE	Installation of Kingship First Dynasty (Solar Eclipse)
	3516 BCE	Unification of the Two Lands under pharaoh Narmer

Upper Egypt:

	ca. 6000 BCE	Settlement at El Kab
	ca. 5000 BCE	Concentration of Settlements around El Badari (Badarian)
	ca. 4000 BCE	Rise of Abydos, El Amra, Nagada (Nagada I)
	ca. 3900 BCE	Proto-development of Hierakonpolis into a location of observation of the heliacal rising of the star Sirius
	ca. 3650 BCE	Hierakonpolis/El Kab develop into a twin-town
	ca. 3600 BCE	Proto-development of the Upper Egyptian Kingdom between This and Hierakonpolis, Dynasty 0 with 7 or 11 pre-dynastic kings?
	3541 BCE	Warfare between the Followers of Horus from Lower Egypt and the Children of Seth from Upper Egypt
	3516 BCE	"Unification of the Two Lands" under Narmer. Founding of the State, beginning of Dynasties.

Sumerian Chronology II

Beginning	**5205 BCE**	Big Bang of Civilisation Rise of Sumeria: Ur, Erech, Ubaid, Eridu
-/-	2,171 years	First Dynasty of Civilisation Gilgamesh and his Epic
Subtotal	3033 BCE	End of Djemdet Nasr Period in Egypt

At the same time as the breaching of traditions by the Third Dynasty. Pharaoh Snofru of Egypt radically changed architecture and sculptural arts during his rulership

30 years	Ur-Nungal
15 years	Utul-Kalamma
9 years	Labasher
8 years	Ennunadanna
56 years	...he-de
6 years	Me-lam-an-na
36 years	Lugal-ki-aga

2,873 BCE

Egyptian Chronology III

From the Founding of the State in 3517BCE - 1650 BCE:

Sumerian Chronology III

From Dynasty I of Ur ca. 2895 - ca. 1655 BCE:

Dynasty I from, together with Dynasty II	3516 BCE. 363 yrs.	
Dynasty III	3153 BCE. 143 yrs	
Dynasty IV	3010 BCE. 185 yrs	
Dynasty V	2825 BCE. 165 yrs	Dynasty I of Ur 2898 BCE. 177 yrs

General Remarks during the Old Kingdom:

Transition from Star-cult to Sun-cult ca. 2900 BCE, under pharaoh Djedefre.

Introduction Sun-cult at the start of Vth Dynasty.

After the last Pharaoh Unas, the Turin papyrus shows a red line to denote a subtotal. This line probably suggests a specific end.

Note: Syncellus specifically mentioned a beginning of the rulership of the first Egyptian Kings. Earliest Pyramid Texts. Aridity of the climate takes on serious forms.

Hekla 4 (catastrophe)	ca. 2690 BCE. Cause of Hekla 4 catastrophe, precession in conjunction with Pleiades; this constellation is traditionally linked up with the myth

around the Deluge of Chaldea and other widespread nations.[7]

Egyptian Kings:

Dynasty VI	2,660 BCE 133 yrs	Dynasty II of Ur	2,721 BCE. 108 yrs
Dynasty VII	?	Dynasty Akshak	2613 BCE. 93 yrs

Catastrophe, rulership interrupted from 2,527 BCE for 6 years

Catastrophe   2520 BCE.

Drastic climatological changes   Ur no longer a seaport?

Dynasty VIII   2521 BCE   Governors of Lagash
                    97 yrs   ca. 2600 until 2380 BCE.

Proto-Dynasty Akkad
Lugalzaggesi   ca. 2380 BCE.

Dynasty Akkad:
Sargon I   ca. 2355 BCE.
                        180 yrs

Synchronous Dyn. Akkad:
Dynasty IV of Kish 2267 BCE for 92 years

and Dyn. Gutiu 2,228 BCE
End Gutium   2,137 BCE

First Intermediate Period until Dynasty XI:

Dynasty IX and X: 2424 BCE
                         Ca. 273 yrs

Regional Governors at Heracleopolis reigning together after
Collapse of Old Kingdom for 409 'years' x 2/3 = 273 solar years.
Remarkable: Manetho registered as well as for Dyn. IX and X:
19 Kings of Heracleopolis. My opinion is that his mentioned
409 'years' reign for Dyn. IX is included the 185 'years' for Dyn. X.
(Egypt of the Pharaohs, Gardiner, Appendix)

Continuation of Akkad:
Dynasty III Erech 2175 BCE
                        25 yrs

Dynasty IV Erech 2150 BCE
                        30 yrs

		Dynasty V Erech 2120 BCE
		7 yrs

Dynasty III of Ur 2113 BCE
108 yrs

Dynasty XI   2151BCE

Inyotef prince
Mentuhotep I
Inyotef I
Inyotef II
Inyotef III
Mentuhotep II   2076 BCE
Year 12,
Union of the Two Lands: 2064 BCE

Dynasty Isin   2004 BCE
92 yrs
Overlapping Isin:
Dynasty Larsa   1973 BCE
97 yrs

Transition-period 6 or 7 yrs. under vizir Amenemhat I
Dynasty XII   1996 BCE (213 yrs, 1 month, 19 days)
77,794 days = 2,634 Moon-periods

General Remarks during Middle Kingdom (XII Dynasty):

Joseph arrives in Egypt; translation of hieroglyphs into Semitic ca. 1,930 BCE, discovered by Egyptologist Darnell. Semitic alphabet was developed from hieroglyphs (Wadi el Hol). Synchronous with Biblical Chronology.

Heliacal rising of Sirius on IV Peret 16, year 7 of Sesostris III,
New Moon on Peret 17(18th July 1873 BCE; JD.1,037509)
(Parker 1875 or 1872 BCE)

Dynasty I   1876 BCE
Babylon   226 yrs

Second Intermediate Period until Dynasty XVIII:

Dynasty XIII	1783 BCE	Sinmubali	(1876-1847BCE)
Era of Aseth		Hammurabi	(1847-1804 BCE)
		Et al. until	
Start Era of Decline in Egypt		Ammizaduga	(1701-1681 BCE)
		Samsuditana	(1681 – 1650 BCE)

Dynasty XIV to XV?
Libyan Garamants invade Egypt

Dynasty XVI	ca. 1655 BCE	Hittites invaded Babylon in
	Domination by the	1650 BCE
	Hethites;	

King Mursil I, known as Hyksos, founded Avaris in the Delta

Thera eruption	1628 BCE

General Remarks during the First Dynasty of Babylon:

The chronology of Hammurabi has been determined on the basis of the Venus tables of Ammizaduga. In Year 1 of Ammizaduga, day 15 of the month Sabatu occurred on 15th November 1701 BCE (JD 1,100,452). On this day, a partial lunar eclipse was visible on the horizon in Babylon at approximately 14h00 GMT. This date was established by comparing the relevant texts (***Anfänge der Astronomie***, p. 35ff) and the details included in them. The planet Venus became invisible for 67 days in year 10 of Ammizaduga, day 10 of the month Arahsamna, 10th August 1691 BCE (Disappearance in the morning, *Morgenletzt*), and regained visibility on 16th October 1691 BCE (First Appearance in evening, *Abenderst*). Venus remained in the immediate vicinity of the sun for 67 days and was thus "invisible" from the Earth. This particular position of Venus is not mentioned in either the "Middle" (1645 until 1627 BCE) or in the "Short" chronology (1571 BCE). Cf. also ***Astronomy before the telescope***, p. 45 (Hammurabi 1848-1806 BCE).

Survey hieroglyphs Egyptian Grammar, Sir Alan Gardiner

M44   N27   N24   N15   T14 and 15   D21   D22   O24   D40   L2   R13   Q1   Q2
Z8

Footnotes

Chapter 1

[1] *Pyramid Texts*, Faulkner, Utterance 477
[2] *Nieuwjaar in het Oude Egypte*, Borghouts, p. 5 and Edfou V, 351. 3-4.
[3] *De Neanderthaler*, Holleman, p. 85.
[4] Ibid, p. 32-33.
[5] *Le Tchad depuis 25000 ans*, Schneider, p. 35-36 diagram.
[6] *Ice-core dating of the Pleistocene/Holocene Boundary applied to a calibration of the 14 C time scale*. Radiocarbon, vol. 28, no. 2a, 1986, p. 284-291.
[7] *Le Tchad depuis 25000 ans*, Schneider, p. 42 en 43.
[8] *Ancient Egypt, a Cultural Topography*, Kees, p. 18-19.
[9] *Le Tchad depuis 25000 ans*, Schneider, diagram. Corresponds with Hekla 5/ Thjorsa from the detailed isotopic research on the ice-core borings at Camp Century (Greenland) by Hammer et al (1980).
[10] *Archéologie Africaine*, M. Cornevin, p. 69.
[11] *Chronologie der Aegypter*, Lepsius, p. 472 and p. 486.
[12] *Mythical Origin of the Egyptian Temple*, Reymond.
[13] *Piramides*, Lehner, p. 66.
[14] *Keeper of Genesis*, Bauval/Hancock, p. 325.
[15] *Zeitrechnung*, Sethe, II, p. 37.
[16] Cf. also *Astronomy before the Telescope*, Wells, p. 29-32.
[17] *Star Names, Their Lore & Meaning*, Hinckley Allen, p. 307.
[18] Cf. also *Piramides*, Lehner, p. 106-107.
[19] *Thesaurus*, Abteilung II, Brugsch, p. 525 schedule by astronomer Dr. von Gumpach. His schedule runs until 2700 BCE. We add the following data, pertaining to the summer solstice:
July 17th 2800 BCE G.M.T. 07h:l0 AM.
July 18th 2900 BCE G.M.T. 0lh:l5 AM.; the Sun in 0°Cancer. Heliacal rising of Sirius at Heliopolis on July 18th.
[20] *Zeitrechnung*, Sethe, II, p. 31ff; p. 37ff and p. 49ff.

Chapter 2

[1] *Herodotus over de 26 ste Dynastie*; de Meulenaere, p. 4
[2] *De Piramiden van Egypte*, Silotti/Hawass, p. 18.
[3] *Histories*, Book II-43. Herodotus,
[4] Ibid, Book II-144.
[5] Ibid, Book 11-145.
[6] *Myth and Symbol in Ancient Egypt*, Rundle Clark, p. 263.
[7] *The Orion Mystery*, Bauval & Gilbert, p. 180.
[8] *Egyptian Astronomical Texts*, I, Neugebauer/Parker p. 24-5.
[9] Cf. *The Death of Gods in Ancient Egypt*, Sellers. p. 13.
[10] *The Pyramid of Unas*, Piankoff, p. 5.
[11] Plutarchus, *Moralia V* on the Myth of Horus and Seth; cf. also *Osiris*, Vol.I, Wallis Budge, p. 386.
[12] *Gods of the Egyptians*, Vol.II. Wallis Budge, p. 126-128.
[13] *Die Sterne von Babylon*, Papke, p. 140-141 and p. 277-281.
[14] *Gods of the Egyptians*, Vol.II, Wallis Budge, p. 47.
[15] *Nag Hammadi Texts*, NHL VI, 8:70, 3-10.

[16] *Coffin Texts*, Faulkner, Vol.III, p. 132, Spell 1035.
[17] *Kingship and the Gods*, Frankfort, p. 192.
[18] *StarNames, Their Lore & Meaning*, Hinckley Allen, p. ix.
[19] *L´Egypte Céleste*, Georges Daressy, p. 31.
[20] *Ancient Egyptian Science*, Vol.I, Clagett, p. 570.
[21] *Götterglaube*, Kees, p. 59.
[22] Ibid, p. 59.
[23] Ibid, p. 403.
[24] Ibid, p. 266.
[25] Ibid, p. 321.
[26] Ibid, p. 313.
[27] Ibid, p. 325.
[28] Ibid. p. 331.
[29] *Nag Hammadi Texts*, NHL VI. 8:70, 3-10.
[30] *Knaurs Lexicon der Agyptischen Kultur*, p. 183.
[31] Coordinates rounded off down to minutes of arc; adapted from *The Atlas of Ancient Egypt*, Baines and Malek, p. 233ff.
[32] *Corpus Hermeticum*, Stob. Herm. XXIV, 13. Stricker, Horus III, note 2421; v, note 7068. Mahé. Hermès II, 230.
[33] *Ag. Rel.* 46 and 47, Morenz. The last ..... also refers to pseudo-Apuleius, Th. Hopfner, *Fontes historiae religionis aegyptiacae*, Bonn 1922 and Hopfner, Fontes 620, who praises Egypt as "the temple of the entire world" and as "the image of the heavens".
[34] *Papyrus Leiden* I 344 verso x, 9.10.
[35] *The Complete Pyramids*, Lehner, p. 142.
[36] *Götterglaube*, Kees, p. 90, note 5.
[37] *Lexikon der Agyptologie* (LÄ) Vol.I, kol. 844.
[38] *De Ibis* 18, no. 2, p. 45, ed. Egypt. society "Sjemsoethot", Amsterdam.
[39] *LÄ.*Vol.I,kol.844.
[40] *De Ibis* 18, no. 2, p.46

Chapter 3

[1] *BIFAO* 74, 1974. p. 135-147.
[2] *Kepler's Geometrical Cosmology*, Field, Chapter I.
[3] *Thesaurus* I/II, Brugsch, p. 86.
[4] *Calendars*, Parker, § 193.
[5] *Nieuwjaar in het oude Egypte*, Borghouts, p. 6.
[6] Ibid, p. 13.
[7] *Ancient Records of Egypt*, Vol.I. Breasted. § 619.
[8] *Götterglaube*. Kees, p. 178.
[9] Ibid, p. 178.
[10] *Woordenboek der Oudheid* (WdO), col.3232.
[11] *The Followers of Horus*, Ed. Friedman and Adams, contrib. by von der Way, p.221.
[12] Ibid, p. 223.
[13] Ibid, p. 220-221.
[14] *Atlas of Ancient Egypt*, Baines and Malek, p. 78.
[15] Ibid, p. 80.
[16] *Beiträge*, Sethe, p. 3ff.
[17] *Egypt of the Pharaohs*, Gardiner, p. 421.
[18] *Götterglaube*, Kees, p. 119.
[19] *The Complete Pyramids*, Lehner, p. 82.
[20] *DE* 24, The Heliacal Rising of Sirius, van Oosterhout, p. 92.
[21] *Götterglaube*, Kees, p. 224-225.
[22] *Sothis-und Monddaten*, Rolf Krauss, p. 49.
[23] *Atlas of Ancient Egypt*, Baines and Malek, p. 73.
[24] Ibid, p. 123.
[25] *Egyptian Grammar*, p. 489.
[26] *Dramatische Texte* 23 and 25, Sethe.
[27] *Nieuwjaar in het oude Egypte*, Borghouts, p. 13-15.
[28] *The Sphinx: Who Built It and Why*, Archeology. Hawass/Lehner, Sept/Oct. 1994, p. 34.

[29] *Pyramid Texts*, Faulkner, Utterance 527.

[30] Ibid, § 1650.

[31] *Egypte, Het land van defarao's*, p. 12.

[32] *Chronologie der Ägypter*, Lepsius, p. 472.

[33] *Archéologie Africaine*, M.Cornevin, p. 66.

[34] *Secrets du Continent Noir Révelés par l'Archéologie*, M.Cornevin. p. 79.

[35] *LÄ*, Vol.IV, kol. 609-610 and note l and 2.

[36] *Egyptian Grammar*, Gardiner, O 36; R 12; T 3.

[37] *Egypte, Het land van defarao's*, p. 6.

[38] *The Palermo Stone and the Archaic kings of Egypt*, O'Mara. p. 154.

[39] *Grundzüge der Ägyptischen Geschichte*, Hornung, p. 10.

[40] *BIFAO* 74,1974, p. 135-147.

[41] *Rock Tombs of El Amarna*; Part V, p. 23-27.

[42] *Studiën zur Altägyptische Kultur* 14, 1987, p. 239-246.

[43] Ibid, p. 239-246.

[44] *Egyptian Grammar*, p. 199.

[45] *Egyptian Grammar*, p. 66 note 27.

[46] *Ancient Egypt*, Kemp, p. 270.

[47] According to the Egyptologist Goyon, 1 royal cubit equals 52.36 centimetre. Cf. *Le Secret des Bâtisseurs des Grandes Pyramides Khéops*. p. 156.

[48] *SAK* 14, 1987, p. 239-246.

[49] *De Ibis* 17, p. 117-118.

[50] *Ancient Egyptian Construction and Architecture*. Somers Clark and Engelbach, p. 46 and   52-53.

[51] Ibid. p. 64-65.

[52] *Egyptian Grammar*, Gardiner, § 266.2.

[53] Ibid, § 266.2.

[54] *Maps of the Ancient Sea Kings*, Hapgood, p. 113ff.

[55] *Le Secret des Bâtisseurs des Grandes Pyramides Khéops*, Goyon, p. 92.

[56] *Mémoires*, Académie des Inscriptions, XXIV (1756), Fréret, p. 507-522.

[57] *Recherches critiques, historiques et géographiques sur les fragments d'Heron d'Alexandrie*, Letronne, Paris, 1851,133.

Chapter 4

[1] *Astronomy before the telescope*, edited by Walker, 1996, p. 11.

[2] Ibid, p. 28.

[3] Ibid, p. 28.

[4] *The Facsimile Edition of the Nag Hammadi Texts*, J.M. Robinson, Leiden 1972-1979. (NHC) VI, 8:70, 3-10.

[5] *Histories*, Book II-5, Herodotus.

[6] *Histories*, Book II-43, Herodotus.

[7] *Star Names,Their Lore & Meaning*, Hinckley Allen, p. 359.

[8] , *Histories*, Book II-144, Herodotus.

[9] WdO, kol.3171.

[10] *LÄ*.Vol.III, kol.41 and 42.

[11] *Star Names, Their Lore & Meaning*, Hinckley Allen, p. 265.

[12] *LÄ*.Vol.IV, kol.609. and *Life in Ancient Egypt*, Erman, p. 271 and 348.

[13] *The GreatPyramid*, Piazzi Smyth, p. 4.

[14] *Encyclopedia Britannica*.

[15] *Star Names, Their Lore & Meaning*, Hinckley Allen, p. 307.

[16] Ibid, p. 223.

[17] Ibid. p. 307.

[18] *Ägyptische Chronologie*, Meyer, tables p. 125 and 145.

[19] *Die ägyptischen Pyramiden*, Stadelmann, p. 311.

[20] *Egypt of the Pharaohs*, Gardiner, p. 435.

[21] *Ägyptische Chronologie*, Meyer, p. 30, note 2.

[22] *Egypt of the Pharaohs*, Gardiner, p. 436.

[23] Cf. also *Ancient Egyptian Science*, Vol.I, Clagett, p. 629-630.

[24] De l'application de techniques palynologiques à un territoire désertique. *Paléoclimatologie du Quaternaire Récent au Sahara'*, Quézel, p. 245-248.

[25] *Ancient Egypt and some Eastern Neighbours*, Nibbi, p. 2.

[26] Ibid, p. 6.

[27] Ibid, Chapter 1.

[28] *Ancient Egypt and some Eastern Neighbours*, Nibbi, p. 1.

[29] Le *Tchad depuis 25000* Ans, Schneider, p. 94.

[30] Ibid, p. 94.

[31] *Science*, 17 oktober 1969, Vol. 166, n° 3903, 377-381

[32] Three Climatic records revealed by the Camp Century ice record. In: *Late cenozoic Ice Ages* edit. by Turekian K.K., New Haven and London, Yale University Press, 1971, p. 37-56.

[33] *Chronologie des pharaonischen Ägypten*, von Beckenrath, p. 149 and 152. The author of the Turin King-Papyrus reported "six missing years" after pharaoh Nikotris of the Sixth Dynasty.

[34] *The Complete Pyramids*, Lehner, p. 15.

[35] Ibid.p.95,106,120.

[36] Ibid, p. 10-11.

[37] After the unification of Egypt had become a definite fact after the stirrings towards the end of the Second Dynasty (ca. 3150 BCE), and subsequent to developing a plan to build a royal necropolis near the triangle of Memphis, Letopolis and Heliopolis, it was also decided to give the pharaohs of the 0th, 1st and 2nd Dynasty, who had been buried on the graveyard of Umm el Qa'ab in Abydos, a re-interment in the bend at Saqqara. Thus, the founders of Egypt were paid tribute to and were interred into the necropolis.

[38] *Ancient Egyptian Construction and Architecture*, Somers Clarke and Engelbach, p. 223.

[39] *The Obelisks of Egypt*, Habachi, p. 15-25.

[40] *The Complete Pyramids*, Lehner, p. 107,120,138,140-148.

[41] *The Gods of the Egyptians* I, Wallis Budge, p. 340.

[42] Ibid, p. 216.

[43] Cf. 'Die Unterweltsbücher der Ägypter', Hornung, p. 101ff.

[44] *Pyramid Texts*, Faulkner, § 802-803.

[45] *The Complete Pyramids*, Lehner, p. 83.

[46] *Pyramid Texts*, Faulkner, § 959.

[47] It takes around two months before a star in the position of Sirius is passed by the Sun and that this star Sirius rises at dawn shortly before sunrise and becomes visible again for the first time (heliacal rising). *Sothis-und Monddaten*, Rolff Krauss, p. 39 and 61f.

[48] The period from May 11th until November 13th lasts for 180 + 5 epagomene days, followed by another 180 days.

[49] *Atlas of Ancient Egypt*, Baines and Malek, Plaatsnamen register, p. 233.

[50] Ibid, p. 233.

[51] ASAE 3,1899, 77.

[52] *Histories*, Book II-15 and 97, Herodotus.

[53] Cf. also *Cercasorus et l'Ancien Observatoire*, Goyon, BIFAO 74, p. 135-147.

[54] *The Geography of Strabo*, Vol.VIII, The Loeb Classical Library, Book XVII, 1.30.

[55] Liv.I, a. Pomponius Mela,

[56] *Histories*, Book II-97, Herodotus.

[57] *Egyptian Grammar*, Gardiner, T 14 and T 15. p. 513.

[58] *Star Names, Their Lore & Meaning*, Hinckley Allen, p. 303.

[59] *The Complete Pyramids*, Lehner, p. 107.

[60] *Atlas van het Universum*, Moore. p. 216.

[61] Ibid.p.216.

[62] *Star Names, Their Lore & Meaning*, Hinckley Allen, p. 310 and 308.

[63] LÄ.Vol.IV, kol. 609-610 and note 2.

[64] *Coffin Texts*, Vol. III, 263.

[65] *Star Names, Their Lore & Meaing*, Hinckley Allen, p. 313.

[66] Ibid.p.308.

[67] Ibid.p.235.

[68] *The Complete Pyramids*, Lehner, p. 96.

[69] *Ancient Records of Egypt*, Vol.I, Breasted, p. 280ff.

[70] *The Complete Pyramids*, Lehner, p.154.

[71] Ibid, p. 154.

[72] *Ägyptische Chronologie*, Meyer, p. 57.
[73] Cf. also LÄ, Vol.I, column 42ff.
[74] *LÄ*, Vol.I, kol.45.
[75] *Star Names, Their Lore & Meaning*, Hinckley Allen, p. 235.
[76] *Moralia* V on the Myth of Horus and Seth, Plutarchus.
[77] *Gods of the Egyptians*, Vol.II, Wallis Budge, p. 126-128.
[78] *Astronomy before the telescope*, p. 11.
[79] Ibid.p.11.
[80] *The Complete Pyramids*, Lehner, p. 77.
[81] Ibid. p. 118-119.
[82] Cf *The Complete Pyramids*, Lehner.
[83] *Kingship and the Gods*, Frankfort, Ch.2, p. 27.
[84] *Kramer's Latijns WoordenBook*.
[85] *The Complete Pyramids*, Lehner, p. 78.
[86] *Götterglaube*, Kees, p. 90, note 5.
[87] *LÄ*,Vol.III. kol.41 and 42.
[88] *Histories*, Book II-148, Herodotus.
[89] *The Complete Pyramids*, Lehner, p. 54.
[90] *WdO*, kol.1935-1936.
[91] *Star Names, Their Lore & Meaning*, Hinckley Allen, p. 332.
[92] *Histories*, Book II-91, Herodotus.
[93] *The Geography of Strabo*, Vol.VIII, The Loeb Classical Library. Book XVII, 1.3.
[94] *Atlas of Ancient Egypt*, Baines and Malek, p. 14-15.
[95] Cf. also *Kingship and the Gods*, Frankfort, p. 190ff.
[96] Ibid, p. 195ff.
[97] *Pyramid Texts*, Faulkner, § 819-820.
[98] *Kingship and the Gods*, Frankfort, p. 166.
[99] *LÄ*, Vol.I, kol.45.
[100] *Egypt before the Pharaohs*, Hoffman. p. 218.
[101] *National Geographic*, Vol.193, no.2, p. 38-39. Feb. 1998.
[102] *De Ontdekkers*, Boorstin, p. 583.

Chapter 5

[1] *Histories*, Book 1-1 Herodotus,
[2] *The Legacy of Egypt*, Glanville. Oxford, p. 12.
[3] *Phaedo*, 108-109, (58). Plato,
[4] Ibid, 110, (59).
[5] Cf. *Maps of the Ancient Sea Kings*, Hapgood, p. 182.
[6] WdO, kol.1418.
[7] The translation may be open to question, since Ro may mean land or earth; Egyptian Grammar, Gardiner, D 21, cf. D 25 for mouth and Cf. Rhind papyrus.
[8] *The Geography of Strabo*, Vol.VIII, The Loeb Classical Library. Book XVII, 3.20.
[9] WdO, kol.2409-2410-2411.
[10] WdO, kol.2409-2410.
[11] *The Geography of Claudius Ptolemaeus*, Stevenson, Book l, Ch.I, p. 26.
[12] *Times World-Atlas*, index of names of towns.
[13] HBA I; Weidner, p. 107.
[14] Ibid, p. 107.
[15] *Neue Untersuchungen zur Topographie des babylonischen Fixsternhimmels*, Koch, p. 57.
[16] *Die Sterne von Babylon*, Papke, p. 28.
[17] Ibid, p. 29. Tontafel L4 (K 3050 + K 2694).
[18] HBA I; Weidner, p. 107.
[19] Ibid, p. 108.
[20] Ibid, p. 112.
[21] *Neue Untersuchungen zur Topographie des babylonischen Fixsternhimmels*, Koch, 1989, p. 56-61.
[22] HBA I; Weidner, p. 110.
[23] *Anfänge der Astronomie*, v.d. Waerden, p. 294-297 and table III by Koch, in appendix IX.

[24] HBA I; Weidner, p. 109.

[25] Ibid, p. 109.

[26] *Neue Untersuchungen zur Topographie des babylonischen Fixsternhimmels*, Koch, p. 60, note 228.

[27] Cf. table III, Koch, p. 59.

[28] HBA I; Weidner, p. 111.

[29] *De Stenen Spreken*, de Jonge and IJzereef. p. 20ff and *The Megalithic Art of Western Europe*, Shee Twohig.

[30] *Geschiedenis van de Cartografie*, p. 11.

[31] *Stob. Herm.* XXIV.13. Stricker, Horus III, note 2421; v, note 7068. Mahé. Hermes II, 230.

[32] *The Complete Pyramids*, Lehner, title page and p. 34.

[33] *Egyptian Grammar*, Gardiner, p. 183 and p.495, Mn-nfr = Memphis.

[34] ANET, Sachs translation, p. 332,1.274f.

[35] *Das Wiedergefundene Paradies*, Ungnad, p. 11.

[36] *Anfänge der Astronomie*, v.d.Waerden, p. 66ff and Hamlet's Mill, De Santillana & von Dechend, p. 435.

[37] *Ancient Records of Egypt*, Vol.I, Breasted, p. 280ff.

[38] Cf. also *Die Beziehungen Ägyptens zu Vorderasien im 3. und 2.Jahrtausend v.Chr.*, Hekk. p. 12-17, 38-39.

[39] Cf. also *The Complete Pyramids*, Lehner, p. 127-133.

[40] *Atlas of the World*, National Geographic Society. Washington. 1981. Maps 207 and 208. Scale l : 8.250000.

[41] *The Followers of Horus*, Ed. Friedman and Adams, contrib. by von derWay, p. 217.

[42] Ibid, p. 221.

[43] Ibid, p. 223.

[44] *Egyptian Grammar*, Gardiner, M 44.

[45] *Thesaurus* I/II, Brugsch, p. 86.

[46] WdO, kol.3232.

[47] WdO. kol.2613-2614.

[48] *Le Tchad depuis 25000 ans*, Schneider, p. 19-27.

[49] *Art rupestre et préhistoire du Sahara*, Jean-Loïc Le Quellec, p. 184 and Roset, Archéologia, 183. p. 43-50.

[50] *Le Tchad depuis 25000 ans*, Schneider, p. 42-43.

[51] Cf. eg. Wainscoat, Nature 319, p. 491-493 and the mitochondrial DNA research by Cann, Stoneking and Wilson in Nature, 1987.

[52] Cf. also *Archéologie Africaine*, M.Cornevin, Ch.4.

[53] *Art rupestre et préhistoire du Sahara*, Jean-Loïc Le Quellec, p. 187-188.

[54] Cf. *Secrets du Continent Noir révélés par l'Archeologie*, M.Cornevin, p. 79.

[55] *Tetrabiblos* 11,3, Claudius Ptolemaeus.

[56] Ibid

[57] Ibid

[58] *Das Wiedergefundene Paradies*, Ungnad, p. 11.

[59] *Die Sterne von Babylon*, Papke, p. 151ff.

[60] ANET, Pritchard, p. 60ff.

[61] Ibid. p. 57 and 181.

[62] *Kingship and the Gods*, Frankfort, p. 313-314.

[63] *The Gods of the Egyptians*, Wallis Budge, Vol.II, p. 109.

[64] ANET, Pritchard, Akkadian Myths and Epics, Translator: Speiser, p. 60.

[65] *The Genius of China*, Temple, p. 35.

[66] ANET, Pritchard, p. 69 and 503 with note 109.

[67] *Kulturgeschichte des Alten Ägypten*, Wolf, p. 203-204.

[68] *Geschiedenis van de Cartografie*, p. 160-161.

[69] *Egypt's Making*, Rice, p. 249.

[70] *Osiris*, Wallis Budge, Vol.I. p. 31ff.

Chapter 6

[1] See also *Histories*, Book IV, 168-185 Herodotos,

[2] *Archéologie Africaine*, M.Cornevin, p. 37.

[3] Nature, Vol. 339, June 15th 1989, p. 532-534.

[4] *Archéologie Africaine*, M.Cornevin, Ch.4 and 6 and *Le Tchad depuis 25000 ans*, Schneider.

[5] *Le Tchad depuis 25000 ans*, Schneider.

[6] *Archéologie Africaine*, M.Cornevin, p. 61-63.

[7] LÄ, Vol.I, kol.515,905,980; Vol.II. kol.120; Vol.III. kol.307,479; Vol.IV. kol.1196; Vol.V. kol.1269; Vol.VI, kol. 231,1269,1343.

[8] *Wisdom of the Egyptians*, Sir William Flinders Petrie, Plate III, London, 1940.

[9] *StarNames,Their Lore & Meaning*, Hinckley Allen, p. 45-46-47.

[10] *De Rotstekeningen in de Sahara*, Lhote, p. 138ff.

[11] Ibid, p. 144.

[12] *Exact Sciences*, Neugebauer, 2nd edition, Dover, p. 140.

[13] *Gilgamesh Epos*, Heidel, p. 82, note 173.

[14] Cf. *Art rupestre et préhistoire du Sahara*, Jean-Loïc le Quellec, p. 104-106, 305 and 549.

[15] *StarNames, Their Lore & Meaning*, Hinckley Allen, p. 303.

[16] *Histories*, Book 11-123. Herodotus

[17] Cf. *Griekse Mythen [Greek Myths]*, Graves, op. cit.8. Neith was, amongst others, Goddess of the island Elephantine (Lady of Abu), which is why the glorious Hathor temple was built at a later stage on Philae, the island nearby. See also The Gods of the Egyptians, Vol.I, Wallis Budge, p. 450-465, esp. p. 463.

[18] *Griekse Mythen [Greek Myths]*, Graves, op. cit.8.

[19] *Götterglaube*, Kees, p. 211.

[20] *Art rupestre et préhistoire du Sahara*, Loïc le Quellec, p. 443.

[21] *Predynastic Egypt*, Adams, p. 17.

[22] *Histories*, Book IV-189, Herodotus,

[23] WdO, kol.1992.

[24] *Rär*, Bonnet, p. 514. and LÄ Vol.IV, kol.393.

[25] *Pyramid Texts* § 289, 508,1059,1065,1131; Faulkner

[26] *Rär*, Bonnet, p. 514.

[27] *Die Unterweltsbücher der Ägypter*, Amduat Book, eleventh hour, Hornung, p. 171.

[28] *Gods of the Egyptians*, Vol.I, Wallis Budge, p. 450-465 and Herodotos, *Histories*, Book II-59 and 62,170 and *Griekse Mythen [Greek Myths]*, Graves, 8 (amongst others).

[29] *Kingship and the Gods*, Frankfort, p. 159.

[30] *Le Renard Pâle [The pale Fox]*, Griaule and Dieterlen, p. 458.

[31] Meyer Enzyclopädie and WdO, kol.3136.

[32] *De Rotstekeningen van de Sahara,[La Découverte des Fresques du Tassili]*, Lhote, p. 146-156.

[33] *The World of the Phoenicians*, Moscati, p. 63-64.

[34] *The Bible*, Dutch authorized version of 1747, based on the Decree by the National Synod of Dordrecht in 1618 and 1619; Judges 16: 23 en 24; Cf. Notes: Dagon the Philistinian idol, who acquired this name because the lower part of his body resembled that of a Fish, while the upper part of his body was like that of a human being; cf. also I Samuel 5: 3, 4, and 5. In a similar way, other heathen tribes also worshipped sea-idols, such as Neptune, Triton, Leucothea, etc. It is claimed by some that the name of this idol is derived from the Hebrew word dagan, i.e. corn, since they believed him to be the god of agriculture.

[35] *Egypt's Making*, Rice, p. 293.

[36] *Griekse Mythen [Greek Myths]*, Graves, register, p. 726.

[37] Ibid, 1,5.

[38] Ibid, 82.6.

[39] *Rär*, Bonnet, p. 512.

[40] Ibid, p. 512.

[41] *Egyptian Grammar*, Gardiner. p. 468 and 502 under signlist R 13.

[42] *Urgeschichte*, Sethe, § 67, 85.

[43] WdO, kol.3136.

[44] *Astronomica*, Manilius, *Map of the heavens*, van Wageningen.

[45] WdO, kol. 153.

[46] *Rär*, Bonnet, p. 514.

[47] WdO, kol. 3136.

[48] *Götterglaube*, Kees, p. 102ff.

[49] *Kingship and the Gods*, Frankfort, p. 392, note 62.

50 *Götterglaube*, Kees, p. 29.
51 *StarNames, Their Lore & Meaning*, Hinckley Allen, p. 52.
52 *Art rupestre et préhistoire du Sahara*, Loïc le Quellec, p. 448.
53 *Geschichte des Altertums*; Meyer, § 312.
54 WdO, kol.974-975.
55 Encyclopedie Winkler Prins
56 *The Twelfth Planet*, Sitchin, p. 152.
57 Does this maybe point to the Egyptian term imyw-h3t, meaning "person from former times", who was a goat-herd holding a whip? Cf. also *Egyptian Grammar*, Gardiner, A 50 and 51, p. 447 and S45, p. 510
58 Excerpt from *"Journaal van een Woestijnreiziger"*, Mathieu Berden, 1943.
59 *Grootste Mysteries Aller Tijden*, p. 298.
60 Meyer Enzyklopädie, p. 802.
61 *Looking for Dilmun*, Bibby, p. 60 and 62.
62 *Egypt's Making*, Rice, p. 244.
63 *Bahrain through the ages, the Archeology*, p. 157-165.
64 *Egypt's Making*, Rice, p. 254.
65 Ibid. p. 253.
66 Ibid, p. 253.
67 *Gilgamesj Epos [Gilgamesh Epic]*, Dr.De Liagre Böhl, 133-134; 169; 166 and 95.
68 *Die Sterne von Babylon*, Papke; p. 148-152.
69 *Star Names, Their Lore & Meaning*, Hinckley Allen, p.47-48.
70 Ibid, p. 51.
71 *Geschichte des Altertums*, Meyer, § 182.
72 *Egypt's Making*, Rice, p. 252-253.
73 Syncellus, Chron. 28 and Eusebius, Chron. 5.8. from *The Ancient Fragments*, Cory, London 1828;1832 and 1876.
74 Cf. legenda *Le Renard Pâle [The pale Fox]*, Griaule and Dieterlen, p. 60.
75 *The Egyptian Heritage*, Lehner, p. 128-129.
76 *Le Renard Pâle [The pale Fox]*, p. 336-337 and fig. 116-117.
77 *Art rupestre et préhistoire du Sahara*, Loïc le Quellec.
78 *Atlas van het oude Egypte [Atlas of ancient Egypt]*, p. 109.
79 *The World of the Phoenicians*, Moscati, p. 23.
80 *Pyramid Texts*, Faulkner, § 802-803.
81 *Oxford Companion to Archeology*, Fagan, p. 532.

Chapter 7

1 *Götterglaube*, Kees, p. 177.
2 *Egypt´s Making*, Rice, p. 248.
3 Cf. *Thesaurus I/II*, Brugsch, p. 255:46, 266:16, 258-272 and Parker in *Calendars* § 86 and § 214-216.
4 *Egypt´s Making*, Rice, p. 248.
5 *Pyramid Text*, Utterance 265 and *Egypt's Making*, p. 248.
6 *Mythical Origin of the Egyptian Temple*, Reymond, p. 262.
7 Ibid. p. 263.
8 Ibid, p. 127 and p.153, p.158-159.
9 Ibid. p. 55.
10 Ibid. p. 13 note 4
11 Ibid. p. 13 esp. the Edfu Records VI.14,15; 176.9; 181.16 and Edfu Records VI.170,5; 328.15; 330,8.
12 *Egypt's Making*, Rice. p. 250.
13 Ibid, p. 248.
14 *Maps of the Ancient Sea Kings*, Hapgood, p. 222.
15 *Mythical Origin of the Egyptian Temple*, Reymond, p. 65.
16 Ibid, p. 69. and the Edfu Records IV. 392,16.
17 *Maps of the Ancient Sea Kings*, Hapgood; p. 224.
18 *Mythical Origin of the Egyptian Temple*, Reymond, p. 93.
19 Ibid, p. 109.
20 Ibid, p. 109.
21 Ibid. p. 17.

[22] Ibid, p. 107,108,126,127 and first par. on p. 323 and Eg. Grammar, Gardiner, D 10, p. 451.

[23] *Pyramid Texts*, Faulkner, § 872-873.

[24] *Pyramid Texts*, Faulkner, § 1746-1752.

[25] *Pyramid Texts*, Faulkner, § 1022.

[26] *Myth and Symbol in Ancient Egypt*, Rundle Clark, p. 177.

[27] *Pyramid Texts*, Faulkner, § 628-629.

[28] Cf. WdO. col.995.

[29] *Egypt's Making*, Rice. p. 249.

[30] *The Ancient Inhabitants of the Canary Islands*, Harvard Afr. Studies, Vol.VII; E.A. Hooton, Cambridge. 1925, p. 56.

[31] *Art rupestre et préhistoire du Sahara*, Le Quellec, p. 447.

[32] *Nat. Hist.* II. Book VI, p. 487, Plinius.

[33] *Histories*, Book IV, 184-185. Herodotus.

[34] *Atlantis and Egypt with other selected Essays*, Gwyn Griffiths.p. 8

[35] *Timaeus*, 24-25. Plato.

[36] *Atlantis in the light of modern research*, Earth Sci. Rev. 21 (1-3) VII (224p.), Kukal. Elsevier, Amsterdam, 1984.

[37] *The Geology of the Atlantic Ocean*, Emery and Uchupi, Fig. 10 and 13 C, beside the Middle-Atlantic Ridge, west of Portugal and Spain. Cf. also *De Zondvloed*, Tollmann, p. 467-469.

Chapter 8

[1] *Pyramid Texts*, Faulkner, Utterance 477, § 956-961.

[2] *Kingship and the Gods*, Frankfort, p. 26-31.

[3] *Star Names, Their Lore & Meaning*, Hinckley Allen, p. 366.

[4] *Lexicon der Ägyptischen Kultur*, p. 192-193.

[5] *Kingship and the Gods*, Frankfort, p. 32.

[6] *Götterglaube*, Kees, p. 94 note 5 and 295 and 296.

[7] *Pyramid Texts*, Faulkner, § 1520.

[8] *Götterglaube*, p. 296 note 3.

[9] *Le Renard Pâle*, p. 160.

[10] *Hamlett's Mill*, p. 385 and *Star Names, Their Lore & Meanings*, p. 445-446.

[11] Ibid. p. 385 note 8.

[12] Ibid, p. 385.

[13] Ibid. p. 384-385.

[14] Ibid. p. 385.

[15] *StarNames, Their Lore & Meaning*, Hinckley Allen, p. 406.

[16] *Egyptian Grammar*, Gardiner, F 23 and 24, p. 464.

[17] *StarNames, Their Lore & Meaning*, Hinckley Allen, p. 443.

[18] *Studiën zur Ägyptischen Astronomie*, Leitz, p. 35ff.

[19] *Osiris*, Vol.II. register. Wallis Budge, p. 389.

[20] *Götterglaube*, Kees, p. 42.

[21] *Urgeschichte* § 61, Sethe, Anm.

[22] *StarNames, Their Lore & Meaning*, Hinckley Allen, p. 204.

[23] Ibid, p. 204-205.

[24] *Papyrus Leiden*, I 346 and I 348.

[25] *Papyrus Brooklyn*, 3.10, 3.17.

[26] *Nieuwjaar in het Oude Egypte*, Borghouts. p. 15.

[27] *Ancient Records of Assyria and Babylonia*, Vol. II, § 523.

[28] WdO kol. 2725.

[29] Cf. also *Pyramid Texts*, Utterance 477.

[30] *The Gods of the Egyptians*, Wallis Budge, Vol.II. p. 109.

[31] ANET, Pritchard, Akkadian Myths and Epics, Translator: Speiser, p. 60.

[32] *Histories* II-5, Herodotus.

[33] *Pyramid Texts*, Faulkner, p. 115, note 7 and *Kingship and the Gods*, p. 190.

[34] *Kingship and the Gods*, Frankfort, p. 210.

Epilogue

[1] *Mythical Origin of the Egyptian Temple*, Reymond. p. 92.
[2] Ibid, p. 13 and p. 13 note 8.
[3] Ibid, p. 65 - 74 (incl.).
[4] *Stob. Herm.* xxiv, 13. *De Geboorte van Horus III*, p. 244, B.H. Stricker, note 2421; note 7068. Mahé, Hermès II, 230.
[5] *Calendars*, Parker, § 152-153
[6] *World-Maps for Finding the Direction and Distance to Mecca*, David King, p. 27, note I,52 and passages on p. 82, note II-83 and 85, p. 158, note III-83.
[7] *Maps of the Ancient Sea Kings*, Hapgood, p. 248-250, esp. item 3.

Appendices

[1] *Anfänge der Astronomie*, van der Waerden, p.220-221.
[2] *Histories*, Herodotus, Book II-123.
[3] *Anfänge der Astronomie*, van der Waerden, p.221.
[4] Ibid, p.223.
[5] Ibid, p.224. The 3000-year period almost equals 151 conjunctions between the planets Jupiter and Saturn.
[6] *Pharaonic King-lists, Annals and Day-books*, Redford, p.190ff .
[7] Joseph Scaliger, *Historical Chronology*, Grafton, p.243 and 249.
[8] Ibid, p.329.
[9] Ibid, p.251.
[10] Ibid, p.188 and 190.
[11] Ibid, p.729.
[12] Ibid, p.262.
[13] Ibid, p.263.
[14] Ibid, p.733.
[15] Ibid, p.348.
[16] Ibid, p.716.
[17] Ibid, p.717.
[18] Ibid, p.284.
[19] *The Romance of Bible Chronology*, Vol.I, Anstey, p.227.
[20] Joseph Scaliger, *Historical Chronology*, Grafton, p.664.
[21] *Chronology of the Ancient World*, Bickerman, p.83.
[22] *Egypt of the Pharaohs*, Gardiner, p.67.
[23] *Thesaurus*, Brugsch, p.525.
[24] *Sothis- und Monddaten*, Krauss, p.47.
[25] Ibid, p.48.
[26] *Discussions in Egyptology*, van Oosterhout, DE 24, 1992
[27] *The Exact Sciences in Antiquity*, Neugebauer, p.80ff.
[28] Ibid, p.80-81.
[29] *Sothis- und Monddaten*, Krauss, p.44.
[30] bid, p.38.
[31] *Excavations at Giza*, Hassan, p.195.
[32] *The Death of Gods in Ancient Egypt*, Sellers, p.116.
[33] *Egyptian Grammar*, Gardiner, § 265, p.197.
[34] The New Testament, Revelation 13:18.
[35] *Kingship and the Gods*, Frankfort, p.380 note 2.

Chronology

[1] *Ancient Egyptian Science*, Clagett, Vol.I.p.630.
[2] *Ancient Egyptian Science*, Clagett, Vol.I.p.631.
[3] WdO col.890.
[4] Memphis, Herakleopolis, Theben; die epigraphischen Zeugnisse der 7-11. Dynastie Ägyptens, W. Schenkel, p.22-23.
[5] *Pharaonic King-lists, Annals and Day-books*, Redford, p.280 shows the translation of

the text and the status quo of research up to the present.

[6] *De Zondvloed*, E & A Tollman, p.236.

[7] *Star Names, Their Lore & Meaning*, Richard Hinckley Allen, p.398.

Bibliography

Adams, B.   Predynastic Egypt, Shire Publications, 1988.
Adams , W.Y.   Nubia, Corridor to Africa, London: Allen Lane, 1977.
Aldred, C.   Egypt to the end of the Old Kingdom, Thames and Hudson,
                     London, 1984.
Anstey, M.   The Romance of Bible Chronology, Vol.I en II, Marshall
                     Brothers, London, 1913.
Arnold, D.   Die Tempel Ägyptens, Bechtermünz Verlag, Augsburg,
                     1996.
Assmann, J.   Ägypten Eine Sinngeschichte, Fischer Taschenbuch
                     Verlag, 1999.
Baines, J./   Atlas of ancient Egypt and Atlas van het oude Egypte,
Malek, J.   Published by Agon, Amsterdam, 1981.
Bauval, R./   The Orion Mystery, Heinemann, London, 1994 and Het
Gilbert, A.   Orion Mysterie, Fibula, Houten
Beaujeu   Histoire géneral des Sciences, PUF, 1, 1957.
Beckenrath, von J.   Chronologie des pharaonischen Ägypten, Mainz, 1997.
Berden, M.   Journaal van een Woestijnreiziger, Eindhoven, 1943.
Berthelot, A.   L'Afrique Saharienne et Soudanaise, Parijs, 1927.
Bethencourt   The Canarian, or Book of the Conquest and Conversion of
Jean de   the Canarians, London, 1872.
Pierre Bontier,
Bibby, G.   Looking for Dilmun, Harmondsworth, 1972.
Bickerman, E.J.   Chronology of the Ancient World, Rev.Ed, London, 1980.
Bonnet, H.   Reallexikon der Ägyptischen Religionsgeschichte, Berlin,
                     1952.
Boorstin, D.   The Discoverers, Random House, New York, 1983 and De
                     Ontdekkers, Published by Agon BV, Amsterdam, 1989.
Borchardt, L.   Die Mittel zur Zeitlichen Festlegung von Punkten der
                     Ägyptischen Geschichte und ihre Anwendung, Kairo
                     Selbstverlag, 1935.
Borghouts, J.F.   Nieuwjaar in het Oude Egypte, Leiden, 1986.
Breasted, J.H.   Ancient Records of Egypt, Vols I-V, London, 1988.
Bricker, C./   Geschiedenis van de Cartografie,
Tooley, R.V.   Atrium, Alphen a/d Rijn, 1975 en 1981.
Brugsch, K. H.   Thesaurus Inscriptionum Aegyptiacarum, Vol.I en II,
                     Akademische Druck- und Verlagsanstalt, Graz, 1968.
Brugsch-Bey, H.   Egypt under the Pharaohs, Bracken Books, London, 1902.
Clagett, M.   Ancient Egyptian Science, Vol.I, 1989 en Vol.II: Calen-
                     dars, Clocks, and Astronomy, American Philosophical
                     Society, Philadelphia, 1995.

Cornevin, M.	Archéologie Africaine, Maison Neuve et Larose, Parijs, 1993
Cornevin, M.	Secrets du Continent Noir révélés par l'Archéologie, idem, Parijs, 1998.
Crawford, H.	Sumer and the Sumerians, Cambridge, 1991.
Dieter, K.	Treffpunkt der Götter, 1994.
Dilwyn Jones	Boats, British Museum Press, 1995.
Diodorus Siculus	Works I-XII, Loeb Classical Library, London, 1933-1967.
Edwards, I.E.S.	The Pyramids of Egypt or De Piramiden van Egypte, Published by Hollandia, Baarn, 1987 and adapted in 1993.
Emery, W.B.	Ägypten, Geschichte und Kultur der Frühzeit, Wiesbaden, 1964.
Emery, K.O.& Uchupi, E.	The Geology of the Atlantic Ocean, Springer, New York, 1984.
Erman, A.	Life in Ancient Egypt, New York, 1971.
Fagan, B.M.	The Oxford Companian to Archaeology, Oxford, (Ed.) 1996.
Faulkner, R.O.	The Ancient Egyptian Pyramid Texts, Oxford University Press, 1969.
Faulkner, R.O.	The Ancient Egyptian Coffin Texts, Vols 3, Oxford University Press, 1973-1978.
Field, J.V.	Kepler's Geometrical Cosmology, University of Chicago Press, Chicago, 1988.
Frankfort, H.	Kingship and the Gods, University of Chicago Press, Chicago, 1948.
Fréret, N.	Mémoires, Académie des Inscriptions, XXIV, Paris, 1756.
Friedman, R. /Adams, B.	The Followers of Horus, Egyptians Studies Association Publication No 2, Oxbow Monograph 20 , Oxford, 1992.
Gardiner, Sir Alan	Egyptian Grammar, 3rd Edition, London, 1973.
Gardiner, Sir Alan	Egypt of the Pharaohs, Oxford University Press, London, 1974.
Gardiner, Sir Alan	The Royal Canon of Turin, Griffith Institute, Oxford, 1987.
Goyon, G.	Le Secret des bâtisseurs des grandes Pyramides Khéops, Pygmalion, Parijs, 1990.
Grafton, A.	Joseph Scaliger, A Study in the History of Classical Scholarship, Vol.I, Textual Criticism and Exegesis, Clarendon Press Oxford, 1983 and Vol. II, Historical Chronology, Oxford, 1993.
Graves, R.	Greek Myths, 1955 and Griekse Mythen, Houten, 1993.
Griaule, M./ Dieterlen, G.	Le Renard Pâle, Institut D'Ethnologie, Museé de l'Homme, Parijs, 1991.
Griaule, M.	Conversations with Ogotemmêli, Oxford University Press, 1970.
Gundel, W.	Neue Astrologische Texte des Hermes Trismegistos, Gerstenberg Verlag, Hildesheim, 1936.
Habachi, L.	The Obelisks of Egypt, The American University in Cairo Press, 1984.

Hancock, G./ Bauval, R.	Keeper of Genesis, Mandarin Paperback, London, 1996.
Hapgood, Ch.	Maps of the Ancient Seakings, Kempton, USA, 1966.
Hassan, S.	Excavations at Giza, Government Press, Cairo,1946.
Haywood, J.	Atlas of the Ancient World, Andromeda, Oxford, 1998.
Helck, von W.	Die Beziehungen Ägyptens zu Vorderasien im 3. und 2. Jahrtausend v.Chr., Wiesbaden, 1971.
Herodotus	The Histories by R.Waterfield, Oxford University Press, 1999 and Historiën, vert. Dr. Damsté, Houten, 1987.
Herzog, R.	Punt, Abhandlungen des Deutschen Archäologischen Instituts Kairo, Band 6, Verlag Augustin, Glückstadt, 1968.
Heyerdahl, T.	Tussen de Continenten, De Boekerij, Baarn, 1975.
Heyerdahl, T.	Tigris, De Kern, Baarn, 1979.
Hinckley Allen, R.	Star Names, Their Lore and Meaning, Dover Books, New York, 1963.
Hoffman,M.A.	Egypt before the Pharaohs, Ark edition, London, 1984.
Holleman, T.	De Neanderthaler, Amsterdam University Press, 1998.
Hooton, E.A.	The Ancient Inhabitants of the Canary Islands, Harvard African Studies, Cambridge, 1925.
Hornung, E.	Die Unterweltsbücher der Ägypter, Aramis, Zürich, 1992.
Hornung, E.	Untersuchungen zur Chronologie und Geschichte des Neuen Reiches, Harrassowitz, Wiesbaden,1968.
Hornung, E.	Grundzüge der ägyptischen Geschichte, Wissenschaftliche Buchgesellschaft Darmstadt, 1988.
Ideler, L.	Beobachtungen der Alten, Berlin, 1806.
Ideler, L.	Handbuch der Chronologie, Vol.I and II, Berlin, 1825 and 1826.
Johnson, D.S.	Phantom Islands of the Atlantic, Walker and Company, New York, 1996.
De Jonge, R./ IJzereef, G.	De Stenen Spreken, Kosmos-Z&K Uitgevers, Utrecht/ Antwerp, 1996.
Kees, H.	Der Götterglaube im alten Ägypten, Akademie Verlag Berlin, 1977.
Kees, H.	Ancient Egypt, a Cultural Topography, University Press of Chicago, Chicago, 1961.
Kemp, B.	Ancient Egypt, Routledge, London, New York, 1993.
King, David A.	World-Maps for Finding the Direction and Distance to Mecca, Brill, Leiden, Netherlands, 1999.
Kitchen, K.A.	The Third Intermediate Period in Egypt, second edition with supplement, Aris & Phillips, Warminster, 1986.
Koch, Joh.	Neue Untersuchungen zur Topographie des babylonischen Fixsternhimmel, Harrassowitz, Wiesbaden, 1989.
Kramer, S.N.	The Sumerians, their History, Culture and Character, Chicago, 1972.
Krauss, R.	Sothis- und Monddaten, Hildesheim, 1985.
Kukal, Z.	Atlantis in the light of modern research. Earth Sci. Rev.21 (1-3) VII (224p.), Amsterdam, 1984.

Landström, B.	Ships of the Pharaoh, 4000 years of Egytian Shipbuilding, London, 1970.
Langdon, S.	The Venus Tablets of Ammizaduga, Oxford University Press, Oxford, 1928.
Lanman, J.T.	Glimpses of History from Old Maps, Herts, England, 1989.
Lauer, J-P.	Die Königsgräber von Memphis, Pawlak Verlaggesellschaft, Herrsching, 1991.
Lehner, M.	The Complete Pyramids and Piramides, Bosch and Keuning, De Bilt, 1998.
Lehner, M.	The Egyptian Heritage, Virginia Beach, 1974.
Leitz, C.	Altägyptische Sternuhren, Peeters, Leuven, 1995.
Leitz, C.	Studien zur Ägyptischen Astronomie, Harrossowitz, Wiesbaden, 1991.
Lepsius, R.	Chronologie der Aegypter, Neudruck der Ausgabe Berlin 1849 in Osnabrück 1981.
Lepsius, R.	Die Alt-Aegyptische Elle, Berlin, 1865.
Letronne, A.J.	Recherches critiques, historiques et géographiques sur les fragments d'Heron d'Alexandrie, 1851.
Lhote, H.	La Découverte des Fresques du Tassili and De Rotstekeningen in de Sahara, Sijthoff, Leiden, 1959.
Lhote, H./ Bandi, H-G.	Het Stenen Tijdperk, Elsevier, Amsterdam/Brussel, 1961.
De Liagre Böhl, F.M.Th.	Het Gilgamesj Epos, Uitg. Paris, Amsterdam, 1958.
Luft, U.	Die chronologische Fixierung des ägyptischen Mittleren Reiches nach dem Tempelarchiv von Illahun, Wien, 1992.
Manilius, M.	Astronomica, Brill, Leiden, 1914 (vert. van Wageningen, J.)
Manley, B.	Historical Atlas of Ancient Egypt, Penguin Group, London, 1996.
Mendelssohn, K.	Das Rätsel der Pyramiden, Weltbild Verlag, Augsburg, 1993.
de Meulenaere, H.	Herodotus over de 26ste Dynastie, Leuvense H. H. Universitaire Uitgaven, Instituut voor Oriëntalisme, Leuven, 1951.
Meyer, E.	Geschichte des Altertums, Vol.I t/m VIII, negende uitgave, Phaidon, Essen, 1952-1958.
Meyer, E.	Aegyptische Chronologie, Verlag der Königl. Akademie der Wissenschaften, Berlin, 1904.
Moore, P.	The New Atlas of the Universe, Spectrum Boek, Utrecht, 1984.
Moore, P.	Astronomy before the Telescope, British Museum Ed. C.Walker Press, London, 1996. Chapter 'Astronomy in Egypt' by R.A. Wells.
Moortgat, A.	Entstehung der Sumerischen Hochkultur, Leipzig, 1945.
Moscati, S.	The World of the Phoenicians, Cardinal, London, 1973.
Neugebauer, O.	History of Ancient Mathematical Astronomy, 1975.
Neugebauer, O.	The Exact Sciences in Antiquity, Dover Books, New York, second edition, 1975.

Neugebauer, O./ Parker, R.	Egyptian Astronomical Texts, 3 Vols (1960-69), Rhode Island.
Nibbi, A.	Ancient Egypt and some Eastern Neighbours, Noyes Press, New Yersey, 1981.
Nibbi, A.	The Sea Peoples and Egypt, idem, 1975.
O'Mara, P.F.	The Palermo Stone and the Archaic Kings of Egypt, Paulette, Publ., California, 1979.
Oosterhout, van G.W.	The Heliacal Rising of Sirius, Discussions in Egyptology, DE 24, 1992.
Otto, Eberhard	Geschiedenis van Egypte, Het Spectrum, 1962.
Parker, R.	The Calendars of Ancient Egypt, University of Chicago Press, Chicago, 1950.
Papke, W.	Die Sterne von Babylon, Lübbe Verlag, Bergisch Gladbach, 1989.
Petrie, Fl.	Wisdom of the Egyptians, Vol. LXIII, The Sheldon Press, London, 1940
Petrie, Fl.	The Making of Egypt, The Sheldon Press, London, 1939.
Piazzi Smyth	The Great Pyramid, Bell Publishing Company, New York, 1978.
Plato	Collected works, Published by Ambo, Baarn, 1980. (Transl. by Dr.X.de Win.)
Pliny	Natural History, Vols. I-X, Loeb Classical Library, H.Rackham, Harvard University Press.
Plutarch	Moralia V, Myth of Horus and Seth, Loeb Classical Library, Harvard University Press.
Pritchard J.B.	Ancient Near Eastern Texts Relating to the Old Testament, 3rd edition with suppl, Princeton (Ed) University Press, Princeton, 1969.
Ptolemy, C.	Tetrabiblos, vert. Robbins, Loeb Classical Library, London, 1940.
Ptolemy, C.	The Geography, Dover Books, New York, 1991.
Le Quellec, J-L	Art rupestre et préhistoire du Sahara, Bibl. Scientifique Payot, Parijs, 1998.
Quispel, G.	De Hermetische Gnosis in de loop der eeuwen, (Red.) met name Het Hermetisme en het Oude Egypte van J.Zandee, p.96-174, Tirion, Baarn, 1992.
Redford, D.	Pharaonic King-lists, Annals and Day-books, Benben Publ. Mississauga, Ontario, 1986.
Reymond, E.A.E.	The Mythical Origin of the Egyptian Temple, Manchester University Press, Barnes and Noble Inc. New York, 1969.
Rice, M.	Egypt's Making, Routledge, London, 1991.
Rice, M. and and Shaikla Haya	Bahrain Through the Ages: The Archaeology (Proceedings of the Bahrain Historical Conference 1983), London, 1986.
Robinson, J.M.	Nag Hammadi Library in English, Brill, Leiden, 1984.
Rundle Clark, R.T.	Myth and Symbol in Ancient Egypt, Thames & R.T. Hudson, London, 1991.
Samuel, A.E.	Ptolemaic Chronology, Becksche Verlagsbuchhandlung, Munich, 1962.

De Santillana/ von Dechend	Hamlet's Mill, paperback 3rd edition, Boston, 1992.
Schneider J.L.	Le Tchad depuis 25000 ans, Masson, Parijs, 1994.
Schoot, van der A.	De ontstelling van Pythagoras, Kok Agora, 1999.
Schott, S.	Altägyptische Festdaten, Wiesbaden, 1950.
Schulz, R./ Seidel, M. (Red.)	Egypte, het land van de farao's, Könemann, Köln, 1998.
Sellers, J.B.	The Death of Gods in Ancient Egypt, Penguin Books, London, 1992.
Sethe, K.	Zeitrechnung der Alten Ägypter im Verhältnis zu der andern Völker, 1920.
Siliotti/ Zahi Hawass	De Piramiden van Egypte, Zuid Boekproductions., Lisse, 1998.
Siliotti, A.	Egypte, Tempels, Mensen en Goden, idem, 1994.
Smith, W.	Dictionary of Greek and Roman Geography, Vol. I and II, New York, 1966.
Somers Clarke/ Engelbach, R.	Ancient Egyptian Construction and Architecture, Dover Books, New York, 1990.
Stadelmann, R.	Die Ägyptischen Pyramiden, Verlag von Zabern, Mainz, 1991.
Strabo Transl. Jones	The Geography of Strabo VIII, Book XVII, Loeb Classical Library, Harvard Univ. Pr. and Heinemann, London, 1982.
Tadema Sporry/ Auke A. Tadema	De Pyramiden van Egypte, Fibula, Bussum, 1971.
Temple, R.	The Genius of China, Prion, London, 1986.
Tollmann, E & A.	De Zondvloed, Tirion, Baarn, 1994. Translation of: Und die Sintflut gab es doch, Munich, 1993.
Tompkins, P.	Secrets of the Great Pyramid with Appendix L.C. Stecchini, Harper and Row, New York, 1971.
Vergote, J.	De Godsdienst van de Egyptenaren, Romen, Roermond, 1971.
Waddell, W.G.	Manetho, Cambridge, 1971.
Waerden, v.d. B.L.	Anfänge der Astronomie, Noordhoff, Groningen, 1956.
Waerden, v.d. B.L.	The Venus tablets of Ammisaduqa, 1946.
Wallis Budge, E.A.	The Gods of the Egyptians, Vol.I and II, Dover Books, New York, 1969.
Wallis Budge, E.A.	A History of Egypt, Vols I-IV, 1968.
Wallis Budge, E.A.	Osiris and the Egyptian Resurrection, Vol.I and II, Dover Books, New York, 1973.
Wallis Budge, E.A.	The Book of the Dead, Routledge & Kegan Paul, London, 1974.
Weidner, E.F.	Handbuch der Babylonischen Astronomie, 1915
Weir, J.D.	The Venus Tablets of Ammizaduga, Ned. Hist.-

	Archeologisch Instituut in het Nabije Oosten, Istanbul, 1972.
Wellard, J.	Lost Worlds of Africa, London, 1967.
Wildung, D.	Egypte, Taschen/Librero, Cologne, 1997.
Wilkinson, Toby. A.H.	Early Dynastic Egypt, Routledge. London, New York, 1999.
Woolley, Sir L.	Het Midden-Oosten, Elsevier, Amsterdam/Brussel, 1962.
Woolley, Sir L.	Excavations at Ur, Benn Limited, 1954.

General

National Geographic Society, Atlas of the World, Washington, 1981.
Times, de Grote Wereldatlas, Ede, 1983.
The Cambridge Ancient History, Vols. I-XII, Cambridge University Press, 1974.
The Cambridge Ancient History of Africa, Vols. I-II, 1978-82.
African Archaelogy, 1985 and 2nd edition 1993.
Oude Geschiedenis van de Joden, Flavius Josephus, Vols. I-II, Ambo, 1996.
Knaurs Lexikon der Ägyptischen Kultur, Munich/Zürich, 1960.
Lexikon der Ägyptologie, Bnd. I-VII + Index, Harrassowitz, Wiesbaden, 1975.
Woordenboek der Oudheid, Vols. I-III, edited by Prof. Dr. Nuchelmans en Prof. Dr. Vergote e.a., Bussum, 1976.
De Ibis, quarterly of the Egyptological Society 'Sjemsoethot', vols. 1986-1999.
Encyclopedia Winkler Prins, 8th edition, Elsevier, Amsterdam/Antwerp.
Meyers Enzyclopädisches Lexikon, Mannheim/Wien/Zürich, 1971.
Grootste Mysteries Aller Tijden, 1977.
The New Encyclopaedia Britannica, 1985.
The American Ephemeris, Michelsen, ACS Publications, 1980-83.
Tuckerman Ephemeride 601 BCE until 1649 CE, Vols.I-II, Philadelphia, 1962/64.
Lunar Tables and Programs from 4000 BCE to 8000 CE, Chapront Touzé en Chapront, Richmond, 1991.
Uranometria 2000,0, Vols. I-II, Tirion-Rappaport-Lovi, Willman-Bell, Virginia, 1993.
Star catalogue
Atlas van de Sterrenhemel, Dunlop-Tirion, Becht, Amsterdam, 1985, maps
Cosmic the Universe of Stars, edition Sculptures-Jeux, Paris (distributed by Sarut Inc., New York)
Redshift 3
Skyglobe 3.6
NRC Handelsblad, articles:
Sterren in steen, d.d. 01-02-1996 (interview egyptologist Dr. A. Egberts).
Oudste Steencirkel werpt nieuw licht op Egyptische beschaving, d.d. 04-04-1998.
Kleine Verandering in Aardbaan deed Sahara Ontstaan, d.d. 31-07-1999.
National Geographic, February 1998.
Kramers' Woordenboek Latijn, Amsterdam/Brussel, 1984.

Computerprogramma Universiteit Utrecht, afd. Geografie, onderdeel Cartografie.
Internet:http://WWW.SOTON.AC.UK/-TJMS/ADAMS2.HTML   http://WWW.ESD.ORNL.GOV/ERN/QEN.NERC.HTML.
For the maps on the paleo-vegetation of North Africa from 18.000 up to 2500 BCE.
BBC Horizon, television 28-10-1999/04-11-1999, Atlantis Uncovered and Atlantis Reborn.

Magazines and articles

Batrawi, A. The Racial History of Egypt and Nubia, Part 1 en 2, Journal of the Royal Anthropological Institute 75 (1945); p.81-101; idem 76 (1946); p.131-156.
Bell, Barbara. The Dark Ages in Ancient History, American Journal of Archeology 75 (1971); p.01-26.
Clark, S. El Kab, Journal of Egyptian Archeology VII; p.54-79.
Comes, M. Geographical Co-ordinates of al-Andalus (Cordoba) and North-Africa, Journal for the History of Arabic Science 10 (1994); p.41-51.
Daressy, G.M. L'Égypte Céleste, BIFAO XII, 1916.
Derry, D.E. The Dynastic Race in Egypt, Journal of Egyptian Archeology; p.42 (1956).
Frankfort, H. The Origin of Monumental Architecture in Egypt, American Journal of Semitic Languages and Literaturs, LVIII; p.329-358.
Goyon, G. Kerkasôre et L'Ancien Observatoire, BIFAO 74; p.135-147.
Goyon, G. Les Ports des Pyramides et le Grand Canal de Memphis, Revue d'Égyptologie 23 (1971); p.137-153.
Howard Carter, H. The Tangible Evidence for the earliest Dilmun, Journal of Cuneiform Studies 33, 1981; p.210-233.
Kennedy, E.S. en Regier, M. Prime Meridians in Medieval Islamic Astronomy, Vistas in Astronomy 28 (1985); p.29-32.
Rinsveld, B. van Le dieu-faucon égyptien des Musées royaux d'Art et d'Histoire, Bulletin KMKG Brussel 62 (1991); p.15-45.
Roset, J.P. Art rupestre en Aïr, Archeologia, no. 39; 1971.
Tagalagal: un site à céramique au 10 millénaire avant nos jours dans l'Aïr (Niger); 1982. Comptes Rendus Acad. des Inscriptions et Belles Lettres, juillet-octobre.
Les plus vieilles céramiques du Sahara, Archeologia, no. 183, p.43-50; 1983.
Neolithic development in the Early Holocene of Northern Niger, in Close, ed., p.245-266; 1987.
Néolithisation, néolithique et post-néolithique au Niger nord-oriental, Bull. AFEQ (Ass.Française Etude du Quaternaire), 4, p.203-214; 1987.
Iwelen, site archéologique de l'époque des chars dans l'Aïr septentrional (Niger) in: Libya antiqua, Unesco, p.121-156.
Trimble, V. Astronomical Investigations concerning the So-called Air-Shafts of Cheops' Pyramid in: MIOAWB, band 10, p.183-187, 1964.

Miscellaneous

Bull. d'Égypte 30 (Cairo 1960) Observations sur les Piramides.
BIFAO 47   (1969), p.71-86.
BIFAO 69   (1971), p.11-41.
Bull. SFE 69,9
JARCE 26   (1989), p.191-206.
JARCE 28   (1991), p.155-186.
JEA 31   (1945)
MDAIK 49 (1993)
MDAIK 52 (1996), p.11-81.

Index

Picture Credits

THE SECRET VAULT
Philip Coppens & André Douzet

Is Notre-Dame-de-Marceille the true centre of the mystery of Rennes-le-Chateau? The authors report on the discovery of a secret vault in that location, which has been at the focus of attention of the main players in the mystery of the nearby village - and its priest, Bérenger Saunière.

*152 Pages. Paperback. Euro 16.90 * GBP 9.99 * USD $ 14.95.*

SAUNIERE'S MODEL AND THE SECRET OF RENNES-LE-CHATEAU
André Douzet

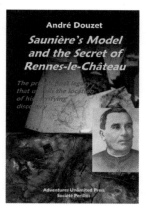

After years of research, André Douzet discovered a model ordered by abbé Bérenger Saunière. Douzet reveals that Saunière spent large amounts of time and money in the city of Lyons... trips he went on in the utmost secrecy. Douzet finally unveils the location indicated on the model, the location of Saunière's secret.

*116 Pages. Paperback. Euro 14,90 * GBP 7.99 * USD $ 12.00.*

THE TEMPLARS' LEGACY IN MONTREAL, THE NEW JERUSALEM
Francine Bernier

Montréal, Canada. Designed in the 17th Century as the New Jerusalem of the Christian world, the island of Montreal became the new headquarters of a group of mystics that wanted to live as the flawless Primitive Church of Jesus. But why could they not do that in the Old World?

*360 pages. Paperback. GBP 14.99 * USD $21.95 * Euro 25.00.*

THE CANOPUS REVELATION

Stargate of the Gods and the Ark of Osiris
Philip Coppens

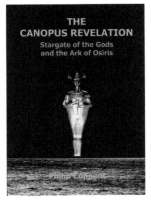

The identification of the constellation Orion with the Egyptian god Osiris has become engrained in human consciousness, yet it is one of the biggest misunderstandings. Canopus, for Egypt the South polar star, is the second brightest star in the sky and interplays with Sirius in such a way that ancient accounts say they control time. Furthermore, Canopus was believed to allow access to the Afterlife - the domain of Osiris. Canopus was specifically identified with his Chest, his Ark, in which he was transformed from mere mortal to resurrected supergod. This book radically reinterprets the most powerful myth of Osiris and Isis in its proper context, offering full understanding both from historical and cultural perspectives, and shows the way forward... what did the ancient Egyptians believe that would happen to the soul?

*216 pages. Paperback. USD $ 17,95 * GBP 11,99 * Euro 20.90.*
Code: CANO

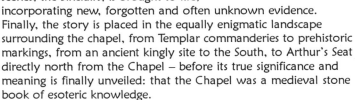

THE STONE PUZZLE OF ROSSLYN CHAPEL

Philip Coppens

This book will guide you through the theories, showing and describing where and what is being discussed; what is impossible, what is likely... and what is fact.
The history of the chapel, its relationship to freemasonry and the family behind the scenes, the Sinclairs, is brought to life, incorporating new, forgotten and often unknown evidence. Finally, the story is placed in the equally enigmatic landscape surrounding the chapel, from Templar commanderies to prehistoric markings, from an ancient kingly site to the South, to Arthur's Seat directly north from the Chapel – before its true significance and meaning is finally unveiled: that the Chapel was a medieval stone book of esoteric knowledge.

*136 Pages. Paperback. Euro 14,90 * GBP 7.99 * USD $ 12.00.*
Code: ROSC